MORRIS

THE CARS AND THE COMPANY

Jon Pressnell

First published in June 2013

A catalogue record for this book is available from the British Library

ISBN 978 1 85960 996 5

Library of Congress control card no 2013932256

Published by Haynes Publishing,
Sparkford, Yeovil, Somerset BA22 7JJ, UK
Tel: 01963 442030 Fax: 01963 440001
Int. tel: +44 1963 442030 Int. fax: +44 1963 440001
E-mail: sales@haynes.co.uk
Website: www.haynes.co.uk

Haynes North America Inc.,
861 Lawrence Drive, Newbury Park, California 91320, USA

Graphic design by Eric Péro (spyro): www.imageric.fr

Printed and bound in the USA by Odcombe Press LP,
1299 Bridgestone Parkway, La Vergne, TN 37086

Jacket illustrations
Front 1925 Morris Oxford 'Bullnose' two-seater (James Mann).
Back 1933 Isis and Minor Special Coupés (LAT); 1937 Hope-bodied Morris 25hp (Colin Schiller); Morris 1100 (Jaguar North American Archives).

Contents

Acknowledgements

This book would not have been possibile without the help of countless people. I am particularly grateful to Peter Seymour and Robin Barraclough for their many insights and for generosity with their time, as well as for the provision of photographs and much fascinating material. Sincere thanks also go to Anders Clausager of Jaguar Daimler Heritage Trust, who provided a magnificent set of statistics. Another major source of help was Ken Martin of the Morris Register, guardian of the archives of former club historian the late Harry Edwards. Ken spent an inordinate amount of time helping me select photographs and then providing scans – a vital contribution.

Also much appreciated was the kindness of Barbara Robinson at Caffyns in Eastbourne, who loaned precious 1930s publicity material. In France, Hubert Achard de la Vente, Rainer Hindrischedt and Marc-Antoine Colin were of great help in unravelling the Morris-Léon-Bollée story, and in providing illustrations. Over in Australia I am grateful in particular to Nairn Hindhaugh and Kerry Kaehne for assistance with information and documentation, and to my old friend Paul Blank; thanks also to Ruth Dowthwaite, Colin Schiller and Mostyn Upton. Much valued was the warm welcome at the Modern Records Centre of the University of Warwick, and at the archives departments of Nuffield College and the London School of Economics.

Many photographs have come from LAT Photographic and from the British Motor Industry Heritage Trust. A big debt of gratitude is owed to Kevin Wood at LAT and to Gillian Bardsley, Lisa Stevens, Jan Valentino, Richard Bacchus and Derek Tew at BMIHT for their efficient and friendly service – with special thanks to Lisa Stevens at Gaydon for her scanning work and last-minute provision of photographs. A large number of former press photographs in the public domain have been acquired by the author in the course of his thirty years as a journalist. All publicity materials originally produced by the British Leyland Motor Corporation (subsequently British Leyland Ltd and later Rover Group Ltd) and its constituent companies including Austin, Morris, MG, Rover, Standard, Triumph, Riley, Wolseley and Vanden Plas, is the copyright of the British Motor Industry Heritage Trust and is reproduced here with due acknowledgement.

Further photos have been provided by Richard Barton, Phil Jennings, John Seddon, Bill Munro, Nick Georgano, Howard Dent and Richard Monk of the Morris Cowley, Oxford and Isis Owners Club, Nuffield College, Rob Symonds and Ray Frampton of the Morris Register, and Mike Cook of Jaguar North American Archives.

This project has been very much a collaborative venture with award-winning designer Eric Péro, who has shown patience and understanding beyond the call of duty, and done a superb job in giving the book a lively and readable look; to Eric and wife Claire go sincere thanks for their tolerance and hospitality. I am grateful in addition to the following for their help and encouragement: Christopher Balfour, Mike Brears, Rik and Marie Blote, and Isabelle, Olivier, Jane and all the team at the Bar à Trucs in Lherm. Finally, a big 'thank you' goes to my partner Alice for her forebearance and for all the very many things she has done to help this book along the way.

Jon Pressnell, Lherm, France

Bibliography

Adeney, Martin: *Nuffield – a Biography* (Hale) • Adeney, Martin: *The Motor Makers* (Collins) • Andrews, PWS and Brunner, Elizabeth: *The Life of Lord Nuffield – A Study in Enerprise and Benevolence* (Blackwell) • Bardsley, Gillian and Laing, Stephen: *Making Cars at Cowley* (The History Press) • Bardsley, Gillian: *Issigonis – The Official Biography* (Icon) • Barraclough, RI and Jennings, PL: *Oxford to Abingdon* (Myrtle Publishing) • Buckle, David: *Turbulent Times in the Car Industry* (David Buckle) • Church, Roy: *Herbert Austin – The British Motor Car Industry to 1941* (Europa) • Clare, Anthony: *The Nuffield Tractor Story* (Old Pond) • Edwards, Harry: *Morris Commercial Vehicles* (Alan Sutton) • Edwards, Harry: *The Morris Motor Car 1913–1983* (Moorland) • Fairfax, Ernest: *Calling all Arms* (Hutchinson) • Fenby, Charles: *The Other Oxford* (Lund Humphries) • Garnons-Williams, Philip: *Morris Cars 1913–1930* (Bullnose Morris Club) • Georgano, GN: *A History of the London Taxicab* (David & Charles) • Howlett, John: *The Guv'nor* (John Howlett) • Jackson, Robert: *The Nuffield Story* (Muller) • Jarman, Lytton P and Barraclough, Robin I: *The Bullnose and Flatnose Morris* (David & Charles) • Jennings, PL: *Early M.G.* (PL Jennings) • Kaehne, Kerry: *Morris 8/40 – Australia 1935 to 1948* (Kerry Kaehne) • Lanning, Greg *et al* (Television History Workshop): *Making Cars* (RKP) • Maxcy, George and Silberston, Aubrey: *The Motor Industry* • (George Allen and Unwin) • McComb, Wilson: *MG by McComb* (Osprey) • McKinstry, Leo: *Spitfire – Portrait of a Legend* (John Murray) • Minns, John: *Wealth Well-Given – The Enterprise and Benevolence of Lord Nuffield* (Alan Sutton) • Munro, Bill: *A Century of London Taxis* (Crowood) • Munro, Bill: *Carbodies – The Complete Story* (Crowood) • Newbigging, Carole, Shatford, Susanne and Williams, Trevor: *The Changing Faces of Cowley Works, Book One* (Boyd) • Newbigging, Carole and Williams, Trevor: *The Changing Faces of Cowley Works, Book Two* (Boyd) • Overy, RJ: *William Morris, Viscount Nuffield* (Europa) • Painting, Norman: *'Buy British and be Proud of it' – The history of Morris Commercial Cars Ltd* (Rossendale) • Pressnell, Jon: *Mini – The Definitive History* (Haynes) • Pressnell, Jon: *Morris Minor – Exploring the Legend* (Haynes) • Pressnell, Jon: *Morris Minor – The Official Photo Album* • Richardson, Kenneth: *The British Motor Industry 1896–1939* (Macmillan) • Seymour, Peter: *The Development of 8 & 10 cwt Morris Light Vans 1924–1934* (P&B) • Seymour, Peter: *Wolseley Radial Aero Engines – Lord Nuffield's Thwarted Venture* (Tempus) • Sharratt, Barney: *Men and Motors of 'The Austin'* (Haynes) • Skilleter, Paul: *Morris Minor – The World's Supreme Small Car* (Osprey) • Thomas, Sir Miles: *Out on a Wing* (Michael Joseph) • Turner, Graham: *The Leyland Papers* (Pan) • Ware, Pat: *Quarter-Ton – The Story of the Quarter-Ton 4x4 in British Military Service 1941–1958* (Warehouse) • Wood, Jonathan: *Alec Issigonis – The Man who made the Mini* (Breedon) • Wood, Jonathan: *Wheels of Misfortune – The Rise and Fall of the British Motor Industry* (Sidgwick & Jackson).

Preface

The cars carrying the Morris name are to a greater or lesser degree known, but the industrial context in which they were made and sold – the history of the company behind them – is less satisfactorily documented. All the protagonists from the most significant years of the Morris business are long dead, and have left little behind them in the way of recorded memories.

As a result, writers have tended to rely on two principal sources. The first is the 'official' biography of Lord Nuffield by Philip Andrews and Elizabeth Brunner, commissioned by Nuffield College in a bid to efface the ill-feeling that Nuffield felt towards the University of Oxford. The second is *Out on a Wing*, the engagingly readable memoirs of long-time Morris high-up Sir Miles Thomas. The Andrews and Brunner biography is detailed and wide-ranging, but was steered by two Nuffield loyalists, his former personal secretaries Wilfred Hobbs and Carl Kingerlee, along with the rather less reverential George Dono, a senior manager and director of the company; it was then approved for publication by Lord Nuffield himself. Described by its authors as 'an act of piety', it is inevitably partisan and selective. Indeed, Nuffield put pressure on Andrews and Brunner, sometimes successfully, not to mention certain people or episodes. Thomas's delightful book naturally enough gives a personal spin to events, although it is generally both accurate and fair.

By good fortune, however, the transcripts of the interviews carried out by Andrews and Brunner have been preserved, in the archives at the London School of Economics. They are an extraordinary resource that has rarely been used, and I am grateful to Roy Church for his 1996 article in the *Economic History Review* that brought the papers to my attention. Andrews and Brunner interviewed all the key players in the history of the company, and their testimony was far-ranging and often trenchant. Alas, much of this material was judged too sensitive, and fell on the cutting-room floor. I have drawn extensively on the Andrews and Brunner papers, and make full acknowledgement: I do not seek to appropriate their work as my own. Typed up from the notes of the authors, the text is in the form of indirect speech, but is evidently pretty much a direct transcription of the words of the interviewees. I have therefore used double quotation marks throughout, with appropriate modifications in square brackets. Where a quotation is not attributed to Andrews and Brunner or to another source, it can be assumed that it is drawn from these interviews.

With the support of this material, along with other previously unpublished documentation, it has been possible for the first time to tell the true story behind the cars. It is not always a happy tale, but then the history of the British motor industry never has been. I hope this account will all the same make readers appreciate the important role Morris played in the development of that industry, and the significant place it – and its founder, Lord Nuffield – occupy in the history of the 20th century. **JTP**

William Morris, Viscount Nuffield

William Morris received his first honour in 1917, when he was awarded the OBE (Order of the British Empire) for his war work. In 1929 he became Sir William Morris, and in 1934 he was elevated to the peerage as Lord Nuffield. Finally, in 1938 he was given the title of Viscount Nuffield in the County of Oxford. It is difficult to be consistent in how one refers to Morris, especially as many of those interviewed in later life are not themselves consistent. The author trusts readers will pardon him any historical infelicities in this matter...

William Morris, cycle-maker and garage-owner

A well-known photo of the Morris showroom at 48 High Street, Oxford; next door is the tobacconist's shop of sometime partner George Cooke. (Author's collection)

William Morris showed enterprise and a forward-looking spirit right from the start of his career. He had a chequered start to his professional life, but by 1912 he had built up a substantial and thriving garage business in the city of Oxford.

So many times have William Morris's early days been recounted that the story has entered into myth – and myth into the story. The essentials are briefly told. William Richard Morris was an enterprising and able young man who started out repairing and building bicycles in Oxford, moved on to make motorcycles, and by 1912 had a thriving garage business servicing and selling motorcycles and cars.

Morris was born on 10 October 1877 in Worcester, and grew up in Oxford with two sisters. His father Frederick was one of a long line of Oxfordshire yeoman farmers – self-employed tenant farmers who ran their farms with their own capital. At a time when farming was a key part of the economy, such people were the backbone of the rural middle classes. Both his parents were well educated, and William Morris was not born into a disadvantaged or povety-stricken family, something he was keen to stress in later life. Frederick Morris, evidently a bit of a rolling stone in his younger days, was also an able horseman, and had spent a period in Canada driving a Royal Mail coach; on his return to England, he married and was articled to a draper's shop in Worcester, but in 1880 he returned to farming in Oxford. This was as a bailiff – what we would today call a farm manager – running his father-in-law's farm at Headington Quarry.

The first bicycles

It was soon evident that William Morris had a practical bent. When he was 14 he taught himself to ride on a borrowed penny-farthing and then bought a secondhand solid-tyred 'safety' bicycle that he was forever taking to bits and re-assembling. After his father had developed asthma and had to give up farming, Morris left school, at the age of 15, in order to help support the family. Accordingly he joined local bicycle shop Parker's, but when in 1893 he was denied a pay rise he set up on his own.

He worked from the back of the family home in James Street, in the Oxford suburb of Cowley St John, operating from a brick outbuilding – not a tumbledown shed, as some romanticising biographers have it – and exhibiting his bicycles

William Morris's initiation to cycling was on an old penny-farthing. (Author's collection)

in the front window of the house. Morris repaired and sold bicycles and sold cycling accessories, and moved on to build his first cycle when a local vicar commissioned a machine from him. The bicycle, which survives to this day, had an unusually tall 27in frame, to accommodate the gangly Reverend Pilcher; to finance its construction Morris had to borrow £4 from a lady living nearby.

Other orders soon followed, and it is said that in his first year Morris sold 50 bicycles – presumably not just those he built around his own frames. He was a painstaking craftsman, and in later life even those who had ambivalent feelings about him admitted that his brazing work was beautiful. An oft-told story is of how

Morris was an extremely successful cycle-racer, winning countless championships. (Author's collection)

The bicycle built for the Reverend Pilcher: it was still in excellent order when it turned up at a jumble sale in the late 1930s. (Author's collection)

Having entered the local postal directory in 1896 as 'cycle-maker', by 1901 Morris was trading from 48 High Street, Oxford, and had won the contract to service the city's post bikes. By 1902 he had further premises at 100 Holywell Street, on the corner of Longwall Street. For relaxation Morris was a competitive cyclist – from early on with his own cycles. Muscular and compact, he was a top-flight racer, winning a goodly number of championships and being regarded as one of the finest riders in the county.

Next, a motorcycle

Having built a motorcycle in 1900, using bought-in components and his own frame, in 1902 Morris branched out into this field, with a 2¾hp model using a proprietary engine. It innovated in its frame, which looped around the bottom of the engine, and had other clever and advanced details. Two models were exhibited at a show in London, and to commercialise the motorcycle Morris took on a partner, Joseph Cooper, who was a friend and fellow cycle-dealer and racer. The two traded as Morris & Cooper but the partnership lasted less than a year, ending when Cooper disagreed with Morris committing himself to the purchase of three engines so he could build three motorcycles at the same time, thereby reducing costs. Morris bought Cooper out – but he returned to Morris Garages as an employee, worked on the first Morris car, and ended up as foreman of the axle department at Cowley. He was left £5000 in Morris's 1927 will, but pre-deceased his former partner.

The company carried on, making a steady number of motorcycles, including some fore-cars with passenger seating in front of the rider. At the end of 1902 an apprentice was taken on at Longwall, Alf Keen, to work alongside Morris and the one other employee. Additionally there was a man and a boy at Queen Street, looking after the storage, cleaning and repair of undergraduates' bicycles. Meanwhile Frederick Morris ran the High Street shop, and kept the accounts; he was apparently a meticulous book-keeper.

he brazed together a part on a linotype machine at the *Oxford Times* when it had been judged beyond repair – and of how the brazing was still holding up when the machine was scrapped in 1937. From the start he was prudent in his business practices: stock and expenses were kept to a minimum; sometimes he would cycle to Birmingham to get parts.

On to four wheels
– and an ill-fated partnership

Morris's next move was to expand into motor cars, and in a 1903 Oxford directory he is described as 'Sole maker of the celebrated "Morris" cycles and motor cycles' – with in addition the words 'Motor Repairs a Speciality'. That year Morris entered into another partnership, a venture

Morris (far right) and his workers with the frame of a Morris motorcycle. (Author's collection)

that would constitute one of the more colourful episodes of his early life. The prime mover was Walter Launcelot Creyke, a dilettante former Oxford undergraduate in his early twenties.

Born in 1880 into a wealthy family of Yorkshire landowners, Launcelot Creyke had been a rather less than model pupil at Eton, from which he had run away, and would appear to have been something of a wastrel when he went up to Christ Church in 1899. When he inherited the family fortune in 1901, he left Oxford University without a degree and threw himself into the motor business. In 1902 he helped set up the Speedwell Motor and Engineering Co of Reading, and sat on the board of another company in London; Speedwell was agent for various makes, soon acquired an expensive Knightsbridge showroom, and would unveil its own Speedwell car at the end of 1903.

Creyke's final investment was in establishing the Oxford Automobile Agency in 1902, with Frank Barton, who was proprietor of three cycle shops – in Oxford, Abingdon and Bicester. Morris joined the pair in October 1903, to look after the workshops, as he was regarded as the best man in Oxford when it came to cars. The business was now known as the Oxford Automobile and Cycle Agency, and was based at 16 George Street, where Creyke had set up a showroom, with motorcycle assembly in New Road, behind

The Morris motorcycle had several unusual features, not least its frame. (Author's collection)

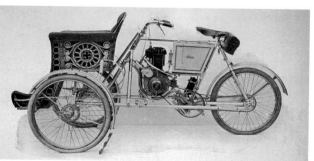

The motorcycle was also available with a fore-carriage. (Robin Barraclough)

The Oxford Automobile & Cycle Agency in 1903; at this stage Morris still wore a cap, later replaced by a felt hat to reflect his more exalted status. (Richard Barton)

help of a small loan from his bank, he picked up the pieces, and carried on trading from his rented premises in Oxford High Street and at Longwall.

Frank Barton, meanwhile, stayed in the cycle trade as manager of two shops, before returning to work for Morris in 1911 as general manager of Morris Garages. He stayed in this post, pretty much as Morris's right-hand man, until he moved to Devon in 1918. In 1923 he became Morris distributor for Devon and East Cornwall, and with personal financial support from William Morris he built up a substantial business.

Revival – and the 'Oxford Motor Palace'

Much is made of how the Creyke episode was a salutary experience, and of how thereafter Morris vowed never again to have a partner. In fact, in June 1905 Morris did enter into another business partnership, with George Cooke, who had a tobacconist's shop next door to Morris's High Street premises. Cooke put £400 into the enterprise to launch the partnership, with Morris contributing £150 represented by fixtures, fittings and book debts. In June 1906 Cooke put a further £150 into the business, but the two men went their separate ways in April the following year, when Morris bought Cooke out with a payment of £650.

The revived business took on the garaging and care of undergraduates' cars. Keeping its finger in the two-wheeled pie, it also set up plating and enamelling operations. But the emphasis was starting to shift to cars. Morris had one of his own, and in 1905 he began hiring out cars with drivers. This was followed by a taxi service – a new thing at the time – and the provision of driving lessons. Morris's reputation built up, and he took on agencies for Arrol-Johnston, Belsize, Humber, Hupmobile, Singer, Standard and Wolseley cars, plus Douglas, Enfield, Sunbeam and Triumph motorcycles. As for the bicycle side of operations, this was sold in 1907 to another Oxford cycle dealer.

By 1910 Morris was described in the Oxford directory as a motor car engineer and agent and garage proprietor, and was operating as The Morris Garage from newly built premises on the corner of Longwall Street – known as 'The Oxford Motor Palace'. He also had premises in St Cross Road and by this stage was probably employing 15–20 people. The business was doing well. Sales almost doubled that year, from £8500 to £16,000, and the profit of £1500 was

Barton's Oxford bicycle shop and garage. The arrangement was that Creyke would provide finance and be a sleeping partner, Barton would look after sales, as general manager, and Morris would be works manager. Makes handled include Panhard et Levassor, Renault, De Dion-Bouton, Daimler, MMC and Mors. The enterprise attracted plenty of attention, if only because of Creyke's transport: when he wasn't driving a 30hp Panhard racer, the flamboyant young man charged around Oxford in Léon Serpollet's record-breaking steam car, the 'Easter Egg'.

It would all end in tears. Creyke spent extravagantly, and Barton was unable to rein him in, as the company's capital disappeared in extravagant dinners and boozy parties – the old 'entertaining clients' routine. After barely a year the business failed, in April 1904. Most of the debts were met by the sale of assets; Morris escaped with his tool set, which he supposedly had to bid for, in the rain, and had to pay off £50 in liabilities.

Morris had not realised that when you were in partnership you did not need any deed setting out your obligations, but were liable for all the debts of your partner. It was a wretched end, and came the very month that Morris married a companion from his cycling club, Elizabeth Maud Anstey, generally called Lillian. With the

WHAT HAPPENED TO LAUNCELOT CREYKE?

All sorts of tall stories have been retailed about Creyke, not least by Morris himself, who told Andrews and Brunner that he 'ended up in South America running a gin palace'. Fortunately, Bullnose historian Robin Barraclough has researched Creyke's subsequent life – and at the very least the gin palace story can be discounted. After the debacle of the Oxford Automobile and Cycle Agency, Creyke's family used their connections to get Launcelot shipped out of the country to Canada. Having found him a job with the Hudson's Bay Company, he ended up in Telegraph Creek, British Columbia, employed as a clerk. Apparently he worked well, and learnt the language of the local Indian tribe.

But he started cooking the books and embezzling the company, as well as drinking and card-playing, and then he made a local Indian pregnant. His mother set about repatriating her wayward son, who naturally enough had by now lost his job. Meanwhile he married the Indian and went to live on her reservation – but only until a boat home could be arranged at the end of 1909. To make amends, he made over some of his money to his wife, who in the interim had given birth to a second child but was alas to be murdered shortly afterwards; her descendants thrive to this day.

What Creyke did in the First World War is not known, although he was briefly commissioned into the Royal (Garrison) Artillery in London. Afterwards he lived with his mother in London. 'It is said that he got through a second fortune, spent mostly on girls he met at stage doors,' writes Barraclough. He died in 1940, after falling in front of a train. An open verdict was recorded, suggesting the possibility that he took his own life.

Launcelot Creyke in the 'Easter Egg' in which he created such a stir around Oxford. (Richard Barton)

higher than in the four previous years combined. In 1911 the results would be even better.

Morris wasn't just a successful local businessman. By all accounts he ran a happy ship. He was more often than not in overalls, worked long hours, and was very much part of the workshop team – who nicknamed him 'Uncle'. He picked and kept good men, and brought out the best in them. He had great self-belief without being arrogant, a characteristic he would retain throughout his life.

During this time he was also striking up acquaintances which would serve him well when he launched himself as a motor manufacturer. His garage was advertised as 'The Rendezvous of Varsity & County Motorists' and among those from Oxford University who became customers was the Earl of Macclesfield, who would take £4000 of Preference shares to help launch WRM Motors; another was John Conybeare, an undergraduate who would become an eminent doctor and a key figure in the administration of many of Morris's charitable activities in later life.

The Longwall Street garage in c.1907. As well as servicing and selling cars, Morris had a small hire fleet. (Author's collection)

William Morris with his wife Lillian – an austere and difficult woman. (LAT)

He was small in stature, wiry, friendly and yet remote… he combined a working knowledge of engineering and tremendous attack as a mechanic with a magnetic personality which attracted people, made people anxious to serve him, proud to work for him and with him. But at the same time they never got to know him because he was so brittle, so exclusive and unpredictable in his likes and dislikes."

Morris was evidently as tense and energetic as his 5ft 10in frame was wiry and muscular. To Richard Newitt of distributors Wadhams, talking to one-time Nuffield Place curator Dorothy Silberston, he was 'temperamental, full of go, like a violin string… a man who had to have his own way and could be difficult to deal with'. Beatrice Nermberg, who painted the portrait at the entrance to Nuffield House at Guy's Hospital, found him 'shy, rigid and self-conscious'. Eventually she broke through his reserve, and he said he liked talking to 'down-to-earth people'.

He fitted into that category himself. 'I think among the really big men William Morris… was at once the most remarkable and unremarkable,' writes WO Bentley in *The Cars in my Life*. 'I recognised him at once as a complete contrast both in appearance and character to the popular conception of the loud, bustling, extravagantly phrased, successful industrialist. With Morris there was none of this barking down a multitude of telephones, restlessly pacing the floor and 'big talk' that might be expected of someone in his position. When Morris talked it was at a practical down-to-earth level, modestly phrased and with never a wasted word; and his appearance might be described as that, say, of a legal clerk dedicated to his calling and determined to do well in it… Certainly no one meeting him in the street would have associated him in any way with engineering, and I have never met a more un-tycoonish tycoon.'

Reginald Rootes, used to the flamboyance of his larger-than-life cigar-chomping brother Billy, found Morris dull company when he accompanied him on a boat to Argentina, as he recalled in an interview for BBC programme *The Car Makers*. 'Morris was a more popular man in the trade than Austin, but a man of not much personality. He couldn't talk much, but he was very honest, very straightforward. He was admired by his dealers. He never left the boat. He just sat on it, and didn't mix with other people at all. I had dinner with him; he had nothing to talk about except the motor business.'

This book does not seek to be a biography of William Morris: enough of these have been written. But some sort of gauge of the character of the person is necessary, in order to understand his history as a businessman.

Perhaps the essence is summed up in the description of Morris in *Out on a Wing* as a 'bright-eyed tight little man'. Thomas more expansively portrayed him in his conversations with Andrews and Brunner. "There was something about him which gave people more than normal confidence.

Always prudent with his money, Morris was a modest man of modest tastes, as will be appreciated by anyone visiting his former home, Nuffield Place. He was not a man of culture, had no hobbies other than tinkering with old clocks and cigarette lighters, and he read little and had unrefined music-hall tastes in entertainment. That said, he gave long-term financial support to the Oxford Theatre Company. If he was no intellectual, he was mentally very sharp, as Thomas impressed on Andrews and Brunner. "Whereas the college professor could talk and impress by rarified logic, Nuffield had not got that ability. But he would make a devastatingly simple remark which went right to the root of the matter. That was one reason for his success."

He didn't drink much, although he was proud of his ability to hold his liquor and was not averse to the odd gin-and-French. He did, however, smoke intensely and intensively – either a pipe or cigarettes. Despite this, he was an obsessive to the point of crankiness about his health – which in fact seems to have been impressively robust.

Perhaps his one real extravagance was the purchase of Huntercombe Golf Club. But even this was a pragmatic decision: until he moved into what became Nuffield Place, it provided him with board and lodging, while it was always a congenial venue for him to meet business contacts and people associated with his charitable activities. His own game of golf, incidentally, was not particularly skilled, it is said.

Although he was always smart, with beige slacks and a blazer being his favoured leisure wear, he never spent much money on his clothes, his suits being modest and loyally purchased from the same tailor in Oxford.

In his early days he cut a dash by using special-bodied Morrises as his personal transport, but in his final years he contented himself with a pre-production example of the Wolseley Eight, punctiliously buying it off the company for £75 in 1955 and being maniacal about its fuel consumption. A friend of the author, a one-time Nuffield engineer, once recalled how he was torn off a strip by His Lordship when he replaced the worn tyres on the Wolseley: he was instructed to put them back on the car, 'as they weren't yet down to the canvas'. This was typical of his natural reflex not to waste things. To the end of his days he untied parcel string and saved it, and used old envelopes as rough paper,

and there are stories of having old wastepaper bins repaired rather than replaced, and of his returning from walkabouts in the factory with nuts and bolts and washers in his pocket that he had picked up off the floor.

By the time of the Andrews and Brunner biography, Lord Nuffield was a dispirited man, as Philip Andrews recorded in his notes of a 1953 interview. 'Lord Nuffield said his batteries had run down. His body was healthy and strong. If a man annoyed him, he could still give him a good punch. In fact, his body was really that of a man of fifty. But if his opponent hung on, he would collapse completely. Lord Nuffield was tired and it was a great effort to arouse an interest any more... Lord Nuffield really had complete nervous exhaustion. He did not want to go on living.'

The Morrises never had any children and Nuffield, although kindly with children, was always a little awkward in their company. Lillian Morris, Lady Nuffield, kept herself very much in the background. She was not liked. She was, said senior Nuffield manager George Dono, "a woman with a small village mind who had never grown up". Miles Thomas was generously discreet when talking to Andrews and Brunner. "As [Nuffield's] fortune grew, his protective mechanism grew, and that was aided by Lady Nuffield, who was frugal to the point of parsimony," he told them.

Nuffield's personal secretary, Carl Kingerlee, said that he refused to have anything to do with the Nuffield Trust for the Forces of the Crown or the Elizabeth Nuffield Home, because it would have meant dealing with Lady Nuffield, and having endless arguments about the cost of curtains and suchlike. He also said that she was the origin of much of the tittle-tattle at the Cowley works.

Former company secretary SGK Smallbone said that Lady Nuffield was "very economical, not to say mean". You always knew when she had guests for the weekend, he said, "because she would send to Hill Upton and say she would like to try some electric light fittings on approval. Then, on Monday, she would tell them to take them away again – because she did not like them."

Although Nuffield insisted that the section on his wife in the Andrews and Brunner biography be baldly perfunctory, her death in 1959 clearly left a hole in his life, at a time when he was already depressed and listless now that he was no longer at the helm of the company he had created.

The 'White and Poppe' Oxford

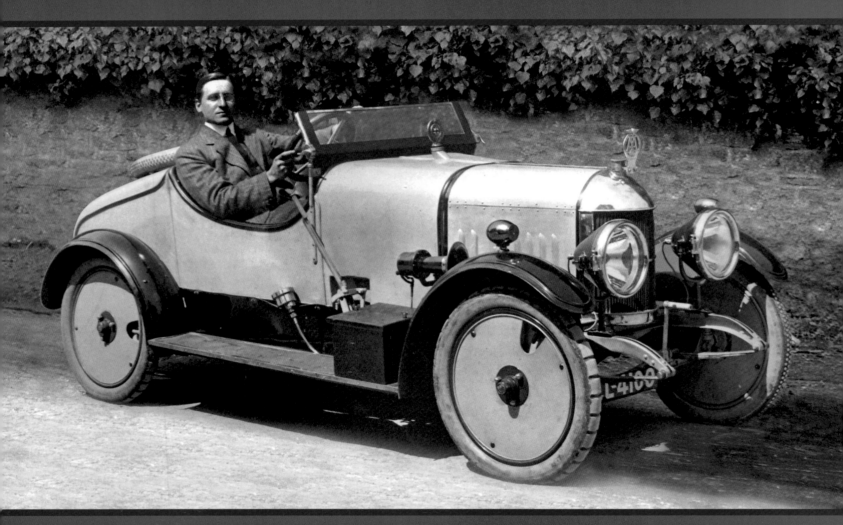

Gordon Stewart of Stewart and Ardern looking every bit the young blade in his special-bodied De Luxe Oxford, complete with rather over-the-top five-lamp electrics and an outside speedometer. (Nuffield College archives)

With his first Morris-Oxford, Morris demonstrated a vision and an intelligence that set him apart from other producers of cars from bought-in components. The little runabout soon built up a good reputation.

William Morris at the wheel of a very early W&P car, with Frank Barton as passenger. (Richard Barton)

As so many who had begun as cycle-makers, William Morris sought to make the transition to being a manufacturer of motor cars. But unlike so many such people, he was not a trained engineer, versed in the theories – arcane or otherwise – of the discipline. Nor was he, despite occasional early-days dabblings, an enthusiastic participant in motor-sport[1]. Rather differently, Morris approached car design via the garage trade. As opposed to an exercise in engineering vanity, the car he conceived was one based on his practical experience of what worked and what did not work, borrowing as appropriate from existing designs.

By 1912 he was ready to put his thoughts into action, thanks to a £4000 loan from Lord Macclesfield. It was both a good and a bad time to enter the market. The industry was in full expansion, with total national output set to rise to 34,000 in 1913, against 10,800 cars made in 1908. Competition, on the other hand, was fierce. Between 1911 and 1914 a substantial 64

firms would be founded, of which 46 would still be in business at the end of that period. Ford, meanwhile, was to begin production in Britain at the end of 1911. From sales of 400 in 1910, when it was still imported, output of the Model T would exceed 8000 units in 1914 and the price would fall from £220 to £135, giving the rustic but unbreakable Ford an easy sales leadership.

The fully enclosed drivetrain prevented the ingress of dirt and dust and added to the reliability of the car; Morris was very proud of this feature. (Author's collection)

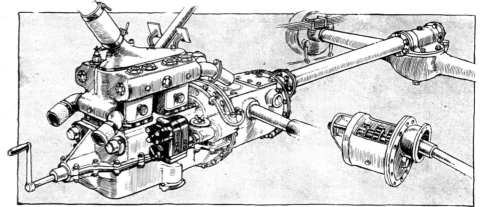

[1] *Morris won an Oxford hillclimb in 1908 or thereabouts in an Enfield car from his hire fleet. He won by keeping in bottom gear and going up at full revs. He used the same technique to win the Coventry Hillclimb in an early Morris-Oxford.*

A week's output of early W&P Oxfords outside the former Military Academy in 1913. In all, 495 narrow-track models and 980 De Luxes were made. (Author's collection)

A very early Oxford. The windscreen is adjustable, and is generally shown at a more raked angle than here. (Author's collection)

The De Luxe with its hood erected; side curtains were available as a 25s extra. (Author's collection)

Creative thinking – and an industrial logic

Morris did not need to be hugely perspicacious to work out where the market was going. The motor industry was developing in the same way as had the cycle industry, with a progressive democratisation of what had started out as a plaything for the aristocracy. The future lay in producing a car at an accessible price – not a gimcrack cyclecar, though, but a proper automobile, lightweight and simple, but fully equipped, and capable of being a serious rival to the Ford.

In reality this was the only option open to Morris. He did not have a lavish engineering shop; nor did he himself have the engineering abilities to design and build a car from scratch. So he would have to assemble a car from bought-in parts, as in the bicycle trade. Perforce that meant something small and cheap, as opposed to a costly hand-built bigger model that could command a higher price on account of its bespoke construction.

Morris was fortunate in that he was entering the field just as a new genre of vehicle was coming onto the market – the so-called 'light car'. In the same way as the Austin Seven of a decade later, these were literally big cars in miniature rather than half-baked motorcycle-powered marginalia, and they were enthusiastically championed by a new magazine, *The Light Car and Cyclecar*. In Britain, Singer and Humber were the first serious players, respectively with their Ten and Humberette, both introduced in 1912; the following year the French would join the fray with the Bugatti-designed Bébé Peugeot. Morris was able to plug into this new trend, which corresponded exactly to his perception of what the market needed – and what he could most happily produce.

The idea of an 'assembled car' was regarded with disdain in some quarters, *Automobile Engineer* magazine observing in 1911 that 'the manufacturer who buys finished parts and puts them together has generally been regarded rather contemptuously and it is usual to assume that cars made in this way cannot be really good'. Although at the time an industry leader, making vehicles in relatively substantial numbers, Wolseley would proudly claim in 1914 that it made everything for its cars but the ignition coil and the tyres – including its own castings.

Thanks to his bicycle experience and his good network of contacts in Coventry, Morris knew such arguments were fallacious. He could obtain better-quality parts at lower cost if he went to specialist producers who manufactured in large quantities. Also he would need relatively little capital. Had he been making his own components, he would have needed to invest in plant; as it was, he could build a respectable turnover from a small base, whilst at the same time achieving a relatively high output. In thinking this way, rather than trying to be an artisan building small numbers of his own cars from scratch, Morris was a genuine innovator, ahead of the game in an industry that would only wake up to mass-production after the experience of manufacturing munitions in the First World War[2].

This, indeed, was another plank of Morris's business plan: right from the start he would quantity-produce his car. At the time it was industry practice to take orders at the Motor Show and then organise production accordingly. It was building to order, or in other words playing it safe, but the downside was that it tied the manufacturer to small and less economic contracts with his suppliers. Following such a rhythm, a sanction of 50 engines might represent several weeks of work for a supplier. Morris, however, wanted up to 50 power units a week – with 300 for his first order.

In negotiating component prices with suppliers on the basis of substantial contracts, Morris showed an early awareness that increasing production would bring unit costs – and thus prices – downwards, even if that meant that suppliers might have to bring in fresh tooling to achieve the required output. Despite being new to the field, he inspired sufficient confidence to win over his intended suppliers, helped by the fact that early on he had secured a contract with respected engine manufacturer White and Poppe; thanks to backing from the Earl of Macclesfield, he could also demonstrate that adequate finance was in place.

Good components, intelligently assembled

The cornerstone of the Morris car was indeed a White and Poppe engine – Morris already being a customer, as he fitted the firm's carburettor to some of the vehicles that passed through his garage. Of 1018cc, with a 60mm bore and 90mm stroke, the in-line 'four' was specifically designed for Morris, and featured a somewhat old-fashioned T-head configuration in conjunction with a fixed cylinder head; the carburettor, naturally enough, was a W&P unit. Although commissioned by him, Morris apparently had little input into the engine's layout. He volunteered "no idea at all" about the detail of its design, according to Hans Landstad, the Norwegian-born chief draughtsman at White and Poppe who laid it out. This slightly sour observation is at odds with a 1928 article

in *The Autocar*, in which editor H Massac Buist told of how all the suppliers to whom he had talked recalled Morris as requesting quite specific changes to the design of their parts. 'All agreed on one point,' wrote Buist. 'They never knew anybody who wanted so many alterations and yet they had to recognise the fact that each detail was dictated as the result of a practical user's and repairer's experience.'

Built by Hollick and Pratt for Lancelot Pratt's personal use, this 1914 Oxford De Luxe has an extended body featuring two additional inward-facing folding occasional seats. (LAT)

This Oxford was used for a 1400-mile tour in late 1913, and tackled all the major hills comfortably whilst returning 38–42mpg. Morris claimed the car was capable of 50mph and 50mpg. (LAT)

From 1914 a drophead coupé by Hollick and Pratt was a catalogued model. (LAT)

[2] 'In Britain the engineers were obsessed by the technical product rather than by the technique of production,' comments SB Saul, in his article 'The Motor Industry in Britain to 1914'. In this he echoes a prescient observation in a newspaper of the period. 'To put it bluntly, the fact is that there is no firm at present which has been sufficiently enterprising to lay down a large enough plant to make cheap cars in sufficient numbers to make their production really cheap,' said The Times, in its 20 August 1912 edition.

Another Hollick and Pratt creation, this three-quarter coupé from 1914 may have been a personal car for William Morris. (LAT)

Bodied in aluminium, the Sporting Model featured disc wheels. It cost £220 in 1914, against 190 guineas (£199.10s) for a De Luxe two-seater. (LAT)

The Limousine Coupé was bodied by Hollick and Pratt. It was upholstered in Bedford Cord. (LAT)

The gearbox was mounted at the front, in unit with the engine, as on the Model T Ford. This was at a time when many gearboxes were separately mounted or integrated into the back axle, arrangements which only added complication; the clutch, meanwhile, was a multiple-plate type, running in oil shared with the engine and gearbox. This last would also be manufactured by White and Poppe, and at Morris's instigation was a direct crib of the gearbox used on the Belsize car, of which he sent up an example from Oxford to be copied. "It was an absolute infringement, but it worked alright," Landstad told Andrews and Brunner, admitting to admiration that Morris had been prepared to take the risk of brazenly pirating another car manufacturer's design.

There was in fact an excellent rapport between Morris and Landstad, and this resulted in not just the engine and gearbox being schemed at W&P's Coventry factory: in the end the whole car was laid out by Landstad, with Morris – "a good chaser" – breathing down his neck, and dropping in at any time from 7am to 10pm, in the course of the two or three days a week he latterly spent in Coventry during the gestation of the car. This was indicative of Morris's approach to his suppliers, and one of the secrets of his success. 'WR Morris was fortunate in his suppliers and he drove them hard,' comment Andrews and Brunner. 'He believed in personal contact to keep them up to the mark, and always preferred to go over and see them rather than let them come to see him. In this way, he kept in close touch with what was happening in their works and made personal acquaintances which he kept for years, generally refusing to deal with anyone else in the firm.'

Whilst Landstad was working on the engine, the decision was taken to source the front axle, the worm-drive rear axle and the worm-and-wheel

If that meant imitating the practice of other manufacturers, so be it. A very concrete example was the decision to adopt a fully-enclosed torque-tube transmission – for the first time on a quantity-produced British car. This was directly inspired by that of the Hupmobile, Morris Garages being an agent for the American make, and would enhance the reliability of the Morris, as well as eliminating snatch as the driver let in the clutch. In old age Morris remained proud of this feature – and of his use of enclosed internal-expanding brakes rather than the horse-and-cart external-contracting type some manufacturers still used.

steering gear from Wrigley's – who had first made a precautionary phone-call to White and Poppe, as Landstad related to Andrews and Brunner. "One day Wrigley's phoned up White and Poppe and said there was a man from Oxford, Mr Morris, and did they know anything about him, because he was talking about wanting 300 sets of axle parts and did we think he was safe? They said they could not imagine anyone starting to make cars in Oxford. White and Poppe replied yes... that Macclesfield was behind [him], and after that, there was no question about it."

Morris's main contact at Wrigley's was chief draughtsman Frank Woollard, to whom he outlined his requirement for robust easy-to-repair components. "Morris had his say... he did not do the design as we understand it, but he said very definitely what jobs they were to do," recalled Woollard. Wrigley's didn't take Morris seriously at first. The manager refused to see him and he and his fellow directors used to refer patronisingly to him as 'Woollard's little garage friend from Oxford'.

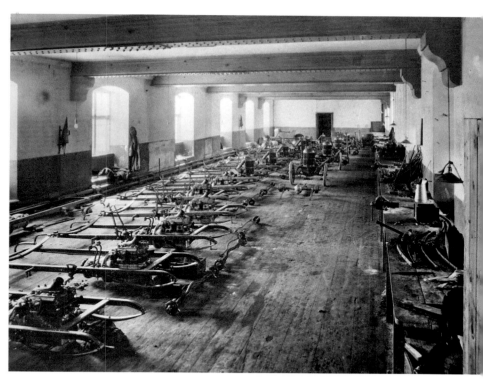

The chassis erection shop in the former Military Academy, during 1913. (Author's collection)

The top floor of the building housed the body shop. Soon relatively few bodies were coming from Raworth, Hollick and Pratt having established themselves as the principal supplier. (Author's collection)

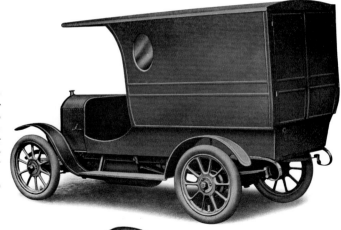

The delivery van had an open cab and a mahogany body. This 1914 catalogue image shows a car on the Standard chassis, but most were built on the more stable wider-track De Luxe underpinnings. (Author's collection)

The De Luxe chassis retailed at £180; it can be identified by the rear springs. These sit below the axle – rather than above it, as on the Standard/Popular. (Author's collection)

Morris always saw Woollard instead, and the two men become very friendly. Attitudes higher up the company tree changed when the Morris-Oxford was in production and Morris had proved himself to have some standing as a motor manufacturer, but the conduct of the Managing Director meant that relations remained glacial. As related by Woollard, the gentleman in question was very proud of being descended from ancient Scottish kings – "and was going to let everyone know it". On a visit to Cowley, "Morris... had about an hour of this Scots kings business, and was absolutely furious. When the war was over, instead of coming back to Wrigley's, he went elsewhere for his axles..."

Morris wasn't going to be treated as a second-rate citizen. When he decided to increase his order for 1914, Wrigley's asked for a guarantee. Morris, with a characteristic love of the dramatic, paid the full sum for one month's supplies directly into the company's bank.

Other suppliers included Coventry firm Doherty for the radiator, Raworth in Oxford for the body, and Sankey of Hadley in Shropshire for the wheels. Morris was one of the first British manufacturers to take up Sankey's new pressed and welded steel artillery wheels; reducing costs, the dies ended up being shared with the Perry company, who used the same wheels on its own short-lived light cars.

Into production – in an old school

Meanwhile, in August 1912 a new business was established for the manufacture of the Morris motor car. WRM Motors Ltd had Morris as Managing Director, and friend and local coroner Henry Galpin as Junior Director and secretary. Morris's principal backer, the Earl of Macclesfield, had £4000 in Preference shares and the title of President. Galpin would resign in late 1913, at which stage Lillian Morris became a director.

Morris had planned to exhibit the car at the 1912 Motor Show, but there were delays in the supply of components, not least of engine castings. In the end, White and Poppe brought in five draughtsmen from Coventry car manufacturer Maudslay, to speed things up. Whether it was one of these hired hands or not, one draughtsman contributed to the hold-up in the arrival of parts: he drew up the engine half-size, but did not indicate this on his drawings, and legend has it that the first example of the casting in question came back half-size.

With no car to display, Morris ended up publicising his Morris-Oxford with nothing more than blueprints and a specification sheet. Despite this, Gordon Stewart of Stewart and Ardern placed a firm order with a deposit, for 400 cars, and was duly appointed distributor for the London area. When it came to a distributor for the South of England, Morris appointed WHM Burgess, who had represented White and Poppe and secured the contract for the company to build the Morris engine. Burgess was appointed wholesale and shipping agent, and sole distributor for all territory south of Aberystwyth and The Wash, excluding Oxfordshire, Buckinghamshire and Berkshire.

THE OXFORD BUS WAR

It was in the very early days of the Morris-Oxford that William Morris became involved in an extraordinary and controversial affair in Oxford, when he briefly ended up running a bus company.

The only public transport in Oxford at the time was horse-drawn trams. The City Corporation had given an option to a company to operate electric trams but nothing had happened. Then the horse-tram drivers had gone on strike, and there was no public transport at all. With the council in turmoil, in November 1913 Morris asked for a licence to run two public buses. When he received no reply, he made contact with local solicitor Frank Gray.

A more inappropriate associate for the sober Morris than Frank Gray it is difficult to imagine. The son of a property developer and former mayor of Oxford, this larger-than-life character was a chancer, a hustler, a showman, and a calculated eccentric. A businessman with interests ranging from steam laundries to cinemas, he had a circle of dubious acquaintances, from horse-dealers and gypsies to dog-breeders. He would go on to be a Liberal MP and to set up the *Oxford Mail*, but would also spend time as a tramp, and would try to be a miner in the mid-1920s. His home, Shipton Manor, was evidently a madhouse, with a wing at one stage given over to 'gentlemen of the road'.

According to his biographer, Charles Fenby, Gray quickly appraised the situation. 'It was obvious that the Corporation could never grant a licence which would cut right across its contractual engagements and form a precedent, and so Frank decided that the only hope of success was to marshall public opinion and whip it up to the point where it would carry all before it; in other words, the mob was to rule'.

Morris and Grey decided to put two buses on the streets without a licence. Fares were not paid on boarding, but bought in advance as coupons sold in the shops. When the City Solicitor applied for a warrant for the arrest of the drivers and conductors and of Morris and Gray, the latter organised an immediate public meeting. All the roads were blocked by people trying to get in, and to a packed house Gray made a rabble-rousing speech – 'an inflammatory speech, in a nature inciting to riot,' according to Fenby. It had just that effect: the crowd rushed out and turned over a horse-drawn tram and tried to set fire to it, whilst battling with the police.

As threats of litigation flew, Morris and Gray found themselves in a three-cornered fight with the City Corporation and the company originally contracted to provide the electric trams. "All the council had fingers in this pie. He had had detectives on the job and found that they were having champagne parties in London at the expense of the tramways company," Morris told Andrews and Brunner. In the end, he said, he had taken a page in the *Oxford Times* every week, and exposed one councillor each week, to the point that they were "shaking in their shoes as to who was to be the next victim". With a loan of £8000 from Gilletts Bank, Morris managed to acquire two buses intended for Salford, re-painting the lettering to read 'Oxford' and rushing them into service. Soon there was a fleet of 16 buses, offering a complete service for the city.

The temperature continued to rise, with meetings, petitions and a soap-box orator paid to stir things up by talking about a 'bus war'. At one stage a mob made for the Town Hall and there were fears that it might be sacked. Then four rival buses were put on the street – and the crowds threatened anyone trying to board.

Finally the Council decided to hold a special meeting to allocate the bus licences. Gray and Morris again used intimidation, taking all their buses out of service and using them to block access to the Town Hall. In this febrile atmosphere, with crowds baying outside, the meeting was adjourned. When it took place a few days later, in early January 1914, twelve licences went to Morris and twelve to the other company; Morris almost immediately sold on his licences, and his buses, to the horse-tram company. He had made his point, and had no wish to be a bus-operator.

This colourful episode did much to raise Morris's profile in Oxford: he was respected for having the guts to stand up to an incompetent and possibly corrupt local administration, and for delivering a modern bus service. At the same time, a friendship had been struck up with Frank Gray, to the point that the two men would later go to the United States together, to source parts for what would become the Morris-Cowley. Subsequently, however, the two would fall out over the issue of Protectionism.

Morris had of course to find a suitable works. Not wanting to move to Coventry or Birmingham, he ended up renting – and latterly buying – the former Hurst's Grammar School site at Temple Cowley. Since ceasing to be a school it had been used as premises for the Oxford Military College and had then been sold to London-based mechanical engineers and manufacturers Alfred Breese Ltd. The company had never taken up occupancy, as it had gone into liquidation after spending a fortune expanding the site – estate agents estimated that the east and west wings alone had cost £50,000. As well as the 35,000 square feet of factory space in these two wings, according to the description of the estate agents there was a quadrangle at the rear, 'adapted as a Trial Track for Motor Cars, including a Canteen or Pavilion' and an ensemble of a 17th-century Manor House, a chapel, a Master's House, a lecture hall, 'numerous classrooms or workrooms', an engine house (containing 'up-to-date plant for Electric Lighting and Power'), a clock tower, engineers' workshops, fives courts and a detached cottage. Morris, whose father had been educated at the grammar school, took up residence in the Manor House, and the new wings were used as his factory.

The Express Carrier of 1915 was built on the Popular chassis and had a removable carrier box which could be swapped for a low-line tail section for normal touring use. (Author's collection)

Production methods were rudimentary, and handicapped by the old Military Academy being a three-storey building. Such minimal machining and drilling as was required took place on the ground floor, chassis assembly was carried out on the middle floor, and body-fitting and final finishing was the domain of the top floor – Charles Raworth apparently moving in to supervise the body operations directly. In these early days there were no moving lines, the chassis being laid out in a row and assembled on the spot; it was said that it took only four hours to assemble a running chassis. In 1913, according to Carl Kingerlee, the workforce numbered 130 people.

A happy baby, with few teething pains

Alf Keen recalled that the first engines were delivered from White and Poppe at the end of February 1913 or in early March. On 28 March, Gordon Stewart collected the first car. As the oft-repeated story has it, the poor Mr Stewart had an eventful start to his long association with Morris: the cast-iron universal joint on which Peter Poppe had insisted broke before the car had even left the works, and the replacement failed not many miles further on. Morris was beside himself with fury, and demanded that White and Poppe henceforth supply phosphor-bronze universals. After this initial mishap, the first Morris-Oxford evidently settled down to give good service, as in the early 1920s the then owner wrote to Cowley requesting a replacement stub axle. Morris offered to swap the car for a new one, but the owner said that he just wanted the stub axle, and so William Morris was alas denied the chance to buy back his very first motor car.

Retailing at £175 with full equipment including a spare wheel, Powell and Hanmer acetylene headlamps, an adjustable screen and a cape hood, the Morris-Oxford was advertised as 'The High-Grade Small Car' – with much stress being placed on the top quality of all the components used, whether the Hoffmann ball bearings or the 'practically indestructible' Sankey wheels. Finished in Pearl Grey with green leather trim, the Oxford was a dainty creature, sitting on a 7ft wheelbase and a 3ft 6in track, with an overall length of just 10ft 5in – or five inches longer than a Mini. The narrow track made the cockpit too tight for anyone bigger than the wiry Morris, and after 150 or so cars had been built the track was widened by 2in, allowing a slightly more spacious body and improving stability a little. According to Jarman and Barraclough, 43 surplus narrow-track component sets were built into export-market cars.

The press – particularly the ultra-enthusiastic *Light Car and Cyclecar* – gave the Morris a warm reception, one that it essentially merited. The Oxford was well sprung, uncapricious to drive, and in the words of *The Autocar* had the 'revviest small engine sold to the public'. This meant that it was a car that demanded to be driven with spirit to get the best out of it: it didn't pull well at low engine speeds.

Teething troubles were few, and mainly limited to the alternate steel and bronze plates of the 36-plate clutch sticking when the oil was cold. This was rapidly redesigned, with two fewer plates and stronger springs, which solved the problem – although Morris was understandably a bit grouchy about having to send mechanics around the country to change the clutch on customer cars. There were also problems with engine lubrication, which was looked after by oil being scooped up by the flywheel and 'splashed' around the engine: the faster the engine went, the less oil was distributed.

Such worries were soon overcome, and the only bugbear that stayed with the car was a tendency to overheat, notwithstanding the 'extremely handsome v-type radiator of novel design, and of the greatest possible efficiency' of which Morris boasted – or indeed the engine's supposedly well-cooled valve pockets. This latter claim was apparently misplaced, as the plugs tended to get too hot, resulting in misfiring. Morris always denied that there was a problem, saying that the fault lay with people not using the correct plugs, an argument not without foundation, as it was generally found that the Oxford performed most happily with the specified Bosch plugs.

Better cars – and more of them

The first sanction was for 400 cars, which tallies with the official figure of 404 cars made during 1913. For 1914 a new De Luxe model – 'a car of super-excellence at a modest price' – joined the range. Offered in dark green or grey, it had a track widened by a further three inches, to 3ft 9in, and sat on a longer 7ft 6in wheelbase that resulted in an overall length of 11ft. The steering was improved, with a different design of axle and the drag link above rather than below the axle, and grooved rear tyres were fitted. As well as the mainstream two-seater, the De Luxe was also available as a drophead coupé and as a rather racy aluminium-bodied 'Sporting Model' with a chassis 'specially picked and tuned-up'. Also catalogued was a delivery van, again based on the De Luxe. The original 7ft-wheelbase Oxford continued, as the Standard Model, still on a 3ft 6in track, and was accompanied by a new Commercial Model with a narrower body and less good finish, 'introduced to meet the requirements of Commercial Travellers and the like'. For the general customer, however, it was the more spacious and better-to-drive De Luxe that had greater appeal than the more basic models: according to Jarman and Barraclough a full 827 found homes in the calendar year 1914, against only 61 Standard Oxfords.

Supported financially by the Earl of Macclesfield, output was increasing to 100 cars a month by this stage. Macclesfield loaned Morris £500 in each of the years 1911–1914 inclusive and £2500 in 1915, when Morris himself ploughed £8000 back into the company. The Earl's financing would be even more generous in subsequent years, with a loan of £4500 in 1916, of £9500 in 1917 (when the banker Gillett additionally put in £5000), and of a further £9500 in 1918. Given Morris's mealy-mouthed attitude to Macclesfield in later life, it behoves one to record the Oxfordshire aristocrat's contribution to the company in its formative years.

The regular two-seater in 1915 De Luxe form. The body of the De Luxe and Popular had softer lines and a shorter door that did not extend to the bottom of the body. (Author's collection)

With 908 cars produced in 1914, Morris was in the top peleton of British manufacturers, alongside Singer, Wolseley, Rover, Austin and Humber. With 2000 or so vehicles delivered in the 1914 season, Wolseley and Rover were top of the pile, but Morris was already level-pegging with Austin, who produced 866 vehicles in that model year. Ford, however, made 8352 Model Ts at its Trafford Park factory in Manchester. To cope with further expansion, a new building was erected in the early days of the war, on the old college parade ground. This steel-framed building, which became known as 'The Old Tin Shed', gave an extra 100,000 sq ft of space, and would allow line-assembly to be introduced. The new facility's entry into use was troubled, however: a gale blew it down, and every piece had to be taken back to makers Rubery Owen at Darlington, and re-rolled.

The range was slightly modified for 1915, with a five-window Limousine Coupé added, along with a second type of delivery van, with a detachable canvas top. The sports Oxford was no longer offered, and nor was the Commercial Model, in place of which Morris proposed the Express Carrier, which was a two-seater with a large box compartment added to the rear. The Standard Model continued, but was renamed the Popular. War or no war, production continued through 1915, at the end of which year a further 159 Oxfords had been made – a way short of fulfilling the second sanction of 1500 cars that had been established. The split this time was less kiltered towards the De Luxe, with 98 being made, against 61 Standard models. The reason for this is not difficult to discern: during 1915 would-be buyers of the De Luxe had the possibility of transferring their automotive affections to a new, more powerful and more spacious Morris model.

The Continental-engined Cowley

This 'cruiser-type' Cowley was built in 1918 by Hollick and Pratt, for Morris general manager Hugh Wordsworth Grey. The upper body was in apple green and the lower body and wheel discs in a light green merging into a darker green. (LAT)

The American-sourced components of the Cowley allowed it to be sold at a competitive price, and allowed Morris to extend the appeal of his range. But production was held back by the First World War.

The Oxford having swiftly established itself as a reference among small cars, Morris naturally enough sought to build on this success. A higher level of production was desirable not just in itself, but also as a way of driving unit costs downwards. Not only would this be beneficial to profits, but it would allow him to lower prices, which in turn would ramp up demand. Whilst he could have stuck to producing the existing Oxford, there were two fundamental obstacles to expanding his business on the back of the little 10hp light car.

Firstly, his British suppliers were unable – or unwilling – to furnish him with components in the quantities he required. In particular, White and Poppe were apparently working at full capacity for their various customers, and said they could not increase output of engines for Morris. One also imagines that established suppliers were hesitant about making serious commitments to this ambitious newcomer to the British motor industry, lest he fatally over-reach himself and leave them with a pile of unpaid bills.

Secondly, the Oxford was to a degree a prisoner of its status as a light car: it had a small engine and could happily carry only relatively compact two-seater or occasional-four-seater coachwork. In order to offer four-seater open tourer bodies – and perhaps rather more heavyweight closed cars than the various Oxford coupés – a more powerful engine was needed, implying more robust running gear. Put simply, a new design was the best way forward.

Morris looks to America

With the British engineering industry not in a position to supply Morris, he turned to the United States. This was a brave internationalist move by the parochial standards of the time, and all the more so given that he was still relatively small fry: in 1914 he would produce 908 cars, against the 8352 Model Ts made at Trafford Park by market-leader Ford. Morris's output was more than honourable in a British context, but the domestic motor industry was a pygmy in relation to that across the Atlantic. Total British production in 1913 was of roughly 34,000

The Continental engine and Warner gearbox were to play a key part in Morris history; the presence of a dipstick was a novelty for the time. (Author's collection)

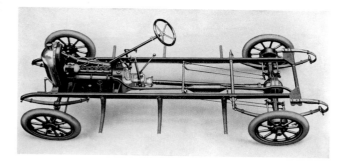

As on the Oxford, drive from the gearbox to the rear axle was totally enclosed; the bronze universal was lubricated from the gearbox. The Cowley was the first volume-produced British car to have a helically-cut crownwheel and pinion. (Author's collection)

vehicles, when US motor production was in the order of 485,000 units. This perforce meant that the American components industry was geared up for larger numbers, and could thus produce at lower cost.

Consequently in early 1914 Morris made the first of two trips that year to the United States. As much as anything this turned into a reconnaissance, Morris visiting key suppliers and coming to appreciate the advance the Americans had in mass-production techniques. No deals were signed at this stage. Vickers had preceded Morris, placed a lot of orders on behalf of Wolseley, and then cancelled them. Consequently the companies concerned were understandably wary of this unknown Englishman. Despite

The two-seater resembled an enlarged Oxford. The electric lighting set Morris back £10.10s – a big proportion of the car's cost, which he calculated, including overheads and a 10 per cent profit, as being £125.3s.0d. (Author's collection)

this, Morris returned home with drawings for a suitable engine and transmission, and for the steering and axles he would need – in other words, all the basic components. The prices quoted were attractive indeed: according to Andrews and Brunner the power unit, from the Continental Motor Manufacturing Co, was costed at £25, when the comparable price from White and Poppe was £50 an engine[1]. To put such figures in perspective, by 1915 Continental – described by Morris in subsequent publicity as 'the World's largest and most prominent producer of petrol engines' – would be making 46,000 engines a year, more than the entire output of motor cars achieved by the British industry and a production rate that inevitably gave them enviable economies of scale.

The drophead coupé was by Hollick and Pratt, who were now responsible for most of Morris's bodies; in all, 117 were produced. (Author's collection)

Morris arranged to return to the States in April 1914, accompanied by Frank Gray and Hans Landstad – who was still chief draughtsman for White and Poppe. The idea was that Landstad would get a job with Continental so that he could study mass-production techniques, and that Morris would tie up the necessary contracts with suppliers; meanwhile, the two would scheme up a new chassis to take the US-sourced components. These would ultimately comprise a

1495cc Continental side-valve engine, a gearbox from Warner, and axles and worm-and-wheel steering gear from the Detroit Gear Company; Morris requested that the engine's pressed-steel sump be replaced by a more up-market sand-cast aluminium item, judged more in line with British tastes.

On the transatlantic crossing, Landstad, working in the second-class dining room, started drawing up the frame for the new Continental-powered model, a task he soon had to abandon as he couldn't cope with the rough seas. Morris, he told Andrews and Brunner, was 'quite good' on the chassis. "He could not draw, but he said he wanted this and that, a strut here and a strut there..."

In Detroit, as has often been related, Morris and Landstad set up base in a modest hotel, sharing a room to which were sent samples of the components they wished to use. In a fug of tobacco smoke in this pokey hotel room the two men drew up the bare bones of the new Morris car, Landstad perching his drawing board first on the bed, then on some boxes. Morris soon returned to Britain, but Landstad stayed in Detroit, where he had indeed been given a temporary position with Continental. He was thus able to monitor the progress of Morris's contracts, and send back such engineering drawings as were necessary. After seeing the first engine through its tests, he returned to England after the outbreak of war, joining WRM Motors in December 1914 as a draughtsman, on a salary of £350 a year.

Britain's entry in August 1914 into what became the First World War naturally caused Continental to question if Morris still intended to go ahead with his new car. Surreal though it may seem, whilst Europe was being dragged into the remorseless bloodshed of trench warfare, leisure motoring continued in Britain. Morris confirmed his initial order for 1500 units, part of a plan to build 2500 Continental-engined cars in the first year and 5000 in the second year. Contracts with the other US suppliers were maintained, apparently to the anger of British component manufacturers, many of whom had already switched to munitions work but who, even in peacetime, could not hope to compete with American firms.

---

[1] *According to Andrews and Brunner the engine ended up costing Morris $85, or £17.9s.3d at the then current exchange rate of $4.87 to the pound; this figure excluded freight and insurance. Morris's own costings for the Cowley, dated June 1915 and reproduced in the Andrews and Brunner biography, quote £17.14s.2d, with the gearbox coming to a further £8.6s.6d. Did the price quoted for the Continental engine thus fall even further, in the course of Morris's negotiations? This is conceivable, but it is more plausible that the figure* of £25 in fact represents a combined price for the engine and gearbox, in line with the combined price that White and Poppe would presumably have quoted for their supply of both engine and gearbox for the Oxford. Lending credence to this supposition is that in Morris's 1915 costings the combined total for the engine and gearbox comes to £26.0s.8d – within spitting distance of that £25 quoted.

The Morris-Cowley
– a new approach to the light car

So it was that in April 1915 the new Morris-Cowley was announced. This was preceded – or so it appears – by what today's motoring press would herald as a scoop. As related in its 15 March issue, *The Light Car and Cyclecar* chanced upon a Morris Oxford 'which appeared somewhat longer than the standard model'. Closer inspection revealed it to have an 8ft 6in wheelbase, a central gearchange, a bevel-drive rear axle, and Lucas electric lighting. The engine and gearbox were said to be unchanged, but whether this was really the case is another matter. It seems that the journalist in question might in fact have stumbled upon the prototype Cowley. Told by Morris that the bevel rear axle was an alternative because of supply difficulties with the regular worm-drive unit, the magazine duly reported on the car as being 'An Improved Morris-Oxford' – which could be regarded as being broadly true.

There could be another explanation for the sighting of this car. According to Andrews and Brunner, Morris had intended that a four-seater Morris-Oxford with a longer wheelbase and a bevel-drive rear axle would also be introduced for 1915, this model retaining British parts including a longer-stroke version of the White and Poppe engine. Another story, expounded by Jarman and Barraclough, has this car being how Morris had originally envisaged broadening his range, but with the idea being discarded on account of its higher costs. This version of events suggests that it was the likely costs of such a car that convinced Morris to look to the United States, after which the project was abandoned.

Whatever the identity of this 'mystery' Oxford, attention naturally switched to the new Cowley. There was no attempt by Morris to conceal the car's American origins, which led to some carefully worded explanations in the British press, which was aware how damaging too close an association with the regularly mocked Ford Model T could be. 'The car is not in any way a cheap American car, but in design and workmanship it is well up to English standards, and it cannot be too clearly understood that the American components are made to English designs and specifications,' *The Motor* reassuringly if inaccurately informed its readers. Similarly *The Autocar* wrote that the engine 'was planned and specified to the tiniest detail by John Bull, but made in America under Uncle Sam's miraculous output methods.' Such

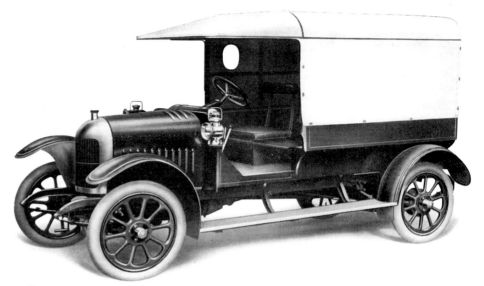

A canvas-topped Cowley delivery van was offered, but only 37 were made. (Author's collection)

talk was hokum. The engine, also to be used by US marque Saxon, was designed in all its essentials by Continental, while the gearbox could be found in various makes of American car.

Deliveries of the new Morris were planned to start in June 1915, but in fact the first engines only arrived in September, in which month the first dozen cars were eventually made. Launched at 158 guineas (£165.18s) for a two-seater, or 185 guineas (£194.5s) for a four-seat tourer, the car was built around a similar simple ladder-frame chassis to that of the Oxford, and like that car it featured semi-elliptic front springing and three-quarter elliptics at the rear. Transmission remained by torque tube but the back axle was now a cheap-to-make lightweight pressed-steel 'banjo' design with bevel drive rather than the Oxford's worm drive; this was claimed to be 25 per cent quieter, and was designed so that the driveshafts could be removed without disturbing the brakes, allowing easy removal in turn of the crownwheel-and-pinion assembly through the detachable back of the casing. As was normal for the time, only the rear wheels were braked.

Moving away from the rather Edwardian T-head arrangement of the White and Poppe unit, the Continental 'Red Seal' Type U engine was of conventional L-head side-valve configuration, with three main bearings and a detachable head; the main bearings were pressure-fed while the big ends were splash-lubricated. Mated to a two-plate dry clutch, it drove a compact three-speed gearbox equipped with a typically American ball-change central lever; also centrally positioned was the handbrake, meaning that a driver's door could be fitted, greatly adding to ease of use. Equipment included Lucas five-lamp electrics – for the first time on a Morris, and something of a feature for the price – along with five detachable wheels and a complete set of tools; the interior was in buttoned diamond-pattern leather, and just one coachwork colour was offered, a khaki-buff shade.

To offer a 1½-litre engine, four-seat coachwork and full equipment for such a cost was a genuine achievement, and made the Morris something of a category-buster: 'It is really a link between two existing types, the light car and the Rover type,' observed *The Motor* in its initial description. True though this undoubtedly was, the Cowley was very different in character from the Oxford, its 50-per-cent-larger engine being a torque-rich 'slogger' as opposed to the revvy little White and Poppe unit.

The extra bulk of the Cowley relative to the Oxford is apparent in this shot of a two-seater at an early post-World War One sporting trial. (LAT)

Life in wartime

The motoring press was predictably warm about the newcomer. 'It may be stated at once that the new Morris-Cowley car is likely to cause quite as great enthusiasm among users as its predecessor has done, as it is remarkable both for the very thorough equipment and generous specification as well as the remarkably low price at which the complete car is offered,' cooed *The Light Car and Cyclecar* in an April 1915 issue. A more detailed assessment came in September 1916, by which time the two-seater had risen in price to 190 guineas (£199.10s) and the four-seater to 212 guineas (£222.12s). In its four-page appraisal – headed 'A Car of Superlative Merit' – the magazine, which had become something of a cheerleader for Morris, was fulsome in its praise of the Cowley, which it had tested over 500 miles. It was, said the writer, 'one of the most wonderful cars I have ever driven'. The Morris's hill climbing was 'astonishing' and the transmission was 'dead silent' while fuel consumption fetched out at an impressive 33–38mpg. 'So excellent is the car throughout, so astonishing its behaviour on the road, that one is tempted to indulge in

superlatives, but they are certainly deserved,' concluded the glowing report.

Despite some consignments of parts being lost at sea, Morris nonetheless managed to make 1344 cars between January 1915 and December 1918. Whether the exercise was as profitable as Morris would have liked is another matter, as government action in the closing months of 1915 considerably changed the fiscal landscape. With the United States initially neutral in the war – it was only to join hostilities in 1917 – its manufacturers had an opportunity to profit from the fact that British car-makers had been obliged to turn to the production of war materiel. With American cars being freely imported into the country in increasing numbers, British firms felt they were being penalised for their patriotism.

The government responded in September 1915, Chancellor Reginald McKenna introducing what became known as the McKenna Duties. Supposedly intended to conserve foreign exchange and to avoid having valuable shipping space tied up in transport of non-essential luxury goods, the duties constituted a 33.3 per cent levy on imported cars and automotive components. These tariffs helped Morris by keeping out foreign competition, but also meant that US-sourced components arriving at Cowley after the imposition of the duties became a third more expensive for him; hence the price rise mentioned above.

Although supply problems meant some chassis were bodied by other companies, the cars principally had coachwork by one of the business's two main pre-war body suppliers, Hollick and Pratt. Styles latterly included a folding-head Cabriolet Coupé and a Commercial Van. With only 37 being made, the open-cab van was an item of marginalia, but the Cabriolet Coupé body was carried through essentially unchanged to the post-war generation of Bullnoses.

At the end of November 1918 – the month the Armistice was signed – the works still contained sufficient material for the production of 336 Continental-engined Cowleys. Thanks to his investment in US-sourced parts, Morris had enjoyed a good war as a motor manufacturer. His output of 320 cars in 1915 had admittedly been well down on that of the preceding year, but this reflected the drying-up of British-made components for the Oxford and the slow coming-on-stream of the Cowley; in 1916, however, he had produced 697 cars, of which all but 13 were Cowleys. This had fallen to 125 Cowleys and a sole – and final – W&P Oxford in 1917, but in the last year of the war output had surprisingly climbed: the Oxford works had manufactured 163 cars in the period up to the Armistice, plus a further 35 in the remainder of the year. Talk of small-scale assembly 'in a corner of the works' (of 'a trickle' according to Andrews and Brunner) is thus slightly misleading, even if output had sharply fallen away after 1916 – a hardly unexpected state of affairs, given that in March that year the government had banned the import of American cars and parts.

What is true is that car manufacture inevitably became a sideline, as the Cowley works turned itself over to war production. Making a remunerative contribution to the war effort initially proved a challenge, as the factory was essentially an assembly operation, with just very basic machinery. Morris was also financially extended, with fresh buildings still being completed and paid for during 1915, capital tied up in stock, and the need to pay for parts coming in from the United States. There was thus an urgent need to obtain government contracts. 'Morris himself haunted the ministries in London,' recounts Miles Thomas in *Out on a Wing*. His assiduousness paid off: early in 1915 a first contract, to make hand grenades, was secured, and this was followed by another for the machining of cases for the shells of Stokes trench howitzers. Despite this, total turnover more than halved, and a loss of over £1000 after tax and dividends was recorded that year, against a £13,700 profit after tax and dividends in 1914.

The year 1916 saw a revival in the company's fortunes. Success with the shell contract meant that Morris found himself on various committees concerned with munitions production. This led to a major contract, for the assembly of mine sinkers, large quantities of which were needed for sowing the North Sea minefield. Morris, drawing on his experience putting together cars from bought-in parts, said he could assemble 250 per week – but that this would be dependent on sub-contractors supplying components as required, in the right quantities, and made to a standard specification.

This would demand meticulous planning. Fortunately Morris's expertise dovetailed with the thoughts of Arthur Rowse, the superintending engineer for the Ministry of Munitions in Birmingham, who had suggested that manufacture of the mine sinkers should be broken down into components, with different firms making the various parts rather than assembling the whole sinker, and with all parts standardised and interchangeable. Hans Landstad was enrolled to design the jigs, a task he accomplished within three weeks, working until late at night, and Rowse had them made in Nottingham by firms who in peacetime made machinery for the lace industry.

After six months, production began at Cowley, using female labour. Manufacture was under the administration of the Ministry of Munitions, with Morris appointed Controller, at an annual salary of £1200. Peak production of sinkers hit 2000 per week, against a pre-Morris weekly output of 40 sinkers, and the cost dropped from £40–50 to £30. So successful, indeed, was the operation that supply ended up outstripping demand; for his efforts Morris was awarded the OBE.

Did he end the war a rich man? Morris took out up to £1500 a year as a salary, but once dividends had been paid all profits were ploughed back into the firm. After the good year of 1914, he clearly sailed close to the wind in getting the Cowley into production, recording pre-tax profits of only £700 for 1915. Thereafter the company performed well, with pre-tax profits of £23,500 in 1916 and of £16,200 the following year. The 1918 balance sheet showed profits before tax of £18,900 and cash-in-hand of a relatively slender £4666. The company was thus on a reasonably satisfactory footing, but there could be no grounds for complacency as Morris entered what was sure to be a turbulent post-war period. Perhaps it was in nervous anticipation of the struggles to come that early in 1919 he ran into health problems, with suspected – but never confirmed – diabetes, this resulting in his being despatched by his doctors to Germany for a cure.

William and Lillian Morris in Morris's personal polished-wood boat-tail Cowley, in 1919; the same car, equipped with rear tyre chains and driven by Alf Keen, was the only car to climb Alms Hill, Henley, during a Junior Car Club rally. (LAT)

The post-war Bullnose
1919–24

Madam attends to her grease nipples. The car is a 1924 Oxford two-seater, with the three-piece windscreen current only for this season. (BMIHT)

By boldly cutting prices, Morris increased his sales and became a dominant player in the British market. Along the way he acquired his major supplying companies, establishing the basis of his business empire.

At the end of the war Morris had sufficient components in stock for 336 cars, equivalent to roughly a third of his sales in his best year of 1914, when he had delivered 908 vehicles. He also had a proven design and a factory unburdened by newly redundant munitions-making machinery. An assembler of bought-in parts before the war, an assembler of bought-in parts during the war, he could revert seamlessly to being a car-assembly operation on the same principle after the Armistice – with the added benefit that he had learnt a lot about flow-line production techniques when manufacturing grenades and mine-sinkers.

He had also learnt that small suppliers could work efficiently when properly tooled-up to produce accurately and in quantity. He put this knowledge to practical use in this immediate post-war boom period, contracting with smaller companies to help get around the supply bottlenecks that existed with bigger firms. 'Morris was perhaps the first to make systematic use of such suppliers on a large scale,' say Andrews and Brunner, citing the use of small suppliers as an important ingredient in his success. By 1923 he would have over 200 businesses of various sizes supplying him.

In this he was immeasurably helped by Arthur Rowse, who had been persuaded to join the company after the war. Rowse's contacts in the Midlands meant that he knew which factories had the necessary machine tools for a particular job. "Rowse got around and placed orders before anyone else," observed Landstad. Rowse had no specific title, so he ended up suggesting his own, duly becoming Production Manager. "Nobody had any authority. They were simply got together on the lines of this was a wonderful adventure," he told Andrews and Brunner. "There was no factory, practically no plant, and the problem was after the war to make a motor car without a factory, and [I] produced the scheme for doing that."

Morris was then in size a small-to-medium company, employing roughly 200 workers in 1919; Austin, in comparison, emerged from the war with 20,000 people on its payroll. In motor-

For 1920 the Cowley had no side valances. A total of 304 two-seater Cowleys were made for the 1920 season. (Author's collection)

manufacturing terms it was a lean operation. Assembly was concentrated on the ground floor of the old Military Academy building, initially while it was still being cleared of ammunition stocks; axle assembly took place on the first floor, and the top floor stores. After about a year, assembly moved to the new steel building erected in 1914. This was laid out for line production, with operations broken down and with chassis being pushed from one work station to the next as soon as they were on wheels. This was not an innovation: other than Ford, companies such as Wolseley, Rover and Singer had adopted the same system.

A fresh start: the need to re-tool

But if Morris was more fortunate than some, he was faced with one fundamental challenge: thanks to the McKenna Duties – which remained in operation – he could no longer source all his key mechanical components from the United States. In the case of the engine, the question was academic, as Continental did not wish to carry on its production, judging it too small a unit to find customers in the US motor industry. Morris thus had to find alternative sources of supply in Britain – and perhaps even a new engine – if he wished to stay in the motor-manufacturing business.

Morris explored two seperate avenues. Continental had ceded to him the design rights for the 'Red Seal' Type U, along with some tooling, and he also had drawings – and one assumes design rights – for the other components he had previously sourced from the States. There was

The headlamps of the Cowley remained on the wings until the 1924 model year, when they adopted a conventional position. (Author's collection)

A nice on-the-road shot of a 1921 Cowley two-seater; the leathercloth side valances are clearly visible. (Morris Register)

A very early post-war Oxford two-seater, distinguishable from a Cowley by its five-lamp electrics, with scuttle-mounted sidelamps. (Author's collection)

Poppe was keen to work with Morris, but fellow Managing Director Alfred White judged him too marginal a client and was more interested in developing the company's relations with truck-maker Dennis, for whom it had supplied large numbers of engines during the war. At the end of 1919 White would sell out to Dennis, and Poppe would move to a position at Rover; in the interim the firm turned down the Morris proposition.

Morris approached Oldham's, a Coventry enterprise that had manufactured heavy artillery during the war, but apparently the price he proposed, for making the Continental engine, was not considered viable. He then turned to Dorman, well known as engine manufacturers, with a view to using one of their power units. Landstad stripped down a sample engine and was not impressed by its rough finish; in any case a potential deal fell by the wayside when the Staffordshire firm demanded a £40,000 deposit. An approach by small-time Stamford car-manufacturer Jack Pick was doubtless more opportunistic than anything else, and soon foundered when it was clear that the maker of Pick and New Pick cars simply did not have the facilities to mass-produce engines for Morris.

In the end the problem was solved when the English branch of French car and armaments manufacturer Hotchkiss got wind of Morris's quest for someone to make engines for him. Hotchkiss had established a satellite plant in Coventry during the war, to turn out its celebrated machine guns. Now it was desperate for work; so desperate, in fact, that when Morris hesitantly asked whether a deposit might be required, the Hotchkiss managers quickly said that they were happy to forge ahead without any money up front. What the official version of events does not say is that a £40,000 guarantee was demanded, and that this was provided by the Earl of Macclesfield.

So it was that a deal was signed, to make the Continental engine and a version of the Warner gearbox. Morris said that he wanted the engine to cost around £50, and Hotchkiss undertook to get the price down to this level, even if not straight away. The first engine was delivered in July 1919, with sales of Hotchkiss-powered cars able to start in September 1919, in time for the 1920 model year. Although this might appear a relatively quick turnaround, there were delays, not least because Hotchkiss had difficulty getting castings at the right price and quality at a time when their was a brief post-war boom

thus the possibility that he could find a firm to make the Type U engine for him, along with a suitable gearbox. The other option was to start anew with a different engine from one of Britain's various makers of proprietary power units.

Morris's first instinct was to turn to his original engine supplier, White and Poppe. During the war the company had drawn up a new L-head 'four' and Poppe offered this to Morris, when it was still – or so it appears – at the state of a paper project. According to the testimony of Hans Landstad, Morris also suggested that another option might be that the company make the Continental engine for him. But White and Poppe was a business pulling itself apart. Peter

in industrial activity; it tried sourcing engine blocks from Belgium, apparently, but this proved unsatisfactory. As a result Morris felt constrained to set up a foundry of his own at Cowley. This allowed castings to be produced more cheaply, while quality could be closely monitored[1].

It wasn't just a question of having the engine re-sourced; there was also the question of the running gear. Wrigley's was already tied up in making components for the ill-fated Angus-Sanderson, and in any case Morris felt disinclined to favour them with his business after their snooty treatment of him in pre-war days. Instead he drew on his wartime experience, and the axles and steering were broken down into components and forgings sourced individually and then machined by outside businesses, before everything was assembled at Cowley.

Morris didn't just sign a contract with these suppliers and leave them to it. He bought the raw material, inspected it, and with Rowse and Landstad laid down methods of machining, supplying gauges and jigs and fittings if need be. Long contracts meanwhile allowed the subcontractors to amortise the cost of their own investments in production apparatus. This was Morris in his element, as Leonard Lord acknowledged to Andrews and Brunner. "His best asset was his keen appreciation of price and costs. Basically he was a buyer and a very keen buyer indeed. Anything he bought he bought at a keen price and went to endless trouble to get what he needed, and got it in the end."

Amongst the principal suppliers, Joseph Lucas was signed up to supply lighting and electrics after a Smiths dynamotor failed in testing. Coming after an initial order from Morris in 1914 that represented the company's first bulk commission, this deal was to make Lucas the industry leader in car electrical systems; by 1923, over half of its business was with Morris. As for Smiths, it was given in compensation the contract for clocks and dashboard instruments. Chassis continued for a while to come from Belgium, but manufacture then passed to Rubery Owen, and later to the Projectile and Engineering Co in London; axle casings came from Fisher and Ludlow, who could press out these for a lower price than a traditional cast axle casing would have cost. Radiators came from Doherty Motor Components in Coventry. When it became clear that the company would not be able to supply Morris in the quantities he needed, it was encouraged in 1919 to set up a

branch in Osberton Road, Oxford, in a former skating rink purchased by Morris. Later, Morris bankrolled the factory's two foremen, Ryder and Davies, to buy out the company, and Osberton Radiators was to grow into a major enterprise.

Bodies were now almost exclusively the domain of Hollick and Pratt, with only small numbers still coming from Raworth – whose quality of workmanship was apparently considered as inferior. But with Hollick and Pratt serving other clients as well, output for Morris was insufficient. A bodyshop was therefore set up in 1919 at Cowley, on the former allotments across the road from the factory. Managed by Lancelot Pratt, and with much of the labour coming from the nearby railway-carriage works at Swindon and Wolverton, it operated as a satellite to the main Hollick and Pratt works in Coventry, which henceforth concentrated on the more specialist body styles, leaving Cowley to major on the mainstream tourer and two-seater coachwork. Cementing this closer relationship, Pratt put £10,000 into the Morris business, and in 1920 a further £10,000.

This delightful two-tone oak-strake Cowley was built by Hollick and Pratt in 1920 as Lancelot Pratt's personal car. (LAT)

The work of Buckingham coachbuilder Phillips, this vee-front saloon Oxford was completed in 1920 for a Dr Sankey of Oxford. (LAT)

[1] It was less than ideal, all the same, to have the foundry so far from the engine works, and in the 1930s it would be transferred to Coventry; costs duly came down.

The Sports was rakish, and supposedly good for approaching 60mph; only 80 were made in 1921. (LAT)

At £398.10s in 1921, the Sports was appreciably cheaper than a regular two-seat Cowley at £465. (Author's collection)

The first sum, a loan, was part of a company restructuring in 1919, when WRM Motors Ltd went into voluntary liquidation and in July was reborn as Morris Motors Ltd. This was so Morris could end his contract with WHM Burgess, dating from 1913, which gave Burgess exclusive distribution rights for the South of England outside London, and exclusive export rights, along with a substantial commission structure. Morris had to pay compensation to Burgess, but he could now establish his own network of distributors and have closer control over exports. Shareholders in the new business included the Earl of Macclesfield, with shares worth £25,000, banker Arthur Gillett, Witney engineer HW Young, and Reginald Thornton, Morris's auditor. Morris himself put £16,185 into the business ahead of this reconstruction, which was bolstered by a £10,000 loan from Gillett in 1920 and a temporary £60,000 loan facility from Barclays bank. In 1923 all these loans would be paid off – and as Andrews and Brunner recorded, 'the Morris business… never again borrowed from outside sources, except for purely temporary finance from bankers in the ordinary way'.

For all its promise, 1919 was a difficult season for Morris, as he reconstructed his business and his network of suppliers. As a consequence it ended with only 63 of the 387 cars he sold having the Hotchkiss engine. Unsurprisingly, the company posted a loss of nearly £8000 in this first troubled year of peace.

1920: Morris begins his ascent

The range that Morris presented for the 1920 model year held no great surprises. Although the Oxford was in addition offered as a drophead Cabriolet-Coupé, he concentrated on the two mainstream body styles, the two-seater with dickey and the four-seat open tourer. Roughly twice as many Oxfords were tourers rather than two-seaters, whereas approaching eight out of ten Cowleys were two-seaters. Partly this was because at the launch of the new Hotchkiss-engined cars the Cowley was not offered as a four-seater, this body type only becoming available late in the season. As this sales pattern broadly repeated itself the following year, one can assume that the more moneyed folk who bought the Oxford could reach to the more expensive four-seater, whereas the Cowley attracted those on a tighter budget who plumped for the cheapest option. This phenomenon would not last, for reasons that will become clear.

With all the key elements in place, Morris got off to a good start. After the war years, there was a pent-up demand for cars, and this was further fed by a short-lived industrial boom, built on the back of easy credit. Morris planned to make 4000 cars in 1920, a huge jump. Perhaps this was over-ambitious, but output rose steadily during 1920 and by April was at 140 cars a month; by September that figure had nearly doubled, with 276 cars and chassis leaving Cowley in the course of the month. Morris would finish the calendar year having produced 1563 cars in 1920, his best result to date.

Morris "came in at the right time" according to Sir George Kenning, who became Derbyshire distributor in 1919. "There was just a market for that particular car. It just grew… He chose wisely in his distributors and a good deal of work was put into sales. The quality was there and he just had the imagination to touch what he public needed." Ford was still dominating the market, all the same, selling 25,665 cars and 20,697 light commercials, out of total British sales of roughly 60,000 vehicles. Morris was still small fry, not just in relation to Ford but also in relation to other British companies: Bean was producing 20 cars per day during 1920, which was more than Morris was achieving.

From boom to bust

For 1921 the cars were changed only in detail. In particular, the Cowley became additionally available as a better-equipped De Luxe and gained the leathercloth valances already worn by the Oxford, whilst the latter benefitted – from November 1920 – from a revised mounting for the dynamotor. This put the combined starter/dynamo in a housing in the gearbox bellhousing as opposed to its previous position on top of the geearbox and protruding into the passenger compartment. Further to this, from March 1921 a sports version of the Cowley became available. Fitted with a skimpy polished-aluminium body, it had what was described as a 'specially-tuned' engine – in fact just a set of aluminium Aerolite pistons – along with a bigger-bore exhaust and a raised back axle ratio. Although no claims were made for the performance, the Sports Model (as it was called) was guaranteed, said Morris, to average 40mpg 'at normal speeds'. Quite how fast the car was doubtless remained a mystery to owners, as a speedometer was not fitted, but *The Motor* wrote that 'on good roads it could be driven up to its maximum speed, which... we should estimate at over 60mph'. The Sports was not listed after the 1923 season, and production in fact ended, except for special orders, at the end of the 1922 model year. It was evidently a minority interest, as a mere 107 were made in total.

But the early post-war boom did not have robust underpinnings, and in April 1920 a rise in bank rates from 6 per cent to 7 per cent had already put the brakes on growth. By the autumn Britain was in an economic slump, with all too many companies suddenly looking shaky. It wasn't a pretty picture. 'The slump of late 1920 left many companies in the unhealthy position of having over-expanded plant and watered-down capital, often the result of new share issues and unwise investment or borrowing,' comments Kenneth Richardson in *The British Motor Industry 1896–1939*. 'This led to an inflation of prices, while wages, which had reached record levels during wartime, did not keep pace. This, in turn, inevitably produced acute industrial unrest and a spate of strikes for improved rates of pay.'

Needless to say, the motor industry soon felt the cold. The sellers' market that had allowed

The two-seater 1923 Cowley had a one-piece screen; paint on the Cowleys was a roughly finished buff. (Author's collection)

them to charge high prices started to evaporate. By October, demand was falling away, and the Motor Show was a disaster for the order books of British companies. Making matters worse, the downturn was global, and cars were stacking up on the docks in Australia and New Zealand, because agents had too much stock.

Morris sales dropped in November 1920 to 137 units, before crashing to 74 in January – admittedly always a depressed month for sales. Rising wages and costs and transitorily strong demand had pushed British car prices upwards but then the slump had meant that business users had cut back on such expensive purchases as a motor car, whilst private buyers, hit by a fall in income, had similarly kept their wallets closed. UK car production, which had been of 24,000 vehicles in 1919, had risen to 50,000 in 1920 but would fall back to 32,000 in 1921. With most manufacturers – and there were too many – making cars in penny-packet numbers, costs of manufacture were just too high to allow prices to be adjusted to match demand. Meanwhile, Ford had cut its prices, in response to the end of the US boom, shaving £25 from the price of its four-seat tourer in August 1920. Despite the McKenna

In contrast, the Oxford had a two-piece screen and a better paint finish – with more coats, and flatting-down between coats. (Author's collection)

The Oxford coupé – here a '23 model – retailed at 425 guineas in 1923, making it the most expensive Bullnose. (Author's collection)

Duties, Ford sold over 15,000 cars in Britain in 1920, against Austin's 4319 and Morris's 1932 cars and chassis. A shake-out in the industry was inevitable.

Morris, geared to produce at least 60 cars per week, saw his debts mount, his overdraft double to over £84,000 and the sum owed to suppliers reach £50,000. Output was maintained, but this only worsened the situation, especially as the company had raised its prices for 1921. Stock piled up at the Cowley works, to the point where it actually hindered assembly. Morris was at least in the right place in the market, offering two relatively low-priced cars of moderate horsepower rating. Austin had based its post-war programme on a big 20hp model, which was expensive to tax and cost £200 more than expected; as a result the slump pushed Longbridge into receivership.

But with a factory full of unsaleable cars, this was a crisis for Morris, whichever way you sliced it. Barclays, his principal bankers, lost confidence and according to Arthur Rowse they threatened to withdraw their loans. Arthur Gillett, however, stood by Morris, and apparently said that if this happened he would sell his Barclays shares, resign from the bank's board, and back Morris himself. In the end Morris got the additional £200,000 overdraft he was requesting, while Gillett loaned the company £10,000, as did Lancelot Pratt, with the latter increasing his loan by a further £10,000 in 1922.

Lucas and Dunlop, meanwhile, gave three months' credit, a succour Morris never forgot. Fisher and Ludlow, who supplied Morris with radiator shells, petrol tanks and some chassis parts, also supported him, holding back deliveries and in all likelihood also accepting deferred payment of their bills. Such acts of generosity were used by Morris to persuade other suppliers into giving better terms of credit. Hotchkiss, Morris's principal supplier, on the other hand demanded three months' bills, with the requirement that they be backed. Macclesfield duly underwrote the cheques, to the tune of £50,000, a generous and vital act that makes subsequent events even more unfortunate. "Macclesfield and Gillett really saved the company," Morris Motors secretary Kimpton Smallbone told Andrews and Brunner.

During this time morale hit rock-bottom. "They had a very difficult time, and Morris was worried to death," Rowse recalled. "At the height of the crisis he tucked himself up at Huntercombe and they could not get him to come near the factory… They could not get Morris to come in and decide anything, and the person who went out to bring him in was Macclesfield, because he was the only person independent of Morris." So depressed was Morris, in fact, that according to Landstad he was thinking of chartering a steamer and taking all Cowley's machinery and fittings, and any men who wanted to accompany him, and setting up in Australia.

The 1921 price cuts

William Morris pulled out of this spin with an act of calculated commercial bravery that would become part of motor-industry legend: in February 1921 he cut his retail prices. He was not the first manufacturer to take such a step: he was following in the wake of Bean, who in September 1920 had cut their prices by up to £95. The difference, though, was that Morris had funds behind him and although the situation was serious he did not yet quite have his back to the wall. Bean, in contrast, was massively indebted and within a month of its cuts had to shut down, albeit temporarily.

The four-seat Cowley was reduced by £100, to £425, and the two-seater Cowley by £90, to £37; the Oxfords, meanwhile, were reduced in price by only £25, with the exception of the top-of-the-range coupé, on which margins were presumably higher and which shed £80. Although it hardly required one to be a genius to work out that cutting prices would boost demand, the gamble paid off. Sales in February bounced back to 236 units, and then jumped to 400 in March; for April, May and June they were 361, 352 and 361 respectively. By the end of May the stock of unsold cars had been cleared, along with all debts.

According to the official Morris-endorsed account of events, the sales manager, Hugh Grey, told him that his profit was only £15 per car, and

This vee-front all-weather Oxford was the work, in 1922, of the Ideal Motor Carriage Works of Fulham. (LAT)

that such a cut was madness; Morris, aware that accounts showed the profit to be more like £36 per car, over-rode him, saying that with a factory full of unsold cars they weren't making any profit at all. According to this version, retailed by Morris to Andrews and Brunner, he expected the price cuts to restore the market for his cars, and asked for parts supply to be doubled, but the frightened Grey didn't follow through on these instructions. The initiative was reckless – he had, he said, never taken such a decision in his life – but it was just intuition as in those days he did most of his reckoning 'on the back of an envelope'. It was, he told his biographers, "all done in five minutes – no discussion, no figures or anything".

As the unpublished testimony of Landstad and Rowse confirms, this presentation of the '£100 cut' as a stroke of inspired genius on the part of William Morris is self-serving myth. It was not only a considered act, but also one that had been suggested by others rather than pulled out of a hat by Morris himself[2] – although of course the ultimate responsibility for implementing the cut rested with him.

Arthur Rowse told Andrews and Brunner that although the profit on engines and bodies was always hidden from him it was clear that the Cowley bodyshop, run by Lancelot Pratt with Morris backing, was making 'a fantastically high profit'. Rowse told Pratt that Morris was paying £100 too much for his bodies. "In the meantime Grey... was worried to death. He was agitating for a price reduction... So they had a meeting...

Grey, who was primed, said he wanted a drastic reduction in price... Morris replied that he did not know whether it could be done, but that he and [I] would go into it after the meeting and see if it could be done. Of course, [I] knew already it could be done, and it was."

Landstad gave Morris's biographers a similar account, describing Pratt's body figures as 'hopelessly high' – not least as the costings were done on the same basis as at the main Hollick and Pratt works in Coventry, where labour costs were much more expensive. The reductions were possible because according to Rowse the pre-cut prices of Morris cars had been unrealistically high even without the over-charging for the bodies. "In 1920 [Morris] revamped that car for price increases three or four times, and every time they re-costed them, [they] added a bit on for luck and, as a result, the price of the car became fantastic. By the end of 1920 they had built up such a dizzy price structure that by the spring of 1921 they had arrived at a fantastic price and war gratuities came to an end and they could not sell anything."

Helping make the cuts viable, Morris asked his distributors to accept a reduction in commission from 17.5 per cent to 15 per cent. This lasted for five years, the 17.5 per cent being restored in 1926. Additionally Landstad and Rowse streamlined body production and trimmed other manufacturing costs and the company reduced inventory time for the components it bought – what we would today call lean production, in other words.

Morris's action created waves in the motor industry, and in April 1921 other manufacturers started to cut their prices. But many waited until

the autumn Motor Show – and even then at best only matched Morris's cuts. But the slump was continuing, and after the first burst of interest it became clear that the boost to Morris sales had been short-term, even allowing for seasonal fluctuations: having risen to 361 cars in June, monthly sales had dropped back to 261 in September, and would fall to 172 in October.

Morris saw that his profit levels would allow him to absorb a second price cut, especially as labour and materials costs were now falling. Additionally Rowse and Landstad had renegotiated prices with the company's suppliers on the basis of higher quantities, as Morris was confident that lower prices for his cars would further boost demand. Rowse said that he approached Morris's suppliers and negotiated a 15 per cent cut for the next year, giving a personal guarantee that the price of the car would be cut by at least the same amount. He also promised that he would not go to other suppliers over the next 12 months, and

This pre-1924 Cowley two-seater was converted in 1926 to a coupé by Armstrong and Co of Shepherds Bush, London, for a cost of roughly £32.10s. (LAT)

that the company would automatically get repeat orders at the same price. Further helping these subcontractors, instead of batches, Morris put through orders of up to 10,000 units a time.

All this was based on the trust people had in Rowse personally – and over and above that, in Morris himself. 'We have not heard a single story to suggest that Morris was an unfair buyer,' comment Andrews and Brunner. He standardised requirements and contracted for long runs, without changes to specification, and didn't try to renegotiate the contract during the season. As long as suppliers remained competitive on price, he would remain loyal to them. Further to this, he did not seek as tight terms for the Oxford, where margins were higher. Finally, all suppliers were paid promptly, whether small or big – regularly, at the end of the month. Naturally enough, acknowledge Andrews and Brunner, some suppliers accepted Morris's terms under protest, but in the end they tended to find that the contract was in their financial interest, because of the quantities involved: 'many of the motor car industry's suppliers were earning the economies of large-scale production on their Morris contracts'.

Morris, who was very much in control of all aspects of company in these early days, allied canny buying to tight financial control, with rigorous weekly budgeting. Distributors paid on delivery – 'cash on the cylinder head' – while Morris had 60-day credit with his suppliers when he was building a Bullnose in six days. Profits, meanwhile, were ploughed back into the business: Morris did not live an extravagant life on the back of his company. Nor did he build up big reserves. When Arthur Gillett suggested that he should create a cash reserve, Morris said that his priority was to reinvest in the business. It would only be towards the end of 1924 that he started to build up a strategic reserve.

With all this in place, the company duly reduced prices a second time at the 1921 Motor Show. The competition were discomfited, to say the least, but Morris ended the year with output up by over half, from 1932 cars and chassis the preceding year to 3076 at the end of 1921.

His action, he told Andrews and Brunner, "saved the motor trade from complete calamity, because the Americans were pouring in at that time. Had the motor trade gone on as it was doing, the foreigner would have captured the motor trade of this country". He had, he said, "put Ford off the road".

Consolidation: the 1922 and 1923 seasons

As for the cars themselves, again there were few modifications to the cars for 1922, the most obvious being that the radiator – now of honeycomb rather than gilled-tube construction – lost its decorative horizontal strip; in addition metal wing valances were fitted, to both the Cowley and the Oxford. Hidden changes included a leather-diaphragm SU Sloper carburettor, which was phased in to replace the Zenith, a petrol filler under the bonnet rather than inside the car, and pressed-steel brake backplates separate from the axle casing rather than a part of it as previously. Later in the season a revised four-port engine was introduced.

Having hoisted himself ahead of weaker and less visionary competition, Morris was able to profit from the upturn in the business cycle in 1922–23, especially as he now had the financial firepower to repeat his price-cutting, initiating one round of cuts before the 1922 Motor Show and another during it.

Sales responded, as was only to be expected, Morris explained in a 1924 article in *System* magazine in which he outlined his business principles.

We have never waited for the public to ask for a reduction. We get in with the reduction first. Is it quite sufficiently realized in this country that every time you make a reduction, you drop down on what I call the pyramid of consumption power to a wider base? Even a ten-pound price reduction drops you into an entirely new market. If the man cannot pay the last £10 in price, he cannot buy the car. When the £10 is knocked off, he very often can and will. The one object in life of many makers seems to be to make the thing the public cannot buy. The only object of my life has been to make the thing they can buy.

In driving down manufacturing costs, lowering car prices and ramping up production in response to rising demand, Morris was creating a virtuous circle, and one other manufacturers were forced to emulate, if they wished to stay in business. He thus drove costs down for the rest of the industry. Inevitably the casualties were the small firms, who either couldn't compete or whose attempts to reduce prices often resulted in lower quality. Morris made sure he never fell into that trap: he always produced cars of good manufactured quality, a point he stressed in his advertising. This was of course, another part of that virtuous circle: mass-production with

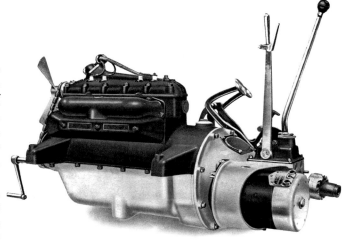

The Hotchkiss-built engine for a 1923 Oxford, showing the dynamotor in its housing. (Author's collection)

standardisation of parts and processes meant better and more consistent quality than with hand finishing.

For 1923 the Oxford and the Cowley started to grow further apart, with the Oxford optionally being available with a larger-bore engine of 1805cc. Rated at 13.9hp for fiscal purposes and delivering an estimated 30bhp, its fitment was given away by a larger radiator – and by the engine being painted in blue as opposed to the red of the 11.9hp unit. Only fitted in quantity from January 1923, the bigger engine was nonetheless specified for 1580 – or 37 per cent – of the 4261 Oxfords made for the 1923 season.

Whatever the engine, the Oxford now had a Smith's five-jet carburettor, as the previous year's SU had proved unreliable. The design of the Smith's unit was defective – 'the mixture was tied in a reef knot on its way to the induction manifold' in the words of Jarman and Barraclough – so it was doubtless just as well that the Cowley shed its SU in favour of a simpler single-jet Smith's carb.

The Oxford was also equipped with Gabriel snubbers as standard, the fitting of these spring-loaded webbing-strap dampers requiring the headlamp brackets to be mounted on top of the dumb irons rather than on their sides. This was not an issue on the Cowley, on which Gabriels were offered as an option, as this kept its mudguard-mounted headlamps. Also available at extra cost on the 1923 Cowley was a package comprising a dynamotor and full instrumentation including a speedo, a clock and oil and petrol gauges – plus a folding 'park bench' dickey on the two-seater.

Morris's cars were now extraordinary value, as a November 1922 advertisement proclaimed. 'Two years ago the lowest-price Morris car sold at £465. To-day we are marketing a BETTER car at £225 complete', ran the copy. This was the same price as a new Austin Seven, so it is

A jolly day by the seaside for these three ladies in their factory Chummy. The two side-mounted jump seats are unfortunately not visible. (Author's collection)

The railway-carriage door handles are a giveaway that this is a Morris Garages Chummy rather than the later Cowley-built car. (LAT)

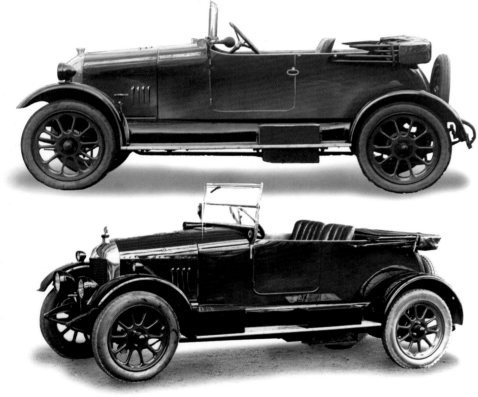

The Chummy cost £215 for 1924, meaning it slotted in between the £198 two-seater and the £225 tourer. (Author's collection)

The acquisition of suppliers

The period from late 1922 until the beginning of 1923 saw an important further development of Morris's business, when he purchased three of his principal suppliers. All were integrated into the Morris Motors portfolio in January 1923 but in 1924 were transferred to William Morris's newly-formed personal holding company, the Morris Company Ltd.

Morris's deviation from his policy of relying on outside specialists was motivated by a simple concern: as he planned to ratchet up production in 1923, he was frightened of not having enough of three key components: bodies, engines and radiators. He was also worried that he had become as dependent on his suppliers as they on him, and if a firm decided to sell out to a competitor, Morris, principal customer or not, risked being put out of business. Meanwhile, from the supplier's point of view, if the company was near-exclusively supplying Morris then it was in the process of effectively becoming a branch of the Morris business, but without the security of belonging to it. The company could of course limit the work it carried out for Morris, to spread the imagined risk, but then they wouldn't get costs down to the level required by Morris. It was a bind, and so Morris decided to acquire Osberton Radiators, Hollick and Pratt and ultimately – for more complex reasons – Hotchkiss Engines.

By 1922 the Morris and Hollick and Pratt businesses were intimately entwined. Morris had tried other suppliers for at least some of his bodies, but they had not proved satisfactory,

easy to understand why Morris was not moved – initially at least – to offer a smaller car, even when Austin slashed the price of the Seven to £165 in December 1922. As things were, Morris had through his commercial success himself largely defined where the centre of gravity of the British market sat: by 1927, according to *The Economist*, the 12hp–15hp category was accounting for 102,000 out of 164,000 cars made in Britain.

THE SNUBNOSE VANS

Morris entered the light commercial market for serious at the 1923 Olympia Show, when an 8cwt van was introduced. Based on the Bullnose but with a flattened radiator, it soon became known as the Snubnose. Fitted solely with the 11.9hp engine, it was offered as a Standard and a De Luxe. The Standard had a domed roof, a single door the on the nearside, oval side windows and black-painted screen while the De Luxe had a flat roof, gently curved in profile and fitted with a roof-rack, and featured two doors, arch-shaped side windows and a nickel-plated screen, whilst inside there was a sliding partition behind the driver. The body elements, in Plymax aluminium-armoured plywood, were provided by Davidsons of Trafford Park, Manchester, and assembled at Cowley.

Initial sales were slow, with probably many of the first vans going to Morris dealers for their own use: for the 1924 model year 283 Standard vans were made and 171 De Luxes, rising to 753 Standards and 540 De Luxes for the 1925 season. Part of the reason for this gentle take-up was that the McKenna Duties did not apply to commercials, so Ford's 7cwt Model T van remained very cheap, at £125 in 1924, against £198 for the Standard Morris. Furthermore, the horsepower tax didn't apply to light vans.

Morris, unsurprisingly, campaigned to have the McKenna Duties applied to commercial vehicles. Their exemption might have been valid when imported commercials had been needed for the war effort, he said, but now British manufacturers needed to ramp up volume so they could reduce prices. This would only be possible 'when they are freed from the menace of foreign competition,' he was quoted as saying in *Motor Transport* magazine for May 1925. Eventually, in May 1926, the import duties were applied to commercials – at a rate of 33.3 per cent on vehicles from the United States. Imports dropped by 85 per cent in a year. As Morris's main competitor was Ford, who was making the Model T van in England, the gesture was all the same largely symbolic. In any case, Ford discontinued the Model T in 1927, and the Model A van was more expensive – although still cheaper than the Morrises – and had a big engine of 3.3 litres, this just at the time the fuel tax was reimposed.

The big fish to be snagged, of course, was the Royal Mail, then running Model T vans, and Morris was quick on the draw, despatching the first of two trial vans in March 1924, with a 105 cu ft body by an outside coachbuilder. After some polemic in the press, the GPO started to convert its fleet to Snubnoses, the first six being despatched in March 1925. The vans had special 70 cu ft or 105 cu ft bodies and were supplied up until 1928, when the Post Office moved across to the Morris-Commercial L-type with a 105 cu ft body.

The Standard van; both types were supplied ex-works in grey primer. (Peter Seymour)

This De Luxe dates from 1924 and is a rare survivor. (Mark Dixon)

On the De Luxe van the spare wheel moved to the rear of the offside running board. (Mark Dixon)

The hood on the Chummy provided ample weather protection but not much visibility. (Peter Seymour)

This head-on view of a 1924 Cowley shows the new two-piece screen and five-lamp lighting. Note how the radiator is narrower than that on the Oxford shown on page 30. (Peter Seymour)

and two had gone into liquidation. Meanwhile, Hollick and Pratt had served Morris well, and Lancelot Pratt was in charge of the efficient on-site bodyshop at Cowley. Then in August 1922 the main works in Coventry suffered a severe fire. Pratt proposed that as Morris was now their only customer, he buy the company. This he duly did, for a shade under £100,000, promptly investing £10,700 in new buildings. With no bodybuilders in England capable of the rate of production Hollick and Pratt achieved at Cowley and Coventry, the move made industrial sense, as

it safeguarded Morris's body supply by bringing it in-house. Pratt continued to run the business, while becoming Deputy MD of Morris Motors.

This was the first time such a position had existed, and the arrangement functioned well, owing to an evident bond between the two men. Morris regarded Pratt as his closest colleague and as not really being a deputy as such – "because he had his own business and they were friends, they would sit and discuss things". He also had another virtue, according to Morris: "he never interfered". Working in Pratt's favour was that – although according to Carl Kingerlee "he could really argue" – he had a profound knowledge of coachbuilding, an area where Morris had limited aptitude and as a result was prepared to defer to him. According to Miles Thomas, in *Out on a Wing*, Pratt was 'the nearest that Morris ever came to having a close business friend'.

Alas, the collaboration came to an early end with Pratt's death from cancer in 1924, at the age of 44. Morris was deeply distressed. Pratt, he said in his funeral oration, was "a rock of confidence and the finest comrade any man could wish – always cheerful, open as a book and yet possessed of an amazing aptitude for and foresight in business..." In the view of Thomas, the loss was a significant one in terms of the management of the business. Pratt, he wrote, 'could have increased the coherence of the team at Cowley.' Kimpton Smallbone was of the same opinion. Pratt was "God's own man" and affairs at Cowley "would have been quite different had he lived," he told Andrews and Brunner. "[He] was the one man who could handle WRM, who thought the world of him." Such judgements are particularly pertinent in light of the future evolution of the Morris business.

Morris's second acquisition was that of Osberton Radiators, which by this stage was virtually exclusively supplying Morris Motors. Morris, who already had a financial interest in the company, acquired it for £15,000 – keeping Harold Ryder as manager. The company would thrive under Morris ownership, and by the end of the 1930s would be employing 1300 people and carrying out a considerable amount of press work – bonnets, petrol tanks, exhausts, and the like – as well as being Cowley's main source of plating.

It was whilst the 1923 Bullnoses were being launched at the 1922 Motor Show that Morris took the decision to make his final and most important acquisition of this period, that of his engine supplier Hotchkiss. There was some unease about the company, as it seemed doubtful that as a subsidiary of a French firm it would seek to expand in England in pace with Morris's ambitions; perhaps it might even decide to pull out, and centre all its operations in France, leaving Morris high-and-dry, with no engine supplier.

Morris also felt, perhaps exaggeratedly, that Hotchkiss was not wholeheartedly behind him, as it was also supplying other manufacturers, making a vee-twin for the 10hp BSA[3] and an overhead-valve version of the ex-Continental Morris engine for Gilchrist. Whilst it might have peeved Morris that the latter company was using an adaptation of a power unit to which he had rights, in practical terms the arrangement with the fledgling Scottish motor-maker was a passing irrelevance, as the company only made 20 or so cars before folding; the BSA, though, was arguably a competitor of sorts to his Cowley.

Over-riding all this was a much more fundamental issue: Morris wanted a weekly consignment of 500–600 engines and gearboxes for 1923, and Hotchkiss said it could only manage 300 a week. This low rate was not a question of capacity, according to Frank Woollard, one of Morris's key collaborators on the original Morris-Oxford, who at the time had just left his employer Wrigley's after a difference of opinion. The MD of the company, Henry Mann Ainsworth, "had not got too much belief in Morris's capabilities" and as a result, said Woollard, he was not prepared to

A 1924 Cowley two-seater with its sidescreens in place; the Cowley now had five-lamp electrics. (Author's collection)

extend himself on his behalf, preferring instead to seek supplementary business elsewhere. There was therefore a certain amount of friction between the two companies. Indeed, according to Reginald Thornton, about a year before this Morris had contemplated switching engine production to Tyler, who had made the Angus-Sanderson engine, but negotiations fell through. In the end the issue was straightforwardly resolved: Ainsworth suggested that Morris buy the business.

Morris asked Woollard to go around the works in Coventry with him, and then put him on the spot by asking him to give a valuation for the business. Woollard wrote what he described as an 'impressionistic' report – just three-quarters of a sheet of foolscap. Morris read this at the Motor Show – he read very slowly, according to Woollard – and then said "Right. I am buying it." It was, according to Woollard, "a pretty quick decision, but he was always like that." So Hotchkiss was bought, largely blind, but in essence because, said Woollard, Morris could see its potential. On 1 January 1923 the business was made over to Morris; Ainsworth, who harboured ambitions to carry on running the operation, and who doubted Morris's ability to manage without him, was given 14 days to pack his bags. It seems there was no love lost between Morris and the dandyish and haughty Ainsworth. According to Landstad, Ainsworth one day had an argument with Morris and told him "Morris, you're no engineer!" Morris never

The Oxford cabriolet was pretty much a minority interest: just 307 were made for the 1924 season, against 3871 tourers. (Author's collection)

[3] It has been said that Hotchkiss was making the Rover Eight air-cooled twin-cylinder engine. This is not correct.

A 1924 Cowley at the factory. Grey was the sole colour offered on Cowleys, whatever their body. (Peter Seymour)

The Traveller's Car was intended for commercial travellers or 'reps' – hence its name. (Author's collection)

forgave this slight, said Landstad – "and after that, when he bought Hotchkiss, Morris would not take Ainsworth on. He was given a nice gold watch and sent back to France..."

The genius of Frank Woollard

Hotchkiss was an expensive purchase, and one that stretched Morris's finances. He paid £150,000 for the Ordinary shares, plus £49,423 cash, immediately injected £20,000 in working capital, and had an option to purchase the Preference shares for a further £150,000. This he would take up, in May 1923, to eliminate the remaining Hotchkiss presence on the board: ostensibly this was because he was not happy with this arrangement, when Hotchkiss was selling its own cars in England. More likely it was because he didn't want his control diluted, or to be obliged to work with Frenchmen.

Under its new ownership the factory was replanned, and an extra shift introduced. Output rose by 66 per cent in the January to July 1923 period, and weekly production went from 475

engines in July to 500 from January 1924. Morris soon had his 600 engines a week, but by this time he was wanting 800 per week, a target that was duly met and exceeded, output reaching 1200 units in 1925. That to achieve this he spent a further £300,000 on extending the factory, and £150,000 on new machinery, is a demonstration of Morris's belief in investment to move ahead – and evidence that by 1923 he had the financial means to prime the pump in this way. His acquisition was paid for within two years; further proof that the economics stacked up was that when Morris raised weekly output from 300 to 500 cars, on the back of this enhanced Morris Engines productivity, his manufacturing costs fell by 30 per cent.

The credit for the extraordinary rise in output at Morris Engines Ltd goes to Frank Woollard, whom Morris immediately installed as General Manager. Hailed by Miles Thomas as a genius, Woollard was a pioneer in the technique of flow production, aspects of which he had started to apply as early as 1904, when working for a company making steel railway carriages[4]. At Wrigley's he had initiated a move from batch to flow production, and for his work on improving the design and manufacture of tank gearboxes during the First World War he was awarded the OBE in 1918.

At Morris Engines the factory was reorganised according to these precepts, with a smooth flow of operations, the establishment of standardised

[4] For information and insights on Woollard, the author acknowledges his debt to Peter Seymour, and to his paper 'Frank George Woollard: forgotten pioneer of flow production', co-authored with ML Emiliani and published in the Journal of Management History, 2011.

operations on a short time-cycle, and tight control of inventory. Working with a bright young man by the name of Leonard Lord, who had become Assistant Chief Engineer in 1922, Woollard also introduced mechanised transfer machinery for producing gearbox cases and flywheels. In this he was well in advance of his time – Renault, a future European leader in this field, would only introduce automated transfer machinery in 1947. Unfortunately reliability issues with the electrical, pneumatic and hydraulic systems led to a return to a manual system in late 1925. In a very real sense Woollard anticipated today's lean production methods and the just-in-time control of material inputs that lay behind the success of Toyota, in particular, in Japan. In 1926 Woollard would become a director of the reconstituted Morris Motors (1926) Ltd. Influential in applying flow production principles across the entire company, his role in the development of the Morris business should not be under-estimated. 'The acquisition of these three businesses and the establishment of the foundry marked a definite stage in the development of the business,' comment Andrews and Brunner of Morris's 1922–23 absorptions. 'Henceforward, it could contemplate growth without being hampered by supply bottlenecks, for the specialist suppliers of electrical equipment, etc, grew with the industry and the more usual run of engineering supplies could be confidently expected to be fairly readily available.'

The breach with Macclesfield

It was during the 1923 season or thereabouts[5] that Morris and his long-term backer Lord Macclesfield parted company. Morris bought out Macclesfield's participation in the company with a cheque for the full amount, delivered personally to his Shirburn Castle residence by solicitor Andrew Walsh. As a car enthusiast and as a substantial investor in the business, Macclesfield naturally liked to keep abreast of affairs at Cowley, and as well as attending management meetings he had a tendency to visit the factory for informal tours of inspection. This came to rankle with Morris, whilst for his part Macclesfield became increasingly irritated by Morris's erratic chairing of meetings.

When saloon bodies came in, Morris used an outside supplier. But when demand went up, he made the bodies in-house. This is a regular 1924 Oxford saloon. (Morris Register)

'What had started as a warm business friendship degenerated into an atmosphere of near squabbling, accentuated frequently by Macclesfield's kindly but gruff enquiries into the reason behind some decision Morris had unilaterally taken,' recounts Miles Thomas in *Out on a Wing*. Thomas was not then himself part of the company, so his information was perforce secondhand. Fortunately, Hans Landstad furnished a detailed account of the breach to Andrews and Brunner, whilst Macclesfield and Morris himself gave their own versions of the episode.

The falling-out, said Landstad, was 'a silly thing' and was over the new carburettor used on the 1923 Oxford. "Morris was very touchy, and they had a lot of difficulty with the new carburettor – the Smith's five-jet. They had one foreman… who was very good on carburettors, but Morris reckoned he was the only one who knew anything about carburettors, and he was going to show them how to adjust it. Nothing came of it and they were getting late with the cars. Macclesfield came up then and said why not leave it to the man in the shop who knew the job. That did it. The day after, Morris sent Andrew Walsh over to Shirburn with the cheque for the £20,000 which Macclesfield had put in."

[5] Macclesfield dated the breach to 1923. Andrews and Brunner give an earlier date of February 1922 that does not ring true, while Hans Landstad thought it was 'about 1924' – which seems a bit late. Macclesfield was 'a really nice man' who every year still sent him a pheasant he had shot himself, Landstad told Andrews and Brunner. "Years afterwards, Lady Macclesfield was interested in something to do with hospitals and she asked Morris if he would contribute, and he would not," said Landstad. "That was another thing which Macclesfield never forgot." Landstad thought Morris was resentful of the Earl because he had never been asked inside his castle – while Macclesfield was equally 'a bit sore' because he had never been asked inside the door of Morris's manor house at Cowley.

Photographed in June 1924, this Oxford most unusually has wire wheels. 1924 Oxfords – but not Cowleys – had an electric horn on top of the battery box. (BMIHT)

There is some ambiguity about the nature of Macclesfield's financial involvement, as well as conflicting memories about the sums involved. Figures provided by Morris's accountant, Thornton, show that Macclesfield loaned Morris £500 in each of the years 1911–1914 inclusive, then £2500 in 1915 (when Morris himself put £8000 into WRM Motors), £4500 in 1916, £9500 in 1917 (when the banker Gillett put in £5000), and a further £9500 in 1918. This sum totals £28,000.

Figures obtained by Philip Andrews show that Macclesfield had 21,000 Preference shares in WRM Motors and that when the company was re-formed as Morris Motors Ltd this £21,000 investment was converted to Preference shares in the new company. At the same time Macclesfield advanced another £4000 and some time later a further sum of £9000. This last contribution was supposed to be converted into Preference shares but this never happened because of the dispute with Morris.

It would seem therefore that Macclesfield held £25,000 in Preference shares, this tying in with Macclesfield's recollection that the cheque was for about £25,000. Morris, however, said he thought that Macclesfield didn't have Preference shares and that the sums involved were loans.

What one imagines happened is that Macclesfield's loans were largely converted into shares, and that Morris tried to present matters otherwise, to give the more favourable impression that he had merely been repaying a loan rather than forcing out of the company one of its principal early-days financial backers.

According to Macclesfield the dispute over the carburettor that sparked the break was symptomatic of a deeper malaise. "The atmosphere at Cowley was dreadful," he told Morris's biographers. Things came to a head when he was lunching one day at Cowley with Rowse, Pratt and Young. "They said they could not go on. They could get no decision out of [Morris]. He would not attend the business, but at the same time he wanted to make every decision himself, and he was playing around with something, [I] thought a carburettor, at Huntercombe. What was discussed with the others was the fact that the business was going downhill and something had got to stop it, because Morris was not attending to business and was playing about with a carburettor or whatever it was at Huntercombe... Pratt, Rowse and Landstad had certain things coming along which they wanted Morris's OK for, and Morris was playing about. These men were looking to the future, and it was the management that was going to pieces."

Macclesfield said he let the affair ride for a week or two, and then tracked Morris down at Huntercombe, playing golf. A tearful conversation ensued, according to Macclesfield, and shortly afterwards Morris sent Walsh with the cheque. It was obvious long before this that he was not wanted, Macclesfield said, instancing that he was never invited to anything that went on in the works. The break obviously remained a painful memory for Macclesfield, as he asked Andrews and Brunner to cut out a passage in the book about Morris being grateful to him – "because he had never shown it."

Morris's recollections were somewhat different, unsurprisingly, but seemingly equally bitter when he spoke to Andrews and Brunner about the episode. At one stage he said that he wanted a reference in the book to Macclesfield to be excised, "because Macclesfield mistrusted him and dealt with others behind his back". The final break came, he said, when they were having trouble with the radiators of the cars boiling and Macclesfield asked then why they were doing nothing about it.

"In fact they had got on to it long before he had and they had done something. [I] said he could see [Macclesfield] was frightened of losing his money, so in the end [I] said 'Why don't you take it out?' and wrote him a cheque... [I] said to him 'Take your money and get out' and cancelled the loan with a cheque."

New styles, better specifications

For 1924 both the Oxford and Cowley gained further body styles. The new Oxford models were a cabriolet and a saloon, with most of the latter being made made at Poole, in Dorset, by Chalmer and Hoyer – better known as Hoyal. The new Cowleys, meanwhile, were an Occasional Four or Chummy and a Commercial Traveller's Car. The former was pretty much a direct crib of the model

that Morris Garages had commissioned the previous year, and had offered, in conjunction with Buist of Newcastle and Parkside Garage of Coventry, on both Oxford and Cowley chassis.

Models in both ranges took on a more substantial look. The 13.9hp engine became standard wear for the Oxford, a move accompanied by the fitment of a taller and wider radiator to counter the overheating problems that had been enountered with the larger engine. This meant that the scuttle was also taller and wider – allowing in turn a bigger petrol tank, up from 5 gallons to 7 gallons – and prompted a widening of the body of the four-seater tourer, to keep the lines harmonious. Additionally a three-piece screen was fitted, and external door handles became standard on all Oxfords.

As for the Cowley, this went over to a five-lamp lighting set, meaning that it abandoned the rather cyclecar-like mounting of the headlamps on the mudguards; the headlamps were of a smaller size than those of the Oxford. Additionally there was a two-piece fully-framed windscreen on the four-seater and the Chummy, with the two-seater retaining its single-piece screen. Sidescreens were now standard on the Cowley, as was a full set of instruments, although it still did without a rear-view mirror, a wiper, or a dash lamp. Bulking out the Cowley's looks a little, finally, the wheels were increased in size to 710mm x 90mm, as on the Oxford.

By now Morris wasn't just selling a motor car. He was also facilitating its purchase and its maintenance, and enhancing the ownership experience. To draw in new customers, in 1923 he financed a hire-purchase scheme in conjunction with the United Dominions Trust – an invaluable initiative, as proven by the fact that by mid-decade half of all car purchases were on the 'never-never'. Free insurance was another Morris innovation.

He had also understood early on that one didn't just sell a car and walk away, and in 1924 he had instituted a system of standardised parts prices and servicing charges, at the same time stressing the importance of dealers having an adequate stock of parts. That same year he launched in-house magazine *The Morris Owner* and in 1925 printing of this was transferred to a new company, The Morris Oxford Press Ltd, which henceforth would look after all Morris publishing needs. Finally, to promote use of his cars, a Touring and Travel Bureau was set up, dispensing free advice to Morris motorists.

The later Bullnose
1924–26

With the final Bullnoses Morris took market leadership. In this period he also moved into commercial vehicles. There were approaches to join forces with other companies, but nothing came of these. Meanwhile a key figure joined the company.

An early T-type Morris one-tonner; it was only from 1927 that the radiator carried the 'Morris-Commercial' name. The engine was a 13.9hp Bullnose unit, and there was a worm-drive rear axle. (Morris Register)

In 1924 the Bullnose underwent the most comprehensive round of modifications in its post-war career. It was also a year in which Morris carried on making acquisitions, and one in which he made what was to prove one of his most significant managerial appointments.

Morris began the year with the purchase, formalised on 1 January, of his former axle supplier EG Wrigley, and he ended it with the take-over of French car manufacturer Léon Bollée. In between, he considered buying the HE company, which made quality sporting tourers in Caversham, near Reading. The deal fell through when Morris judged the asking price to be too high; quite why the idea was ever entertained in the first place is another matter.

Whilst the Léon Bollée purchase (see Chapter 7) was to prove a grave misjudgement, with Morris pulling out in 1931 after his French-built Morris-Léon-Bollées proved unsaleable, the acquisition of Wrigley's was to add an important further leg to his business, in becoming the home of his Morris Commercial Cars operation.

Morris moves into commercial vehicles

Wrigley's had entered receivership in December 1923, having burnt its fingers badly by being part of the consortium behind the Angus-Sanderson, a failed venture to make a quality mid-sized car from assembled parts – including an engine made by Tylor, a reputed manufacturer of lavatory cisterns. Frank Woollard, as a former senior staffer, had early information that a grouping was being constituted to buy Wrigley's and re-start Angus-Sanderson production, and he tipped off William Morris, who agreed to buy the company as a going concern. He paid a little over £200,000, possibly more than had he hung on in hope of the company being dissolved, but told Woollard that he hadn't wanted Archie Kendrick, the chairman, for whom he had great respect, to 'go through the hoop' of a prolonged and possibly messy receivership.

During William Morris's first Super-tax hearing (see page 85) it was suggested that Wrigley's was an unnecessary purchase that had nothing to do with his core business, and was in fact a

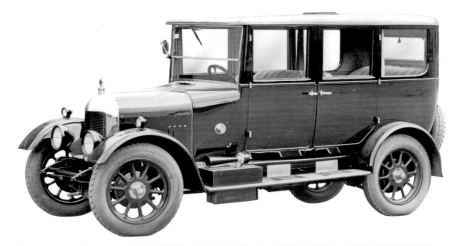

The four-door body and front brakes indicate this is a 1925-on Oxford saloon; the lack of a headlamp cross-bar identifies it as a '25 rather than a '26 model. (Author's collection)

The Oxford saloon's interior was trimmed in Bedford Cord with patterned banding; note the opening roof vent. (BMIHT)

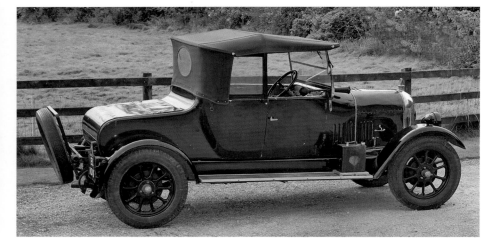

This is a 1925-season Oxford two-seater. For the final two model years the Oxford windscreen reverted to a two-piece unit. (James Mann)

The Oxford Coupé for 1925 was offered in blue, claret, bronze green and grey. (Author's collection)

way of sinking money into a further enterprise as a way of avoiding Super-tax. Whilst Morris was undoubtedly a canny operator when it came to his financial affairs, it is far more plausible that he bought the company because he recognised that its well-equipped works, in Soho, Birmingham, would be ideal as a site for manufacturing the one-ton lorry he wanted to bring into production to compete with Ford's market-dominating TT truck. If the evidence – perforce including a degree of special pleading – that was presented for the Super-tax case is any guide, Morris sailed close to the wind in buying Wrigley's, running down his reserves to about £5000 by the time he had made a further investment of £107,757 for extensions and working capital. 'They went carefully into the position… and they could see themselves just getting through, which they did,' company auditor Reginald Thornton is quoted as having said in his evidence.

Miles Thomas arrives… and Morris is No.1

January 1924 also saw Miles Thomas arrive at Cowley. A motoring journalist who had impressed Morris with his abilities, Thomas was brought in with the idea that he would take over sales from Hugh Wordsworth Grey, who Morris felt was losing his grip. Grey was in fact ill, and would ultimately leave the company at the end of 1926. Once a robust character, at least physically, he had become progressively more unwell. "Grey gradually altered completely. Instead of being burly, he got weak and cried at meetings. His brain was affected," recalled Landstad. The dynamic Thomas, not yet 27 years old, provided an energetic contrast. Given a vague remit to look after sales and promotion, one of his first tasks was to set up a house magazine. As recounted on pages 56–57, he soon rose up the management ladder, and eventually became Vice-Chairman of the entire Morris group.

He arrived at a key moment in the ascension of the company: it was to be in 1924 that Morris would finally out-sell Ford and take first place in the British market. After the huge jump in sales in 1923, Morris production rose a further 64 per cent to 32,910 cars, or 28 per cent of national output. An additional reduction in prices surely helped, and was part of a virtuous circle. Other manufacturers tried to match Morris on price, but because they lacked his volume, the result was that either profitability or quality – or both – would invariably suffer; alternatively, in the case of rivals who could not or would not reduce the

The author at the wheel of a 1925 Oxford tourer. Despite the addition of front brakes, the price in 1925 dropped from £320 to £285 – or to £275 if you didn't want four-wheel braking. (LAT)

The dashboard of open Oxfords remained a plain aluminium panel. (LAT)

cost of their products, their cars would simply cease to have appeal, on account of their higher price. Provided that Morris maintained the quality of his cars – and on this he was unyielding – then his winning run would continue.

Merger talk – the real and the possibly imaginary
Displacing Ford from market leadership had been a long-term aim, but it was all the more piquant as in the previous year rumours had been circulating that Ford had been trying to buy Morris. Whether there was any substance in these stories is another matter; what is true is that in the 1924–26 period various potential alliances were mooted. In particular, during 1924 Austin proposed a three-way merger with Morris and Vickers-owned Wolseley. Austin was still financially rickety in 1924 and the Labour government's repeal of the McKenna Duties with effect from August 1924 had the British motor industry feeling vulnerable. Herbert Austin proposed a unified product range, with many interchangeable components. Longbridge would make 7hp, 15hp and 20hp cars, plus a 30cwt lorry, Morris at Cowley, Birmingham and Coventry would concentrate on a 12hp car and a one-ton van, and Wolseley on an all-new trio of 14hp and 18hp cars and a three-ton lorry.

First year output would be of 64,000 cars, with

Vertically-pleated trim was introduced for 1925 on both the Oxford and Cowley, and is clearly visible on this Oxford tourer. (Author's collection)

The road-test 1925 Oxford Tourer of The Autocar with its improved weather equipment in place; there was now just one upright hood iron each side. (LAT)

more components manufactured in-house. The main forge and foundry would be at Longbridge, as would the press shop, with Wolseley's Adderley Park works providing further foundry facilities and heavy pressings being possibly sourced from the Wolseley factory at Ward End. Recognising

A 1925-season Cowley two-seater in later life. Advertising of the time claimed 'A Morris Car Never Wears Out'. (Morris Register)

The Cowley saloon introduced in spring 1925 was finished in black over blue with blue leathercloth trim; it retailed at £250, against £195 for a Cowley tourer, including a year's insurance. (LAT)

This Hollick and Pratt Cowley saloon has an Oxford radiator and bonnet; it was designed by Lancelot Pratt and built in 1926 for a lady member of the Hollick family. The vee-screen and vee'd dashboard are rather nautical. (LAT)

with two competitors who were in fundamentally poor health? Austin didn't give up, though, and clarified that Morris 'would virtually be in command'. He also raised the possibility of leaving Wolseley out of the deal. Morris was unmoved, writing to Austin that 'the organization would be so great that it would be difficult to control and might tend to strangle itself'. These were just and prophetic words, when one considers the later history of the company.

A rather less ambitious potential alliance was with Bentley, then underfunded and struggling. WO Bentley approached Morris in the winter of 1925/1926, in search of financial backing, visiting Cowley in a 6½-litre Bentley. 'It was my aim to convince him that it would be good business to branch out into a more exotic and exciting field... He said many pleasant things about the car, but although he was non-committal about the possibility of taking a financial interest in us I was left with the impression that he didn't think it would work. Later, he wrote a very courteous letter, saying that he didn't think he could successfully market both a cheap car for the masses and an expensive sporting motor car,' recounts Bentley in *The Cars in my Life*.

The final possible merger or take-over in the air during this period is the most bizarre of all – if indeed the proposal ever existed. According to Morris biographer Robert Jackson, in 1926 the US giant General Motors offered to buy the Morris business. Jackson uses the story of this as the opener for his book, suitably dramatised with plenty of direct speech. He describes GM chairman Alfred P Sloan personally making an offer of £11m, in Morris's office at Cowley – and Morris rejecting this offer, for roughly twice the company's value, saying "the Morris organization is not for sale. Even if it were, we should not be for sale to an *American firm*." Jackson later has Morris telling 'a friend' that had he accepted "I should have been selling my country to another country and that I refuse to do. I should have felt a traitor".

Despite the fact that Morris in 1926 was Britain's leading motor manufacturer, there is no mention of any approach to him in Alfred Sloan's detailed business autobiography, *My Years with General Motors*. He talks of looking at buying Citroën in 1919 and of seriously examining the purchase of Austin in the 1924–25 period. Sloan did not personally visit England to inspect Austin, but relied on a report from the GM vice-president in charge of exports. From his book it seems that

Cowley's lack of engineering strength, chassis and body design would be looked after by Longbridge, from where management control would be exercised.

Under this scheme, Austin and Wolseley would have seen their financial position reinforced, and Morris's relative strength undervalued: at the time Morris's profits were nearly three times those of Austin, whilst Wolseley was loss-making and spiralling towards bankruptcy. Unsurprisingly, Morris saw no virtue in Austin's proposals: why lose his autonomy, just to ally

The Oxford Landaulet was trimmed in Bedford Cord and had a single folding jump seat facing the rear seat. (Author's collection)

This 1925 Cowley has an Australian-built 'occasional-four' body. (Jim Bruce/Morris Register)

he was next in Europe in 1928, to inspect export and assembly operations and visit potential purchase Opel; in other words, when in 1925 GM acquired Vauxhall – 'as a kind of experiment in overseas manufacturing' – it seems that Sloan was not in England to progress the deal. That he would have been in England for putative discussions with Morris, despite not deeming his presence necessary during the purchase of his one and only British acquisition, seems hard to believe. That a potential take-over by General Motors was not mentioned by anybody to whom Andrews and Brunner talked is to the author's mind further proof that Jackson's account is pure fantasy.

Four-wheel brakes for the Oxford

Meanwhile, September 1924 saw a comprehensive revision of the Bullnose. In particular the Oxford moved further away from the Cowley by being built on a chassis with an extra 6in let into the wheelbase. This allowed for more roomy bodies, and for the saloon to move to a four-door format; the two-seater and coupé retained the shorter 8ft 6in wheelbase for a while, but soon switched to the longer chassis. The frame on the Oxford had deeper side members and a tie-bar between the front dumb irons to further improve rigidity, something demanded by the other important change, a move to four-wheel brakes. This was only on the Oxford, which could also be specified with just rear-wheel brakes, at a lower cost, in which case the tie-bar was not fitted. Early 1925 cars were mainly two-wheel-braked, suggesting there may have been initial supply problems.

Well-base wheels and matching wider-section balloon tyres became standard on both Oxford and Cowley, having been a dealer-fit option for 1924, and a much-improved 'straight-through' Smith's five-jet carburettor was now used on both models. Other shared changes were a larger magneto, a steering-column lever for the

Two further '25 Cowleys with Australian bodies. Closest to camera is a two-seater with Sydney-built coachwork; behind is a Chummy-style body of unknown provenance. (Rob Dowthwaite)

JULY 1926 Vol.III No.5

The MORRIS OWNER 4D

The only All British Motor Journal

"Summer Joys"

The Oxford saloon on this 1926 The Morris Owner cover is finished in claret with a black upper body; other colours – all with a black top – were blue, brown and grey. (Ken Martin collection)

Finished in two-tone brown, this Chalmer and Hoyer – or Hoyal – Oxford was described by The Autocar as a landaulet; this may be a mis-captioning. (LAT)

In 1926 Armstrong & Co of Shepherds Bush was offering this saloon-top conversion for Morris tourers. (LAT)

choke, and an internally operated scuttle vent; the upholstery, meanwhile, moved to a pleated pattern, and became detachable.

Specific to the Cowley was a revised two-seater body that was now flat-sided at the rear, with a dickey seat newly fitted in the boot, and had a two-piece windscreen. As yet there was no saloon version of the Cowley, but just such a model was announced in April 1925, at the same time as a landaulet was added to the Oxford line. With the Cowley being on the short-wheelbase chassis, the saloon variant was a two-door design. Oddly, but perhaps to distinguish it from its more prestigious sister car, the body was not that of the previous season's two-door Oxford saloon, from which it could be distinguished by its squarer rear side windows. The Cowley saloon was preceded by the arrival in March 1925 of a three-window fixed-head coupé. Again the styling differed from the comparable Oxford model, having a more square-cut turret and a different shape to the rear deck.

Yet again, prices were lowered. With better cars and a wider range, Morris continued, unsurprisingly, to make hay. Bullnose production rose from 32,939 units in 1924 to 54,151 in calendar-year 1925 – and this despite the growing competition from Austin's Seven. Profits before tax reflected the company's commercial success, rising by nearly 80 per cent, from £870,000 to £1,556,000.

It should be pointed out that this performance took place at a time when the McKenna Duties had been temporarily repealed, resulting in imports of motor vehicles doubling in 1924. Morris had fought hard against Labour chancellor Philip Snowden's intention to abandon the duties, claiming this would cost a million men their jobs. Using Miles Thomas as his lobbyist and propagandist, he set himself up as a spokesman for British industry. Snowden in turn accused him of a 'ramping, raging, lying campaign' – with some justification, it would appear reasonable to conclude, judging by Morris sales during this period.

Last year for the Bullnose

After the mechanical modifications and new models of the 1925 season, the changes to the Cowley and Oxford for 1926 were minor. In essence they consisted of front-wheel brakes – with 9in drums as opposed to the Oxford's 12-inchers – becoming a £7.10s option on open Cowleys and standard wear on the closed models, and the Oxford being equipped with Barker dipping headlamps. These were quite literally headlamps that dipped, swivelling downwards on their tubular mountings when a floor-mounted

The Three-Quarter Coupé was a new style for 1926; this is the folding-head Oxford variant. (Author's collection)

London coachbuilders Alford and Alder showed this occasional-four all-weather Oxford in 1926. (LAT)

lever was operated. They could also be pivoted upwards, which was doubtless useful for reading signposts.

A final detail was that the Boyce Moto-Meter water-temperature gauge mounted on the radiator top of 1925 Cowleys and Oxfords gave way to a very similar device made by Wilmot-Breeden, a firm in which Morris had a personal financial interest. So similar, indeed, were the two gauges that an aggrieved Boyce took Morris to court for patent infringement – and won. Morris was unabashed. The Wilmot-Breeden Calormeter was redesigned, with a longer stem so that it took the temperature of the water rather than that of the air space above the water level, thereby getting around the original patent.

Body styles for the cars were also re-jigged for the 1926 model year. A 'Three-Quarter Coupé' was introduced on both the Oxford and Cowley chassis, this being a five-window design offered as a fixed-head in Cowley form and as a drophead in Oxford guise. The three-window style was still available – as a drophead – in the Oxford range, but the equivalent Cowley derivative – which had been a fixed-head – was deleted. Meanwhile the

This Weymann fabric-bodied 'Saloon-Coupé' was built by Morris Garages for Lillian Morris, on a 1926 Oxford chassis; it was finished in two-tone crimson. (LAT)

MILES THOMAS – A POWER BEHIND THE THRONE

In Miles Thomas, William Morris had recruited a man who would prove to be one of his longest-serving, most loyal and most able executives, someone who would become enormously respected both inside and outside the industry and would ultimately end up running the entire Morris organization. The multi-talented Thomas would also leave behind him the absorbing and entertaining *Out on a Wing*, the sole account from an insider of life in the Morris business. The only child of a retired furniture dealer, Welsh-born Thomas was educated at the King Edward VI School in Bromsgrove and went on to be an engineering apprentice with a firm making

Miles Thomas (far right) with Edgar Blake (left) and visiting Arabian dignitaries, in mid-1932. (Morris Register)

components for diesel engines. As a schoolboy he had already started submitting articles to motorcycling magazines, and he had developed an interest in photography; now he gained practical machine-shop experience and in evening classes picked up drawing-office skills.

A keen motorcyclist, on the outbreak of war he joined the Midland Motor Volunteer Corps as a despatch rider, moving on to drive armoured cars and ultimately to join the Royal Flying Corps. By 1918 he was a test-pilot, decorated with the DFC and in line for a permanent commission in the

RAF. Rather than become a career officer, instead Thomas joined the staff of *The Motor*, and was soon also contributing to *Motor Cycling*, *Commercial Motor* and *The Light Car and Cycle Car*; in 1922 he became editor of the last-named magazine.

Once at Cowley, Thomas set up *The Morris Owner* – for which he wrote and photographed extensively – and then started in-house print operation the Morris Oxford Press, later re-named Nuffield Press. Soon after his arrival, Thomas courted and married Morris's much-valued personal secretary, Hylda Church. Bringing the two men closer together, it was not just a happy marriage but one that served Thomas well in his ascent up the company, as future Nuffield Metal Products director George Dono acknowledged. "[Hylda Thomas] was a power in the land all right. Both she and Thomas had an eye on the main chance. She had strong social aspirations. She was the only woman, as far as [I] knew, who persuaded Lady Nuffield to go to the Motor Show, and took her round..."

By 1927 Thomas had been appointed Sales Director, an influential position for one so young. When Leonard Lord arrived as MD of Cowley, Thomas was aware that between two such strong characters there was a potential for conflict, and happily accepted moving to Morris Commercial Cars in 1934 as General Manager. His responsibilities soon expanded to a role at Wolseley, to which he transferred full-time in 1937 as Managing Director.

By all accounts he re-dynamised the apparently pretty sleepy Birmingham subsidiary, and he was well regarded for his tenure at Wolseley. '[We]... always say that Tommy was the man who took the wool out of Wolseley,' wrote Stanley Reece of Liverpool dealers Blake's. Others recognised his journalist's nose for a story. When a Wolseley on a record run to the Cape in 1939 fell off a bridge in the Belgian Congo but was hauled, battered, out of the river and carried on, Alexander Duckham of the oil company jokingly wrote to Thomas 'Did you stage the accident? It was worthy of you!' With the death of Oliver Boden in 1940, Thomas stepped into his shoes as Vice-Chairman, a position he held until finally parting company with Morris in 1947, as recounted in Chapter 18.

Future BMC senior manager Geoffrey Rose, quoted by Jonathan Wood, remembered Thomas as 'a good manager of people' – something that was undoubtedly true. "He... generated a team spirit in a way that others didn't. When in 1939 I joined the Territorial Army, every six months or so those of us in the Services had a note from him asking 'How are you doing? What is happening?' He'd got that touch and inculcated a sense of loyalty which had great impact on us younger people. He had a flair for publicity, was a bit of a showman and ran a beautiful red Wolseley Super Six."

From his surviving papers[1], dating from the late 1930s until his departure, a compelling picture emerges of Thomas in his later years at Cowley. This was a man who occupied himself with every aspect of the firm's activities, firing off memos on matters ranging from future engine programmes to whether a new 5cwt van could be found for his milkman. Switching from questions of administration to questions of engineering, he was crisp and judicious, and clearly had a fine grasp of both disciplines. On top of this, it was Thomas who prepared Lord Nuffield's public pronouncements, and who himself became a very visible spokesman for the motor industry, dashing around the country making speeches and schmoozing with politicians. At ease on the national stage, he became as much the emblematic face of the Nuffield group as 'WRM' himself.

Thomas was a networker, a canny operator who held the ring between the squabbling senior executives of the various Nuffield companies. He was also a proficient courtier, anticipating and accommodating Lord Nuffield's wishes and if necessary carrying out the sackings his master demanded but himself lacked the courage to implement.

It was a difficult line to walk, and Thomas's apparent involvement in cabals with the likes of fellow directors Harry Seaward and Kimpton Smallbone (see page 150) leaves a nasty taste in the mouth. "He was able and ambitious and not very scrupulous and went out of his way to ingratiate himself with Morris," Arthur Rowse told Andrews and Brunner. In the hothouse atmosphere of Cowley's executive corridors, friendships certainly needed to be robust to survive: Miles and Hylda Thomas were chummy with Smallbone and his wife, yet it must have been Thomas who in 1945 had to inform Smallbone that his services were no longer required.

Thomas seemed to get things done. He obviously had a prodigious appetite for work. But was a lot of it just showmanship and PR flannel? George Dono

told Andrews and Brunner that he had spoken to an executive at state airline BOAC – of which Thomas became Chairman in 1949 – who said that he was the perfect publicity man 'but between you and me he could not manage a tea-party'.

This might be unfair, but it is interesting that in the desperate battle to get the post-war Morris Minor into production (see Chapter 18), Thomas only very late in the day imposed his will on those who were trying to sideline the car. Ultimately he made the right decision, and politically it was no doubt astute to play along with Lord Nuffield's cranky obstructiveness, but one can't help thinking that as Vice-Chairman he should – and could – have knocked heads together sooner. That enough respected voices have regarded Thomas's departure from the Nuffield Organization as a tragedy for the British motor industry is perhaps, all the same, a more reliable barometer of his worth.

Miles Thomas with William Morris; in his later BOAC years. Thomas, never a shrinking violet, was known as the 'Aplombable Showman'. (Author's collection)

[1] Held by the BMIHT at Gaydon; the two quotations above are taken from letters to Thomas in these papers.

The Special Saloon Landaulet had a fully enclosed driving compartment; the standard colour was brown, with blue or claret to special order. (Author's collection)

The engine of the '26 Oxford tested by The Autocar, showing the dipstick combined with the oil filler cap; the carb is a Smith's five-jet. The thermostat in the top hose was a 1926-only Oxford feature. (LAT)

This rather fine Bullnose ice-cream van has an elevated centre section to the roof. (Morris Register)

A new man at the top – of a new company

The year of 1926 was important on several levels in the history of the Morris organization. Firstly, on a purely administrative level, the dynamics changed, with the appointment in July of a new Deputy Managing Director. Morris had been working in tandem with Sales Director Hugh Grey, but the latter's illness meant that he had never fully stepped into the boots of the late Lancelot Pratt. Unusually, Morris's choice was someone he brought in from outside: Edgar Blake, formerly General Sales Manager at Dunlop. He had known Blake for many years, and regarded him as "a very straight man", he told Andrews and Brunner, It is likely, too, that he felt a sense of gratitude to Blake, for the way in which Dunlop had not pushed for payment of bills during the 1921 crisis.

It was not a good pick. Blake was evidently a fundamentally decent man, but as Morris's first proper long-term deputy he was in above his head. In retrospect, several key Morris figures, including Lord Nuffield himself, regarded the appointment as a grave misjudgement. "Blake was a wonderful administrator. There was no letter written by any administrator which he did not see," recalled Carl Kingerlee. "He was a nice man, but he tried to hold all the strings in his hand, and he was not big enough to do it."

The task confronting Blake was all the more challenging, as Morris had made it clear that he wanted to step back from the day-to-day running of the company, as Miles Thomas explained to Andrews and Brunner. "While Pratt was alive, Morris was the boss, Captain on the Bridge, the Director of the Ship, etc. But when… Blake… was made Deputy Managing Director, Morris said 'Here you are, you take the reins. I am here if I am wanted, but you get on with it.' He did that, and [I] would say that at that point the direct executive control, of the Cowley factory at any rate, went out of his hands and it never came back."

Cowley saloon took on a four-door format, only with the twist that there were only two doors, both on the nearside. This was claimed to give far easier access for both front and rear passengers but resulted in somewhat peculiar styling. Finally a Special Saloon Landaulet joined the Oxford line-up, this having normal glazed front doors rather than the open driving compartment of the regular Landaulet.

Characterised by Kingerlee as "slow-moving [and] always afraid of Morris", Blake was in an unenviable position, and one compounded by two things. Firstly, he was not a technical man; secondly, he had to cope with Cowley politics, described by Woollard as "too fierce for words". On the first score he made an unfortunate mark straight after his arrival, commissioning a paint installation without consulting the other directors. It was out-of-date, and when he tried to reverse out of the deal, the suppliers refused, and the plant had to be scrapped, at considerable cost. In an effort to master the technical side, Blake apparently relied on advice from Reggie Hanks, then Assistant Service Manager, but even then he was humiliated in board meetings by Arthur Rowse. For Kimpton Smallbone the Blake era would be characterised by what he termed 'slackness' – Blake, he said, "was no more a Managing Director than a fly". As for Morris himself – who surely should shoulder much of the blame – "the business seemed to come to a standstill" under Blake.

This is perhaps an over-statement, but it is undoubtedly true that management did start to lose focus and begin to drift as the 1920s drew to a close and as a new and more complex decade threatened. Such worries were in the future, as Morris devoted his energies in mid-1926 to a second major re-structuring of his business.

In essence Morris tidied up his affairs in June 1926 by bringing into one new company the subsidiaries he had acquired earlier in the 1920s. At the same time he floated the new company on the Stock Exchange, selling £3m in Preference shares to fund the purchase of the constituent businesses and provide extra capital. The newly-created Morris Motors (1926) Ltd incorporated Morris Engines Ltd, Osberton Radiators Ltd and Hollick and Pratt. Morris remained the sole ordinary shareholder, thereby retaining full control of the business. As he wrote in his *System* article, 'I can get things done while a Board would be brooding over them'.

Morris now had funds for further expansion. In particular, it made available the £500,000 he needed for his investment in the new Pressed Steel Company, as discussed in Chapter 8. In the first three years, no dividend was paid to Morris for his Ordinary shares, despite the company's good profits. The costs of forming the company – approximately £150,000 – had to be written off, and then a total of £2m went to a special reserve fund.

Where were the cars in all this? With the economy suffering a blip in 1926, sales were well down on the preceding year, with just 32,183 Oxfords and Cowleys being despatched – or roughly the same as in 1924. But by now the Morris, which could trace its design back to 1913, was looking somewhat old-fashioned. Although it pained William Morris, the company needed to move forward, and modernise its product line.

Richard Barton of the Barton Motor Company competed in this late two-seater Cowley. (Richard Barton)

The Cowley version of the 1926 Three-Quarter Coupé had a fixed head. (Ken Martin collection)

The 1926 Cowley saloon looked like a four-door but in fact there were only two doors, both on the nearside. (Author's collection)

F-type and the M.G. Super Sports Bullnoses

This four-seater Morris Garages Super Sports is a long-wheelbase model, recognisable by the offside door no longer having a bevelled rear edge. (Author)

The first attempts to make a six-cylinder model were not successful, unlike the modified sporting Bullnoses made by the Morris Garages retail business, which laid the foundations of the MG marque.

Preserved at Gaydon, this is the prototype F-type that William Morris ran as his personal car. (Author's collection)

The interior was suitably well appointed. Note the vertical capillary fuel gauge, and the 'smoker's companion' in front of the driver. (Author)

The engine of the F-type was essentially a 'Hotchkiss' Cowley/Oxford unit with two extra cylinders. (Author's collection)

Although William Morris made much of his mission to offer an affordable light car to counter the Ford Model T, it seems that almost from the start he had ambitions to make an additional higher-priced six-cylinder model.

In the 1915–16 period Hans Landstad was accordingly tasked to develop a six-cylinder engine. He wanted it to be monobloc – "but Morris wouldn't have it because he was afraid it would look too like an American engine," Landstad told Andrews and Brunner. It thus ended up with separate cylinders on the crankcase. At the same time Morris wanted a detachable cylinder head, and the plugs over the valves, which meant the engine was 9in taller than it needed to be. Only one of these engines was made, according to Landstad, and eventually it appears that a car was built up for Morris's personal use: the testimony of Landstad is not totally clear about the various different six-cylinder cars, experimental or otherwise.

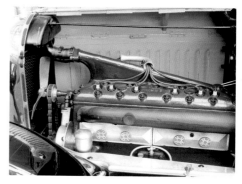

From E-type to F-type

After the war Morris returned to the idea of a six-cylinder model, and two overhead-valve 2355cc engines were built, one being fitted into a chassis extended by 9in and featuring centre-lock wire wheels and half-elliptic rather than three-quarter-elliptic rear springs. Bodied as a saloon, this was shown at the 1920 Motor Show. 'We are informed that all tests have been completed

small flywheel on the camshaft to serve as a vibration-damper. There was also a funnel cast into the exhaust manifold, to channel hot air to the Smith's five-jet carburettor, via a long intake pipe that wrapped around the rear of the engine, whilst the front offside bearer arm for the engine doubled up as a water outlet. These quirky details all seem to have been soon abandoned. Other items of the specification included a twin-plate cork clutch and all-round Hartford friction dampers; the steering, clutch, gearbox and transmission were said to be the

The F-type that The Autocar *took to Scotland: it found the acceleration 'undoubtedly good' and the roadholding 'truly admirable'. (LAT)*

This Hollick and Pratt F-type coupé was completed in 1925 for William Morris. Its body, with a polished and lacquered copper lower section and a polished aluminium upper portion, was later transferred to a Morris Six. (LAT)

and the production programme mapped out, but that it is unlikely that any private buyers will be sufficiently fortunate to be able to secure examples of this new model till well into 1921,' wrote *The Autocar*. In fact, the growing economic crisis meant that in 1921 Morris had other things on his mind, as has been seen, and the E-type six-cylinder car remained a one-off.

The notion wasn't dormant for long, as in the autumn of 1921 a new car was built for Morris's personal use. The chassis, according to Jarman and Barraclough, was almost identical to the E-type; the engine, however, had reverted to side valves, and was now of 2320cc, as a result of commonising bore and stroke with the 11.9hp Hotchkiss unit. Output was said to be around 39bhp at 2800rpm. From this prototype – which survives to this day – was developed the production F-type six-cylinder Bullnose, which was duly announced at the 1922 Motor Show. As first seen, unusual features of the engine included a chain drive for the dynamotor, taken off the first-motion shaft of the gearbox, and a

same as those used on four-cylinder Bullnoses, with the final drive and back axle 'strengthened proportionately' according to *The Autocar*.

A suitably glowing set of road impressions appeared in *The Motor* during December 1922, almost certainly written by Miles Thomas. The Morris was described as being 'deceptively fast' and having a performance at low speeds in top gear 'as refined as the most discriminating might wish' – as well as being 'utterly devoid of period throughout its whole range'. Over-soft rear suspension and a steering column not braced to the dashboard were deemed minor quibbles.

After this write-up the press was largely silent, until in February 1924 *The Autocar* published an article on a trip to the Glasgow Motor Show in an open six-cylinder tourer. In its introduction the magazine commented that although the model had been on the stocks for some time, 'its development has in no way been hurried' – clearly suggesting that only then, in early 1924, was the F-type going to become available to the public.

In fact the 'six' never really made it into series manufacture. According to Jarman and Barraclough only 49 were built, with production as such ending in July 1924, but with three cars assembled in 1925 and a final example in 1926; Landstad is variously quoted in the Andrews and Brunner transcripts as saying that 69 or 29 were made, but these figures are quite possibly either a mistake on the part of Landstad or a mistranscription. In the main it appears that the cars went to company insiders or people close to Morris, with most being despatched in 1924. In February 1923 the first production car went to Lord Redesdale, father of the Mitford sisters, and Lancelot Pratt and the Earl of Macclesfield each had one. Having joined the company in early 1924, Miles Thomas also briefly ran an example. Morris, meanwhile, used three of the cars, in addition to the prototype, with his final F-type having four-wheel brakes and artillery wheels. As for the car built in 1926, if the testimony of a former MG employee is any guide, this was constructed by Morris Garages for the New Theatre in Oxford, to appear in a play entitled *Six-Cylinder Love* and starring well-known stage and screen actress Edna Best.

A car doomed from the start

So what went wrong with the F-type venture? Landstad suggested that simply it was the wrong car for the time, and also that the chassis dimensions did not allow enough room for a suitably spacious body. Arthur Rowse made it clear, however, that there were fundamental failings with the engine – because it was in essence a four-cylinder 'Hotchkiss' unit with two extra cylinders tacked on, and a crankshaft of unchanged dimensions. "That engine was quite impossible... [The] agents ordered a few, as they always will, but within a matter of weeks there were reports of serious knocks in the engine and, of course, the centre crankshaft bearing had gone... The car was a complete and utter failure. About 2000 engines were made and lay about the factory for a considerable period, and it was not diplomatic to refer to their existence at all," he told Andrews and Brunner. Rowse duly wound up the supply contracts "and buried the thing decently and got people not to press for compensation, by arguing that they would get it back on later contracts". The only good thing that came of the F-type, he said, was when he bought a light boat and installed one of the engines. "[It] was perfectly alright. [I] geared it down so that

One of the six Raworth two-seater M.G. Super Sports, ready for the 1924 Land's End trial. (Russell Chiesman)

On the way home after the event; the Raworth's long tail is clearly shown. (Russell Chiesman)

the engine never had to run at more than 1000 revs a minute, and that was the only one of those engines that found a useful home."

Jarman and Barraclough confirm the Rowse story, speaking of the F-type having a 'gluttony for crankshafts' as a result of two vibration periods that caused the slender crank to fracture. Apparently at least nine cars had to have their engine changed before they left the works. According to Landstad there had been an approach to Rolls-Royce to make the engine for Morris; it is thus piquant to recount that in 1925 William Morris showed his personal F-type to Sir Henry Royce, who immediately recognised the nub of the problem, the under-dimensioned three-bearing crankshaft.

There were other problems, according to Richard Barton, son of Frank Barton, who recalls Miles Thomas and his wife visiting in an F-type Bullnose. "Those cars were trouble. William Morris had insisted there should be no clearance on the piston rings, and as a result you had to start the car with a crowbar. I think Dad had the

A familiar photo of a Morris Garages vee-front saloon, with Kimber's wife Irene – known as Rene – stepping out of the well-appointed interior. (LAT)

The fabric-bodied Morris Garages Weymann saloon; despite its gothic looks it was latterly available as a Super Sports. (Phil Jennings)

pistons out and gave the rings some clearance." Quite how the evident failings in the design of the engine can be squared with the 1922 report in *The Motor* or indeed the equally enthusiastic 1924 *Autocar* write-up is another matter.

The F-type fiasco was a humiliating episode, one that according to a 1926 letter from Rowse to company accountant Thornton had cost Morris £20,000 in all. He had planned to make 65 six-cylinder engines per week, but in the end most of the surplus parts were used as hardcore to fill in a lake at the Osberton Radiators factory; an exception was the stock of Hartford dampers, which ended up being used by Morris Garages.

Morris had originally wanted to lay down a sanction for 5000 of the cars, Landstad told Andrews and Brunner. In the end he and Rowse,

convinced the 'six' would never be a success, had whittled this down to 500 cars. "But at the same time the market dried up and nobody wanted it. Meanwhile, they had bought all that material. They had it in stock, and Morris noticed it every time he went round. [I] said they must do something. So they dumped it in the lake up at Radiators..."

Adding sparkle: the Morris Garages Bullnoses

Rather more successful as an up-market and better-performing Bullnose were the cars created by the Morris Garages retail business. Sold as Morrises, they soon came to carry the initials 'MG' on their badges and in their advertising, and constituted the starting-point for the world-famous sports-car marque.

Cecil Kimber had joined Morris Garages as sales manager in 1921 – having moved from Wrigley's, where he had been involved with the Angus-Sanderson project and is said to have designed the car's radiator. Soon after becoming general manager of Morris Garages in 1922, he had created the Chummy occasional four-seater, as discussed in Chapter 4. With Morris adopting this body style as a catalogued model for the 1924 model year, Kimber had the ground cut out from under his feet.

It seems he anticipated this state of affairs, as in the summer of 1923 he commissioned six sporting two-seater bodies from Raworth, for fitment to 11.9hp Cowley chassis on which the steering had been raked and the springs flattened. Key features of what was described as 'the most delightful two-seater body imaginable' were a raked screen with triangular side-panes, and nautical vents in the scuttle – characteristic touches carried through to later sports-bodied Morris Garages Bullnoses. The first example was delivered in September 1923 and by December the car was being promoted as the 'M.G. Super Sports Morris'. It was, said the advertisements, 'an exceptionallly fast touring motor car, capable of 60 miles an hour on the flat, and wonderful acceleration' – and with the modified steering and springing giving 'a glued-to-the-road effect producing finger-light steering at high road speeds'.

In the end only six of these two-seaters were built, and they seemed slow to find buyers. Cecil Cousins, one of those who built the cars, and who stayed with the MG company until 1967, regarded them as the first products that could be considered MGs; marque historian Wilson McComb was more circumspect, calling the two-seater 'the first Morris Garages sports car'.

It is apparent that Kimber was casting around for a formula that would give him a product to be made in decent numbers to replace the Chummy. In early 1924 he advertised a smart vee-fronted saloon, but with Morris offering its own perfectly presentable D-back Oxford saloon for £395 there was never going to be much of a market for the £460 Morris Garages version. Various other bodies were mounted on Bullnose chassis in the course of the year, not least two landaulettes.

A winning recipe

McComb gives the most detailed account of what happened next, one that is corroborated in its essentials by the reminiscences of Cecil Cousins. It seems that Kimber was visited by Reg Brown, a staffer from Sunbeam motorcycles – for whom Morris Garages was an agent – and was shown a special Morris Oxford he was running. It had a polished aluminium sports body, and sat on a chassis with flattened springs, raked steering and wire wheels. The body was the work of Clarey Hughes, a sidecar-maker in Birmingham, and was supposedly modelled on that of a 30/98 Vauxhall; Kimber was impressed.

At around the same time a Morris Garages salesman called Jack Gardiner had bought a 13.9hp Oxford chassis in preparation for fitting a sporting body, and started modifying it, lowering

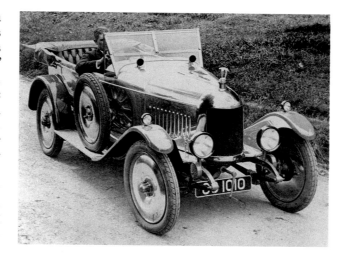

An early four-seater Super Sports in the all-aluminium finish; note the bevelled edge to the rear door. (Ken Martin collection)

Catalogue image of a 1925 four-seater; the upper body was in Smoke Blue or Dark Red. Maximum speed was approaching 65mph. (Phil Jennings collection)

The two-seater was promoted as 'The Car for the Connoisseur'. The triangular quarterlights limited side-draught. (Ken Martin collection)

the springs and in addition (or so he recalled in later life) raking the steering column. Gardiner showed Kimber sketches of what he had in mind for the body, and his boss ended up taking him up to Birmingham and Coventry. It is not known whether Gardiner saw the Brown car or not, but he said that he did visit Carbodies, where according to his account Kimber showed him a

The shapely rear deck housed a dickey seat. In all, 101 two-seater Bullnose Super Sports were made, against an estimated 220 four-seaters. (Ken Martin collection)

steering column raked to anything like the same degree as later cars, if at all. In all other respects, though, it was the clear starting point for the first generation of MG-badged Morris Oxfords built by the Morris Garages. Bullnose MG authorities Robin Barraclough and Phil Jennings estimate that perhaps six further cars were built as 1924-season models. The specification now included a bracket to rake the steering, allowing a lower line to the scuttle. The flattened springs meant that the Gabriel Snubbers at the rear were replaced by Hartford friction dampers but at the front the Gabriels remained. In addition

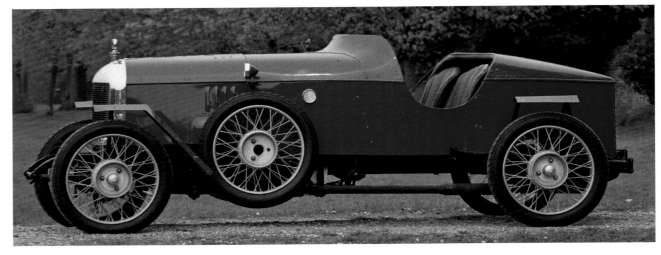

Often erroneously described as the first MG, 'Old Number One' was a one-off special completed in 1925 for Cecil Kimber; it used one of the ohv engines built for Gilchrist. (LAT)

four-seater aluminium body and said that this was the type of body that would be used on his chassis.

Gardiner's car was duly built with polished-aluminium coachwork exactly in this style. McComb is unsure about whether Hughes or Carbodies were responsible, but as the body is largely identical to that of subsequent M.G. Super Sports Morris Oxfords, which were definitely bodied by Carbodies, it is reasonable to suppose that they can claim paternity of this car. A fly in the ointment, however, is the version of events recounted by Carbodies historian Bill Munro. This has the car as being built by Hughes, and Kimber asking the company to build more like it. But Hughes apparently were not in a position to take the Morris Garages order, said to be for six cars, states Munro, and so Kimber commissioned Carbodies, thereby setting in motion a lucrative collaboration that would last into the following decade.

The Gardiner tourer sat on undisguised artillery wheels and did not have the scuttle ventilators of the earlier two-seaters; nor was the

the engine was lightly modified, an SU sloper carburettor generally replacing the Smiths unit and the ports supposedly being polished, while the back axle ratio was raised to allow more relaxed cruising. A special exhaust system was also fitted, and the looks were sharpened by the fitment of Ace wheel discs. The revised steering, which brought with it a longer drop arm, meant that there was no room for a central throttle, so the pedal was moved to the right; additionally the central handbrake was soon displaced to a position beside the driver.

When for 1925 the wheelbase of the Oxford tourer, saloon and cabriolet was extended to 9ft, the Super Sports four-seater followed suit, while two new Super Sports models, an open two-seater and a closed Salonette, retained the 8ft 6in chassis. All three cars used the smaller Cowley radiator, for greater elegance of line; for the same reason narrower running boards were fitted. Naturally enough, the four-wheel brakes of '25 Oxfords were standardised on the Morris Garages productions, although a few cars may have been supplied with two-wheel braking.

The extra six inches in the wheelbase enhanced the lean look of the four-seater, as did the introduction of a painted top half to the body, applicable equally to the two-seater. This upper portion of the body was now in steel, but the lower panelling remained in aluminium.

These were appealing cars, combining trusted Morris mechanicals with racy looks and a dose of extra performance. All this came at a reasonable price: £350 for a two-seater and £375 for a four-seater, against £260 and £285 for the respective mainstream Oxford models. Morris Garages had found the way forward, and in 1925 a full 142 two-seater and four-seater Super Sports were made, as well as six Super Sports Salonettes and three apparently ordinary-chassised Salonettes. The Oxford workshops in Alfred Lane couldn't cope. The cars were assembled after-hours, sometimes up until 10 o'clock in the evening or even midnight, and during the day had to be pushed out into the street to allow regular work on customer cars to continue. In September 1925 Kimber therefore moved operations to a part of the Radiators Branch factory in Bainton Road: with 50-odd employees and their own premises, the car-building arm of Morris Garages was on its way to becoming the MG Car Company.

For 1926 the Super Sports gained a Dewandre brake servo and Barker dipping headlamps, and the long-wheelbase chassis was standardised for all models. Wire wheels came in, too, for the open Super Sports, with the option of Ace wheel discs, and still in conjunction with narrow beaded-edge tyres. On the engine side, a Solex carburettor was henceforth used, along with a special magneto, and power units were now dismantled and inspected and the reciprocating parts balanced and the ports polished. Bodies, meanwhile, were 2in wider, and had steel wings. One distinguished owner was the heir to the Spanish throne, the Prince of the Asturias, who while up at Oxford had a four-seater finished in the Spanish royal colours. The combination was certainly striking: purple wings and upper body, a red-and-gold coachline, and a red-painted chassis with gold pinstripes. Capitalising on this royal patronage, the Morris distributor in Madrid advertised the M.G. Super Sports Morris Oxford tourer as the 'Prince of the Asturias' model.

The 1926 season was even more successful, with 167 two-seater and four-seater Super Sports made, plus twelve Salonettes. All these cars were registered as Morrises, and advertising generally but not invariably mentioned that the

Salonettes had a folding rear seat and were finished in duo-tones. The Motor hailed their 'harmonious yet racy lines'. (Phil Jennings)

By 1926 the Salonette was being called the Sporting Salonette. The alloy coachwork was by Carbodies of Coventry. (Phil Jennings)

cars were built on a Morris chassis, even if it was the M.G. Super Sports name that was most prominent in the advert. The radiator badging, meanwhile, always read 'Morris-Oxford' – albeit with a surrounding ring on the badge reading 'The M.G. Super Sports'.

With their smart coachwork and sensibly-honed mechanicals, the 350 or so sporting Morrises made by Kimber and his team were a perfect complement to the regular Cowley products, and made the ill-fated Six seem a foolish caprice on the part of William Morris. Perhaps the last word should go to Bullnose author and Super Sports owner Lytton Jarman. 'On the road... the 14/28 M.G. and the contemporary Morris Oxford seem two entirely different cars, in spite of the similarity of the chassis specification, and the only features common to both which are immediately recognisable are the delightfully sweet clutch and the gearbox,' he wrote in a 1960 edition of *Safety Fast*, the MG Car Club magazine. 'The M.G. has a much higher and more effortless performance than one would anticipate, but the very real charm of the 14/28 M.G. cannot be measured in terms of performance alone. I think Kimber's real genius lay in the way he could completely transform a car with the minimum of modification, and consequently offer such excellent value for money.'

The Morris-Léon-Bollée

Un salon sur la route

Morris-Léon-Bollée artwork was generally excellent. This 1926 brochure cover picks up on two often-used themes, comfort and spaciousness. (Hubert Achard de la Vente)

A Morris made in France, the Morris-Léon-Bollée was an attempt by Morris to break into the French market with a locally-made product. A mid-range car of no particular distinction, it proved an embarrassing failure.

In 1924 began one of the more bizarre episodes in the life of William Morris, one that today continues to perplex historians: in December that year he bought marginal French manufacturer Léon Bollée, and started making cars in France. The project was not a success, and Morris abandoned the business in 1931.

The story began, according to Hans Landstad, when Morris bought the Hotchkiss engine works in Coventry and became friends with Dunlop (or Archie) Mackenzie – "who knew France very well and was an independent gentleman". Mackenzie apparently suggested that Morris set up an agency in France. The Société Française des Automobiles Morris was duly founded in October 1924 and a showroom opened in Paris. This, said Landstad, was "a wash-out" – although how this conclusion could have been reached in such a short period is another matter. Mackenzie then said that if Morris actually manufactured his cars in France then the French might be prepared to buy them.

The upshot of all this was the purchase, as a going concern, of Automobiles Léon Bollée. Based in Le Mans, this pioneer French business had fallen on hard times after the death of founder Léon Bollée in 1913. Just about keeping its head above water in the hands of Bollée's spendthrift widow Charlotte, it was typical of those small provincial manufacturers who were losing the struggle against mass-producers Citroën and Renault on one hand and against more competent specialists on the other. By 1924 it was producing just one model, the Type M, a pushrod 2-litre of no notable character.

The mysteries of a purchase most peculiar

So why did Morris buy this decaying automotive minnow? As in so many instances, a personal element intruded, according to Carl Kingerlee, who was to become chief tester for Morris-Léon-Bollée. "Madame Bollée's husband had died... and she had the factory round her neck," Kingerlee told Andrews and Brunner. "She had a daughter called Bella, who was partly educated in England, and [who] before that had an English governess, Miss Cheadle... Bella fell in love with

This four-light coachwork is by Chapron, and is probably the style shown in catalogue artwork as the Malakoff saloon. (Rainer Hindrischedt)

An early advertisement, from June 1926, depicting what would appear to be a fabric saloon. (Hubert Achard de la Vente)

Again this advertisement for a torpédo stresses the seven-seater capabilities of the car. (Hubert Achard de la Vente)

In the metal, the tourer is rather less sleek than in MLB artwork. The catalogued style was latterly known as the Saigon. (Rainer Hindrischedt)

coming to Slough to compete with them, [so he] would go to France and have a go at him."

Whether or not this is what happened, it should be pointed out that the Citroën story, which occasionally surfaces in other accounts, is likely to be a red herring: the chronology is wrong. It was only after the 1925 reimposition of the McKenna Duties that André Citroën decided to set up a factory in England, the deal to rent the works at Slough being signed in July that year. Morris's decision to buy a French firm is likely to have been a straightforward response to France's own import controls: if he wanted to sell in a then-buoyant continental market the only solution was to set up shop there, and the simplest way, as ever, was to buy an existing firm that at least had some market presence.

Morris had therefore asked Hans Landstad to go over to France and see whether there might be a suitable firm he could acquire. According to Landstad there were two possible companies. "One was a big one in Lyons, and the other was Bollée." The facilities at the firm in Lyons were old and so were the machines, and Landstad's judgement was that they would have to scrap everything and start again from scratch. Bollée, on the other hand, was "a good firm, with decent machines". Landstad recommended they purchase it.

The puzzle here is Landstad's assessment of the Bollée works. "I've never understood why Morris bought Léon Bollée. It was a nothing. It's a bit as if Citroën had at the time bought say Jowett," says French historian Marc-Antoine Colin. "Bollée had never regained their footing after the First World War. It was a small provincial factory from the pre-WWI era, that at its peak was capable of building about 500 chassis a year. By the early 1920s it was engaged in nothing more than small-scale production of solid but uninspiring cars for a mainly local customer-base. The workforce was second-rate, because all the best people had gone to the big makes or to the garage trade, and there was no dealership network. I can't fathom it..."

Quite who the Lyons companies were that were judged to be far worse a prospect is another puzzle. Of the smaller fry who might possibly have been amenable to a Morris buy-out, La Buire and Luc Court were probably in no better or worse a state than Bollée, Cottin-Desgouttes had an average-sized works, and Rochet-Schneider might have been suffering from under-investment but at least had a sizeable

a dentist. Her mother objected, and Bella tried to commit suicide. And when she was very ill, the only person she wanted to see was Miss Cheadle, so she came back... as a friend of the family. Madame Bollée was so worried about all these things that Miss Cheadle said 'Why not sell the factory?' And it was she who thought of Morris, and eventually, through Archie Mackenzie, who used to go to France a lot, they got [Morris] interested, and he said André Citroën was factory and a good reputation. Any of these would arguably have been a more attractive buy, and would have had the advantage of being part of a motor-industry cluster second only to that of Paris. There was also De Dion-Bouton, with an acceptable and conveniently situated factory at Puteaux for which the Marquis de Dion was known to be seeking a purchaser.

Perhaps quite simply Landstad and Morris were to a degree innocents abroad, and allowed themselves to fall for a charm offensive from the apparently beguiling but somewhat eccentric Charlotte Bollée. When Morris came over to France with Wilfred Hobbs and company secretary Andrew Walsh, "she fell around his neck and cried on his shoulder, and every time she cried, up went the price," recounted Landstad. "Eventually he bought it..."

New management – and a new car

Morris in fact moved with his customary decisiveness, with the preliminary agreement to buy the firm apparently being signed and sealed within 24 hours, on 10 December 1924. The contract was not put into proper form until the beginning of January 1925 and completion was delayed, but Morris soon put a team in place. Rolls-Royce's assistant sales manager in Paris, GP Wallis, was made Managing Director of the new business, La Société Française des Automobiles Morris-Léon-Bollée, with G van Vestrant recruited from Rover as chief designer and Harry Smith of Morris Engines appointed works manager. The firm was – and would remain – Morris's own property, with working capital supplied in regular but never over-large tranches, from his personal holding company.

Hans Landstad and chief Cowley draughtsman Stan Westby were put to work briefly with van Vestrant to draw up a new car. As early as 1 February 1925 a contract was agreed with Hotchkiss. This was for the supply of 2500 engines and gearboxes for a new Morris-Léon-Bollée model, the whole to be delivered by the end of June 1926 at a maximum weekly delivery rate of 50 units. Meanwhile the existing 10CV Léon Bollée continued to be offered, under the new Morris-Léon-Bollée name. Known as the Type M, this had a 1947cc overhead-valve engine and left-hand drive. Keeping the car in production was a prudent move, as four months after placing an order for chassis parts for the new design it seems as if not even a single sample of some components had been received.

Early advertising and catalogues made much of the Anglo-French collaboration behind the car. (Hubert Achard de la Vente)

Meanwhile Morris made it clear through the medium of an editorial in the May 1925 number of *The Morris Owner* that he did not intend to sell French-made cars in Britain:

The slogan of Morris Motors Ltd is "Buy British – and be proud of it". This, in effect, means that this country should buy the goods produced by its own labour and resources. And so although the Léon Bollée has been sold in this country since its inception, it will not continue on this market in competition with other British cars. It must clearly be understood, in order fully to realise the full importance of this policy, that the Morris-Léon-Bollée is a car much larger and more powerful than any of the present Morris cars. Thus it would not be competitive with Morris-Oxford or Morris-Cowley cars, but, selling at a lower price than do existing foreign or British models of its size and type, it would be in competition with cars sold by makers other than ourselves.

This is a clear case of sheer patriotism. Mr Morris states that rather than benefit personally (as he would do by selling his

This well-presented 1927 saloon is one of 22 Morris-Léon-Bollées known to have survived. (Hubert Achard de la Vente)

The body is in the house style for a four-light saloon but differs in detail from the catalogued Malakoff model. (Hubert Achard de la Vente)

French-made car in this country) he prefers to help free the British automobile industry from unfair competition, to meet the foreigner on his own ground, employ French labour to make cars to sell in France, and thus to benefit the working men of both countries.

We feel our readers will be fully appreciative of the spirit that prompts the man who made economical motoring possible in this country to take this step. It is possibly one of the most broad-minded actions ever known in the history of international commerce.

Despite the foot-dragging by French suppliers, during 1926 the fruits of the team's labours were unveiled in the shape of the four-cylinder 12CV Morris-Léon-Bollée Type MLB. Powered by the new AM2 pushrod version of the 2413cc Hotchkiss engine in harness with a four-speed Hotchkiss gearbox, the 50bhp MLB featured torque-tube transmission, four-wheel Perrot-shaft brakes, and – in a first for Léon Bollée – the right-hand drive that was the badge of a high-quality French car. The 10CV continued to be listed alongside, as the *Modèle Normal*, with the new 12CV being described as the *Modèle Allongé* – literally the 'longer model'. Advertising made play of how the car had all the attributes of a high-priced luxury car but remained in the affordable 12CV class. Particularly stressed was the car's flexible performance, its comfort, and its ability to carry seven people. These claimed characteristics would become regularly-used themes, with *souplesse* – flexibility – being represented by a special radiator mascot available at extra cost and with advertisements boasting that the car was *un salon sur la route* – 'a drawing room on wheels'.

A difficult start-up

With the factory doubled in size and re-equipped, and now concentrating solely on the new model, production was said to be soon reaching 50 cars a week, aided by a chain-driven production line. Given that the bodies were subcontracted to outside coachbuilders, this figure may relate just to rolling chassis; it may also be wishful thinking. Confirmation that it is almost certainly fantasy is an article in *The Motor* in 1928 which trumpets an output of 150 cars a month, up from the 25 cars a month in pre-Morris days. As will be seen, figures for total production make it clear that if a rate of 150 vehicles a month was ever in reality achieved, it would not have been maintained for long by the multi-national workforce, apparently dominated by White Russian immigrants.

In any case, van Vestrant is on record as saying that the sales manager was in the habit of taking orders for styles not in the catalogue, which can only have slowed down the output of finished cars. Certainly a 1929 catalogue makes play of the availability, alongside three different saloons and a tourer, of 'a range of fancy models in harmony with modern artistic tendencies' – without giving much away about what these might be. If Kingerlee's testimony is any guide, management seems in fact to have been pretty ropey, with Wallis largely an absentee MD, lingering in Paris as he supposedly couldn't find a house in Le Mans. A further handicap, said Carl Kingerlee, was that the company was too far from its component suppliers and its coachbuilders, most of which perforce would have been around Paris. According to Kingerlee it was only when they were able to get a local maker of railway carriages to take on building of bodies that that the latter bottleneck was finally resolved.

That was the least of the problems. According to Landstad, personal animosity between Morris and Henry Ainsworth of Hotchkiss had unfortunate repercussions after Morris had turned to the company to supply engines for the MLB. "[Ainsworth] was always very sorry he had had to leave Coventry. He was a director of Hotchkiss in France, but he would have liked to have kept his own factory, so there was no love lost after that. They decided to place engines with Hotchkiss, and to begin with, they were given absolute scrap. Poor performers were all put in Bollée cars. They had a lot of trouble. If there were ever short deliveries, it was always Morris-Léon-Bollée who suffered." Such was also Lord

The Trocadéro was the catalogued four-light coupé or coach style for 1930. (Robin Barraclough)

The faux-cabriolet saloon was called the Ostende; the rear trunk was an extra-cost option. (Robin Barraclough)

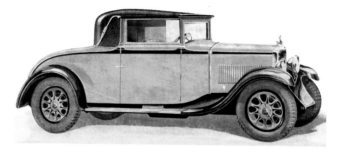

The Dinard drophead coupé was available, as with all styles, on both the four-cylinder and six-cylinder chassis. (Robin Barraclough)

The regular cabriolet, called the Croisette, was in fact a fixed-head. (Robin Barraclough)

Its sister car, the Biarritz, had a lower roofline and a roadster tail. (Robin Barraclough)

Striking artwork for the 1930 catalogue cover; note how the eight-cylinder is not included. (Robin Barraclough)

This late six-light saloon is another survivor with Chapron bodywork. (Rainer Hindrischedt)

fabric saloon, meanwhile, now retailed at 43,900 francs. To cite just one example, that still put the cars above a perfectly respectable 11CV Peugeot in price.

Meanwhile by July 1927 the old 10CV had been deleted, and the MLB offered in a cut-price *Normal* form. In this guise it lost its Perrot front axle and Perrot braking, and its dampers. The regular *Luxe* was now distinguished by a taller radiator and a bonnet without rivets.

There was nothing particular for which to reproach the cars. The Hotchkiss engine had no vices and the coachwork, often by well-known firms such as Chapron, was eminently acceptable. But sales were slow. Money was now leaching out of Morris's personal purse, and the company would run up losses of £150,000 by the end of 1928; the following year it would be a further £80,000 in the red.

Going down the multi-cylinder route

In a bid to make the necessary breakthrough in the French market, the range was expanded for 1929, with new six-cylinder and straight-eight models being shown at the 1928 Paris *salon* alongside the four-cylinder MLB.

The 15CV 'six' was nothing more than an MLB with a 2658cc Wolseley overhead-cam engine – SU carburettor and all – fitted into the existing four-cylinder chassis, a task facilitated by its generous 10ft 3in wheelbase. It was said that the engine would eventually be built in France, but in its report of the following year's Paris show *The Autocar* said that the engine was made by Wolseley in Birmingham, which is reasonably trustworthy confirmation that this never happened. Given the small numbers involved, there was no earthly reason why the engine would have been made at the Le Mans plant.

Already exhibited at the 1927 Paris show, the 18CV eight-cylinder 8D also used a Wolseley engine, although in February 1927 William Morris had paid £104 on behalf of Morris-Léon-Bollée for the purchase from the United States of an eight-cylinder Continental engine; whether this was ever fitted to a chassis is not known. As it was, the new Morris-Léon-Bollée used the Wolseley 21/60 ten-main-bearing unit with its Alfa-like central camshaft drive. Apparently the performance was judged below par, as for the Morris-Léon-Bollée its capacity was raised from 2.7 litres to to 3.1 litres, boosting power to 60bhp at 3200rpm. This was presumably

Nuffield's recollection, in later life. "Hotchkiss sent them all the rejects," he told Andrews and Brunner. He was sure, he said, that Renault and Citroën were behind this skullduggery.

What all this amounted to was that the MLB had a hesitant start-up, and failed to make an impression in the hard-fought French market of the time. By the time of the 1927 Paris show, Morris-Léon-Bollée was forced to slash its prices, the cost of the base open tourer being reduced from 45,000 francs to 33,900 francs; a Weymann

with a view to it coping with heavier coachwork, as a longer-wheelbase chassis was additionally offered for the straight-eight, and coachwork on a long-wheelbase chassis invariably featured in advertising for the car. The standard chassis, however, was the same as that of the four-cylinder and six-cylinder models, and one imagines that with a light body the performance of a swb Morris-Léon-Bollée 'eight' would have been quite satisfactory, although the roadholding may well have been a shade frightening.

Thereby hangs a story. It seems likely that the prototype eight-cylinder car was built in England, with a body commissioned by Morris Garages and perhaps built by Raworth. Certainly a short-wheelbase four-light coupé was photographed in the Morris works in 1927 and is described on the back of the reference print as being an eight-cylinder car built for William Morris. This was corroborated by well-known racer and journalist John Bolster, who married Barbara Skinner, daughter of Carl Skinner of SU Carburettors.

In 1975 Bolster said that the car was broken up fairly swiftly but that its front axle was still lying around at SU in 1934 or thereabouts. 'Do I recall that it was a present to the guv'nor from grateful workmen and was this the car in which he had a nasty accident, in which Lady Morris was injured? Anyway, it was all rather hushed-up, or at least that's my impression,' he wrote in

a letter to *Veteran & Vintage* magazine.

This identification is important, as the car has variously been described as an MG prototype and as a Morris Oxford. It may well have started life as the latter, at least nominally, as the registration WL 1954 was attributed to a 'Morris Oxford 23-6' in the name of Morris Garages; that there was no such thing as a 23hp six-cylinder Morris suggests that it may have started out with an experimental six-cylinder engine before receiving the straight-eight.

Another survivor, photographed a few years ago in a French museum, and unusually wearing the optional wire wheels. (Tony Baker)

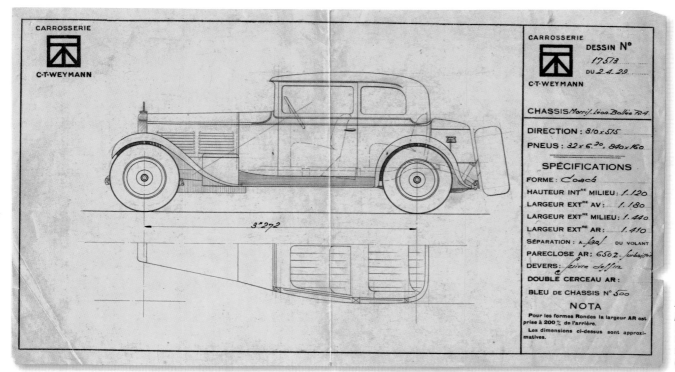

A French coachbuilder's profile drawing for a Weymann close-coupled two-door saloon, dating from February 1929. (Author's collection)

Not waving but drowning...

With a Type T1 light-commercial being listed for 1930 and a new style of bevelled radiator, Morris-Léon-Bollée now had a more attractive range, and one that responded to the fashion for multi-cylinder motoring. It was to no avail. Doubtless the economic downturn that started in 1930 did not help. But even without this, nobody much wanted the cars. According to Jarman and Barraclough only 25 of the six-cylinders were made, and perhaps half a dozen straight-eights. That these figures must be about right – allowing for over-ambitious ordering – is confirmed by Morris's personal

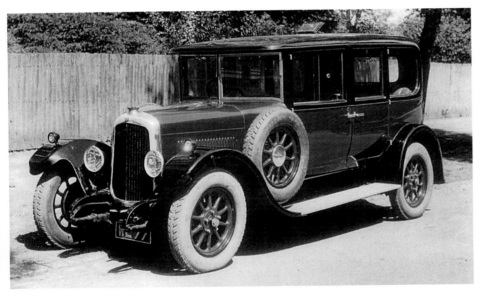

This Morris-Léon-Bollée was bodied on behalf of Morris Garages. (Robin Barraclough)

The 'mystery' two-door eight-cylinder MLB built for William Morris. (Robin Barraclough)

It seems likely the body was provided by Morris Garages, so may well be by Raworth. (Author's collection)

ledger book for the period, which shows that as of January 1929 Wolseley had supplied engines to the value of £3014.10s to Morris-Léon-Bollée; such a sum would be equivalent to perhaps 60 higher-value multi-cylinder engines at 1920s prices. The fact that the 1930 range catalogue did not include the eight-cylinder Morris-Léon-Bollée is likely to indicate that it was no longer regarded as a production model. But even sales of the supposedly mainstream MLB were largely symbolic, and in 1931 William Morris pulled out, ceding the company and its stock for £14,000 to a consortium led by Mackenzie and Smith; Landstad suggests that the duo did quite well out of the deal.

The same trio of models was listed at the 1931 *salon* as Léon Bollées, along with an additional four-cylinder model with a smaller-bore 11CV engine. Despite speculation by historian Michael Sedgwick that this might have been made by Unic, it seems that it was an adaptation of the faithful Hotchkiss AM2 unit; whether any were actually produced is another matter. The following year saw just the 12CV on show, and in late 1932 the firm definitively closed its doors.

Notwithstanding Morris's display of high morality about not selling the cars in Britain, Morris-Léon-Bollées were offered in Australia by some Morris dealers, and the marque was also present in the Republic of Ireland. In addition to William Morris's own car, discussed above, there were some other examples in circulation in Britain. These included a six-light saloon bodied on behalf of Morris Garages and a drophead coupé by Raworth that had again passed through Morris Garages and was apparently built for a well-known Oxford tailor.

Arithmetic of a disaster

How many Morris-Léon-Bollées were made? Jarman and Barraclough suggest 25,000 cars, a total Michael Sedgwick felt unrealistic: his estimate was between 12,000 and 13,000. Fortunately Morris accountant Reginald Thornton had a set of figures, and these survive in the Andrews and Brunner papers. They tell a very different story. At 30 September 1928, a full 879 out of the original sanction of 2500 Hotchkiss engines had not yet been fitted into vehicles, and there were 452 unsold cars. Thus over three model years only 1169 cars had been sold. A note in the margin says that approximately a third of the unsold cars had found homes by September 1929. This suggests

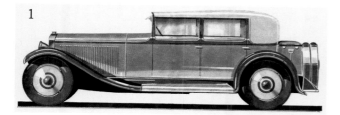

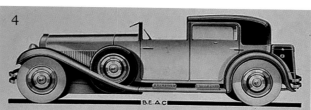

that 300 cars were still in stock at the beginning of the 1930 model year – sufficient for at least another two years of sales.

The most plausible conclusion, therefore, is that the cars sold in the ensuing 1930–33 period were largely and probably exclusively from this stock. This fits in with the implication in the Andrews and Brunner biography that production ceased in late 1928 so that the stock of unsold cars could be liquidated. If there had been a demand for further cars, this could, one imagines, have been met from the component sets presumably still in stock alongside the remains of the Hotchkiss engine sanction. Excluding the handful of six-cylinder and eight-cylinder cars from the calculation, this would lead one to a production of 1621 four-cylinder MLBs – or, at the very most, 2500 if the full stock of Hotchkiss engines and associated parts had all been built into cars, which strikes one as implausible.

As for Morris, the failure of his business in France was bruising, and almost certainly lay behind his dislike of the French, who he felt could not be trusted. Unsurprisingly, he was not forthcoming about the venture, in which he had invested over £420,000. 'He just never talked about it,' says Miles Thomas in *Out on a Wing*. In old age, Lord Nuffield was equally reticent, telling Andrews and Brunner that the French "treated him so badly that eventually he gave the thing away". Wilfred Hobbs, ever the faithful retainer, advised the two that their biography should not mention Morris's mistakes, and suggested that they completely exclude the Bollée episode. This counsel was not followed, and the book deals briefly but fairly with the French venture, concluding that the French had a resistance to buying a car from a foreign firm, and that the Morris-Léon-Bollée was pitched into a stagnant market sector against strong competition.

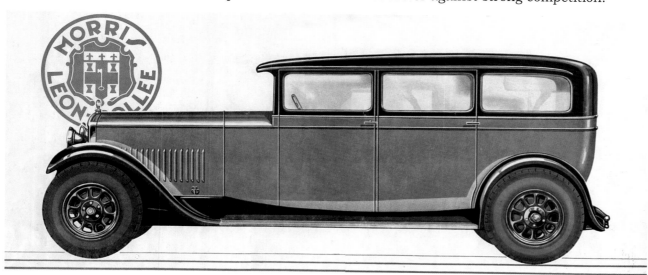

The Flatnose Cowley and Oxford

The flat radiator was not a thing of great beauty, but it was more efficient than the elegant Bullnose item. Here an AA man gives a 1931 Cowley a once-over. (Automobile Association)

Morrises had a new look. But the launch of the Flatnose was traumatic. During its currency the dynamic of the company changed – not necessarily for the best. Meanwhile Morris's personal fortune continued to grow.

Restructuring the business was only part of a packed year for Morris. Before 1926 was over he would also have bought the SU Carburettor Company (see Chapter 9) and – most crucially of all – he would have launched a replacement for the car on which he had built his empire. It is not too dramatic to say that on the success or otherwise of this new model would hang the future of the enterprise.

Something old, something new...

With the Bullnose, William Morris had been a one-hit wonder, successfully offering one design in various forms rather than building up a diverse range of models. Although there was a world of difference between the spindly light car of 1913 and the big-tyred longer-wheelbase four-wheel-braked Oxford of later times, there had also been an essential continuity in that design over the 13 years in question. Equally, though, there had been an evolution in technology and in fashion since Edwardian times, and the charming bullet-nosed prow of the Morris was by 1926 as outdated as its three-quarter-elliptic rear springing. The risk, though, was that in modernizing the Morris car it would lose its character – and at the same time its customer base.

Such fears were misplaced. The evidence shows that the new 'Flatnose' Cowleys and Oxfords with their tombstone-shaped radiator not only arrived at just the right time but also gave a major boost to company fortunes. In 1926 total sales – mainly of the Bullnose – would fall from their 1925 peak of 53,582 cars to a mildly less impressive 48,330 units. In 1927, however, despatches from Cowley would accelerate to 61,632 cars. At the first AGM of Morris Motors (1926) Ltd, in May 1927, William Morris was able to announce that home-market sales had been up a third during the first four weeks of 1927.

Look beyond the brouhaha about the 'Astounding Morris Programme for 1927' and the would-be buyer of a Flatnose would discover that the new car was basically a repackaging of the old mechanicals in a fresh body and chassis – with the bonus of a reduction in prices. The engine, clutch and gearbox were largely unchanged, as were the front and rear axles.

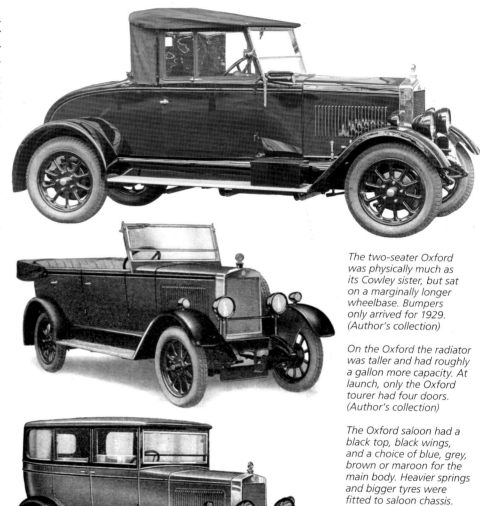

The two-seater Oxford was physically much as its Cowley sister, but sat on a marginally longer wheelbase. Bumpers only arrived for 1929. (Author's collection)

On the Oxford the radiator was taller and had roughly a gallon more capacity. At launch, only the Oxford tourer had four doors. (Author's collection)

The Oxford saloon had a black top, black wings, and a choice of blue, grey, brown or maroon for the main body. Heavier springs and bigger tyres were fitted to saloon chassis. (Author's collection)

The salient feature of the new chassis was that it incorporated semi-elliptic rear springing, damped by Smith single-acting shock-absorbers rather than the previously-used Gabriel Snubbers; the new suspension resulted in better roadholding but a less comfortable ride. The new frame – on a wheelbase of 8ft 9in for the Cowley and of 8ft 10½in for the Oxford – was much more rigid, better able to resist the braking

Barker dipping headlamps were fitted only to the Oxford. For 1929, both the Cowley and the Oxford would have a vacuum-operated dipping system. (Author's collection)

A 1927 Cowley saloon on a French weighbridge. This model was current for only one season. (Ken Martin collection)

Another one-year wonder was the three-light Cowley coupé with its rather abruptly-styled glasshouse. Finished in blue, it sold at £182.10s, against £160 for an open two-seater. (Author's collection)

The two-seater was an occasional four-seater in reality, as there was an upholstered dickey seat, as indeed on the coupé. (Ken Martin collection)

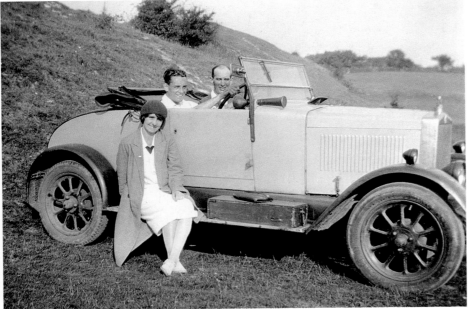

stresses imposed by the four-wheel brakes, and more suited to rough colonial conditions. The side-members were deeper, there were three below-frame cross-braces incorporating the running-board brackets, and further strength was provided by a light and robust pressed-steel bulkhead, this incorporating the seven-gallon fuel tank and the dashboard pressing.

Supposedly as a result of a reserve tap now being fitted, the petrol can on the running board was eliminated; another new feature was a dial gauge on the tank, in place of the rather awkwardly-placed tubular glass gauge found on the dashboard of the Bullnose. Details that differed between the Cowley and the Oxford included the brakes and wheels. The former had 9in drums and three-stud wheels and the latter had 12in drums and five-stud wheels. The appearance of the new Cowley and Oxford was more square-cut, thanks to the flat radiator and the higher scuttle line that accompanied it. Claimed to have 60 per cent greater cooling surface, despite a reduced water capacity, the new radiator eliminated the Bullnose's tendency to boil, but in its original sharp-edged form the cowl was difficult to press, and so had to be given softer radiuses during 1927. The new front was not well received by William Morris. Harry Seaward, at that time manager of the Cowley body shop, recalled Morris asking him why the change had been necessary. "[I] replied that they had got to make progress. Morris said that Rolls-Royce never changed theirs. [I] said that if he

In November 1926 William Morris was obliged for the first of two occasions to appeal against liability for what was termed Super-tax. This was a tax on private persons whose incomes passed a certain threshold, and was payable over and above regular income tax. Without becoming enmired in the finer detail of fiscal policy, it suffices to say that Morris won his appeal, and that this was on two grounds.

Firstly, Morris channelled his money through a holding company, at the time called the Morris Company. It was decided that such dividends as were paid into this entity were not liable for Supertax.

The other argument was that investments Morris had made in other businesses were a tax dodge, and had nothing to do with maintaining or developing the core business. The Inland Revenue focused particularly on the acquisition of Wrigley's, and here Morris was able to

demonstrate that building the firm into his commercial-vehicle arm was a legitimate extension of his existing activities.

Supporting Morris's arguments, Sir Eric Geddes, Chairman of Dunlop, said that the amount of money in quick and fixed assets retained by the Morris Company was not out of relation or excessive, relative to similar companies. Also called as a witness, Austin finance director Ernest Payton testified that Morris was in fact taking a considerable risk in keeping liquid assets so low relative to turnover.

The Commissioner for the Crown perhaps put his finger most astutely on the nub of the problem. "The real trouble is to remember when Mr Morris is Mr Morris, a human being, and when he is one or a collection of separate companies," he commented – one imagines with a tinge of exasperation to his voice.

1928: the recipe unchanged

For the 1928 season there were minor mechanical and aesthetic changes, along with the introduction of some new body styles. The most significant of the modifications to the running gear was the adoption of a new system of brake compensation, using a chain and sprockets; it is doubtful that this Heath Robinson arrangement was any better than the preceding set-up. Further attention to the braking was to come in March 1928, with the fitment of anti-squeal bands to the drums. Beyond this, other mechanical improvements included an SU carburettor to replace the Smiths unit, a better magneto (from May 1928), and a redesigned gearbox top in order to position the handbrake behind the gearlever instead of in front of it, both levers at the same time being lengthened.

Coachwork changes were equally minimal, with the Oxford all-steel saloons, the Cowley saloon and the two coupés all gaining a single-piece windscreen and the Oxford saloon featuring more rounded corners to the windows. The Cowley saloon was now to a four-door configuration – although the two-door saloons continued to be listed until stocks of the '27 model had been exhausted – whilst the Cowley coupé gained rear quarter windows to become a Three-Quarter Coupé. On certain models there was an adjustable front bench seat that could be folded flat. Meanwhile the Oxford cabriolet was deleted and 11.9hp versions of the Oxford tourer and saloon were introduced, identifiable by their smaller Cowley radiator, 19in wheels and Karhyde upholstery. At the other end of

Still with Hoyal, this fabric-bodied coupé was offered in 1928; the fabric was known as Fabrikoid. (LAT)

A rather austere saloon was offered on the Cowley chassis by the South-Western Motor Company of Charlton Adam, Somerset. (LAT)

the range, spring 1928 saw the announcement of a coachbuilt Oxford 'Saloon De Luxe' with a three-piece 'vee' screen. Bodied by Hoyal, this boasted, said the catalogue, 'a scheme of interior decoration and upholstery which is luxurious almost to the point of being ornate' – equipment including high-grade furniture-hide

This 1928 Simplified Cowley was bodied in Australia. It has its headlamps in the normal position – rather than on the wings, as on British examples. (Mark Dixon)

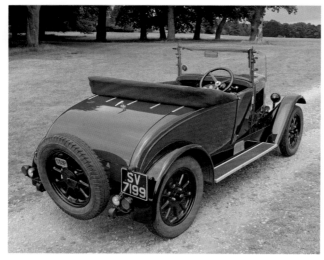

It is thought that the tail incorporates Model T Ford presswork – this being cheaply and readily available to small Australian bodyshops. (Mark Dixon)

The cockpit of a 1930 Cowley two-seater. During the 1927 season, the centre accelerator pedal had been abandoned on the Flatnoses; dials became ivory-coloured rather than silver-faced for 1929. (LAT)

seating, blinds for the rear quarter windows, and mahogany garnish rails. Morris judged it prudent to temper its description with a warning that the wider and more spacious body was 'somewhat heavier' than that of the regular saloon and that 'to some extent, therefore, performance is admittedly sacrificed for comfort and appearance'.

New looks – and the Oxford becomes a 'six'

By the time of the next model year Morris felt more confident about the possibilities of the steel stampings from the Pressed Steel Company. Thus for 1929 it gave the Oxford and the Cowley – which was still wood-framed – a new look characterised by deeper-drawn panels. In particular the rear of the closed cars had a more rounded form, leading to the saloons being dubbed 'Dome-Back' and the coupés 'Dome Head'. The mudguards were also more domed, the headlamps were now on a pressed-steel bar (and had a vacuum dipping mechanism), and the dumb-irons were covered with an apron later characterised by authors Jarman and Barraclough as 'nasty and unnecessary'. Other visual tweaks included a pressed-steel vizor, wings on the Calormeter, and the disappearance of the bulb horn in favour of an under-bonnet Sparton electric unit. Bumpers also became standard wear, these being twin-bladed on the Oxford and single-bladed on the Cowley.

EXIT FROM PRESSED STEEL

In 1930 Morris pulled out of Pressed Steel. The venture had proved problematic on four fronts. Firstly, there was continuing concern over the quality of the bodies and about their sometimes erratic delivery. Secondly, Morris simply didn't have the volume of demand to fill the works. Thirdly, Pressed Steel was finding it a struggle to take on other customers to compensate for this shortfall: other companies were reluctant to place orders with an enterprise part-owned by Morris. Finally, other pressings companies were starting to shy away from Morris, as they felt he was now a competitor; as a consequence, Morris risked losing the flexibility to place his business for smaller press-work with outside firms. An example of this wariness towards Morris was that Fisher and Ludlow at one stage refused to provide quotes for some work, as it was felt that Cowley was trying to benchmark Pressed Steel figures rather than genuinely seeking a contract.

Morris's initial response was to take the whole concern under his control. An offer was made, in 1929 or thereabouts. "It was a very near thing. It looked a push-over, because they only had the one customer and he was dissatisfied," future Pressed Steel Managing Director Fred Cairns told Andrews and Brunner. "But their then Managing Director put up a terrific fight and kept independent. Then, once they got clear of the Morris directors, they started to get the Hillman business[1]".

After this, Morris decided it best to withdraw from the consortium. There was a certain logic to this, in that an independent Pressed Steel could attract the non-Morris business it needed to develop into a viable and healthy enterprise. The pull-out wasn't without its traumas. When it became known that Morris wanted to sell, ambitious up-and-coming William Rootes, owner of Humber and Hillman, tried to buy his shares – but indirectly, via Edward Budd, with whom he had established a friendship.

[1] The Hillman Wizard and Hillman Minx, both announced in 1931, did indeed use Pressed Steel bodies. That used on the Minx saloon would also be employed by Rover for its Ten.

In the end Morris agreed to sell only if none of his shares went to competitors. Apparently he deeply resented Rootes's behind-the-scenes manoeuvres, and thereafter he guarded a lasting animosity towards Billy Rootes.

So it was that in 1930 Morris bowed out from Pressed Steel, taking with him the two positions the Morris company held on the board, occupied at that stage by Edgar Blake, as Chairman, and Arthur Rowse. Six years later, in 1936, Budd in turn sold out to Shroeders, and the business changed name from The Pressed Steel Co of Great Britain Ltd to The Pressed Steel Company Ltd. It would come back into the fold in 1965, when it was acquired by the British Motor Corporation, and merged with Fisher and Ludlow, which BMC had bought in 1953.

The British Paint and Lacquer Company, which had run into some of the same problems as Pressed Steel – it couldn't obtain quotes for cellulose, fillers, and so on – was also eventually unloaded, being sold in the mid-1930s to ICI, apparently for a handsome profit.

With the problems of the early Pressed Steel bodies resolved, for 1929 the saloons took on a more rounded look; this is a 1930 Cowley, and as a fixed-head saloon it has a peak over the windscreen. (Author's collection)

A fabric-bodied Oxford saloon with sliding head was a newcomer, while the Saloon De Luxe was given a restyled body using Cowley saloon panels except for the scuttle, rear panel and roof corner panels; the Oxford Saloon Landaulet was discontinued, as was the Simplified Cowley. The Cowley tourer, meanwhile, was revised to feature a tapering rear edge to the front doors and a waistline level with the scuttle.

Mechanical changes for 1929 were limited to a dipped front axle and a rubber mounting for the steering. As the steering was mounted on the engine, which was itself rubber-mounted, this was not a particularly fortunate innovation: when the cars aged, a combination of play in the steering and worn rubber mounts made directional stability somewhat approximate.

With the arrival of a six-cylinder Oxford for 1930 (see Chapter 12) the four-cylinder model was withdrawn. That left the Cowley, in 11.9hp form only, as the sole representative of the Flatnose line. It was little changed physically: the flanks of the tourer body were altered so they sat roughly an inch below the height of the scuttle, with the doors becoming more parallel-sided, whilst a Kopalapso folding head was fitted to the coupé and available optionally on the saloon. Additionally a Commercial Traveller's Saloon with a side-hinged rear door and a removable rear seat replaced the Commercial Traveller's Car. Triplex glass (soon to be a legal requirement) became standard, and all bright parts were now in chrome; 150 left-over '29 tourers were re-equipped with a Triplex screen and chrome fittings and sold as 1930 models.

The Oxford coupé gained softer lines for 1929 but was no longer a drophead. The dipped waistline moulding distinguishes it from its Cowley sister. (Author's collection)

The Oxford Traveller's Brougham was built by Raworth, who also made at least one Isis with the same body, for the Morris film unit. (Author's collection)

Until the 1930 season, the commercial version of the Cowley was this Traveller's Car. (Author)

Westminster Carriage Co built this fabric-bodied coupé-saloon on an Oxford chassis in 1929, to the patents of a Mr Gregory. (LAT)

The fabric-covered roof slid back and forth on roller-bearing runners, allowing the car to be used at will as either a saloon or a coupé. (LAT)

Far more significant than such cosmetics were two upgrades to the running gear that made the 1930 Cowley a much better car to drive. Firstly the steering box was now mounted on the chassis and became a Bishop cam-and-peg unit. This revision was current from January 1930, and from March 1931 a conversion kit was made available for earlier cars. Secondly, the braking system was simplified by removing the compensation; at the same time, stiffer ribbed drums were fitted. The result was more consistent braking. A minor detail, finally, was that 1930 Cowleys had Armstrong instead of Smith dampers – still of the friction type.

Last of the line: the 1931 Cowley

In what was to be the run-out year for the Flatnose Cowley, it might seem bizarre for Morris's low-cost workhorse to have been given a revised chassis for 1931. But that is indeed what happened. The reason was simple: suitably beefed-up, the Cowley frame could accommodate the six-cylinder engine of the Oxford with no change to the wheelbase, thereby creating a low-priced 'six' to sell alongside the more expensive Oxford and Isis models. The result was the Morris Major.

The uprated chassis, complete with the Major's grouped chassis lubrication – six nipples aligned on the rear-axle casing – was then put to use on the Cowley. Signalling the change, the '31 Cowley had a taller radiator with a deeper bonnet to match, along with a shallower windscreen. Additionally the Major's wire wheels became optional, giving the otherwise staid Cowley a certain air of modernity; they

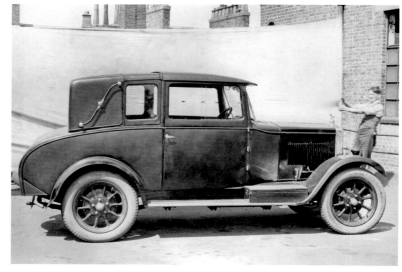

SNUBNOSE AND FLATNOSE VANS, 1927–33

The transition to the Flatnose was less apparent with the Light Van, which continued with the Snubnose radiator and with a largely unchanged body. For the 1927 model year it did, however, switch to to the Flatnose Cowley chassis, only with eight-leaf rear springs; front brakes were now optional, too.

Bodies were henceforth built at Bodies Branch in Coventry and mounted and finished at Cowley. They were essentially as the previous Standard model, and retained that model's oval side windows; the contours to the bonnet to marry the Snubnose radiator to the square-cut Flatnose bulkhead were slightly odd. The front wings were unique to vans and the rears were as the '27 Cowley. Just a single model was offered, rather than a Standard and a De Luxe, but an additional high-roof 10cwt variant was introduced, and during 1927 ultimately replaced the 8cwt low-roof model.

For the 1928 model year, fully-glazed cab doors were fitted and the rear doors cut into the roof top; front brakes were also standardised. A subtle new look arrived for 1929, with body sides that were flat rather than inset at the bottom, giving extra capacity and allowing wider rear doors. The 1930 season, the last for the Snubnose, saw body construction lightened and the semi-circular wood protrusions on each corner deleted. At last the Flatnose radiator arrived for 1931, bringing with it more contemporary lines with a rounded front part of the roof. Revised front wings also featured, except on very early examples, and the 13.9hp type CG engine with its Ricardo cylinder head was standardised. Cam steering was also fitted, but only from October 1930. Now classed as having an 8cwt payload, the van was lightly facelifted for 1932, with wider side doors, the deletion of the behind-cab windows, and oval rather than round windows in the rear doors – which now lost their louvres.

For its final year the van was given a completely new body, although it still sat on a 1929–30 Flatnose Cowley chassis, complete with artillery wheels, and retained the Flatnose radiator. An improved gearbox also featured, with needle-roller bearings for the layshaft. The arrival of the new-generation van for 1934 didn't quite spell the end of the old Flatnose-derived model: a further 164 were built for the Post Office during the 1934 season, the last one being despatched in June 1934.

Chassis were bodied by outside coachbuilders. This elegant 'Esanday' van is by Stewart and Ardern subsidiary Cunard. (John Seddon)

From 1929, the rear wings were unique to the vans; this 1931 example has the domed rather than wedge-shaped front roof introduced that year. (Author's collection)

The 1933 van retained the artillery wheels that had been finally abandoned for 1932 on regular Cowleys. (Author's collection)

were standardized on the folding-head saloon during early summer 1931. Mechanically the recipe was as before, although the engine was given smaller valves and a so-called 'turbulent' head – designed by Ricardo and identifiable by its equally-spaced plugs.

For 1932 there was to be an almost all-new Cowley, so the '31 season's cars marked the end of an era – or almost so, as the 8cwt Light Van continued to be Flatnose-based until the end of the 1933 model year. In all, something over 200,000 Flatnose Cowleys, related vans and four-cylinder Oxfords had been produced, over five years – impressive innings, to be sure.

However, another more telling set of statistics makes it clear that the Cowley's time in the sun was definitely over. In 1927 a total of 86,811 cars had been registered in the Cowley's 11hp–14hp class. By 1929 this figure had fallen to 55,005, in a British market that had risen by 5.2 per cent. In the depressed year of 1931, cars of 11hp–14hp would account for only 31,140

Billed as suitable for business and pleasure, this tall-bodied fabric Cowley saloon offered in 1929 by Stewart and Ardern had a rear door and a removable rear seat. (LAT)

The folding-head Cowley saloon was a newcomer for 1930. It was only available in maroon; the fixed-head saloon, in contrast, was offered in blue or brown. (Author's collection)

Individual front seats were a feature of both Cowley and Oxford saloons from the 1929 season onwards; this is a 1930 Cowley. (Author's collection)

registrations, a drop of 64.1 per cent since 1927, in a market that had shrunk by 11.2 per cent.

Against a background of falling car prices and a wider choice of competent 7hp–10hp models, smaller-horsepower cars were coming to dominate the sales charts. The future of Morris would depend on the company's ability to respond to the market rather than on its previous tactic of seeking to mould it to its own convenience. It needed to return fire against rivals who had created new market sectors while Sir William and his men had allowed themselves to become arguably over-reliant on the emblematic Cowley.

Meanwhile, market share had fallen to a disappointing 27.4 per cent in 1931, and trading profit had nearly halved. The company was still capital-rich and had strong fixed assets. But it was now employing 10,000 people, across ten separate businesses and two subsidiaries, and was a much more unwieldy enterprise to pilot through the troubled waters of an economy knocked for six by the Great Depression.

Politics and personalities: turbulent times at Cowley

If this was the commercial foreground for the battles of the 1930s, the managerial backcloth was equally challenging: as the Morris business entered the new decade, it was with an increasingly absent and remote William Morris, and with a group of bickering, intriguing

Cowley tourers for 1929 and 1930 had a sharp angle to the rear shut of the front doors. Duotone colours were used for 1929 Cowleys: stone-and-brown, blue-and-black, and stone-and-maroon. (Author's collection)

The 1930 Cowley coupé was only available with a folding head; Niagara Blue or Morris Brown were the only colours, in common with all other Cowleys but the folding-head saloon. (Author's collection)

Duple offered multi-purpose bodies for the Cowley. The lift-off top could be to van or shooting-brake format, and the tourer rear could be removed and either a roadster rear or a drop-down tailgate added. (LAT)

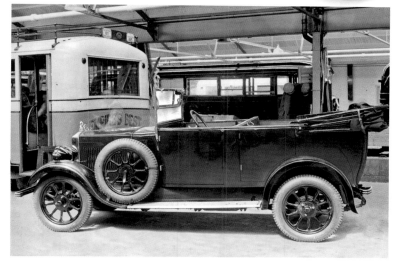

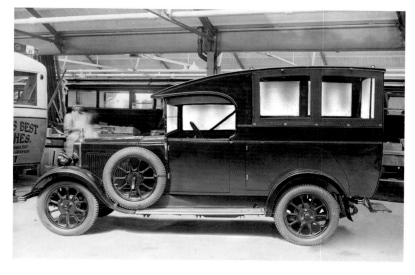

An M.G. Super Sports two-seater from the 1927 season – recognisable as such by the lack of a front apron. (Author's collection)

With the arrival of the Flatnose, Morris Garages had to re-think its M.G. Super Sports, which would perforce now have to be based on the new model. Using the more rigid and better-suspended chassis would be no hardship, even if it added to the car's weight; less welcome was the move to the inelegant tombstone radiator.

The cars that emerged in late 1926 as the flat-rad 14/28 Super Sports and Sporting Salonette looked superficially similar to the Bullnose cars, and were still built by Carbodies, with the exception of a few examples with coachwork by Raworth. But the body, which in open form now had an engine-turned finish to the aluminium panelling, was in fact of revised and lighter construction; to hide the height of the radiator, meanwhile, a blanking plate was soldered to the bottom of the shell.

In 1927 the four-seater Super Sports retailed at £350 – or £110 more than an Oxford tourer. (LAT)

As a further aid to performance, the engines were henceforth dismantled, balanced, and their ports ground and polished, before being reassembled with stronger valve springs. Turning to the chassis, flattened springs aided handling, and the Morris worm-and-wheel steering was replaced by a more precise Marles box, bolted rigidly to the chassis rather than attached to the engine as on the Morris. Brakes were initially the standard Oxford set-up, only boosted by a servo, but the last 50 cars of the 1927 season had a simplified arrangement, described as 'M.G. high-efficiency brake gear'.

The models offered were initially as before, with two-seater and four-seater open cars and a Salonette with or without bustle tail. For 1928, however, a Featherweight Fabric Saloon joined the range and a drophead coupé became available – although very few of the latter would be made.

This 1928 four-seater Sporting Salonette wears the pressed-steel apron introduced for the car's second season, when it was re-named the 14/40 MkIV. (Phil Jennings)

The 1928 season in fact marked the decisive stage in the creation of MG as a separate marque. In September 1927 the car-building operation moved to a new factory in Edmund Road, Cowley. The cars were lightly revised. A pressed-steel apron replaced the previous year's modified radiator shell, a cast-alloy bulkhead was fitted, and the brakes lost their servo and gained shrunk-on bands on the drums to rigidify them. The interior was also re-thought, with octagonal dials, part of a policy of scattering MG octagons all over the cars.

Despite these relatively trifling modifications, the cars were renamed the 14/40 MkIV and were henceforth referred to as an 'M.G.' rather than as a Morris, and were registered thus with the licencing authorities. For the first time, too, Morris Garages had their own stand at the Motor Show in 1927.

The Sporting Salonette with duck-tail rear was billed as a two-seater but had small rear seats. (Phil Jennings)

Manufacture continued for one more season, but sales slowed right off with the arrival of the M-type and 18/80. The last ten chassis were collected from Morris Motors in April 1929, and cars were still available in October that year, at which juncture prices were cut and the stock sold as 'shop-soiled'.

In all, 776 Flatnose MGs had been made, 290 in the first season, 328 in the second, and 158 in the final short 1929 model year. Production amounted to 295 two-seaters, 374 four-seaters, 71 salonettes, 32 Featherweight Fabric Saloons, and just four dropheads.

Gordon England bodied the Featherweight Fabric Saloon. The rag-finish led to one works car being called 'The Old Speckled 'Un' – perverted to 'Old Speckled Hen' and eventually immortalised by the Morland's beer of the same name. (LAT)

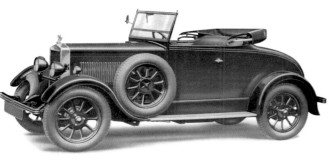

The '31 two-seater was priced at £160, and offered in blue or maroon – as all other Cowleys but the maroon-only folding-head saloon. (Author's collection)

Blink and you'd miss the differences, but the '31 Cowley has a taller radiator, a deeper bonnet, and a shallower glasshouse. (Author's collection)

Deeper sides and a a straight edge to the front doors give the '31 Cowley tourer a different look. Solenoid dipping for the headlamps was a new feature for the season. (Author's collection)

The domed rear of '29-on Cowley saloons is readily apparent in this view. Unlike on the Major saloon, a luggage grid was not standard. (Author's collection)

senior executives who sometimes seemed more interested in internal politics than the well-being of the company. This was the hidden face of an outwardly dynamic concern.

It was generally agreed – in their testimony to Andrews and Brunner, senior figures Seaward, Woollard and Lord all concur – that Morris had ceased to do factory 'walkabouts' by the beginning of the 1930s and had stepped back from daily management. 'After the early nineteen thirties it is fair to say that insofar as the actual business of designing and making motor cars and trucks was concerned Sir William Morris, as he was then, played little or no creative part.

He could give vent to a considerable amount of negative criticism. But that was all,' observes Miles Thomas in *Out on a Wing*.

In the opinion of Leonard Lord, he simply no longer really knew what was going on in his empire. "Nuffield was insular and insulated... his vast manufacturing business was up in the Midlands, and he knew nothing about it," he commented. Yet there was not a coherent decision-making apparatus in place to counterbalance this, thanks to Morris's lackadaisical approach to board meetings – something he himself admitted. 'When Morris Motors was formed into a company, and they

Although dated 1930, the Cowley in this factory shot has all the makings of a prototype of the restyled 1932 car. The black radiator slats did not make it to production. (BMIHT)

The Cowley Traveller's Saloon had a quick-release removable rear seat. In 1931 it retailed at £199, against £185 for a regular saloon, and was only available in blue. (BMIHT)

Many strange fates befell Bullnoses and Flatnoses in their old age. This bizarre rebodying was spotted in 1951 doing sterling service in Vienna. (Author's collection)

had to have a board, in fact they never met at board meetings,' notes the transcript of a 1954 interview for his biography. 'He would just send for the one man he wanted; then they would write the minutes and so on, but it was always a succession of meetings between himself and individuals, never a board meeting. We could not, of course, say this.' Worse, if without his participation there were a meeting of the board, Morris would take a childish delight in calling people out from it, for some specious reason.

The result of all this was an atmosphere in which the Borgias would have felt at home. "It was very difficult to sort out those people who were using you and those who were not," said Frank Woollard. "[Morris] was a strong man, but he was the centre of warring factions." Everyone fought their own corner, jockeyed for position and spread stories about his rivals. Lillian Morris and her brother, Bill Anstey, who ran the transport department, were a conduit for gossip to reach Morris. "She had her spies all over the place," said SGK Smallbone. "The atmosphere at Cowley was lousy. Everybody was cutting each other's throats."

"Tale-bearing and tittle-tattle in this company [were] dreadful and [did] irreperable harm," concurred George Dono, blaming Kimpton Smallbone himself for much of the ill-feeling that prevailed. He was, said Dono, "a snake in the grass" and "fair game for any trouble". Meanwhile, Harry Seaward, MD of Morris Bodies, was in his opinion "a somewhat embittered man and violently antagonistic to Hanks". Carl Kingerlee had no time for either man. As far as he was concerned, Seaward and Smallbone were "pink-eyed rats". After the purchase of Wolseley (see Chapter 10), there was a further source of internal animosities, this time between Leonard Lord, who moved from Morris Engines to Wolseley, Oliver Boden, inherited with Wolseley, and William Cannell, in charge at Morris Commercial. "Each of them hated the other and the games that went on between Lord and Boden in the early days were nobody's business," recounted Dono.

That William Morris latterly developed dictatorial tendencies and ended up preferring yes-men around him seems to have been acknowledged as part of the problem. 'Some

of those to whom he delegated authority may not have been brilliant or even conscientious: but then, it is not every first-rate businessman who would choose to work for a querulous and unpredictable despot,' comments Graham Turner in *The Leyland Papers*. Morris had strong independent financial and legal advice from, respectively, Reginald Thornton and Andrew Walsh, and in his earlier days he had picked his lieutenants well. Landstad, Rowse and Woollard were all outstanding men in their field. So too was Miles Thomas – and of course Leonard Lord, whom he had acquired with the Hotchkiss engines plant. But in the decade to come he would end up shedding most of these talented individuals.

The Barton Motor Company in Devon always created effective showroom displays. Here a Flatnose saloon features in a Christmas scene. (Richard Barton)

The Empire Oxford

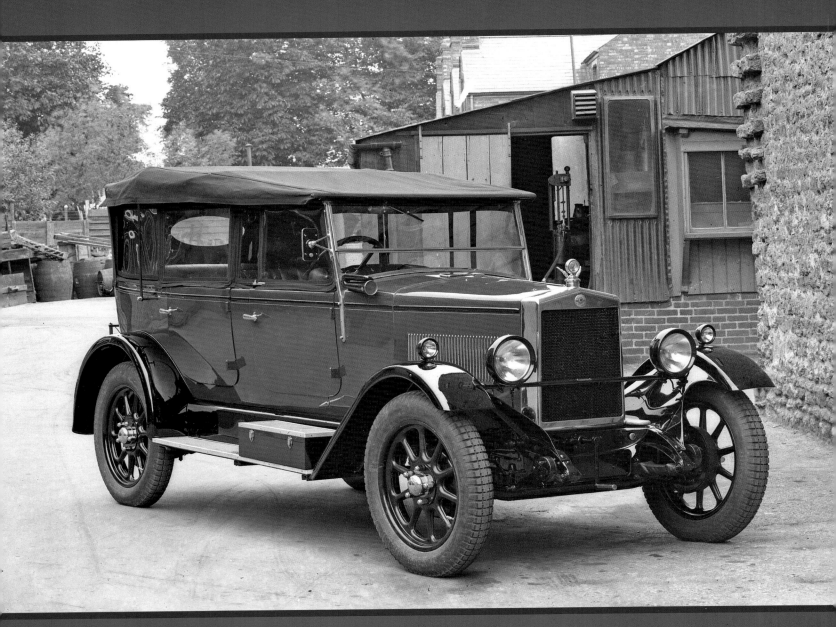

The Empire Oxford tourer looked just like a taller and wider Flatnose; Barker dipping headlamps were standard. At £315 in 1928, it cost appreciably more than the £225 Oxford 14/28 tourer. (BMIHT)

Morris was determined to break into the export markets dominated by the American manufacturers. Alas, the Empire Oxford was not a success, even if something was salvaged from the project.

As well as being the home of Morris Commercial Cars, the former Wrigley's works in Soho, Birmingham, was also to be the birthplace of one of Morris's biggest disasters, the ill-fated EO-series 15.9hp Empire Oxford.

It was said during the first Supertax case that Wrigley's had been bought because of the need for a ready-to-go development department to create a car for export markets: laying down a new factory at Cowley or to have added to the small existing experimental department would have used up too much valuable time. As the Empire Oxford would only emerge in late 1926, nearly three years after the Wrigley purchase, this argument, advanced by MCC Managing Director William Cannell, hardly stands up and is more likely to have been a further example of special pleading. What is true, however, is that Morris Commercial Cars did conceive the new 15.9hp Oxford, under the direction of Cannell, who had joined Morris earlier in the decade, and who as his personal assistant had been functioning as de facto Managing Director at Cowley.

Having reconstituted EG Wrigley as Morris Commercial Cars Ltd in February 1924, Morris rapidly transferred Cannell to Birmingham as General Manager. Personal animosities and internal politics were behind the appointment. Morris had first come across Cannell on a steel committee during the First World War. After the armistice he went to work for Gwynne, who for a brief period in the 1920s made cars under the Gwynne, Albert and Gwynne-Albert names. Cannell had spent time in the United States, working in the machine-tool business, and had the habit of talking in American slang. Morris, with his respect for American industrial success, seems to have warmed to this evidently colourful character – "Nuffield always had that failing of being attracted by a bright lad," commented Carl Kingerlee – and in the 1922–23 period recruited him to the company, slotting him into Cowley's informal hierarchy in such a way that both Landstad and Pratt felt undermined.

A showdown was therefore engineered by Landstad, who had apparently received a job offer from America, and who felt sure that there were also other firms who would be happy to take him. The story as told by Landstad – who clearly despised Cannell and regarded him as useless – is that he said to him that he was going to resign. This got back to William Morris, who snapped to Pratt that if Landstad left he would refuse to write him a testimonial. According to Landstad, Pratt then rejoined, "If you don't, I will – and what's more, I'll go with him and build the bodies." At the thought of losing not just Landstad but the much-respected Pratt, Morris felt a pistol had been put to his head, and moved Cannell to MCC. A more terse account is provided by Reggie Hanks, who told Andrews and Brunner that Cannell had been brought in as General Manager at Cowley "without reference to anyone, and it did not work".

The chassis had a wheelbase 7½in longer than that of a regular Oxford. There was a rear tank, a pressed-steel dash, an adjustable steering column and adjustable brake and clutch pedals. (Author's collection)

The saloon was announced in December 1926, and retailed at £375, or £110 more than a 13.9hp Oxford saloon. The gap narrowed slightly in 1928. (Author's collection)

A Morris for the Empire

At Morris Commercial Cars, Cannell oversaw the design of a bigger 15.9hp engine. This found its first home in 1926's Z-type 24cwt and 30cwt trucks, mated to an MCC-designed – and MCC-built – four-speed gearbox, via a dry clutch; transmission to the rear wheels was by a torque-tube axle with overhead worm drive. When it came to creating a bigger Morris car for export markets, it seemed a natural choice to use this engine, given that it was already in production at Morris Commercial and that using it in a car would increase economies of scale. It also made sense to use the same basic Z-type running gear for the new model.

Given that Cowley in 1926 already had the new 11.9hp and 13.9hp Flatnoses to see through to production – pressed-steel bodies included – it is quite likely that management felt that it had quite enough on its plate, and could see the wisdom of buying in a ready-to-go set of components from

The saloon was lavishly equipped, with furniture-hide seating and blinds to all windows. Colours were blue, grey, maroon or brown. (Author's collection)

The oval instrument panel was identikit Morris. Other cockpit details included a right-hand throttle pedal. (Author's collection)

A two-seater was not a catalogued model; this is one built for the Anglo-Persian Oil Co, who specified an uprated cooling system. Other fleet buyers of the Empire Oxford included the Royal Air Force. (BMIHT)

its commercial-vehicle sister company. Equally, Andrews and Brunner suggest that Cannell held his hand up for the Empire Oxford project, writing in their biography that 'the new company had some elbow room for machining and development and its manager was keen to try his hand at a heavier type of car'.

The need for a model for Empire markets was a real one, if Morris wished to build a presence in these territories, in particular in Australia. Something bigger and more robust than the existing Cowley and Oxford was required, to compete with the dominant products of Ford, Chevrolet, Dodge and the like; US manufacturers would take 81.4 per cent of new registrations in Australia (excluding Western Australia) for the first six months of 1927, against the 14.1 per cent accounted for by UK manufacturers. Morris, however, was almost exclusively selling in the home market: in 1925, for example, out of the 55,000 cars Cowley made a mere 3800 went for export. Whilst building up potentially lucrative 'colonial' trade, it therefore had to ensure that any new car would remain attractive to the tax-by-horsepower British. Consequently it couldn't have too big a power unit. The 2513cc Z-type engine thus seemed an ideal starting-point.

A side-valve unit of 80mm bore and a hefty 125mm stroke, the three-main-bearing engine had pump-assisted cooling and a four-bladed fan; the 12-volt electrics, meanwhile, were looked after by a combined magneto and dynamo on the nearside of the engine and a separate Bendix-drive starter, as opposed to the chain-driven dynamotor of regular Flatnoses. An unusual feature was an engine-driven Smith's Maxfield tyre pump, mounted in front of the timing-gear case.

For the Empire Oxford – an identification it initially carried on its hubcaps – the engine was mated to the Z-type gate-change four-speed gearbox, a first for Morris, via its single-plate dry clutch. The torque tube remained, giving a totally enclosed transmission, and the Z-type overhead worm-drive axle was also retained, allowing greater ground clearance. For the same reason the rods for the four-wheel brakes were mounted above the axles instead of being level with them or hanging below. To make the point that this gave a minimum ten inches of clearance under full passenger load, Morris photographed the car driving over a brick standing on its end.

As for the chassis, this was built on a 9ft 6in wheelbase; the track of 4ft 8in meant it could be fitted with flanged wheels if necessary, for use on railway tracks. The frame was of a straightforward ladder design, with minimal kick-up over the back axle; suspension was by semi-elliptics, claimed to give generous deflection and controlled by friction dampers front and rear. With its generous ground clearance, enclosed transmission and high-mounted carburettor, it was claimed that the car could be driven 'with complete impunity' through 20in of water.

Honest virtues – and hidden vices

Announced at the October 1926 Motor Show in £325 open tourer and £245 chassis forms, the 15.9hp Oxford range was completed with the arrival of a £375 four-door saloon in December. Morris publicity was not reticent about the newcomer. According to the sales catalogue it was 'a highly developed and straightforward car – totally devoid of freakishness – honestly and soundly fashioned in every part'. It would command 'the attention and respect of those who desire a car that will definitely and unhesitatingly cope with any conditions likely to be encountered anywhere the World over'. With an engine able to stand up for hours to 'sheer, slogging pulling', it would successfully negotiate 'backwood tracks, Alpine hill roads, long days of hard work under burning tropical sun, and any other conditions of extreme severity'. This paragon of automotive virtue was made to the very highest standards. 'Only the finest British metals are used in its construction, fashioned by highly skilled operatives, on the finest machine tools in Europe.'

The notion that such hyperbole might possibly have been misplaced is suggested by the fact that both the engine and the transmission were rapidly redesigned: the former to substitute pressure-fed lubrication of the big ends for the original splash-fed arrangement and the latter to enable a switch from the dry-plate clutch to Morris's regular cork-in-oil unit. It was indeed the case that if the specification of the Empire Oxford seemed to auger well for commercial success in export markets, the reality was rather different.

Nobody much wanted the car – and its chances were hardly improved when Ford brought out its thoroughly serviceable Model A in late 1927 and both Dodge and Chevrolet introduced cheap six-cylinder models, for the 1928 and 1929 seasons respectively. With far higher rates of production, and significantly cheaper costs for raw materials – everything from sheet steel to glass and

Morris demonstrated the car's ground clearance by photographing it driving over a brick standing on end. (Author's collection)

This rakish two-seater was bodied in Australia by Brisbane coachbuilder Whatmore and Mackintosh, for local distributor Howard Motors Ltd. (Nick Smith/Morris Register)

Another Australian body, this time by Holden, and to their standard style. (Mark Rendell/Morris Register)

leathercloth – the US manufacturers could sell such cars at a price with which Morris could not compete.

It was a battle lost in advance. Production of what was latterly called the 16/40 Oxford limped on to July 1929, by which time a mere 1742 had been made. Most – 1168 in all – were made during 1927, with 431 being built in 1928 and a final 142 in the first seven months of 1929.

This magnificent saloon with its exposed wood pillars is a further survivor in Australia, with locally-made coachwork. (Eric Cooling/Morris Register)

A fabric-bodied saloon was offered by Hoyal. Other coachbuilders to body the Empire Oxford included Jarvis, who made a four-door all-weather saloon. (Morris Register)

That the Empire Oxford was a turkey became apparent even before production had begun, when in December 1926 Hans Landstad, Miles Thomas and the Cowley head tester took a prototype up to Scotland and put it through its paces in snowy winter conditions, ahead of Morris presenting the car to his antipodean dealers on his visit to Australia in early 1927. According to *The Autocar*, who clearly swallowed the PR line spun by the company, the car emerged from this 1224-mile trial 'with flying colours'. For Hans Landstad, however, the verdict was less flattering, although he was at least impressed that the return journey from Glasgow to Cowley took only eleven hours. "But the engine was very rough," he told Andrews and Brunner. "Thomas said to Morris that it would never do. There were the makings of a good car, but it had got to be differently made. Morris knew [I] had been on the trip and he reckoned they were biased, and would not have it. Eventually they got him to try it himself. Then he said 'Take the engine out and see what's the matter.' It was bad machining.

They told Cannell, and he sent a man down. When he saw its condition he said he was not surprised they turned it down. The crankshaft was not ground properly... Meanwhile the car was being turned out, and they sent out 248, but only the chassis. By the time Morris came to Australia there were 248 chassis on the quayside, waiting. But nobody would take them. They had to come back, and by the time they came back, they were full of wheat and rats. That was the end of that."

Inadequate design – and tough competition

Arthur Rowse was no less scathing of the project when he talked to Andrews and Brunner, and said that the car's problems were more fundamental – and not just related to the engine. "[It] was never properly designed – bits of it were thrown together. It was the responsibility of Morris Commercial Cars, and a certain individual there produced these bits. This was a car to go into the wide open spaces on very rough roads, so it needed a very strong chassis, which it did not have. It was a dreadful bit of stuff."

Rowse realised the chassis design was flawed and that it would be fatal to send the car out to Australia. To make his point, he had it driven over a high kerb, and the chassis so distorted that an electrical connection broke. "Morris saw this and was livid... It was completely designed by Commercial Cars, so Cowley had been snubbed, and any tests which [he] and Landstad did on it were interpreted as jealousy. But it was a dreadful car – very rough, and weak in the chassis."

Part of this disaster Rowse attributed to Morris's mind-set. "He started by buying components and putting them together, and never got beyond that stage. He never realised that the way to get a car was to sit down and design a vehicle to fulfill a particular need, and the way to do that was not to snatch the engine from one place and the axle from another, knock them together and shove the combined effort across to the bodyshop... The original car was built that way, but one could not go on doing that. Harold Taylor had a little workshop beyond the tin shed where Morris's own private cars used to be and Taylor, who was a good mechanic, was always butting into the picture as a car designer. You never knew when he would bob up saying that Morris had told him to put a certain engine in a certain chassis... That sort of thing led to the failure of the Empire car."

Both Landstad and Rowse might be accused of sour grapes, but even mild-mannered Reggie

Hanks described the 15.9hp Oxford as 'shocking' whilst Carl Kingerlee characterised it as 'a rushed job'. Reading the road test in the normally deferential *The Autocar* gives a clear picture of disappointment, one that supports these judgements: the magazine found the gearchange difficult, the steering stiff, the ride choppy, the engine uncouth and the transmission noisy.

In *Out on a Wing* Miles Thomas sums up the car pithily. 'The engine was rough, the body had square-cut box-like lines, and in competition with the then freely exported American cars it was a dismal failure on the Australian and other markets.' Morris, he said, was 'chagrined about the failure... especially as several of his old Morris men at Cowley murmured "We told you so." Attempts to foster a market in Australia... had proved a failure to the tune of £100,000.'

LIFE AFTER DEATH: THE MORRIS-COMMERCIAL TAXI

If the Empire Oxford was dead by 1929, it was, however, not buried. As mentioned by Hans Landstad, the chassis exported to Australia were shipped back to England – not all of them, but 205 of the 250 or so initially sent out. Here Morris distributor George Kenning enters the picture. He apparently went to William Morris and proposed that the Empire Oxford be used as the basis for a Morris taxi-cab. This was prompted by a modest loosening of London taxi regulations, which looked as if it might make the cab market worthwhile to enter – a conclusion also reached by Citroën and Austin at about the same time.

So it was that in January 1929 – a few months ahead of the deletion of the passenger car – Morris announced the Type G International Taxi, with its sales to be handled by Kenning's Sheffield-based International Taxicab Company. The frame and mechanicals were basically identical to those of the Empire Oxford, but the chassis had a wheelbase shorter by 6in and there were at first no front brakes. There are suggestions that the first batch of 840 included mechanical components recycled from the chassis brought back from Australia.

The new taxi was built by Morris Commercial Cars, with a timber-framed steel body from Morris Bodies in Coventry. In all 1700 were made, up until 1932 – some way short of the 50-per-month production for which Morris had been hoping. But the company was not deterred, and introduced a revised International, the G2, with the 13.9hp 'Hotchkiss' engine. This was a response to MCC uprating the Z-type engine to 3041cc, which was rather too large and thirsty for a taxi-cab.

But the G2 proved underpowered, and in 1934 gave way to the G2S, the first six-cylinder London cab. Called the Morris-Commercial Junior Six, this was equipped with the 1938cc LA Oxford Six engine. Whilst the idea of a six-cylinder taxi might seem absurd, the rationale was straightforward: there was no suitable mid-size 'four' in either the Morris car range or the Morris-Commercial range. The Morris taxi continued until 1939, becoming the Super Six – or G2SW – in late 1937, when it was fitted with a 44bhp overhead-valve 1818cc Morris Fourteen-Six

engine for the 1938 model season. Until the end, the chassis used was derived from that of the Empire Oxford, complete with worm-drive rear axle.

The sole Type G taxi known to survive. The owner praises the torque and smoothness of the 15.9hp engine, suggesting that it was much-improved in production form. (Bill Munro)

The G2S taxi had a six-cylinder engine. This example was photographed in London in 1960; under the slightly modernised bodywork there is still an EO-derived chassis. (Nick Georgano)

The Morris Six

This cover image for The Morris Owner dates from June 1929; the car is recognisable as a Six, rather than an Oxford, by the spare wheel having a cover. Wine with maroon was one of five duotones offered for 1929: the other combinations were grey and blue, deep maroon and bronze, blue and black, and beige and brown. (Ken Martin collection)

The six-cylinder version of the Flatnose arrived when Morris was continuing to build up his commercial empire, notably by buying Wolseley. To hold all this together his finances were becoming increasingly complex.

The period immediately after the launch of the Flatnose was one of continued energetic activity for the company. On the product front, Cowley made a second attempt to broaden its range with a six-cylinder model, while Morris himself carried on making business acquisitions. In December 1926 he bought carburettor manufacturer the SU Company Ltd and in February 1927 he took over the once-dominant Wolseley concern. Additionally there was a failed attempt at what would today be called vertical integration, with the purchase of a colliery.

The empire grows: SU joins the fold...
The acquisition of SU, in December 1926, was not just a shrewd move that bought Morris one of the landmark fuelling devices in the history of the motor car. It was also one that played to one of his greatest enthusiasms: all his life he loved tinkering with carburettors, and fancied himself an expert on the subject, to the point that old Morris Garages hands recalled him being nicknamed 'the Carburettor King'.

It was Carl Skinner, co-founder of the SU ('Skinners Union') company with his brother George, who approached Morris with a view to his purchasing the business, then based in London. George Skinner had decided to withdraw from the partnership, and the company was losing money. The carburettor was a good product but was made in too small quantities to be commercially viable; Carl Skinner knew that one sure way to make the economics add up was to have Morris inject capital to raise output, on the basis that he would then fit the SU carburettor to all his cars. The business logic was impeccable, and Morris duly dipped in his pocket to the tune of £100,000. Of this, £14,536 went to paying off directors' loans and £21,662 to settling outstanding debts.

The concern remained Morris's personal property for some years, being folded into a new holding company, Morris Industries Ltd, in June 1927. Carl Skinner was left to run the business, ultimately with a place on the Morris board. Possibly anticipating the problems he would have with Pressed Steel, Morris did not trumpet his ownership of SU, in case this frightened

A head-on view of the original Light Six emphasises its narrow track; it was widened by a full 8in before production began. (LAT)

In its revised form the Six saloon sold at £395 in 1928, against £250 for an Oxford saloon or £275 for an Oxford De Luxe saloon. Duotone colours were standard. Judging by this photo, early – pre-production? – cars had the spare wheel on the driver's side. (Ken Martin collection)

off custom from other motor manufacturers. Instead, he appointed his former distributor WHM Burgess as 'Wholesale Agent' and used the Burgess name in advertising. The carburettor, meanwhile, was fitted to Flatnoses from the 1929 season, and to the Morris Six and the Minor from their inception; additionally SU Autovac and Type L electric pumps would become a characteristic feature of Morris cars. By 1939 over 4000 carburettors were being manufactured each week.

... followed by Wolseley (and a coal mine)

The purchase of Wolseley was a somewhat bizarre exercise, but one which illustrates Morris's determination in business affairs. Once the leading British motor manufacturer, Wolseley was not only suffering from over-capacity but had also invested heavily in re-equipment and extra facilities. In addition it had spent a reputed £¼m on a flash new showroom in Piccadilly. An unwise financial restructuring, finally, exposed it to substantial charges to service the debt it had run up. With a lacklustre product range, disaster was inevitable. In late 1926 one of the company's creditors began proceedings and in November that year Wolseley was declared bankrupt, with liabilities of over £2m. It was, in the words of writer Nick Baldwin, 'one of the most spectacular failures in the early history of the motor industry'.

Morris, who Miles Thomas said had been keeping an eye on Wolseley before it crashed, put in a sealed bid for £600,000. He was bidding against Austin and a third person whose intentions were never clear, according to Thomas. 'There was a third contestant in the field. Try as I would, I

The interior of a Six saloon. The dashboard featured concealed illumination and a full set of gauges. (BMIHT)

A tinted-glass vizor was standard on the 1929 Six, as it was on the Oxford De Luxe saloon with which it now shared body pressings. (Author's collection)

could never find out who he actually represented. Some said General Motors of America, but my hunch was that it was a speculator who, if he had obtained control, could have resold at an inflated price to Morris, to Austin, or to some American company,' he writes in *Out on A Wing*. Carl Kingerlee feels the gentleman in question could have indeed been acting for GM, but it is perhaps revealing that in his memoirs, referred to earlier, Alfred Sloan makes no mention of having any interest in buying Wolseley.

Morris's offer was topped by the mystery bidder, but although the time limit for a fresh bid had passed, he was allowed to submit a higher one. Austin was still in the game, and the two traded bids in the bankruptcy court. Morris said that whatever Austin was prepared to offer, he was prepared to go a bit further. In the end the once-proud company was knocked down to him for £730,000, a sum that represented a large slice of the money he had garnered from the 1926 flotation. "Nuffield brought that court down to the level of a Dutch auction," Thomas sniffily said to Andrews and Brunner.

Why did he buy the Wolseley company? One theory, advanced by Leonard Lord, is that Morris wanted to get his hands on Wolseley's 16/45 'Silent Six' model, which he had apparently studied with interest at the 1926 Motor Show, and for which he felt there was a a strong market. Lord felt the notion to be ridiculous, as to make the car in the numbers Morris talked of would have demanded substantial fresh investment[1]. Miles Thomas, who also subscribed to the 'Silent Six' story, pointed out that the car was an own-goal by Wolseley, thanks to the name. 'The result was that every purchaser who on lifting the bonnet heard the slightest mechanical sound assumed that something was amiss and sent the car back to the garage or the works. This resulted in enormous servicing costs, soaking up what little profit was made on the car,' he writes in *Out on a Wing*.

Another motive quoted is that Morris acted out of patriotism – because he did not want a firm of Wolseley's size and repute being bought up by foreign interests; nor, of course, did he want it to go to his main rival, Austin. Whilst it is surely the case that Morris wanted to fight off Austin

[1] If the transcript of his interview can be believed, Lord told Andrews and Brunner that Morris thought he could sell 1000 of the 'Silent Six' a week – a figure Lord naturally enough regarded as nonsensical, and which in his estimation would have demanded a £1.5m investment in machinery. Possibly the 1000 per week figure is a mistranscription of 1000 per month, which would amount to a high but more realistic aspiration of say 10,000 cars a year. In all, 9958 of the 16/45 and its successor the Viper were made, in the 1926–32 period.

'Built like a big car': Morris's grown-up baby

Morris's Seven rival was announced in June 1928, ahead of its introduction for the 1929 model year. Built around a straightforward channel-section ladder frame, the Minor was a large car in miniature to an even greater degree than the Seven, in that it featured longitudinal leaf springs front and rear, a damper at each wheel, and fully coupled four-wheel braking, cable-actuated and used in combination with a handbrake operating on the transmission. In contrast the Austin had transverse-leaf front suspension incorporating a single damper, and a rear axle hung on two quarter-elliptics – a combination that could give rise to somewhat eccentric cornering behaviour – whilst it was only for 1931 that it forsook separate front and rear braking. Unlike the Austin – and indeed unlike Morris's own Cowley and Oxford – the Minor in addition had a simple open propshaft to take drive to the back axle, rather than a torque tube; the universals were of the fabric rather than metal type.

If the Morris's chassis specification was well considered, the engine, mated to a single-plate dry clutch and a three-speed 'crash' gearbox, was too ambitious for its own good. Possibly out of a wish to impress those at Cowley with its superior engineering skills, Wolseley followed the practice of its larger cars, and drawing on its World War One experience building Hispano-Suiza aero-engines it came up with a dainty overhead-cam power unit of 847cc capacity. Looked at in general terms, this was hardly a sensible choice for a low-cost car, such an engine inevitably costing more to produce than a simple side-valve design[3]. But there was a more specific failing: the overhead camshaft was driven by shaft and bevel with a shaft that went through the centre of a vertically-mounted dynamo, serving at the same time as the armature of the generator. This was conceptually neat, but left the dynamo prey to being drowned in oil, whilst also – initially at least – restricting its size and thus output. Quite why William Morris, a man of conservative mechanical tastes, allowed himself to be talked into such misguided sophistication is something of an imponderable. Was he sufficiently happy

spite of the fact that they designed themselves into bankruptcy. One day we were faced with the Morris Minor...'

For 1931 only, Morris offered a charming miniature fire tender, equipped with a four-section 23ft ladder and with space for twelve large fire-extinguishers. Included was a warning bell, a large first-aid box, and an axe, and the vehicle was promoted as being ideal for villages, factories, schools and the like. One was on the strength at Cowley, and Oxford and Worthing fire-stations also used examples. At least one was exported to India, to be used by the Maharajah Rana Bahadure of Jhalawar. (Morris Register/author's collection)

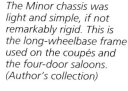

Minors with special bodies were supplied to the War Office as scout cars and latterly as wireless cars. Amongst those using the vehicles was the Royal Corps of Signals; they were also operated by the Indian Army. This scout car dates from c.1929. (Ken Martin collection)

The Minor chassis was light and simple, if not remarkably rigid. This is the long-wheelbase frame used on the coupés and the four-door saloons. (Author's collection)

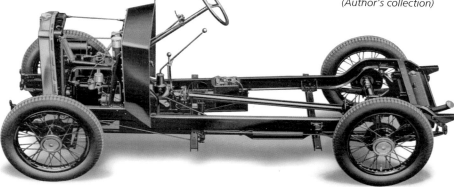

[3] According to Morris's auditor, Reginald Thornton, the company was only making £5 profit on the overhead-cam Minor. This figure might be open to question, as it was used in the pleading on Morris's part in one of the Super-tax appeals, but the point about the car being a low-profit product is surely correct.

❶ A 1934 Minor van in later life. The more curved roof is clearly visible. Note how the original style of radiator is retained. (Morris Register)

❷ As well as the standard GPO type for the postal services and the telephone engineers, there was a high-roof type for engineers, with an additional window at the front of the roof, so the driver could view overhead telephone lines. (Ken Martin)

❸ The van was also offered in chassis form, and coachbuilders such as Bonallack and Cunard offered specialist bodies of various types. This rather top-heavy example is by Cunard, who sold their commercial bodies under the Esanday name. (John Seddon)

❹ Also by Cunard, this butcher's van has a rather more modest raised roof. The Stewart and Ardern subsidiary also built Minor vans with more conventional bodies and had a signpainting operation called Mobility. (John Seddon)

❺ The 'post-production' GPO vans had the Eight's 918cc engine, the final more rounded and valanced Minor wings, and the 1934 model-year radiator shell. Additionally some late cars had Easiclean wheels. (Mark Dixon)

❻ Novelty commercials were popular in the 1920s and 1930s, and this Minor-based Esanday millinery box was shown at the 1931 Commercial Motor Exhibition. (John Seddon)

THE MINOR VAN

As might be expected, Morris followed Austin's example in offering a van version of its smallest model, this being introduced for the 1930 model year. Of 5cwt payload, it had a wooden body frame and as launched it retained the saloon's overhead-cam engine; this made it, said *The Morris Owner*, 'one of the fastest vans on the road' and 'the acme of high performance in the conveyance of small loads'.

The vans moved to the side-valve engine in spring 1931 but otherwise remained largely unchanged until the 1934 model-year. For 1933 they were given Magna wheels and for the 1934 season a more rounded body was introduced, and the fuel tank moved to the rear; but they kept the original 'tombstone' style of radiator to the end, along with flat-topped unvalanced mudguards, the three-speed gearbox, and cable brakes. The van was discontinued – at least for the 'civilian' market – with the arrival of the Morris Eight van.

The General Post Office was an enthusiastic user of the Minor van, the GPO taking its first batch in 1932. These had the GPO's own design of body, rated at a capacity of 30cu ft – later 35cu ft – and replaced the Post Office's motorcycles. Manufacture of chassis for the GPO continued after the arrival of the Eight, until 1939, the vans being bodied as before by outside coachbuilders. The original style of Eight van was as a result never used by the Post Office, which jumped directly from the Minor to the Eight Series Z van. In all, 3660 Minors were supplied as post vans in the 1932–40 period, plus 3710 to Post Office Telephones.

A 1933 Special Coupé, with the side-valve engine. The tall radiator with radiused corners was first seen on the '32 long-wheelbase Minors, before being standardised across the range for 1933. Similarly the domed and valanced wings were a '33 lwb feature that translated across to the whole range the following year. (LAT)

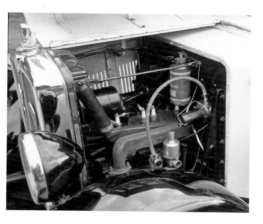

This particular colour was not a standard offering: for 1933 the Coupé was listed in green with green upholstery, red with red interior, grey with blue trim, and black with brown leather; all these were duotones, with the roof being in a darker shade of the colour concerned. Only 120 Minor Special Coupés were made in the 1933 model year, and this is one of six known survivors. (LAT)

The Minor Coupé was 'a luxury car in miniature' according to The Morris Owner. The burr-walnut dash was a unique feature, and the interior was trimmed in leather. (LAT)

wanted something that showed that they had not bought the cheapest product offered... No one wants to keep down with the Joneses!'

It seems that the £100 Minor was indeed a loss-leader for Morris Motors, serving more as bait to lure potential buyers towards a more expensive variant. "When they did the £100 car, they lost money on it," Harry Seaward confirmed to Andrews and Brunner. "There was another peculiar thing – a director had to pay more than if he bought it from an agent. This was because directors paid 5 per cent on the cost of the car, and since they were losing money on it, they could buy it cheaper from Stewart and Ardern."

More models – and a new look

The move away from the ohc engine was consolidated in 1932, when the entire Minor range was restyled, with more rounded 'Eddyfree' bodies, a new-look chrome radiator, and (£100 Minor excepted) the adoption of Magna wheels. A

At the rear of the Special Coupé you sit knees-up and upright – all very cosy. Large blind spots don't help reversing. (LAT)

further change was the replacement of the scuttle tank with a rear tank, fed by an SU Petrolift. At the same time the fabric saloon was deleted, with the coachbuilt saloon now being offered as both a fixed-head and a sliding-head with Pytchley roof. The standard power unit was now the side-valve, but the overhead-cam engine had not breathed its last, being fitted exclusively to two new models built on a 7ft 7in wheelbase, a four-door saloon called the Family Eight and a Sports Coupé in the new corporate style introduced across the Morris range for 1932. Using the Wolseley Hornet chassis, both models had a sliding head and hydraulic brakes, as well as a taller radiator with a curved lower edge to the top of the shell. This last feature, incidentally, was not present on launch-time models photographed for the press.

Falling between the two-door Minor on its 6ft 6in wheelbase and the altogether bigger Cowley, the Family Eight provided a smaller-engined alternative to the 9hp four-door saloons of Singer and Standard, and a rival to Triumph's newly-introduced pillarless four-door version of its Super Seven; Austin, meanwhile, would not offer a four-door Seven until the arrival of 1937's Big Seven. Needless to say, *The Morris Owner* was not slow in talking up the advantages of the newcomer. 'The Family Eight model, while not quite possessing the spacious body of the higher-priced cars, does afford abundant

This artwork from a 1933 range catalogue depicts the Family Saloon in somewhat exaggerated form. But although the four-door Minor was 1ft 3in shorter than a fixed-head Cowley saloon, it had only 4in less rear legroom – or 2in less than on the Morris Ten saloon. (Author's collection)

accommodation for four grown-up persons, yet has a low fuel consumption and high road performance, and withall pays the same tax as a Minor,' it proclaimed. 'This combination of speed and comfort and supreme economy represents a definite advance in motoring for those to whom running expenses are a matter for serious consideration.'

Goodbye to overhead cams

The long-wheelbase models kept the overhead-cam engine for just a year, losing it with the announcement of the 1933 season's cars. These were largely unchanged, but for the incorporation of a four-speed 'twin top' gearbox and Bishop cam-and-peg steering, and the standardisation of the longer radiator shell of the '32 Family Eight and Sports Coupé. An exception to this updating was the £100 two-seater, which kept the earlier radiator cowl, the three-speed gearbox, and worm-and-wheel steering, and had a one-piece rather than a divided screen. It was only available in blue, with brown Karhyde upholstery. For those wanting a better-equipped two-seater, an additional variant built to 'mainline' specification was now available, for an extra five pounds.

Signalling the change to side-valve power, the four-door and the coupé were renamed the Minor Family Saloon and the Minor Special Coupé. Distinguishable from their ohc predecessors by curved and valanced one-piece wings, they also slyly reverted to cable brakes. Supposedly capable of 45mpg, the Family Saloon 'must assuredly represent cost-per-head motoring at its positive minimum,' asserted *The Morris Owner*, claiming that it offered 'abundant seating space for four grown-ups without apology or any suggestion of fatigue on a long run'. As for the Special Coupé, this was 'a luxury car in miniature' and '[an] ideal car for the lady driver – using the word "lady" in its best or worst sense according to your political and social opinions – and for those who place aesthetic appearance before the utmost seating capacity for a given chassis'.

Last and best: the '34 Minors

For the Minor the 1934 season was to be its last. It was also notable for the disappearance of the £100 two-seater from the catalogue. Unsurprisingly, the styling of the Minor was basically unchanged for its run-out year, but the radiator gained a curved stoneguard, and the rounded and valanced wings of the '33 long-wheelbase Minors were standardized across the range.

Radiator shell apart, the 1933 tourer was physically identical to the preceding year's model; note how the tail tucks in at the bottom. The Minors were the only '33 Morrises not to have the ill-fated Wilcot 'traffic light' indicators; trafficators were not fitted, either. (Ken Martin collection)

Photographed at a 1967 Morris Register rally, this 1933 two-seater is typical of these cars during the '60s, being well-presented but in a non-original colour and with anachronistic details such as red brake drums and a black rather than buff hood. With the long radiator and two-part screen it is easily identifiable as a better-equipped four-speed model; these retailed at only £5 more than the bargain-basement £100 two-seaters. (Author's collection)

The body of the open Minors was slightly changed for 1934. Instead of the pert roadster-type body that had been carried forward from the original £100 Minor, the two-seater now had a heavier and more flowing rear, kicking out at the bottom. The new style brought with it a taller hood. (Bernard Chapman/Morris Register and author's collection)

A 1933 and a 1934 Minor together? Not quite. Ignore that non-standard front bumper (and the non-original sidelamps), and the right-hand car (a sliding-head model) shows how a '34 car should look, with the radiator stoneguard. The left-hand car appears at first glance a '33, but is in fact a '34 fixed-head (note lack of drainage slots in roof) with the guard removed. The giveaway is the dipped moulding that runs around the back of the car: on a '33 there is a simpler straight moulding on the side panel. (Pat Curtin/Morris Register)

Maddox of Huntingdon offered a drophead coupé on the Minor chassis, and latterly this fixed-head, which dates from 1933. (Ken Martin collection)

Similarly the tourer had a revised rear for 1934, with the base of the tail flared outwards rather than tucked in; as the open cars were wood framed, such modifications so late in the Minor's career need not have cost much, as costly body re-tooling would not have been required. (Ken Martin collection)

With its short chassis, there was no need for the Minor to adopt the cruciform frame of other '34 Morrises, but it did share with them the installation of a gearbox with synchromesh on third and top gears. Hydraulic brakes also returned, this time for all models, pear-shaped Armstrong hydraulic dampers were fitted, and smaller wheels were shod with larger-section tyres. Further improvements shared with bigger Morrises included a barrel-grip handbrake, a battery master switch, leather upholstery with Moseley 'float-on-air' cushions, and rubber gearbox and pedal-slot draught excluders. Trafficators were standard, and closed models gained interior sunvisors. The Minor was now the best it had ever been, but its perpendicular styling was looking old-hat, especially when

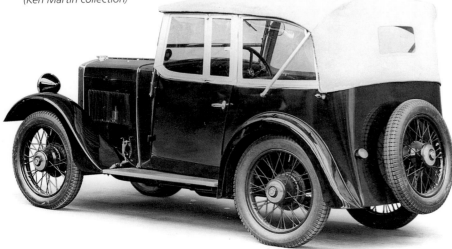

compared to the fluid lines of Ford's 8hp Model Y, a bigger and worrying new competitor. A replacement for Cowley's small car was urgently needed, and in August 1934 the last Minor left the lines, ahead of the introduction that month of the all-new Morris Eight.

In all, 86,310 Minors had been made, comprised of 39,083 overhead-cam models and 47,227 side-valve cars. Over the Minor's six-season currency that amounts to an average of just over 14,000 cars a year – an important slice of Cowley production. But was that good enough? The figures from Longbridge make sobering reading. Austin made 22,709 Sevens in the 1928 calendar year, rising to 26,447 the following year. Output fell back in 1930, but never dropped below 20,000 per annum. In the calendar years 1929 to 1934 – roughly equivalent to the currency of the Minor – Austin produced 134,693 Sevens, or 56 per cent more than Cowley's tally for the Minor. Morris's eight-horse baby might have been a more modern car than its Birmingham rival, and certainly a less quirky one to drive, but in sales terms it can only be regarded as a modest success. As will be seen, many of Cowley's bigger and potentially more profitable models of the early 1930s would fail to set the market alight, so this was a cause for concern.

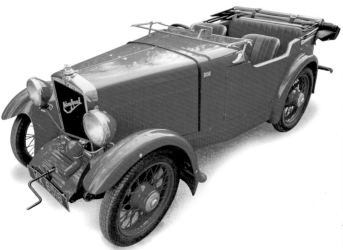

Jensen bodied a number of Minors, initially as McEvoy Specials with tuned engines – these being either a mildly-tuned Model 60 or the Model 70 with a comprehensively upgraded power unit and optional supercharger. Latterly Jensen offered the elegant tourer body under its own name, and with the lengthened bonnet and shorter scuttle of the more expensive McEvoy variants. This is a 1932-registered Model 70 McEvoy, one of approximately eight Jensen-bodied Minors to have survived. (Sarah Gibson/Morris Register)

This charming and well-crafted special was probably constructed around 1950, and is based on a 1934 Minor. Built around a steel frame, the body is mainly steel, with aluminium front wings and nose section; power comes from a Ford Eight engine and gearbox. (Author)

Unusually proportioned, this Australian-built 1933 Minor carries a coupé body by Holden. (Peter Wood)

Another Minor with an Australian body is this trim-looking roadster. (J Wien-Smith)

Properts of Sydney built this two-seater on a side-valve Minor chassis. (David Marshall)

The six-cylinder cars 1929–35

A brace of '34 Oxfords, with the new Coupé to the fore. The sleeker lines and the raked-back radiator shell are readily apparent. (Author's collection)

In the first half the 1930s Morris offered a wide choice of six-cylinder models. By now he was a national figure of some stature, and was becoming involved on the fringes of the political scene.

As the 1920s drew to a close, William Morris still did not have a viable large car, one with which he could attack Empire markets. The 15.9hp Oxford had been a resounding flop, and the company's second serious attempt at a six-cylinder model, the Morris Six, had hardly been a spectacular success. Something better was needed if Morris were to snatch customers from American makes in the colonial markets, and make inroads into the prestige sector in Britain. Mindful of this, August 1929 saw Cowley launch a two-pronged attack on the six-cylinder market, with a re-cast 17.7hp model to replace the Six and a lower-priced six-cylinder Oxford with a new side-valve engine.

Isis – the Morris Six re-thought

First to be announced was the export-orientated 17.7hp Isis. It was designed 'without regard to price, embodying in its specification all that is newest and best in present-day automobile engineering, and introducing innovations all its own,' wrote *The Morris Owner*. At its price, of £385 for the saloon, the Isis called, said the magazine, for 'an entire revision of de luxe car values'.

Behind the gush was a much more saleable vehicle. Built around a new deeper-section chassis on a wheelbase 3in shorter than that of the Six, the Isis was a lavishly equipped and stylish car. The style was frankly American, but that was no surprise: after his disastrous introduction to all-steel coachwork, Morris had gone to the United States, and bought a set of dies for Pressed Steel directly from Budd. As a consequence, the Isis shared its body pressings with the Dodge Victory Six – and, for that matter, the front-drive Ruxton sedan. To get maximum value from his £120,000 investment, Morris used the same body for the Wolseley Messenger, a 21hp model introduced the previous year.

The foundation of the Isis was its all-new ladder-frame chassis, which featured side-members 8in deep, four pressed-steel cross-members and a robust arched pressed-steel bulkhead. With the all-steel mono-side body attached by 25 bolts,

the result was an impressively rigid structure, despite the use of what was described as thin-gauge steel for the frame. 'The strength of the body is extraordinary, and the occupants of the car might easily emerge scatheless if the vehicle rolled over and over down a bank,' commented *The Autocar*. Screwed-down floorboards were proclaimed as a big advance, in that they allowed for a more silent car.

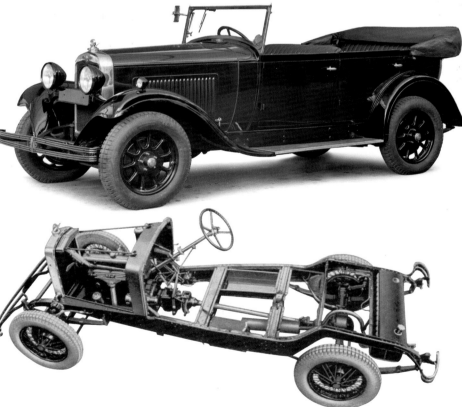

More robust artillery wheels were intended for export markets; for Britain the Isis was generally supplied with wire wheels. The two-toning on this saloon is typical of the first year's production. (Morris Register)

On artillery wheels the 1930 Isis tourer looks somewhat old-fashioned – or just a little bit more American? Over half of all Isis tourers went for export, and roughly the same proportion of chassis. (BMIHT)

The original Isis chassis was shared with no other Morris; it was characterised by its very deep side-members. Luvax rotary-action hydraulic dampers were used at all four wheels. (Author's collection)

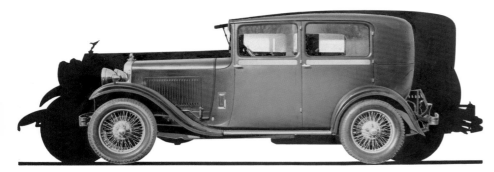

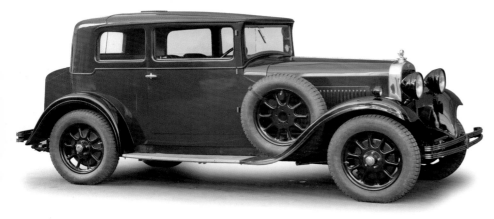

The Gordon England fabric saloon tested by The Autocar *was a sister model to the Club Coupé; whilst the latter was a style carried over from the preceding Morris Six, the fabric saloon was altogether sleeker than the England offering on the Six. (LAT)*

This 1930 Isis carries rather French-looking four-light coupé coachwork and could in fact be mistaken for a Morris-Léon-Bollée; in fact, the body is a dead-ringer for the Weymann design for the MLB R4 shown on page 75, and may well have been a one-off for William Morris himself. (BMIHT)

A catalogue image of a 1931 Isis saloon; for this season the flamboyant American-flavoured duo-toning was abandoned. Compared to the 1932 example shown on page 135, it is clear how the latter sits lower on its revised chassis. (Author's collection)

Equipment was appropriately generous, *The Morris Owner* assuring readers that the car had 'every accessory and aid to comfort, not only [that] the average man, but even the average woman can want'. This included leather upholstery, with pneumatic cushions at the front, that was 'only to be compared for comfort with the expensive lounges of the best London furnishing houses' and details such as a 'Smoker's companion' (with lighter) and a 'Lady's companion' (with powder box) at the rear, an adjustable chrome footrest for rear passengers, and 'enticing little cubby holes' inside the curve of the rear panels. The driver, meanwhile, could appreciate details such as finger-tip controls on the steering wheel and automatic thermostatically-controlled radiator shutters, not to mention an electric fuel gauge on the dashboard rather than the Six's tank-mounted dial.

In addition to the saloon, only available as a fixed-head, a four-seat open tourer was offered from launch, along with a Gordon England fabric-bodied Club Coupé with sliding head. In its October 1929 issue *The Morris Owner* carried a Gordon England advertisement promoting a four-door fabric saloon on the Isis chassis in addition to the Club Coupé, and this new variant seemingly had semi-official status, if its featuring as an *Autocar* road test is any guide. For those wary of fabric coachwork, for an additional £25 the plywood shell of the England bodies could be given a cellulose-painted aluminium cladding, excluding the roof and rear quarters.

The Isis range was further expanded with the announcement of a De Luxe pressed-steel saloon. Described in the July 1930 edition of *The Morris Owner*, this featured louvres over the windows, chrome radiator shutters, and loose cushions and a folding centre armrest at the rear. Costing £10 more than the standard saloon, it was only available in Maroon, with red upholstery, or in a Royal Blue and Ivory duotone.

The Isis certainly appeared a beguiling car, and *The Autocar* made much play of how with its Anglo-American character there was nothing else quite like it being made in England. But was it any good? In *Out on a Wing* Miles Thomas stigmatised the Isis as 'a steel-bodied saloon that was so heavy that it killed itself – commercially'. Reading between the lines, it is clear that *The Autocar* was disappointed with its road-test car. It praised the Isis for a flexibility that allowed it to run from 6–7mph up to a genuine 60mph in top gear, and for its silence at speeds below

Developing something in the order of 50bhp, the 2468cc 'six' with its chain-driven single overhead camshaft was unchanged except for some minor details said to give a smoother top-gear performance, but now had a four-point rubber mounting; the three-speed gearbox and the cork-in-oil clutch were also carry-overs from the Morris Six.

The rest of the running gear was new. Gone was the Six's torque-tube transmission, replaced by an open propshaft with two Hardy-Spicer metal universal joints. Gone too was the mechanical braking system, replaced by Lockheed hydraulics in conjunction with a transmission brake incorporated in the front universal-joint assembly. Finally, the steering was now by Bishop cam-and-peg. Wire wheels were standard for the UK, with steel artillery wheels specified for export markets.

45mph. But the magazine was reticent about the Morris's performance, and drew attention to the way the car rolled on corners and pitched on bad surfaces[1].

With the gentlemanly damning-with-faint-praise approach of the time, it was only when *The Autocar* tested the Gordon England saloon in May 1930 that the truth came out: it seemed probable that the steel saloon was overweight, at just over 28cwt, and 'not doing itself full justice'. With the supposedly lighter fabric body, an indicated 70mph was achieved from the Gordon England, and a timed maximum speed over the quarter mile of 61.6mph. The 10–30mph time in top, meanwhile, was shaved from 14.2 seconds to 10.2 seconds. On this occasion, too, there were no complaints about body roll or a lively ride – suggesting that the less weighty fabric body may additionally have been beneficial in these areas.

The Oxford becomes a 'six'

Meanwhile late August 1929 saw the second of Morris's new six-cylinder offerings, a completely re-fashioned Oxford that in the words of Arthur Rowse represented "the first breakaway from the dismal habit of making cars by scrounging bits of equipment which were unrelated, and building them into a complete vehicle". This was largely because the new Oxford was designed in secret, under Rowse's direction, whilst William Morris was away on one of his long overseas trips.

Morris had already set the ball rolling, announcing that he would himself supervise the design of a new six-cylinder engine, by-passing Morris Engines manager Frank Woollard, who according to Rowse was by then "under a bit of a cloud". A room was set aside in the former Military College, above Morris's office, and Woollard's deputy, George Pendrell, came down from Coventry to draw up an engine under Morris's instructions. The idea was that the new power unit would simply be slotted into the existing four-cylinder chassis, a proposal that appalled Rowse, who deemed the Flatnose frame totally inadequate. Unfortunately Blake's lack of technical knowledge meant that he was quite happy to go along with such thinking. "Blake... had no ideas of his own on subjects of that type, so the car was duly made up with the

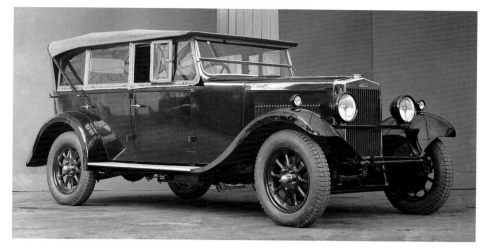

existing body and everything the same except the engine," Rowse related to Andrews and Brunner.

But when Morris went away on his voyage, Rowse decided to have an alternative design prepared in his absence. All the arrangements were made to put the initial proposal into production, but he also ensured it was possible to manufacture the all-new design if it received the green light. Blake – who "implicitly carried out the

An unusual photo, taken at the Morris works in 1929, and depicting an early – possibly pre-production – Oxford-Six tourer on artillery wheels. Small-hub wire wheels were normal wear on 1930-season Oxford-Sixes. (BMIHT

The cheaper LA-series Oxford saloon – by £14 in 1930 – was the £285 fabric saloon. It was offered in black or red with red Vaumol leather upholstery. Magna wires were an option for the 1931 model year. (Author's collection)

The fabric saloon was judged a smart-looking vehicle. The built-out boot put it at an advantage over the sliding-head coachbuilt saloon, which didn't even have a luggage grid. (Author's collection)

[1] In fairness, it should be acknowledged that the road test by The Motor was more favourable, praising the car's 'fine top-gear performance' and its excellent hill-climbing abilities and comfortable ride – along with a structure impressively free of squeaks and rattles. The car's tendency to roll was however mentioned, while maximum speed was recorded as 62mph.

PLAYING POLITICS: MORRIS AND THE LEAGUE OF INDUSTRY

William Morris in his office in the period of the League of Industry; in his lapel is the League's badge. The cigar in the ashtray, admittedly unsmoked, seems out of character: Morris was a voracious cigarette smoker. (Morris Register)

It was during the currency of the second-generation 'sixes' that Morris became a more prominent figure in the world of politics – and during which time he became involved with future British Union of Fascists leader Sir Oswald Mosley.

Morris was not really a political animal. He was a lifelong supporter of the Conservative Party, donating money on both a national and a local level; this was hardly a surprise for a man in his position. At the 1935 General Election he also made substantial donations to the National Liberal Party and Ramsay MacDonald's National Labour Party, a gesture that underlined his basic political position: a belief in a national or coalition government that sat above petty inter-party bickering and espoused 'patriotic' Empire-centric values, import controls and non-partisan support of industry. It was in banging the drum for such a programme that he set up and funded the League of Industry in 1931.

The League was developed out of the National Council of Industry and Commerce, set up in 1930 by Morris and chaired by him. The Council's line, enunciated by Morris, was that for the past 25–30 years England had been financing the world through a suicidal policy of allowing herself to be a dumping ground, thanks to a misguided belief in Free Trade. Industrial protection, strong government and a real workers' leader were what was needed, and the Council would strive to bring together both sides of industry and press for increased colonial and dominion trade while keeping out other producers with protective tariffs. "Party warfare must give place to industrial welfare," he proclaimed.

Although Morris was very much the public face of the League, the key figure was arguably Colonel Wyndham Portal, whose family paper mill printed banknotes for the Bank of England; very much an activist businessman, Sir Wyndham, as he became in 1931, went on, as Baron Portal, to become a minister in the wartime government. Others in the front rank were Gibson Jarvie, Chairman of finance company United Dominions Trust, who looked after all instalment buying of Morris cars, and Sir Alfred Mond, a one-time Liberal minister who created ICI and had a reputation as an enlightened industrialist. Former miners' representative Frank Hodges, who had been a junior minister in the first Ramsay MacDonald administration, was recruited as Deputy Chairman because he was a Labour man and Morris wanted the League to be non-political – or at the very least cross-party.

According to the League's Honorary Secretary, Philip Cambray, the pressure group – which is what we would call the League today – did a great deal of work in bringing together employers and employees through conferences and study schools and helped regenerate South Wales by prompting Portal's involvement in depressed areas and ultimately leading to Morris's Special Areas Trust (see page 284). But fair numbers of manufacturers cold-shouldered the League, some because they were dependent on foreign imports, and didn't want tariffs on them. "A lot of people thought it was a Morris stunt," Cambray told Andrews and Brunner.

In the end, the League outlived its usefulness. The National Government, led by Labour's Ramsay MacDonald, conformed to the League's belief in cross-party governance, and MacDonald showed no inclination to repeal the McKenna Duties. Meanwhile, the economy was rebounding, and Morris in particular was selling plenty of cars, with 1935 in fact being a pre-war record for him, with 96,512 deliveries, comfortably more than double the 1931 figure. So it was that the League of Industry was dissolved, ahead of the General Election in 1935 that would see the National Government reconstructed under the leadership of the Conservative Stanley Baldwin. Cambray thought that Morris hadn't really enjoyed the experience. "It was politics, and Morris did not like or understand politics."

instructions of Morris" according to Rowse – had to be headed off, however, so the new car was put together without his knowledge, in a curtained-off part of the drawing office, with the draughtsmen themselves assembling the chassis.

This secrecy led to one Laurel-and-Hardy comic moment. There was only one engine – and that was in the 'Morris' car. Rowse's men therefore had to borrow it without being found out. They duly whisked the car into the Cowley repair shop, took the engine out, and hoisted it up to the first-floor drawing office, having to tear off an office door in the process. Just at that moment Blake phoned to say someone wanted to see the new Oxford. Could it be sent over? Rowse had to adopt delaying tactics, saying that the engine was out to have something done to it, and the car would not be available until the afternoon. The engine was rapidly put back, and Blake left none the wiser. A new body was also built, but could not be assembled on the chassis before Morris returned. However, he was shown the chassis and an air-brush rendering of the body, and ended up accepting it as 'next year's Morris Oxford'. According to Miles Thomas this was despite his disliking the car; Rowse, however, maintained – with evident self-interest – that Morris immediately approved of the proposed new model. Blake, meanwhile, was completely non-plussed by all these goings-on, said Rowse.

The new car's side-valve engine was a 1938cc unit with full pressure-lubrication and pump-assisted cooling, mated to the existing Flatnose Cowley/Oxford gearbox and cork-in-oil clutch; rated at 14.9hp, it was built around Morris's regular 102mm stroke. Despite its flathead configuration, the four-bearing unit looked as if it had overhead valves, as it had a horsehair-filled 'air-cleaning compartment' – a fume-trap and air cleaner disguised as a rocker cover. Engine breathers exited to the cleaner, which channeled the engine fumes to the carburettor, the oily vapour supposedly aiding upper-cylinder lubrication.

Another unusual feature was an external mechanical oil filter that was claimed to automatically clean the oil every time the clutch was operated: when the clutch was depressed, a rod connected to the clutch pedal rubbed metal discs in the filter against each other, cleaning the discs of any sludge, which then sank to the bottom of the removable filter bowl.

The new drivetrain, retaining torque-tube transmission, was mounted in a ladder-frame chassis which despite having the same 9ft 6in wheelbase was a completely different design from that of the Isis: in particular the side members were less deep and were straight rather than curved at the front, and less swept-up at the rear. Relatively narrow between the side rails, the frame had broad low-set outriggers to support both body and running boards – a feature deemed unusual at the time, and one that allowed the body to sit lower on the chassis. A consequence of this configuration was that all four springs were positioned outboard of the side members. The bulkhead, finally, was a simple firewall-style unit as opposed to the more elaborate Isis steel pressing.

Other features of the mechanicals were hydraulic brakes, Bishop cam-and-peg steering, and Luvax rotary-action hydraulic dampers;

This 1930 Oxford sliding-roof coachbuilt saloon – distinguishable from a '31 car by the lack of window louvres – is in a non-standard colour. As an alternative to Niagara Blue, a red was offered, but it was a deeper maroon. (Rodney Bryant/Morris Register)

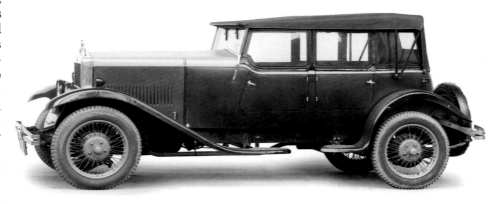

This fabric-bodied and rather sporting four-seater LA Oxford from the 1930 model year was not a catalogued style. (BMIHT)

Another 'rogue' Oxford-Six, wearing a Three-Quarter Coupé body that was never a catalogued option. The photo, dating from 1930/31, was again taken at Cowley. (BMIHT)

The 1931 Oxford coachbuilt saloon was available as a fixed-head with optional Magna wheels at £275 or for £10 more as a sliding-head with Magna wheels as standard. Colours were blue or black. (Author's collection)

A surviving 1931-season Oxford-Six tourer on the optional Magna wheels, which cost £2.10s extra. The colour is again not a catalogued shade, only blue or black being offered on steel-bodied '31 Oxfords; upholstery was in leather. (Morris Register)

Tickford offered its Sunshine folding-head bodywork on the six-cylinder Morrises – and on many other makes. The convertible top wound backwards and forwards on a geared mechanism, and it was claimed could be opened and closed in a mere ten seconds. This advertisement depicts a 1930 Oxford. (Author's collection)

Opened or Closed in 10 Seconds by turning a handle

Tickford Coachwork offers all the comfort of the finest saloon together with the benefits of an entirely open car.

The special model for Morris cars is of that High-class Workmanship for which Salmons & Sons are noted, and can be supplied at the following prices for the complete car:

MORRIS MAJOR with TICKFORD BODY £310
MORRIS-OXFORD with TICKFORD BODY £335

All 1931 Tickfords are fitted with real leather hoods and upholstered in finest soft waterproof leather. Any model can be supplied with Triplex Safety Glass if required.

SALMONS & SONS
13 NEW BURLINGTON ST., LONDON, W.1
Garage and Service - 8 Upper St. Martin's Lane, W.C.2
Works - Newport Pagnell, Bucks.
South-West England Agents - Merlyn Motors Ltd., Bristol

TICKFORD *Sunshine Coachwork*

and a sliding-head four-light coupé. The range 'undoubtedly opens up an entirely new line of thought in medium-powered and medium-priced car values, virtually offering everything the motorist can want, at a price nearly everyone can pay,' announced *The Morris Owner*, claiming that the six-cylinder Oxford created 'new ideals in the medium-powered car class'.

Weekly *The Autocar* was equally enthusiastic, saying that 'the Morris firm has decided to live excitingly' and that the car would 'make history' and set 'a standard hard to equal at the price' – proving that Great Britain could provide 'an Everyman's car at Everyman's price'. With the fabric-bodied saloon at £285 and the coachbuilt saloon at £299 that was perhaps wishful thinking, at a time when the average annual salary was in the order of £200; but the Oxford was certainly good value, when a 20hp Rover six-cylinder saloon cost £398. It looked, too, as if the market liked the car. According to Arthur Rowse the LA 'had an immediate appeal' and made '£½m clear profit in the year it was launched' – helping the company to a £1.5m profit that year. Certainly the car was well received by the press, who praised the Oxford's performance and refinement, and its light controls.

Problems with the Oxford – and exit Woollard

There was, however, a fly in the ointment. Despite Morris boasting of the Oxford having been severely tested in twelve countries, the new power unit suffered from serious design failings, exacerbated by the inadequacies of the hand-me-down clutch and gearbox. 'The engine had been built so compactly that there was not enough water space around the cylinder bores and so, although the radiator temperature did not go all that high, the oil in the sump became boiling hot and disintegrated the cork-faced clutch. The external oil filter warped and every time the clutch pedal was pressed oil spewed out on to the road,' relates Miles Thomas in *Out on a Wing*. 'Edgar Blake, who as Deputy Governing Director was chief executive at Cowley during the Boss's absence, gained no popularity at all for the venture. Profits ran down sadly.' Talking to Andrews and Brunner, Leonard Lord confirmed that when he took over at Cowley the Oxford "was giving trouble all over the world". Less mercurial Reggie Hanks was of the same opinion: "It had the makings of a very fine motor car but it just did not work... nothing was right with it. They made it better but they never got that car right."

all these items featured also on the Isis, but a key difference on the Oxford was the use of a handbrake operating on the rear wheels, via separate shoes.

The headline body style was a six-light fabric saloon, the same design being used on the 1930 Wolseley Viper. Alongside this, three steel bodies were offered – a sliding-head saloon, a tourer,

MORRIS AND SIR OSWALD MOSLEY

It was during the early days of the League of Industry that Morris gave generous support to Sir Oswald Mosley. In September 1930 the National Council of Industry and Commerce had called for 'strong government' and 'a real leader' and in December it had praised the New Party manifesto as a 'ray of hope' and as laying the foundations for an 'industrial party' that could bring the country out of a 'slough of despond'. Before rushing to the conclusion that Lord Nuffield was therefore a closet fascist, it must be remembered that Mosley in this period was a former Labour Party junior minister who was regarded as a brilliant if slightly wayward political figure rather than a raging black-shirted demagogue; in claiming to want a strong non-partisan national government in the midst of a demoralising economic depression, he was advocating something which many Britons – and not least Lord Nuffield – judged an evident truth.

Mosley's New Party was duly set up in March 1931 on just such a platform, and was presented as representing a fresh approach to national governance. Its main organ of communication was the paper *Action*, edited by diplomat, writer and future Labour politician Harold Nicolson, and it was primarily this that Nuffield bankrolled, through a donation to the party of a substantial £50,000. He also guaranteed to cover the salary of union-supported Labour MP John Brown, whom Mosley was hoping to poach for the New Party, and he channelled some of his money towards the party's youth clubs. These clubs went on to have something of a whiff of Hitler's youth movement about them, and were to become one of the recruiting grounds for the young thugs who kept order at Mosley's increasingly heated meetings, but at this stage they doubtless appeared rather more innocent.

Nuffield was introduced to Mosley by Wyndham Portal, who was devoting much energy to fundraising for the New Party among prominent businessmen and was himself a substantial donor to the party. 'My discussions with Lord Nuffield were protracted,' recalls Mosley in his autobiography *My Life*. 'I had practically given up hope of any help from the motor magnate, as nothing seemed ever to come of our talks, when I suddenly received a telegram inviting me to lunch with him at Huntercombe golf course club-house… Like Lord Rothermere, he was a genuine and ardent patriot, but he was even less versed in the technique of politics, a business genius who seemed to be rather lost outside his own sphere… Political conversation with him tended consequently to be tedious, as the only real contribution he could make was through the power of his money, and this point never seemed likely to be reached. However, ennui flew out of the window when at the end of lunch he pulled a cheque from his pocket and handed it to me across the table; it was for £50,000… He was a good and honest man, as well as a business genius; a combination which can occur.'

Morris made no secret of his support. 'At the beginning of the New Party, Lord Nuffield was our chief backer and he told so many people that it became widely known,' writes Mosley. However, the donation remained a one-off. Circulation of *Action* soon crashed, and it was quickly running up losses of £1500 a month. Morris refused to put more money into the paper, and it folded at the end of the year. This was only a short-term set-back, as by 1933 Italian fascist leader Mussolini was subsidising Mosley to the tune of some £60,000 a year – a figure that illustrates how generous was Nuffield's support. All the evidence is that this began and ended with the £50,000 'Huntercombe' donation, and thus that Morris's involvement had been wound down before the New Party morphed into the British Union of Fascists in 1932. When in 1934 the press linked him with the BUF, Morris said he had never been a fascist and denied (possibly disingenuously) that he was anti-semitic[1], whilst making a token £250 donation to the Central Fund for German Jewry. The sum was derisory by his normal standards of giving, but later he made more substantial donations to Jewish causes, suggesting that such views as he may have held in private came to evolve in a more positive fashion during the later pre-war years.

[1] He was a reader of the anti-Semitic *Patriot* paper, and pencilled notes in copies that survive in the Nuffield College archives suggest a certain antipathy to Jews. It is also apparently the case that after the First World War he made donations to far-right grouping the British Empire Union, no friend of the Jewish people.

It wasn't the loyal if largely useless Blake who took the rap for the Oxford's failings – justly enough, given that the car had been designed behind his back. Rather it was Frank Woollard, who as head of Engines Branch had ultimate responsibility for the side-valve engine of the LA, even if he had not had much direct input into its design. As was often the case with William Morris, personal issues also intruded, and the result was that in June 1931 Woollard was forced to resign. 'I have felt for some time that circumstances have made my position at Engines Branch very difficult and in view of this I shall be obliged if you will ask Sir William to accept my resignation as director of Morris Motors Ltd and General Manager of the Engines Branch,' he wrote to Blake.

As well as being accused of incompetence over the LA engine, which was a bit rich seeing as it had been designed under Morris's personal direction, Woollard was judged to not be pulling his weight as a senior manager. When he attended directors' meetings he apparently relied on having his lieutenant Pendrell at his side, and if problems arose he tended to dispatch Pendrell to sort them out. Such, at any rate, were the recollections of Carl Kingerlee – who also said that Wilfred Hobbs and perpetual schemer Kimpton Smallbone "kicked Woollard out".

Lord Nuffield was not forthcoming when talking to Andrews and Brunner, other than to bring up what had really rankled in connection with Woollard: that he ate copiously at lunchtime,

In 1931 Kent-based coachbuilder and Morris dealer Maltby's were offering this rather stub-tailed Oxford roadster. An unusual feature was a hatch on the left-hand side, giving access to a transverse locker for golf clubs, fishing rods and the like. (LAT)

The 1931 Major saloon was only available with a folding head – unlike the Cowley, which was available in a cheaper fixed-head form. The Majors were generously equipped, roomy, six-cylinder cars 'at an astoundingly low price,' said The Morris Owner. Never before, it wrote, 'has such sterling value been available for folk of modest means'. (Author's collection)

The folding-head coupé offered for the Major's first year was the same five-window style as used on the Cowley. The only obvious way of distinguishing the two was the Major's standard wire wheels; but even then these were available as an option on '31 Cowleys. (Author's collection)

The fabric-covered Salonette was unique to the 1931 Major, disappearing in favour of a steel four-light saloon-style coupé for 1932. (Author's collection)

and so was not in a fit state for afternoon board meetings. He needed a post-prandial nap, and as a result preferred to retire to a small room where he had a couch. He locked the door, set his alarm clock, and had a two-hour snooze. "That was not good enough," snorted Nuffield to his interlocutors. Thus was lost to Morris Motors one of the best production engineers in the car industry; as for Woollard, he became MD of Rudge-Whitworth, and then director of the Birmingham Aluminium Casting Company and the Midland Motor Cylinder Company.

Low-cost six-cylinder motoring: the Major

Returning to the cars themselves, Morris now had two modern six-cylinder models in its portfolio, but still felt the need to expand the upper reaches of the range. To do this it was decided to return to the recipe for a low-cost 'six' that had been rejected by Rowse in favour of the LA Oxford. The result was the Morris Major announced for the 1931 season – basically a Cowley fitted with the LA engine. Built on the Cowley's 8ft 9in wheelbase, but thankfully with the chassis reinforced, the Major retained the four-cylinder car's mechanical brakes but gained wire wheels and a rear-mounted fuel tank. Body styles were more restricted, with just a steel-shelled coachbuilt saloon, a folding-head five-window coupé and a fabric salonette on offer. Intriguingly, *The Autocar* found that its test Major saloon was slower from 10mph to 30mph in top gear than the fabric-bodied Oxford saloon, despite the latter being just over 3cwt heavier. Regardless of such detail, the magazine found the engine

This 1932 saloon displays the more sober styling of the second-generation Isis, as well as the new frontal treatment with a large chromium-plated horn integrated into the lamp bar. Only the Isis had valanced front wings for the '32 season. (Mark Dixon)

Doors on the Isis were front-hinged for 1932, but rear-hinged back doors returned for 1933; the Oxford retained its front-hinged doors, and the Major its rear-hinged ones. (Mark Dixon)

'almost unbelievably good' – 'quiet and smooth to the point of silkiness right through the range of speed... and definitely lively in acceleration'.

The other two 'sixes' were given only minor modifications for 1931. Magna wheels with larger hubcaps became standard on the Oxford-Six coupé and sliding-head saloon and optional on all other Oxfords – the range now including a fixed-head coachbuilt saloon. The Isis, which for 1931 was no longer available with Club Coupé coachwork, could also be specified, again at extra cost, with these more stylish wheels. Louvres for the windows were standardized on both the Oxford sliding-head and Isis coachbuilt saloons, whilst both the coachbuilt Oxford saloons gained a rear folding centre armrest. Tourers, meanwhile, were given a redesigned hood. Finally, Oxfords of all types were given a treadle-type throttle pedal, while the Isis received a stoneguard for its petrol tank and the air-cleaner and fume consumer introduced on the 1930 Oxford.

Better cars – and another 'six'

Morris now had three different six-cylinder models, with three different body styles, on three different chassis – a nonsense in anyone's terms, and surely a reflection of the company's disjointed management. For 1932 steps were taken to bring a bit of order to the top of the range, although this was not immediately evident from the tinkering with the underpinnings of the cars.

After just one year the Major sat lower on a new chassis, a wider design with a more downswept centre, straight rather than curved dumb-irons, and diagonal bracing at the front. This was not an adaptation of the Oxford-Six chassis, logical though that might have been, but it was shared with the re-engineered 1932 Cowley, so there was at least some commonality with another model. There was also the undoubted benefit of an extra 4in in the car's front and rear tracks, both in terms of stability and in allowing what was claimed to be a genuine five-seat body.

The Oxford chassis, meanwhile, received a tubular cross-member forward of the kick-up over the back axle, along with an additional cross-member below the engine, in the style of that found on the new Major chassis. The Isis

Newcastle Morris distributor Buist's was responsible for this Isis-based ambulance for the Newcastle Corporation. A more utilitarian use for the Isis chassis was the special Traveller's Brougham built in-house for Morris's film unit. (Author's collection)

This wonderful Isis shooting brake was the work of Cunard. The wheel discs are a nice detail, the hearse-like tall screen rather less so. (John Seddon)

In common with the Major and the Isis, the body on the '32 Oxford was given a new look by removing the peak above the windscreen and restyling the radiator. In the case of the Oxford, though, the basic body looked barely changed. (Mark Dixon)

The cockpit of the 1932 Oxford had plain rather than burr-walnut wood trim. The side handbrake was an Oxford-Six constant until the '33 model year, when a central lever was introduced. (Mark Dixon)

Controls in the steering-wheel hub came in with the Isis and the Oxford-Six in 1929. The oval instrument panel is in the Morris house style. (Mark Dixon)

The big Morrises were certainly well appointed. The Isis, said The Morris Owner, was 'upholstered in the finest automobile hides money can buy, with an interior and exterior finish which only the finest craftsman can produce' – and the Oxford, here a 1932 example, was no less plush. The head cushions were standard. (Mark Dixon)

frame was also modified, with more of a dip to the side rails – allowing a lower-slung body – and was given a 6in extension to the wheelbase.

Common to both the Isis and the Oxford was a modification to reduce the likelihood of wheel shimmy: the offside front spring was shackled at the rear and given an anti-shimmy friction damper. All three cars were given a 'twin top' four-speed gearbox with a 'silent' third gear – along with a lighter-to-operate single-plate clutch, still of the cork-in-oil type, on the Major and Oxford. Additionally the Major benefitted from a move to Lockheed hydraulic braking and a reduction in engine bore to give a capacity of 1803cc, enabling it to fall into the 14hp tax class. The Oxford-Six kept the old 1938cc capacity – so owners were liable for one more pound of tax per year – and was given an improved cork clutch.

It was in the coachwork that logic started to prevail, with the same saloon body shared by the Oxford and Isis. This was of wood-framed construction, a step backwards from the all-steel

The 1934-season Twenty-Five: big P100 headlamps, twin foglamps, wider wheels and a second spare wheel distinguish it from lesser 'sixes'. Duotone colours offered alongside the usual black were blue-and-black, duotone brown, and green-and-black. Although left-hand drive was available, only eleven Twenty-Fives were lhd; eight went to the Anglo-Persian Oil Company. (Author's collection)

With a completely fresh range – from a Ten to a Twenty-Five – due for launch in the course of 1935, for the 1934 Motor Show the six-cylinder models received only minor enhancements, such as a right-hand accelerator on the Oxford, a radio aerial wired into the sliding head, a pull-up handbrake, and the fitment of a Rollsvisor roller-sunvisor. One final range expansion did however take place: the 16hp Oxford was now joined by a 20hp variant with a larger-bore 2561cc engine, bizarrely sold at the same price as the 16hp model. Meanwhile, the Cowley-Six, née Major, changed name again, becoming the Fifteen-Six. With the Oxfords now being referred to as the Oxford Sixteen and the Oxford Twenty, and the Isis as the Isis Eighteen, in retrospect it is clear that Morris was preparing the way for a new naming policy, whereby model nomenclature would be based on fiscal horsepower.

The palatial interior, trimmed in burr walnut, was equipped to the same level as that of the Isis; a bench front seat with folding armrest was an innovation on Oxford and above saloons for 1934, in which year the Twenty-Five saloon retailed for £395, against £370 for an Isis and £285 for an Oxford-Six. (Author's collection)

The Isis and Twenty-Five Special Coupés were subtly changed for 1934: the two-piece winding windows were replaced by a quarterlight and a single winding pane, and the line of the fabric roof was cut back to allow space for trafficators. This is a Twenty-Five Special Coupé, of which only 72 were made in the car's two-season life. (Author's collection)

Too many models, not enough sales

Had the effort in building up a four-car range of 'sixes' been worthwhile? In all, 39,038 Oxfords had been made, an estimated 25,979 of the Major and its successor models, and 7550 of the Isis and Twenty-Five. This suggests that in terms of the time the two cheaper ranges were a justifiable exercise but that the Isis and its big brother were more commercially questionable.

The freewheel and the Bendix vacuum-operated clutch introduced on the '34 Oxford, Isis and Twenty-Five were switched in and out using two dashboard knobs. (Author's collection)

Duple Bodies & Motors Ltd, better known in later years for its coaches, built this roadster, on what would appear to be a '34 Oxford chassis; the customer was the Fife Motor Company of Dunfermline. (Author's collection)

In its last form the 15-Six saloon, as its bigger peers, sat lower on a new chassis. The Wilmot-Breeden 'harmonic stabiliser' front bumper featured on all 'sixes' for 1934: it used dumb-bell end-pieces and a sprung leaf behind the blade, to dampen front-end vibration. (BMIHT)

The new style of Special Coupé introduced for 1934 on the Cowley-Six and Oxford-Six chassis was airy and elegant. This Cowley-Six can be recognised as a '34 by the headlamp bar in front of the radiator. (Author's collection)

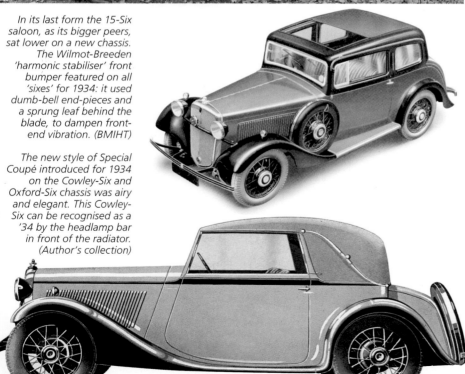

Cunard's Continental drophead on the Cowley-Six chassis was aluminium-panelled and had a twill hood that could be used in a half-furled coupé de ville position. The body, also known as the Lansdowne Continental, was available for other Morris six-cylinder models, and sometimes featured a Bugatti-like 'pen-nib' duotone. (John Seddon)

Break down the figures a little further, and it is clear, though, that a worm was turning. Over its first four seasons – the 1930–33 model years – the Oxford racked up a production of 32,282 units, or an average of roughly 8000 cars a year. The Major managed 18,494 units in the 1931–33 model years, or an average of a little over 6000 cars a year. As a higher-priced model, the Isis was reasonably enough some way behind, with only 3939 cars produced for the 1930 and 1931 seasons, meaning an annual average in the order of 2000 units.

Yet the '34 and '35 Oxfords managed 6756 units in total, over a season and a half, and the Major and its later derivatives an estimated 7485 units over the same model years. Worse, output of the Isis and Twenty-Five amounted to only 3467 cars over the longer period of the 1932 to 1935 seasons – or an average of not quite a thousand examples a year. Indeed, the Twenty-Five was so little wanted that although it was still catalogued for 1935 the last chassis had been laid down in June 1934[2]. In all, a mere 375 had been made, of which 214, including chassis, had been exported.

The obvious conclusion is that both home and export markets were progressively turning their back on the big Morrises. That only 15 per cent or so of Isis production was exported is a painful commentary on the car's lack of appeal overseas.

Despite this, the company had reached mid-decade with no fewer than five offerings in the big six-cylinder class, powered by three different engines, two of which were overhead-cam units that can only have been expensive to produce. On top of that there were three over-2000cc six-cylinder models, unrelated to any Morris, that were being made by the organisation's Wolseley subsidiary. A shake-up was clearly in order.

[2] The Isis continued to be manufactured in small quantities, the last being laid down in May 1935 and despatched in June. The final 208 cars, starting in June 1934, used chassis re-numbered from earlier in the production sequence, an obvious bit of end-of-line house-keeping.

In its final guise, for 1934, the 'perpendicular' Oxford returned to centre-opening doors. With the new cruciform chassis came a lower build and a raked radiator shell with the thermostatic slats behind the false honeycomb. (Author's collection)

Minor excepted, cruciform chassis were the order of the day for 1934. Top left is the new Oxford frame; note the barrel-grip handbrake that replaced the signalman's type on '34 Morrises. (Author's collection)

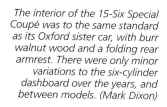

The interior of the 15-Six Special Coupé was to the same standard as its Oxford sister car, with burr walnut wood and a folding rear armrest. There were only minor variations to the six-cylinder dashboard over the years, and between models. (Mark Dixon)

Correctly painted in Green over Cream, this 15-Six Special Coupé is a 1935 model, recognisable by the lack of a visible headlamp bar. Other than all-black, the car could also be obtained in two-tone brown and two-tone green. (Mark Dixon)

The fall-away rear of the second-generation Special Coupés housed an adequately-sized boot by the standards of the time. (BMIHT)

A later Tickford exercise, this folding-head conversion on a 15-Six was a simple adaptation of the existing saloon; the patented winding mechanism was still used, and prices started at £35 in 1934. All closed Morris models could be fitted with the roof. (Author's collection)

The Ten and Cowley 1932–35

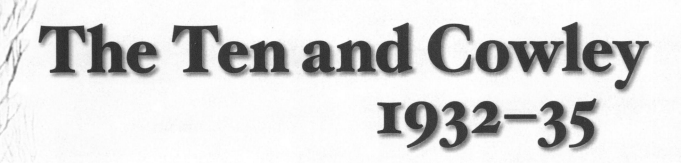

This delightful Morris Owner cover shows a '33 Ten, possibly slightly exaggerating the curve of the lamp bar; this is an easy way to distinguish the Ten from a '33 Cowley, which has a straight lamp bar. (Ken Martin collection)

A much-needed success, the Ten nonetheless claimed the head of its creator, indicating that Morris was perhaps losing his grip on the firm he had created. Meanwhile, the Cowley continued to be be produced, and carried on selling in decent numbers.

By 1932 the Morris house was in better order. The Minor had been brought more in tune with commercial realities by concentrating on the side-valve engine, and the range beneficially enlarged by the arrival of the four-door and coupé variants. The Cowley and its sister car the Major had been modernised, as had the larger Morrises. Emphasising new-found coherence in design, every model in the range was available with snappy Sports Coupé coachwork.

But the market was moving on, and again Morris risked being left behind. Although sales of 11hp and 12hp cars were to stabilise for a few years, after a one-off further dip in 1931, nonetheless the trend was clearly away from larger-engined vehicles. But the growth wasn't just in 7hp and 8hp models. With the arrival of the Hillman Minx in 1931, a new market sector came into being, that for family-sized 10hp cars that slotted neatly between the Sevens and Eights and the more traditional and bulky Twelves. In May 1932 Austin followed suit with his Ten-Four. That year registrations in the 9hp–10hp class jumped from 14 per cent of the market (up from 9 per cent in 1930) to a robust 24 per cent. If William Rootes and Herbert Austin had swiftly read the way the market was evolving, William Morris in the meantime had continued to pin his faith on his much-loved Cowley model.

Arthur Rowse was worried that Morris could not grasp how a problem was building up by this reliance on the Cowley: "That car was designed in 1912 and this was 1932, and the Morris Cowley engine was completely out of date," he told Andrews and Brunner. "We had pushed the power up until the crankshaft was manifestly too weak to sustain the load. We succeeded in getting a better performance with [cars of] heavier weight. The engine was out of date, but it was a very difficult thing for Morris to admit... I felt the thing was to be ready for a large-scale move..."

Rowse duly decided to lay out a new engine, a simple design based on what he had seen on visits to the United States and on the equally straightforward power units used by Austin. When he requested permission to build three engines, Morris tellingly asked him what was

Rear-hinged back doors are a Ten constant. Map pockets are a nice touch, but note how the Ten does without a rear central armrest. (Author's collection)

The Ten-Six is physically identical to the Ten-Four, longer bonnet excepted. This is a 1934 model-year example, but almost certainly a pre-production car, as it lacks the curved radiator stoneguard a '34 Ten would normally wear. (Author's collection)

From the rear the Tens and the Cowley look very similar. But on the former the spare wheel is rear-mounted, as opposed to the Cowley's side-mount. (JE Jewson/Morris Register)

The Ten dashboard follows the house style of the time, with an inset black-painted oval instrument panel. (BMIHT)

The Ten was offered by Stewart and Ardern with a smaller version of its rather inelegant Cunard Calshot drophead coachwork. Billed as an occasional two-seater, it had a folding hammock-type seat in the rear. The body featured a hinged boot-lid and the interior woodwork was in black walnut. Price was £242.10s in February 1933. (Author's collection)

these mechanicals. "I don't think he ever forgave me for that, because it demonstrated that the organisation could build and produce a car on its own."

The result was the Morris Ten, announced in September 1932 as part of the otherwise largely-unchanged 1933 range. The Ten was a classically straightforward design, built around a downswept ladder-frame chassis suspended on semi-elliptic springs front and rear. Rowse's three-main-bearing engine was a side-valve unit of 1292cc, with the same 102mm stroke as the Cowley and Oxford, presumably to allow cost-effective use of existing machinery at Morris Engines. As with the bigger Morris side-valve units, it disguised its flathead configuration by being topped with a horsehair-filled air cleaner and fume extractor. Cooled by pump-less thermo-syphon action and fuelled by the usual SU, in conjunction with an SU Petrolift electric pump, the engine was mated to an unsynchronised four-speed 'twin-top' gearbox via Morris's traditional cork-in-oil clutch. Drive to the rear wheels was by an open propshaft using fabric universals back and front. Other chassis details included friction dampers, Bishop cam-and-peg steering, and Lockheed hydraulic brakes – these last something of which no 10hp competitor could boast. Electrics were 12-volt, putting the Morris at a further advantage over the Austin, which would only receive a 12-volt system for 1934.

At launch only a six-light saloon and a Special Coupé were offered. The latter had a Pytchley sliding roof as standard, along with leather upholstery, and in addition the saloon could be ordered with a sliding head, in which guise

wrong with the existing 'Hotchkiss' unit. Rowse replied, doubtless biting his lip, that the company had to have something ready – "for when public wants a change".

Unbeknown to Morris, then away on one of his overseas trips, Rowse initiated the design not just of a matching gearbox for the new power unit, but also of an entire car to go around

For 1934 the Ten received a new cruciform frame as well as such running-gear enhancements as Armstrong 'pear' dampers. Visible on this Ten-Six chassis are the substantial steel bulkhead, the twin 6-volt batteries, and the upright barrel-grip handbrake that replaced the signalman's type on '34 Minors, Tens and Cowleys. (Author's collection)

it also came with double-blade bumpers and an integral luggage grid. A four-seater tourer followed in December 1932.

Priced at £165 for the fixed-head saloon, and at £195 for the Special Coupé, the Morris Ten was fully competitive with the Minx and the Austin Ten-Four. In its first year a healthy 14,080 were made, representing 32 per cent of Morris output and helping push 9hp–10hp registrations in 1933 to a substantial 34 per cent of the UK market.

Improvements for 1934 – and a new 'six'

For 1934 the Ten remained physically unchanged, but under the skin it was considerably modified. Not least, it received a new cruciform chassis, in common with all the bigger Morrises, whilst the gearbox was given synchromesh on third and top. Aiding refinement, the engine and gearbox received 'equipoise' rubber mountings, comprising two rubber mounts at the front and a single transverse mount at the rear. There was also a more rigid barrel-grip handbrake with a different mechanism and a push-button release. Other detailed mechanical improvements included automatic advance and retard, pear-shaped Armstrong hydraulic dampers, transversely mounted at the front, check straps for the rear axle, and a more accessible oil filler that migrated from low down on the engine block to a position on top of the timing-chain cover. Arguably less of an improvement was a switch from a single 12-volt battery to a pair of 6-volt units, a change necessitated by the revised chassis; presumably also as a result of this, there was a new round petrol tank that fell in capacity from 7 gallons to

6½ gallons. Inside, meanwhile, there were larger seats, with leather now used across the range.

New for 1934 was an open two-seater with dickey and a Commercial Traveller's Saloon, but the arrival of these further body styles was overshadowed by the simultaneous launch of a new six-cylinder Ten. Tapping into the vogue for small-capacity 'sixes', the Ten-Six had a pocket-sized 12hp 1378cc unit derived from the existing four-cylinder engine but with both bore and stroke reduced. 'This engine obtains a further measure of silkiness in a new resilient mounting at the rear end and has excellent acceleration and a maximum speed in the neighbourhood of 65mph, which undoubtedly places it in the very forefront of small Sixes, whether considered as a value-for-money proposition, or putting aside considerations of cost altogether,' trumpeted

A surviving Ten-Six Special Coupé. From this angle the only giveaway to its identity is the 'Six' badge on the radiator stoneguard. (Ewen Macdonald/Morris Register)

The Ten-Six engine was again a side-valve unit disguised by a fume-consumer false rocker-cover. The large cylindrical object on the bulkhead is the SU Petrolift pump. (Author's collection)

The Traveller's saloon was new for 1934, and was available as both a Ten-Four and a Ten-Six. The latter, as the regular Ten-Sixes, had a metal spare-wheel cover. (BMIHT)

Another 1934 introduction was the two-seater with dickey. The dickey was upholstered in Rexine, whereas the main bench was in leather. (Author's collection)

The two-seater in four-cylinder guise was the cheapest Ten, at £165 in 1934, against £169.10s (£169.50) for a fixed-head saloon or a tourer. Hood-up, the tourer looks much like a shrunken version of the bigger Morris tourers. (Author's collection)

The Morris Owner. The reality was slightly less stellar: the saloon tested by *The Autocar* recorded a maximum of 59.2mph, against 57.3mph for the Ten-Four, with a 0–50mph time of 33.4 seconds, against 33.6 seconds for the four-cylinder car. The time for 20–40mph in top gear was barely much better either, at 18.4 seconds for the Ten-Six compared to 19 seconds for the Ten-Four. Maybe, though, it was less what the small 'six' achieved than how it achieved it: tests talk of a smooth and relatively revvy engine.

Built on a wheelbase extended by six inches, the regular Ten-Six was listed with the same range of coachwork as the four-cylinder model, which was re-baptised the Ten-Four. Other than

a longer bonnet, the only distinguishing feature – 'Six' badge on the grille excepted – was the use of a metal cover for the spare wheel, as on all Morris 'sixes'. Alongside the mainstream Ten-Six there was, however, something of a novelty on offer: a sporting variant available either in chassis form or as a low-slung open four-seater.

Called the Ten-Six Special, the newcomer featured twin SU carburettors on a special inlet manifold, an SU electric pump, a remote gearchange, metal Hardy-Spicer propshaft joints, and a Burgess straight-through silencer. The cylinder head was also polished, the compression ratio raised, and a high-lift camshaft fitted. In tune with these enhancements there was a special sloped radiator shell with a stoneguard and bigger Lucas Biflex headlamps (again with stoneguards), mounted on pillars with triangulated cross-bracing; additionally there were twin horns and an apron below the radiator. With a racy dual-cowl scuttle and fake knock-on hubcaps, the Special had a certain allure, and was the first supposedly sporting Morris since the Sports Cowley of a decade earlier. Quite why such a car should have been introduced is another matter, given that Morris already had the Wolseley Hornet Special sitting in virtually the same niche – not to mention a range of more sporting MGs. Perhaps it was simply that it enabled fuller coverage of that sector of the market, for a relatively limited investment; a more uncharitable analysis might be that the Morris was introduced as a way of new Cowley MD Leonard Lord thumbing his nose at his disliked opposite number at Wolseley, Oliver Boden.

Sales, perhaps unsurprisingly, were modest, with a total of 336 being made, through to the end of Ten-Six production. Various coachbuilders bodied the chassis, the best-known being Cunard, who produced a more rakish interpretation of the factory four-seat tourer. A Ten-Four Special was also supposedly to be offered, according to press reports, but this never materialised.

The Ten-Four and Ten-Six carried on into the 1935 model year, physically unchanged but for the addition of a curved radiator stoneguard similar to that worn by the 1934 model-year Minors, and the incorporation of the combined bumper and luggage grid assembly that was again a Ten-and-upwards feature of all the '35 range. It thus benefitted from sundry detail improvements shared with sister cars. These included a new pull-up handbrake lever, larger (4.75 x 18in) tyres, a right-hand accelerator

Two-tone colour schemes with a black upper body were introduced for 1935. Clearly visible on this Ten-Four is the radiator stoneguard of '34 and '35 Tens; the horn tucked down on the right-hand side is not an original fitting. Single-bar bumpers replaced twin-bar units for 1934. (Author)

pedal, rubberised Karvel carpet, and a Rollsvisor sun visor. Additionally there was now an SU L-type electric pump in place of the cumbersome and not particularly reliable Petrolift used until then.

When production of the 'perpendicular' Ten-Four and Ten-Six stopped in April 1935, a total of 49,138 had been made. That was comfortably ahead of the number of post-Flatnose Cowleys produced over a year-longer period. Meanwhile, Austin, beginning earlier than Morris but also ending earlier, manufactured 53,692 of its first series of Ten before a restyled range took over in autumn 1934. As for the Hillman Minx, that lagged behind, with 43,306 of the original 'upright' type being made between 1931 and 1935. In other words, the Ten was a success for Morris. In the judgement of Reggie Hanks, it was the model that "saved their bacon" and "a nice job" that showed how the company had learnt from its past mistakes. Unfortunately this was not to the greater glory of Arthur Rowse. "I never got any thanks for it, but a kick in the pants," he told Andrews and Brunner. What in fact happened was that the Ten caused Rowse's resignation from Morris Motors, in April 1933.

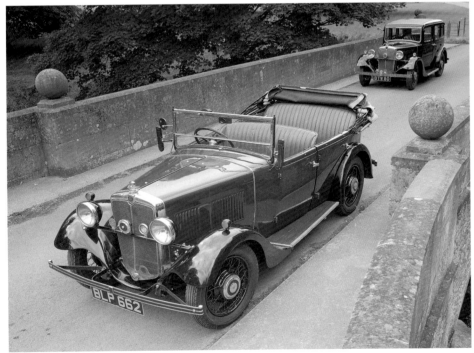

These two Ten-Fours are from the 1935 season; to the front is an open tourer. Whatever the body style, the four-cylinder Tens were good for just short of 60mph, and would cruise happily at around 45–50mph, whilst returning something in the order of 33–34mpg. (Mark Dixon)

Two typical Morris press photos from the time of the Ten launch, showing the only two body styles at first offered. The Special Coupé had a sliding roof as standard. (BMIHT/ author's collection)

As Rowse hints, there was more to the story than this. According to Hans Landstad the fuel pipe problem, hardly in any case the direct responsibility of Rowse, was a pretext, talked up by Smallbone and Seaward – and apparently also by Miles Thomas. Whilst Rowse was in America after the launch of the Ten, these three, along with Blake and Keen, used their influence to convince Morris that there was nothing right with the model. Behind this was some unpleasant political manoeuvering whereby they sought to curry favour with Morris by engineering Rowse's departure, knowing as they did that Sir William had taken a dislike to his Production Director. In very large part this was because Morris, with his habitual insecurity, felt that Whitworth scholar Rowse – 'a man of considerable academic training and with a practical bent to his thinking' according to Miles Thomas[1] – was guilty of being condescending towards him. "Rowse was a very clever technical man… [He] came up from almost nothing and he was proud of his academic knowledge and not averse to shouting it around," Reggie Hanks told Andrews and Brunner. "Nuffield talked in terms of mild steel and Rowse in terms of 3 per cent nickel steel, which Nuffield did not understand, and it was like a red rag to a bull." Miles Thomas confirmed this analysis. "Rowse was a good man and a charming fellow – terrifically capable. But the fundamental reason for Rowse going was that they had a spot of wheel-wobble on the Morris Six and over the lunch-table Rowse tried to explain to Morris what were the causes of gyroscopic 'flick'. He tried to explain it in baby terms to a man not understanding the maths or engineering. Rowse made the mistake of talking down to his boss, and that planted the seeds of [his] going out."

There were other trivial matters. Rowse fitted up his office with carpet and a posh fire grate; he spent firm's money on an elaborate 'progress board'. But above all – and this was the ultimate reason for his downfall – he had supposedly undeclared interests in a business that supplied Morris Motors. A while previously there had been problems with the availability of forgings in the motor industry and Austin had suggested to Rowse forming a small company to make their own forgings. Rowse had spoken to Morris, who said he did not wish to join such a venture but had no objection to Rowse becoming involved on a personal basis.

Rowse thought that because he had talked about this with Morris that no further action

Politics and personalities: the departure of Rowse

Well conceived though it undoubtedly was, at launch the Ten suffered from a fuel pipe that was prone to breaking. Putting loops in the pipe to absorb movement didn't work, but after a short while a move to a flexible pipe provided a solution. However, the market was depressed at the time, and William Morris, unimpressed by the Ten's sales take-up, dwelt unfairly on this minor teething problem, according to Rowse. "All he knew was that it was very difficult to sell cars and all I produced was petrol pipes which broke. The criticism was a valid one. We jumped to it as quickly as we could, and in the ordinary way the thing would have been forgotten."

[1] Out on A Wing

A factory Ten-Six Sports Special; with every sporting accessory – down to a leather bonnet strap – it was certainly not under-dressed. The model was variously referred to in the press as the Ten-Six Sports Tourer, the Ten-Six Special and the Ten-Six Special Sports, but the catalogue appellation was Sports Special. (Author)

The dashboard was unique to the Sports Special and included a combined speedometer and rev-counter. 'Every car is individually assembled in a special factory by men who have made fast cars their life's study,' the catalogue proclaimed, somewhat implausibly. (Mark Dixon)

The Cunard-bodied Sports Special has running boards, a deeper cutaway to the doors and a more rounded tail. (Author)

The dashboard uses the same instruments and switchgear as the factory Sports Special, but disposed differently. (Author)

was required. However, there was an obligation to inform the company secretary, Andrew Walsh, of any shareholdings directors held in outside companies, and Rowse had neglected to do this. Smallbone in particular worried away at Morris about this supposed breach of company protocol, accusing Rowse of improperly enriching himself on the side, and in the end Rowse was obliged to fall on his sword, over what Landstad termed a purely 'trumped-up' charge. "I seem to be very unpopular. I had better put my hat and coat on and go," he is reported as having said. Equally telling is the terseness of his resignation letter to Morris: clearly there was no love lost between the two men.

Not for the first or the last time, a manager of quality had been lost as a result of a lack of vision

The engine is dressed up with a chrome-plated 'fume-consumer' and polished-alloy intakes for the twin SUs. Output was not quoted, but if the 36bhp claimed for the Ten-Four version is any guide, then an increase in power of roughly 25 per cent would seem in order. (Author)

The pillarless Stork saloon on the Ten-Six Sports Special chassis was the work of Kew-based John Charles, and was sold by Moon's Garage in London and by Surrey's Woodcote Motor Company. It was said to have 'special reinforced steel girder construction'. The same coachbuilder also offered a Stork Sports Two-Seater (right) on the Sports Special chassis. (Author's collection)

and a smallness of spirit on the part of William Morris. In *Out on a Wing* Miles Thomas described Rowse as 'a brilliant production engineer' and as a man of great intellect 'who wrung more value out of component suppliers by organizing their production methods than has ever been recognised'. Although condemned by Morris

Commissioned by Liverpool Morris dealer W Watson and Co, this four-light Sports Special saloon was built by Carbodies and retailed at £285 in 1934. (LAT)

Jarvis of Wimbledon offered this three-position Sports Special drophead (with possible coupé de ville position for the hood); the body was by Abbey Coachworks. Price was £293.10s (£293.50) as a Ten-Six and £279 was quoted for a version based on the Ten-Four Sports Special chassis. (LAT)

Another offering from Watson on the Ten-Six Sport Special chassis, this sliding-head coupé was again the work of Carbodies and had a price of £275 in 1934. There was a choice of walnut, mahogany or piano-black interior woodwork. Look closely and you can see how the body is an adaptation of the four-light Carbodies saloon shown above. (LAT)

as being "far too technical" in his approach, in the opinion of Thomas he would have made a far better second-in-command than Blake, and indeed had been acting "in functional fact" as the company's senior executive. "Rowse was one of the geniuses behind this company," concurred future Nuffield Metal Products director George Dono, who went on to tell Andrews and Brunner that Rowse's conduct regarding the forgings company was "all quite honourable".

Rowse apparently had a nervous breakdown after leaving Cowley, but recovered to become a successful businessman-engineer, involved with several companies, one of which was to supply Morris with the grille for the post-war MO-series Oxford. Nuffield, meanwhile, continued to think ill of him, telling Andrews and Brunner that he had played "rather a shabby trick" over the forgings company and that his conduct was "the rottenest stuff on record". Rowse, meanwhile, ended up phlegmatic about his departure from Morris, saying that he owed his life to Lord Nuffield – because had he stayed at Morris he would surely have died on the job. "Life at Cowley would drive you to the grave," he commented.

Life after the Flatnose – the 1932–35 Cowley

If Rowse had pointed the company towards the future with the Ten, past glories continued to be represented by the Cowley. Some in senior management, such as Reggie Hanks, thought that it should be killed off, but it had its

Presumably a pre-production model, this 1932 four-light Cowley coupé wears artillery wheels, whereas Magna wires were catalogued equipment. (LAT)

From the rear the two-seater Cowley really does look like an American roadster. The model was not offered for 1934, being effectively replaced – at the same price of £165 – by the Ten-Four two-seater. (Eric Miller/Morris Register)

prominent defenders, not least William Morris himself and Edgar Blake. The latter told Hanks that there could be no question of dropping such a totemic model, as the whole business had been built up on it. Hanks retorted that if they weren't careful the company would die on it too. Notwithstanding this school of thought, the Cowley was re-modelled for the 1932 season, as mentioned earlier, and carried on until the Series II range was introduced in 1935.

Moving away from the shoebox lines of the Flatnose, the '32 Cowley was completely restyled, with an 'Eddyfree' body and a chassis shared with the second-series Major introduced at the same time. The venerable 'Hotchkiss' engine, derived from the Continental unit of the original 1916 Cowley, received duralumin con-rods and a

The fixed-head Cowley saloon came without bumpers and luggage grid. The solid painting of the waistline fillet is a feature of '32 models only, as are the unvalanced mudguards. For 1933 the waistline fillet was pinstriped and the mudguards were skirted. (Author's collection)

The Sports Coupé was the only Cowley to have window louvres. For 1933 the model was renamed the Special Coupé. (Author's collection)

For its final season the Cowley was renamed the Twelve-Four. The absence of a lamp bar across the grille is an identication point, a detail shared with the '35 Major. (BMIHT)

Renamed the Cowley-Four for 1934, the body of the Cowley – now offered only as a fixed-head or sliding-head saloon – was less upright than before; underneath was a new cruciform chassis. This advertisement targeted women drivers. (Author's collection)

more efficient cylinder head, hidden underneath Morris's 'fume-consumer' false rocker cover; customers could specify either a 11.9hp or a 13.9hp engine, at the same price. Other improvements included a rear tank, feeding the habitual SU carburettor via a Petrolift, Lockheed hydraulic brakes, and ignition by coil instead of the archaic magneto used until then.

Changes for 1933 largely mirrored those for other Morris models, with the arrival of the valanced wings first seen on the '32 Isis and the incorporation of a 'twin top' four-speed gearbox. Additionally the 11.9hp engine became the sole power unit, in the process being given a chain drive to the camshaft and a distributor conventionally driven by shaft and skew gears from the camshaft. Grab straps on the door pillars and silk-cord door pulls meanwhile furnished a lift to the interior.

As with all models but the Minor, the Cowley duly received a cruciform chassis for 1934, along with synchromesh on third and top and a further restyling of the body. In common with the Major, this brought with it the abandonment of torque-tube transmission in favour of an open propshaft with metal Hardy-Spicer universal joints.

Referred to as the Cowley-Four to distinguish it from the re-named Major, the Cowley was now only available as a fixed-head or sliding-head

The Cowley-derived Light Van was completely re-jigged for 1934, even if the body was largely as before. (Automobile Association via Tom Bourne)

The continual sweep of the roofline identifies this van as a '35 model. This was the final year of the regular car-derived Light Van. (Morris Register)

THE COWLEY-DERIVED LIGHT VANS

As the Cowley evolved, so it was inevitable that the second generation of 8cwt Light Van would move away from its Flatnose derivation. This happened with a two-year delay, just as the move to a Flatnose radiator had lagged behind the passenger cars.

It was thus for the 1934 season that the van was remodelled, being given a new lower-slung chassis based on that of the 1932 and 1933 Cowley – with which it shared its rearmost three cross-members. As a consequence of the van not moving onto the cruciform chassis of '34 Cowleys, it retained torque-tube transmission. The dampers remained of the old-fashioned friction type, but the fuel tank moved to the rear – the carburettor being fed at first by a Petrolift and latterly by an SU pump – and the brakes at last became hydraulic. Following the restyle for 1933 the body was largely unchanged, but for the incorporation of the 1932–33 style of Cowley radiator shell and slight modifications to the front doors, scuttle and windscreen; however, as a result of a move from artillery wheels to Magna wires it did suddenly look a lot more modern. As a further bonus, it was now offered in blue, black, brown or green, as well as shop grey, whilst the payload was redesignated as 8/10cwt.

Despite this updating, for the 1935 model year there was a largely new Light Van, even though this was destined to be current for only one season. Known as the TWV, the new model had a redesigned body with a curved straight-through roofline and the 1934–35 style of radiator grille. More importantly, it was given the revised 11.9hp T-series engine, with its pressure-fed big ends and chain-driven camshaft, as introduced on the 1933 Cowley. Cubic capacity thus dropped from 1802cc to 1548cc, bringing with it a shedding of 3bhp in exchange for lower Road Tax; in compensation a four-speed gearbox was now fitted. Whilst on the surface it might appear pointless to have revised the van just for one year of sales, the actual investment cannot have been too significant, as the wood-framed bodies demanded no special tooling and the mechanicals all came from the Cowley parts-bin.

saloon, whilst the Cowley-Six, formerly the Major, could be obtained with the four-light coupé coachwork of the bigger Morrises.

For its last few months of existence, as a 1935 model, the Cowley was re-named the Twelve-Four, and could be distinguished from the previous year's car by the absence of a lamp bar across the front of the radiator grille. A curved edge to the rear armrests was a minor interior enhancement shared with the Fifteen-Six; other changes included a right-hand throttle pedal, improved dampers and brakes, a revised luggage grid integral with the bumper, and a Rollsvisor roller-sunvisor.

Whilst it is certainly clear that Morris's centre of gravity had shifted – with that of the market – to the smaller 10hp class, keeping a presence in the 12hp sector with a rejuvenated Cowley was in no way misguided. Production of 24,205 in the two model years 1932 and 1933 evidently

compared poorly with the 16,786 Cowleys made in the final Flatnose season of 1931. The restyled 1934/35 cars added an estimated 7985 to the tally. That amounts to an approximate total of 32,190, commercial derivatives included, over three and a half seasons, making the last two generations of Cowley the company's third-best-selling line, after the Minor and the Ten. It pays to recall that in the same period fewer than 3500 examples of the Isis and Twenty-Five were made.

In 1935 Vehicle Developments Ltd of London was offering its Osborne cabriolet body on the Ten-Six Sports Special, Twelve-Four and Fifteen-Six chassis. Described by The Morris Owner as having 'sheer beauty of line and resplendent finish', the coachwork was said to have a particularly robust construction, with pressed-steel pillars welded to the sills. (Author's collection)

The Eight

Two Series I saloons, both
fixed-head; the two-door at the
front has been in one family's
ownership since new, and
other than a respray in 1981 is
totally original. (Mark Dixon)

else, the main task facing Lord was to modernize the Cowley works. Without this, new models could not be produced efficiently.

During the preceding years the factory had grown piecemeal. In the 1920s most of the investment had gone to Morris's newly-acquired subsidiaries, although a new body-mounting and finishing plant had been installed in 1928, following the arrival of Pressed Steel bodies. Further planned investments had been put on hold as the arrival of the slump had caused a reining-in of capital expenditure. Now there was to be a big spend: £300,000 – some sources quote £250,000 – in 1934 alone. Morris had the resources to do this because he had been ploughing profits back into the firm: as an illustration of this, 35 per cent of net earnings were retained in the business in the 1929–38 period, against 32 per cent at Austin and 22 per cent at Ford. Morris might have been in the mire, but he did at least have the financial firepower to pull himself out. The poor sales year of 1933, with deliveries their second-lowest since 1934, was a help, with slacker production making it easier to carry out the rebuild of the Cowley works.

The main investment was in a moving assembly line where previously the chassis had been pushed along from work-station to work-station. The new facilities had four parallel lines fed by a claimed 12 miles of conveyor belts and by overhead electric cranes called Telphers. Morris was not alone, of course, in making such investments at this time. Standard was similarly putting down moving assembly lines, and Austin would further expand its facilities in 1936; in

This unusually professional-looking shooting brake has a drop-down tailgate and a roll-up canvas upper section. (Morris Register)

One of three known surviving Jensen-bodied Eights. To achieve its low-slung lines the regular Morris bulkhead was cut-and-shut. Priced at £165, the body reportedly cost Jensen £20 to make. Some cars went to Michael McEvoy, who sold them with his tuning packages. (Author)

Cunard's Foursome Coupé, retailing at £185 in 1934, was similar to the dropheads it offered on other Morris chassis; it was alloy-panelled over an ash frame. There was a conventional rear bench seat in the leather-trimmed interior. One example is known to have survived. (John Seddon)

A certain number of wireless cars were built for the War Department; they had a higher hood and just a single front seat. (BMIHT)

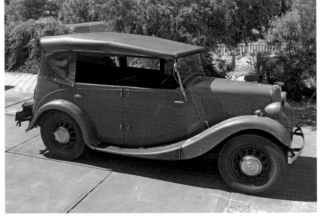

This marvellous Australian catalogue image shows artwork doctored to depict a four-light saloon; whether any such cars were built is not known. In Australia the Eight was called the 8/40. (Kerry Kaehne)

Four-door tourer bodywork on the Morris Eight was unique to Australia. This example is by Bryan's Motor Body Works of Perth, for Comet Motors. (Kerry Kaehne)

Hopes Body Works in Brisbane was reponsible for this smart 8/40 roadster. There was also a similar coupé. (Kerry Kaehne)

France, André Citroën, following the example of Renault, completely rebuilt his main factory in 1933. All the same, with a capacity of 2000 cars per week Cowley was arguably now Europe's largest and most technically advanced motor factory. With workforce numbers largely static – 5500 workers in 1924, 6000 in 1932 and 5000 in 1934 – car production rose from nearly 33,000 in 1924 to just over 58,000 in 1934 and would hit a pre-war record of 96,500 units in 1935 .

This was achieved whilst retaining the system of satellite factories to provide engines, bodies, radiators and other key components – the exact opposite of Austin's in-house approach. Making a virtue out of this, a PR line was spun, giving this method of industrial organisation the term 'Specialisation' and loudly trumpeting its supposed advantages in product advertisements. Within the company this caused a certain amount of amusement. Talk of 'Specialisation' was 'hooey' according to Messrs Tobin and MacMahon, senior managers at Morris Garages – it was nothing more than 'a smart piece of journalism by [Miles] Thomas'.

Part of the Lord reorganization was a brief interlude where American methods were applied to the design process. Robert Boyle, formerly of Rover, moved from Engines Branch to become Chief Engineer at Morris Motors, effectively taking over the function previously exercised by Landstad, nominally the works director. Boyle was sent to the States to see how GM designed its cars, and came back an enthusiast of the General Motors practice of 'sectionalising', whereby each element of a car was designed by an independent team. As a result, at Cowley one engineer was given overall responsibility for back axles, another for front suspension, and so on. This approach had its advantages, but was hardly conducive to an integrated and coherent design process whereby a car was seen as a conceptual whole. The system did not survive the departure of Lord (see Chapter 15), being dismantled by his successor, Oliver Boden; Boyle returned to Engines Branch, and soon rejoined Rover.

Life-saver: arrival of the Morris Eight

The first fruit of the newly revitalized Cowley was the Morris Eight, announced in August 1934 after a crash period of development – "it took about 18 months to design that thing and get it into production," Lord told Andrews and Brunner. Despite its importance to the company's future, Morris himself kept his distance from the project,

said Lord – although his financial support was not in doubt. "Though [he] was worried about it, he never asked me about it. It had to be right when it was put on the market and we had all the money we wanted from him and he never questioned it. In fact, I doubt if he knew exactly what was spent."

Whatever was spent, it was spent wisely. Lord knew where the opposition lay. It wasn't with the Austin Seven. Rather it was with Ford, whose Model Y had been a genuine game-changer. It had rescued Ford in the UK, after a decade in which the marque had fallen from market dominance to near irrelevance, and had simultaneously redefined the market for small cars. With its sassy transatlantic lines, spacious body and 8hp engine, it had created a new sector for something larger, faster and more comfortable – and more stylish – than the Austin Seven and Morris Minor that had become the default choice for budget motorists. Keen pricing helped: at launch the £120 two-door had undercut the equivalent Minor by £2.10s and was a lot more car for the money. The Ford ended up taking over half the 7–8hp market in 1934, a highly impressive achievement, given that production had only begun in August 1932.

Thoughts of replacing the Minor with a model bearing an uncanny resemblance to Austin's future Seven Ruby were thus abandoned, in favour of a bigger car closely inspired by the Ford and built on a wheelbase a foot longer than that of a regular Minor. Not only was the body similarly styled to the 'Y' but the engine – all-new rather than derived from that of the Minor – was a direct crib of Dagenham's 933cc side-valve power unit. What happened was that the Morris Engines draughtsman tasked with drawing up the new power unit – future Jaguar engineer Claude Baily – was given a set of dimensions by the company's Inspection Department, dimensions that had been arrived at by no more involved a process than stripping down a Model Y engine and measuring its constituent parts.

The rest of the car was an exercise in straightforward conservative British engineering practice. The 918cc engine, developing 23.5bhp, had three main bearings as opposed to the Minor's two, and was mated to a three-speed gearbox via a dry clutch; a beam axle was retained at the front, with suspension by semi-elliptics controlled by Armstrong 'pear' hydraulic dampers; the brakes were hydraulic and the steering was by Morris's now-habitual Bishop

The Series II in a period PR photo. The car was mechanically unchanged compared to the SI; it seems that thought was given to fitting a four-speed gearbox, but that this was ruled out on cost grounds. (Author's collection)

Cover image for the SII catalogue. Although the duo-toning of the earlier Eights disappeared, the wings and headlamp shells remained in a black stoved finish. (Author's collection)

Open Eights such as this SII tourer were deservedly popular in both home and export markets; the Eight in all its passenger-car forms was Morris's fourth-best performer in export markets in 1937, with 26.4 per cent of production exported. (Author's collection)

Rather more conventional in style is this Morris Eight 'woodie' – photographed in the 1960s. (Morris Register)

MORRIS 8/40 SOLVES YOUR LIGHT DELIVERY PROBLEMS

SMART, fast, reliable—the Morris 8/40 Utility is the most economical Light Commercial Vehicle in Australia.

It runs for a penny a mile!

Bodies are well-built, handsome, skilfully designed to give you more than the usual amount of carrying capacity. There are four styles—each of which is illustrated in this leaflet—designed to fit the needs of every light delivery.

MORRIS 8/40 WITH ROADSTER FRONT

MORRIS 8/40 PANEL VAN

MORRIS 8/40 WITH COUPE FRONT

MORRIS 8/40 HALF VAN

FULL CHASSIS FRAME AND SPRINGING!

A FULL length box type chassis frame—a frame within a frame—ensures the maximum strength. So that your load will be properly cushioned, the Morris 8/40 is fitted with full length semi-elliptic springs.

A range of different vans and utilities were offered in New South Wales by firms such as York Motors. (Kerry Kaehne)

In Australia the most common locally-built saloon style was very like that of the 8hp Model Y Ford; a boomerang-shaped bumper was generally used. (Morris Register)

This Australian-built Series II Coupé Utility is particularly well executed. (Kerry Kaehne)

cam-and-peg. These mechanicals were installed in a ladder frame having a 7ft 6in wheelbase – one inch shorter than that of the four-door Minor. The open sides of the channel-section longitudinal members were to the outside – a slightly unconventional arrangement – and were boxed at their forward end.

If the Eight wasn't going to win points for technical sophistication, it had two important assets. Firstly, it was available in a wide range of body types, being offered as a two-door and a four-door saloon, with either a fixed head or a sliding roof, and as an open two-seater and a four-seat tourer; Ford, in contrast, offered no open version of the Model Y. Secondly, the Morris was arguably the best-looking small car on the market. The saloons had a crisp, pert elegance, with a chrome radiator shell and two-tone paint adding a touch of class. The open cars, meanwhile, had a sporting flavour that in later years tempted motoring historian Michael Sedgwick to call them 'operational trainers for the MG'. When Singer brought out its Eight-rivalling Bantam the Coventry firm's two-seater and tourer variants were in comparison hopelessly hamfisted.

With a wood-capped dashboard, more generous instrumentation than the 'Y' and details such as ruched map pockets and rear armrests, the Eight saloons could easily justify their £5 premium – in fixed-head form – over the equivalent Fords. That the open Morrises at one stage accounted for 15 per cent of Eight sales indicates in turn the appeal of the two-seater and tourer. Cowley did indeed have a much-needed winner on its hands: by August 1935 53,773 Eights had been sold, or more than the number of side-valve Minors produced over close-on four seasons.

From 'Pre-Series' to Series I and Series II

As its first year on sale drew to a close, the Eight was given Hardy-Spicer metal universal joints in place of the fabric couplings used until then. This coincided with the car being redesignated Series I, to fit in with the new 'Series' policy; this has led enthusiasts to give the preceding Eights the retrospective 'Pre-Series' tag. The only way of distinguishing a Series I from a 'Pre-Series' is to look at the badging: the legend on the radiator badge changed from 'Morris Eight' to 'Morris 8' and the mascot with its 'balanced power' motif was replaced by one carrying two enamelled '8' badges.

Although various small changes took place in the interim, it was only in September 1937 that the Eight was given a facelift. The new Series II model was mechanically as before, the Eight not receiving the four-speed gearbox and ohv engines of its bigger sisters. Cosmetically, however, it was brought into line with the revised Series III cars, being given a painted radiator shell, Easiclean wheels, and a range of single-tone colour schemes; the wings remained in black stove-enamel.

The Series II Eight was current only for one year. Ford had launched new Eight and Ten models during 1937 and Austin had finally started to edge away from its antiquated Seven with the July 1937 announcement of the 900cc Big Seven. Fashion had also moved on, and a trend towards more rounded lines meant that the Eight's taut styling was starting to appear outdated. That 59,000 Series II Eights were made in just one season proves that the car still had considerable appeal, but Cowley couldn't stand still. At the October 1938 Motor Show, a new Eight, the Series E, was introduced; in all, 220,937 of the first generation had been produced over four seasons – vans included – making the Eight the best-selling car in Britain during the later 1930s.

An Eight van was introduced during 1934. It did without bumpers, running boards, or such details as a bonnet mascot; additionally the wheels were spindly 18in small-hub items, rather than the 17in Magna rims of the cars. The panelling was of Plymax alloy-faced ply. (John Seddon)

This half-door van was built in Australia by Gilbert Motor Bodies, one of three firms in Adelaide who bodied 8/40 Morrises. (Kerry Kaehne)

Cunard built this high-top van for London Transport. The top of the part-canvas booth folds down against the rear of the body. (John Seddon)

The 'Series' models

The biggest of the Special
Coupés, the Twenty-Five,
here in Duotone grey; the
other choice, black apart,
was Sports Blue. (BMIHT)

The range of larger cars found a new coherence with the arrival of the 'Series' models. During this time the company was restructured – and Leonard Lord left, slamming the door behind him.

After the Eight, the next stage in the re-making of Morris's range came in May 1935, when the so-called Series II Ten-Four and Twelve-Four were introduced. To be followed by four – ultimately five – related six-cylinder models, they formed part of a company-wide product-rationalisation programme the essentials of which had been put in place in 18 months. Not least, four new families of engines, three with both side-valve and pushrod variants, were put into production, along with their associated gearboxes, both three-speed and four-speed. This was some achievement, even if the design of the gearboxes had evidently being rushed, judging by their lack of reliability in service.

The new models heralded an ostensible change in policy. Henceforth, Morris cars would have a 'Series' identifier and would be modified as and when the company judged appropriate rather than at the beginning of each model year. Indeed, readers of *The Morris Owner* were assured, the Series II label would be retained 'for a considerable period'. No longer would there be a '1935 model' then a '1936 model' and so on.

In such a way the peaks and troughs in the annual sales pattern would be smoothed out: no more would there be a surge in purchases in March and April and a falling away at the end of the summer, ahead of the announcement of the new season's offerings. This indeed proved to be the case, with obvious benefits for Cowley both in achieving regularity of production and in assuring greater continuity of employment for its workers. Morris also trumpeted how the 'Series' system would make depreciation less severe[1]. Other manufacturers cried 'foul' – perhaps predictably – and said Morris had undermined the convention established by the SMMT that new models should properly be announced only from 13 August onwards.

This styling model from 1934 shows an almost definitive Series II – but note those flamboyant bonnet strakes. (BMIHT)

Built on an 8ft 4in wheelbase, four inches longer than that of its predecessor, the Ten Series II was claimed to be as big as an ordinary Fourteen. (Author's collection)

This view of a four-cylinder SII chassis clearly shows the welded-in floorpan, the tubular rear cross-member and the boxed-and-drilled side-members. (Author's collection)

[1] Andrews and Brunner quote figures for August 1935 as proof that the initiative worked. The previous best August had seen 2380 deliveries, of which 1450 were the next season's cars, built for dealer stock. In August 1935, by contrast, despatches rose to 7635 units. In 1938 Morris proclaimed that in the previous three years June to August had been the second-best-selling quarter of the year, wheres previously it had been the slackest period.

Simple engineering and good looks

As for the Series II Ten and Twelve, these were as astutely designed as the Eight, with straightforward mechanicals clothed in graceful fastback coachwork and a well-presented interior with a delightful art-deco Bakelite dashboard.

The six-light saloon bodies conformed to the fashion for 'aerodynamic' styling without being over-stated in any way, and gave the Morrises a litheness of line lacking in the more ponderous 'Flying' Standards of the same era. In comparison the Hillman Minx looked dull and the rival Austins positively frumpy.

In their engineering the cars were pragmatic. Gone was the cruciform chassis introduced across the Morris range with such fanfare for the

This surviving Ten clearly shows the first style of duotone paint. The Twelve was physically identical; at launch, it cost only £5 more. Both models were available with or without a sliding roof. (Mark Dixon)

The interior of a Ten – in fact a SIII, but the only visible difference is the arrival of side armrests. The rear heelboard hinges up to allow access to the back axle. (Author's collection)

As before, the Special Coupé was finished to a higher standard, with furniture-hide upholstery and burr walnut woodwork, as well as a sliding roof; this is a later Ten, with Easiclean wheels. (Mark Dixon)

On the Ten and Twelve Special Coupé there was an exuberant 'deco' look to the door trims and to the wood cappings that were unique to the coupés. (Mark Dixon)

only Morris Garages and Wolseley Aero Engines Ltd were left as private businesses within the Morris empire.

Regarding the garage business, it was apparently felt that it was undesirable for Morris Motors to own a distribution company in competition with private distributors – although such an arrangement was hardly unusual. Sentiment may also have played a part, as Morris Garages was Lord Nuffield's original business. As for Wolseley Aero Engines, this was a new concern, only established in 1935, and was yet to find its feet. In common with other such investments, Morris seemed to be following a policy of supporting the enterprise personally until it had been built up into a viable entity.

Now that Morris was delegating day-to-day management, it was clearly desirable to unify control of all his businesses, something that was already underway as a result of the 1933–34 reorganisation and the setting up of a central export company. But the changes were implemented for more than mere reasons of administrative tidiness. Significantly, too, the structural reforms were accompanied by the issuing of Ordinary shares in the company. These were 'placed' – at a cost of some criticism in City quarters[3]. Only a quarter of the company's Ordinary stock was offered, Morris retaining the rest himself, whether personally or through charitable trusts. The shares all sold at a strong premium, reflecting Morris's wisdom in riding out the recession before offering the shares in a more buoyant Stock Market.

There were various motivations behind this financial remodelling. One was that if all the Ordinary shares remained Morris's personal property there was a risk that tax law would force him into taking larger dividends than he might wish, in order for the company to avoid higher tax liabilities on its profits. Put another way, Morris might personally get richer, but the company's development would suffer from having less of its profits ploughed back. Miles Thomas provided Andrews and Brunner with another reason for the restructuring and its linked share issue. "What bothered the legal and financial pundits was that violent exception might be taken by shareholders to Sir William, as chairman of a public company, buying a considerable value of components from companies of which he was the private owner."

[3] Placing' is the practice of selling shares to a particular institution (in this case a 'jobber' rather than for example a merchant bank), for selling on into the hands of the public.

Morris replaced the Cowley-derived TWV 8/10cwt van in July 1935 with a more purpose-built semi-forward-control van, the TWV Series II. To allow a short bonnet, the 12hp engine and four-speed gearbox were offset, so the driver could sit further forward. (Author's collection)

Another feature was a rear track 4in wider than that at the front, less readily apparent on this ambulance by Cunard. (John Seddon)

A dropside truck joined the van in June 1938, and production continued until 1940; later versions had Easiclean wheels and in van form lost their rear spats. (Author's collection)

By the end of the 1930s 'woody' station wagons were coming into vogue; in 1937 Stewart and Ardern offered this charming Cunard-built 'Utility Car' on the 8/10cwt van chassis; the body could be in stained walnut, oak or ash to choice. (John Seddon)

This delightful streamlined 8/10cwt van was a Cunard creation, for Rayline polishes – 'As used by the Royal College of Surgeons'. The price was £130 in primer. (John Seddon)

FEBRUARY-1937
VOL.XIII
Nº 12

The
MORRIS
OWNER
4ᴰ

During 1936 the lower coloured element of the duotone SII paint scheme was extended to take in the whole lower body, wings excepted. (Ken Martin collection)

Photographed in the Barton Motor Company showrooms in Plymouth is this Series II on Easicleans. (Richard Barton)

Arguments such as this were kept from the public. "We saw they were not forcibly fed with facts," commented Thomas.

Equally, the public was not appraised in detail of another key explanation for the share issue: that it freed up large sums of money for Morris to spend on his multitudinous charitable activities, putting as much as perhaps £20m at his disposal. The part-flotation represented, said Thomas, a 'nodal date' in Morris's personal fortune. Doubtless aware of the potential for adverse publicity relating to his multi-millionaire status, at the same time Morris redirected some of his gains back to his personnel: in early 1937 he set up a special trust with one million Ordinary shares, dividends from these going to his hourly-paid employees as a bonus on top of their wages.

With strong new products, a rationalized three-marque model range, more efficient factories and a tidier financial structure, the effect on the bottom line was bound to be positive – and all the more so as the economy was now growing strongly. The results of this activity were indeed gratifying. Profit before tax jumped from £844,000 in 1933 to £1,168,000 in 1935, and in 1936 reached £2,182,000, including 16 months of trading for Wolseley and MG and 17 months for Morris Industries Exports. Morris's net profits – after tax – had been re-balanced and in the 1932–36 period amounted to a little shy of £4.5m, against roughly £2.7m for Austin and a smattering above £1m for Ford over a shorter

1932–35 span. At the same time the Morris share of the British market had risen from that lowly 20 per cent of 1933 to 31 per cent in 1935. With over 108,000 Morris cars sold in 12 months, crowed a December 1935 advertisement, 'Britain's motor industry has never before known such sensational figures as these – because British motoring has never before known such a sensational policy as Morris-Specialisation.'

Changes for 1937: a return to four speeds

In conformity with the expressed strategy of no longer having annual modifications to its products, the specification of the Series IIs was unchanged for the 1936 Motor Show; the range itself was, however, reduced in size, with the Sixteen and Twenty-One being deleted. There were also new colour schemes on display, although these had in fact been introduced earlier in the year: the duo-toning now extended to take in the whole of the lower part of the main body.

Observing the letter if not the spirit of the 'no seasonal changes' policy, in November that year it was announced that henceforth all but the Twenty-Five could be equipped with a four-speed gearbox. A sleight of hand was involved here. If you decided not to have the hitherto-standard Jackall hydraulic jacking system, there was no extra charge for the new gearbox. You could thus choose to have a three-speed Jackall-equipped car or a four-speeder without Jackalls. What if you wanted both four speeds *and* the integral jacking? Such picky customers could place a special order, and for an extra £5 Cowley would build them a car equipped with these two items. Simultaneously, Easiclean wheels, shod with ELP ('Extra Low Pressure') tyres, became a no-cost option – and this time there was no catch. Such questions became academic in the early months of 1937, when the four-speed gearbox – without the Jackalls – became standard equipment, along with the Easicleans.

High drama – the departure of Leonard Lord

By this time Leonard Lord was observing such changes from the sidelines. In August 1936 he had broken with William Morris, and left the company – "in a tantrum" according to George Dono. Observers were shocked: Lord's departure was described by *The Motor* as 'quite the biggest sensation in the motor industry for some years'.

It has always been understood that Lord's departure was because he had requested a share of the profits that were being generated largely as a result of his own endeavours, and was not prepared to accept Morris's refusal to entertain this. "I make the money. He just sits there and does nothing," Lord was reported as observing to Sir John Conybeare.

Whatever other factors may have intruded (see next page), there is no reason to doubt that a difference of opinion over profit-sharing was indeed at the heart of the dispute: this has been acknowledged by various sources, and not least by Miles Thomas, who in *Out on a Wing* retails the oft-quoted remark by a bruised post-departure Leonard Lord that he was 'going to take that business at Cowley apart brick by bloody brick'. According to Thomas, Lord requested a salary 'which was quite surprisingly high' and a percentage of all profits over and above a figure that at the time was not being realised but which had been achieved in previous years; Thomas calculated that this would have put a tidy £1m in his pocket. Conybeare said that Lord also proposed a profit-sharing scheme for employees and that "this was very greatly resented" by Lord Nuffield – even if he was to introduce just such a scheme not many months later.

So it was that on 24 August 1936 Leonard Lord resigned from Morris Motors. Paid in full to the end of that year, he went off travelling, not least spending time in the United States studying the latest in American production methods. On his return, perhaps proving that the split had not been wholly antagonistic, Lord Nuffield put him in charge of his Special Areas Trust (see page 284).

Lord's annual salary of £5000 – perhaps £150,000 in today's money – was apparently considerably in excess of what he had been paid as MD of Morris Motors. If this was intended to keep him away from the competition, it didn't work: in February 1938 Lord was asked to join Austin, with a free hand to revitalize the Longbridge concern in much the same way as he had turned around the Morris business. According to the memoirs of Lord Swinton, Air Minister at the time, the government had brokered the move, as it wanted Lord's production expertise to be at the service of the shadow-factory scheme, in which Austin was playing a leading role.

Lord later recalled how the two companies differed in their approach to remuneration. 'When the question of salary came up, [Lord] Austin said, "Well, we want him to do my job, so he should get what I am paid"... But that was the difference between them – Austin with the whole jackpot. Nuffield was very mean over his staff's salaries. Cowley had been a very unhappy place, with low salaries and a lot of jealousy between people.'

Whatever arguments there may or may not have been over money, William Morris had let another top-flight manager go. For Kimpton Smallbone, the departure of Lord constituted the biggest loss the company had ever suffered. In his opinion, Lord "had saved the business" – an analysis with which it is difficult to disagree.

A well-known but eloquent picture, from 1935, showing Morris with Leonard Lord, at the time not yet 40 years old. "Lord was a similar type to Morris, a very dynamic man with complete confidence in himself and not prepared not to have his own way," observed Sir John Conybeare. (Author's collection)

In their biography of Morris, Andrews and Brunner gloss over the reasons for Lord's departure – hardly surprisingly, given that Nuffield's own account (see below) was economical with the truth and that at one stage he had wanted neither to mention Lord by name nor dwell on his resignation. They wrote with elliptical blandness that the parting 'was due to Lord's personal decision, one factor in which was that he had begun to think of a break from active management now that he had done what he had set out to do at Morris's'.

Lord himself had however gone into some detail for the two authors. He told them that the issue came about when Morris, by now getting old, began to think of floating the company, as a way of avoiding the business being broken up for death duties after he had died. He asked Lord 'to run the whole show' and was dismayed when Lord said that in that case he wanted a share in the business.

"Nuffield got angry and said that no one was going to have that. So [I] said to Nuffield [that] if that were so, [we] should part. Nuffield said 'Haven't I paid you enough?' and [I] said to Nuffield 'You paid me what you thought my worth was.' [I] asked if Nuffield considered he had overpaid [me], because in that case [I] would write a cheque for it. Nuffield said no..." According to Lord there were "no policy or production problems" and the dispute "happened quite suddenly and we were quite friendly afterwards". In this account, Nuffield then asked Lord what he was going to do and Lord said he had always had the idea of recharging his batteries at 40. He had a bit of money saved and a young wife and they were going to travel.

There is evidence that the break was messier than this version of events suggests. Miles Thomas recounts that in a bid to reconcile the two men Wilfred Hobbs, Nuffield's personal secretary, journeyed back and forth between Cowley and the Isle of Wight where Lord had gone for a holiday break. Whether this shuttle diplomacy was at Lord's behest or that of Nuffield is not known. When interviewed by Andrews and Brunner, Lord Nuffield said that Lord immediately went to see Hobbs "and said he did not mean a word he had said – but that was no good".

If the testimony of Sir George Kenning is any guide, it may well be that Lord repented of his demand for a share of profits. According to Kenning, Lord went to see him and said he had made a mistake and wanted his job back. He then asked the longstanding Morris distributor to intercede on his behalf. This was fruitless, Nuffield saying to Kenning that when a man had left he would never have him back.

However clean or however fraught it was, the departure of Lord may well have had various explanations, as opposed to the single one most commonly given. Firstly, political intrigue may have played a part, doubtless fuelled by the fact that Lord's brusque manner did not always make him friends. Perhaps significantly, amongst those with whom he had antagonistic relations was fellow director Harry Seaward. "Seaward helped to get Lord out," Kimpton Smallbone told Andrews and Brunner. "He... was quite untrustworthy and bit the hand that fed him."

There was also the small matter of Lord showing an improper interest in a young lady in the drawing office. Having surprised the two in Lord's office, Smallbone made allusion to this over lunch, and Hans Landstad and another director apparently reported his remarks back to Lord. As Smallbone's wife had already started to spread tittle-tattle about Lord's friendship with the lady in question, there is every possibility that word reached Lord Nuffield, possibly via Lady Nuffield. Always a conduit for Cowley gossip, she was a well-known prude who would have been sure to have talked up the affair to Lord's detriment.

According to Miles Thomas, this was a time when Nuffield was in a certain mental turmoil about his own role, and this story can only have further influenced how Nuffield perceived his thrusting young Managing Director. After about 1934, said Thomas, he started to become "awfully unpredictable" in his handling of senior executives, because the business had grown "at a rate faster than his personal capacity to handle that type of business [had grown]". He remained a mechanic, "whereas the business demanded engineering ability and directorship".

It was during this period, Thomas told Andrews and Brunner, that Nuffield began to suffer "a sort of psychological conflict with himself, because he knew the business was slipping out of his control, and he made rather desperate efforts to call the thing back into his own control". In the opinion of Thomas, this was what informed the quarrel with Lord. "Lord wanted to go ahead and do this and that, and the stamp of Lord is still visible at Cowley today. But when Nuffield saw that Lord was doing things on his own and taking decisions and being impatient, then the psychological conflict came into operation, which was bad for the business."

One particular area where Lord had taken particular positions, only to find himself countermanded by Nuffield, was in a high-profile dispute with the government over aero-engines, as discussed in more detail in Chapter 17. In essence, Lord had supported the government scheme for the motor industry to build Bristol aircraft engines in secondary or 'shadow' factories paid for by the state. Wolseley was to be one of the seven car manufacturers involved. Lord Nuffield, who rather than participating in the 'shadow' scheme wanted the government instead to buy his Wolseley aero-engines, returned in spring 1936 from one of his overseas trips, forced Lord to pull Wolseley out of the shadow-factory scheme in the early summer, and ultimately, in a fit of petulance, closed Wolseley Aero Engines Ltd. It is impossible to believe that the tensions between the two men during this affair cannot have contributed to the final rupture.

Nuffield's own account is disingenuous. He told Andrews and Brunner that he had given Lord £50,000 in cash "as a present for his work in putting the business right" and that subsequent to this Lord had said he wanted to leave to set up on his own account. According to the transcript of one of the Andrews/Brunner interviews, 'Lord had announced that he wanted to leave very shortly after getting his £50,000. We said that we had heard that he asked for a share in the business, but Nuffield said no, that without any preparation whatever he came in and said he was going to take six months holiday and then start on his own. Nuffield asked him when he was going to hand over the keys. Lord hesitated and then Nuffield said "You need not worry; you have given them now."...'

Further complicating any definitive assessment of what really happened, there is conflicting information about this £50,000, which is perhaps equivalent to £2.8m in today's money. Nuffield's version implies that Lord was either ungrateful or merely following his own agenda, in that he supposedly asked to leave just after he had been given a substantial bonus. However, Robert Jackson's colourful account has Nuffield offering him the £50,000 after the two had agreed to part company – making the sum look like a golden handshake, or quite possibly an attempt to buy Lord's loyalty so that he wouldn't go to work for the competition.

Although Jackson should not be treated as a reliable source, there is an entry for £50,000 to Leonard Lord in Nuffield's hand-written 'Donation Book' – and here the waters muddy a little. The book seems to have been set up retrospectively, in 1938, and significantly it dates the donation to Lord to 1935. However, the entry is in a washable blue ink, whereas all the other entries for the 1935–36 period are in a blue-black. Could it have been added later, deliberately to mislead by suggesting that the donation was before rather than after the row, and thus that this had nothing to do with an argument over Lord wanting a share in the business?

Charles Nichols of instrument supplier Smiths said it had broken his heart when Lord had left; as far as he was concerned, the two people Nuffield should never have let go were Leonard Lord and Arthur Rowse.

Last of the line: the Series III cars

It was therefore under the jurisdiction of a new Vice-Chairman, Oliver Boden, that the next evolution of the family of larger Morrises took place. This was the arrival, in September 1937, of a brand-new Twelve Series III (see Chapter 16) and a revised Ten, Fourteen and Twenty-Five also carrying the Series III appellation. The Eighteen, which had never sold well, was deleted, in half-hearted application of a policy agreed upon at a January 1937 board meeting.

Henceforth, it had been decided, there would be no sub-12hp Wolseleys and Morris would make no cars of over 14hp – thereby restricting badge-engineered Morrises and Wolseleys to the 12hp and 14hp models and leaving Wolseley to field up-market – and higher-profit – cars in the higher-horsepower classes. The continued existence of the Morris Twenty-Five cut across this policy, which would in any case be further compromised in coming years.

With Easiclean wheels and four-speed gearboxes having already been standardised on later versions of the Series II, the main change was the fitment of the overhead-valve engines previously used in the Wolseleys. In the Ten the new power unit – shared with the MG TA and the Wolseley Ten – delivered 37.5bhp at 4500rpm. That of the Fourteen, meanwhile, pushed out 51.25bhp at 4200rpm and could also be found in the 14hp Wolseley and the Morris-Commercial Super-Six taxi-cab, whilst the Twenty-Five, not shared with any other vehicle, mustered a beefy 95.4bhp at 3800rpm in new pushrod format.

Externally the only changes were that the radiator shell was now painted and the cars were finished in a single colour, with all but those in black having the wings and wheels in a slightly different shade. This was in fact making a virtue of a necessity, as the wings were painted in synthetic lacquer, and this more resistant finish was less easy to match to the cellulose used on the main body. Additionally the Twenty-Five was given horizontal chrome strips on the bonnet sides and received an external-access boot, the latter feature being extended to the Fourteen a short time later.

Turning to more detailed changes, trafficators

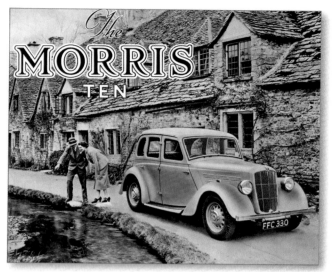

The cover of the SIII Ten catalogue features a typically Nuffield scene, taken in the Cotswolds; but in fact it is a fake, with the car superimposed on a photo previously used to illustrate a Pre-Series or Series I Eight. (Author's collection)

This catalogue image shows the range of single-tone colours available on the SIII Fourteen; the Ten and Twenty-Five came in the same range of shades. Subsequently on the Fourteen the Grey was replaced by Beige with Brown wings. (Author's collection)

The interior of the Fourteen had a flat rear floor – as opposed to the footwells of the Ten/Twelve – and there was a centre armrest at the rear, and wood door cappings to match the dashboard. Other details include a luggage net and cord assist straps. (Author's collection)

In 1938 Whittingham and Mitchel offered this four-seat tourer on the Ten SIII chassis; the sidescreens were stowed behind the rear seat squab and the hood was concealed when folded. (LAT)

became self-cancelling and across the range the electrics gained compensated voltage control. The six-cylinder cars were also given lids for the gloveboxes, and wipers with a hidden motor (with an independent control for the passenger); they also now had a centre folding armrest at the rear, along with an adjustable steering column on the Twenty-Five. The Jackall integral hydraulic jacking system remained a £5 option on the two smaller models but was now standard

on the Twenty-Five; both this and the Fourteen, finally, were now only offered with a sliding head. In this form they would continue until the war stopped production in October 1940.

In a market slightly down on the previous year, these changes kept the key 10hp variant in contention, although an output of 13,721 cars for 1938 suggests that as it entered its fourth season it was starting to lose its appeal. As for the Series III Fourteen and Twenty-Five, in two seasons the combined total for the two models would fetch out at 4940 cars, against 18,391 of the five different Series II 'sixes' that had been made in a little over two model years. The message was clear: Morris's six-cylinder models were of dubious commercial worth. That much had been apparent, indeed, for some while: in 1937 the Twenty-Five accounted for roughly 0.8 per cent of Cowley output.

Looking at the overall picture, Morris's total

EXPORTS: ADDING UP THE NUMBERS

In SIII form the Fourteen sold less well in export markets. Series III cars in black continued to have their wheels and wings stove-enamelled, as opposed to being finished in synthetic enamel. (Morris Register).

Exports began to play an increasing part in Morris's business during the 1930s. Sales outside Britain increased year-on-year by more than 50 per cent in 1931 and continued on an upwards trajectory, helped by the July 1933 formation of Morris Exports Ltd to control exports of all products of the Morris group. At the Morris Motors AGM in May 1936, Morris was able to announce that exports for 1935 had risen 57 per cent over 1934 and in the current year were up 139 per cent over 1933 and 188 per cent over 1932.

The saleability of the 'Series' models was a key factor in this performance. Fortunately export figures for 1937–39 survive, in the Miles Thomas papers held by BMIHT, and their analysis makes interesting reading. Firstly, they show that exports rose from 15 per cent of output in 1935 to 22 per cent in 1938, falling back to 21 per cent in 1939.

Take 1937, and in pure numbers the Eight was the best-seller in export markets, representing 13,196 cars out of a total of 19,030 Morrises exported, equivalent to 69.3 per cent. The next best was the Twelve, with 2223 examples exported, followed by the Fourteen, with 1262 cars sold abroad. But

in terms of the percentage of a particular model exported, the clear winner was the Twenty-Five, with 527 cars or 73.4 per cent of output exported in 1937. In comparison, 31.8 per cent of Twelves, 28 per cent of Fourteens and 26.4 per cent of Eights went overseas.

Comparative figures for 1937 and 1938 have a different statistical base. Take the two years together, and the Eight accounted for 68.6 per cent of exports, the Ten for 6.8 per cent, and the Twelve for 17.4 per cent. Turning to the six-cylinder cars, the Fourteen accounted for 4.6 per cent of exports in the two years and the Twenty-Five for 2 per cent.

Look at the trends, though, and one sees the Eight's share of exports dropping slightly, by 6.4 per cent, over the two years, but the Ten's share rising from 4 per cent to 10 per cent, and that of the Twelve from 13.8 per cent to 21.7 per cent. In contrast, the Fourteen's share of exports fell from 6.7 per cent to 2 per cent and that of the Twenty-Five from 2.8 per cent to 1 per cent. This reinforces the conclusion that the bigger Morrises had become a dead duck in the export market – and bear in mind that for the 25hp model there was no other market. Given that in 1937 you could buy a Ford V8 for £359 in Australia, or a Chevrolet for £349, you would have to have been a dyed-in-the-wool Empire loyalist to want to spend £399 on a Morris Fourteen. In the Dutch East Indies, meanwhile, the Chevrolet was retailing at 2250 guilders, against a Morris Twelve at 2450 guilders.

One final bit of number-crunching confirms that Australia and New Zealand were the major overseas territories for Morris, with 56 per cent of all Eights exported going to these countries in 1937 – and a whacking 84.8 per cent of Twenty-Fives, represented by 441 cars for Australia and a paltry six for New Zealand. Outside Europe, India (including Burma and Ceylon) and South Africa were the next most important markets, with the Eight again being far and away the best seller.

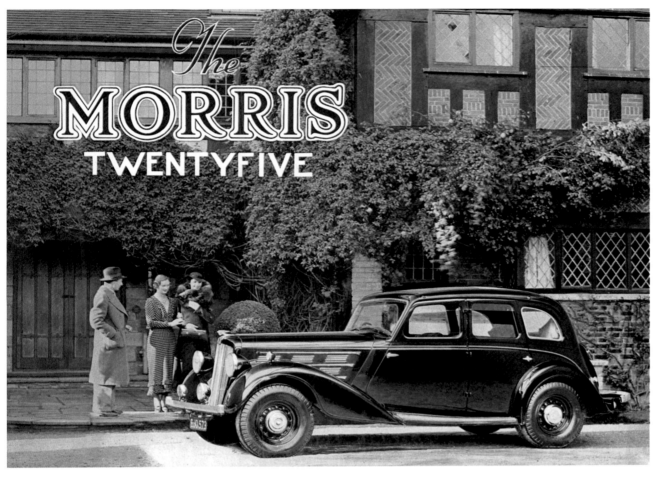

The MORRIS TWENTYFIVE

As well as the sober new look, the SIII Twenty-Five now had an ohv engine: in the hands of The Motor it proved good for over 75mph, and recorded a 0–50mph time of 14.4 seconds. (Author's collection)

The SIII Twenty-Five received an opening boot at launch; the Fourteen (shown) was given one a little later. (Morris Register)

For the Series III 'sixes' – reduced to just the Fourteen and the Twenty-Five – the dashboard (here on a Twenty-Five) gained glovebox lids. (BMIHT)

The SIII Twenty-Five interior remained classily up-market, with splendid sunburst patterns on the door trims and more ornate wood cappings; the rear foot-rail was standard on all 16hp-and-up 'Series' saloons. (Author's collection)

sales in 1938 were down from 89,859 to 72,925 units. This represented a drop of 18.9 per cent when the British market that took most of its cars had fallen by a less steep 12 per cent after the record-breaking previous year, a pre-war best for private-car registrations. The company appeared as if it were losing traction yet again.

To be fair, competition was now fiercer, with Rootes having become a major player, Standard having raised its game, and Vauxhall having completed its transition to a mass-market manufacturer. Ford, meanwhile, had reimposed itself with its 8hp and 10hp models, and seen its market share rise from 3.9 per cent in 1929 to 20.4 per cent in 1936. With re-designed Eights and Tens having arrived from Ford during 1937, along with a technically advanced Ten from Vauxhall, it was hardly a surprise that Cowley had found the going more difficult in the 1938 model year, even with its new Twelve. But would it recover its form during 1939?

The Series E, the Series M and the SIII Twelve

The Series E in tourer form, in Castle Combe village; as before, the windscreen on open Eights folded flat. (BMIHT)

Three new Morrises were introduced in the 1937–1938 period, all to a greater or lesser degree more modern than the cars they replaced. Lord Nuffield also bought the Riley company. But the model range was losing focus.

Modernity and the British motor industry hardly went hand-in-hand during the early and middle 1930s. While independent front suspension had become the norm in Europe and integral construction, front-wheel drive and even independent rear suspension were increasingly on the menu, back in the United Kingdom the customer was still being served up a tepid dish of beam axles, separate chassis, and as likely as not mechanical brakes and side-valve engines. At least Morris had espoused hydraulic brakes from 1931 and had shifted largely to overhead valves in 1937, which is more than could be said for arch-conservative Austin, or indeed for Ford. But there was nothing to match the technological buzz offered by Citroën's Traction Avant, or even the German Adlers and DKWs.

New but not innovatory: the Series III Twelve

All that started to change in October 1937, when Vauxhall completed its transformation into a mass-producer by entering the most important sector of the market with an all-new 10hp model. It was no Traction Avant, but the Type H Vauxhall offered the British buyer of an affordable 'Ten' a raft of modern features: overhead valves, hydraulic brakes, independent front suspension and – above all – the first chassis-less unitary body produced by one of the 'Big Six'.

Morris, meanwhile, had nothing as adventurous to tempt the public at the 1937 Motor Show. It did have a new model, but at first glance it was difficult to see the Series III Twelve as advancing the game in any meaningful way. That is perhaps to sell the car short. If the new Twelve was resolutely conventional, it was intelligently executed, with many clever evolutions of established practice that resulted in a refined and competent 1½-litre saloon.

The Twelve was still built on a separate chassis, but the new frame was a platform type with integral welded-in floorpan. Diagonal bracing around the engine reinforced the front end and in the same way as the Morris Eight and the preceding 'Series' models the body sills

Back in 1936 these proposals for a new Eight (top) and a new Ten (bottom) had the two cars sharing the same basic body: not a stupid idea. The artwork was the work of a French stylist at Cowley by the name of Stella. (BMIHT)

mated with the chassis side-members to form a double box-section. A substantial pressed-steel bulkhead added further strength, and the radiator and shell formed a unit with the front wings. All this resulted in a front structure sufficiently rigid to allow the harmonic stabiliser bumper of previous models to be eliminated.

Upright and not notably graceful, relative to the Series II Ten/Twelve, the new body had a slightly more forward-positioned radiator, which allowed the wheelbase to be shrunk by 4in, to exactly 8ft. This and the less rakish lines gave the car a little more internal room – literally an inch here, an inch there – but above all liberated space for a bigger external-access boot within the same 13ft 4in overall length as the Series II. Claimed to have a 10cu ft capacity, the new boot could be augmented by using the lid as a luggage platform. Body details included a separate spare-wheel compartment, opening rear quarter-lights, and ventpane-equipped front windows that could be counter-wound part of a turn to give a ventilation slot at their forward edge.

First 'new generation' car off the blocks, the Twelve SIII was conservative in its lines – and its engineering. (Mark Dixon)

The sober lines of the SIII are most apparent in this view. The rear numberplate is slightly concave, supposedly to allow it to receive even illumination. (Author's collection)

The dashboard with its high-set instruments and full-width parcel shelf was proclaimed as innovatory; the finish was in imitation wood. (Author's collection)

A more upright rear seat in the SIII Twelve allowed a little extra headroom and legroom within the same overall length – plus a bigger boot. A folding centre armrest was standard. (Author's collection)

Roadster and coupé versions of the SIII Twelve were available in Australia. (Rob Dowthwaite)

Described in the press as being all-new, the engine was in fact the overhead-valve version of the side-valve SII 12hp unit – in other words the engine previously used in the 12/48 Wolseley. There were, however, detail differences, not least the use of a conventional vertically-mounted SU, rather than the on-its-side downdraught unit found on the Wolseley; additionally the air silencer intake extended some way below the carburettor, to act as a balance pipe to smooth out the flow of air. Elaborate rubber engine mounts and diagonally disposed gearbox mounts were designed to limit engine vibration and avoid gearlever flutter; as for the gearbox itself, this was a supposedly new four-speed unit with improved synchromesh, and was adapted to a new clutch that was of the dry-plate rather than cork-in-oil type.

All these efforts to create a more refined car seem to have paid off. In its test *The Autocar* highlighted this very aspect, describing the new Twelve as 'quiet, noticeably free of vibration, and yet possessed of eager acceleration'. The engine, 'if it had any vibrations, was particularly well able to conceal the fact,' it continued, before commenting on how the interior was 'very quiet' when travelling. In terms of performance the magazine found the SIII to be 30 per cent faster to 50mph than its side-valve predecessor, and to have a top speed roughly 10mph higher, at 68mph. Accurate steering and a feeling of stability were also praised, as was the sense of spaciousness imparted by the 'open-plan' dashboard with its high-set instruments.

Absent presence:
Nuffield passes control to Boden

Where was William Morris in all this? The short answer is that he wasn't anywhere very much at all: he was either abroad or busying himself with his philanthropic interests, which had become a dominant part of his life in the post-flotation years. As a public figure, ever ready to give his opinion on matters of economic importance, he was as visible as one would expect the country's most prominent industrialist to be, but within the company his role was diminished. Andrews and Brunner summarise the situation succinctly. 'In this period Nuffield was increasingly remote from day-to-day management,' they write. 'The business had been overhauled and integrated and put into a commanding position in its market. He now left it to his managers to run. He met them regularly round the lunch table and, in general, he expected them to consult, or conform to, his wishes on major policies; otherwise, he was available to settle any internal disputes.' Richard Overy puts it differently: 'He accepted the usurpation of his throne for the sake of the survival of the enterprise,' he writes in his biography.

Day-to-day management was thus in the hands of Oliver Boden, who had under him four principal MDs: Harold Ryder at Radiators, Harry Seaward at Morris, Miles Thomas at Wolseley and John Shaw at Engines. Reports are mixed on Boden, an ex-Vickers man inherited with Wolseley. According to Miles Thomas, in *Out*

The bland grille on this 1937 mock-up for the Series M Ten does it no favours. The bonnet-side flashes were carried through to production. (BMIHT)

The unit-construction Series M body was built around this pressed-steel platform. (BMIHT)

The resultant shell was sufficiently light to shave 3cwt from the Ten's weight, relative to a SIII model. (Author's collection)

on a Wing, he was 'a trained practical engineer and an effective executive... very hard-working, highly competent technically, and completely devoid of intrigue'. Kimpton Smallbone – who by all accounts could not be regarded as 'completely devoid of intrigue' – had a different view. Boden was "a rotter and had got a commission on everything which went into Wolseley", he told Andrews and Brunner.

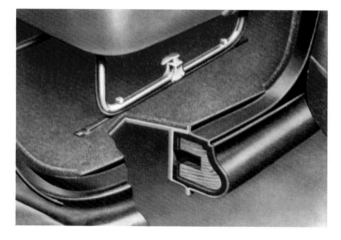

The earliest Series M known to the Morris Register. The blue is correct; other than black, the 'M' was also available in Green, Maroon, and a rather striking Beige with contrasting light brown wings. (Mark Dixon)

On a Maroon Series M the wheels would have matched the coachwork. Back in 1940, one proud owner of an 'M' was the exiled Emperor of Abyssinia – and future Rastafarian cult figure – Haile Selassie, then living in Bath. (Classic and Sports Car)

The all-steel construction of the Series M wasn't quite that: there was wood in the sills. (Author's collection)

The dashboard of the Series M was of bakelite with a fake-wood painted-steel instrument panel. The dials were as the Series E, with the addition of a clock. (Author's collection)

John Howlett, founder of the Wellworthy piston-rings company, came to value Boden as a friend. But on occasion he had found him abrupt to the point of rudeness, abusive and abrasive in his management style, and even 'out of control'. This was a sure sign, he wrote in his memoirs, that Boden had been pushing himself too hard and for too long, as 'he expected from himself every bit as much as Morris expected, which is saying quite a lot'.

Howlett recalled Boden having told him how Morris had rung him up one night to offer him the vice-chairmanship and how Boden had accepted despite his misgivings. "There's going to be a lot of heads rolling over some botch-ups, car engines in commercial vehicles, that sort of thing," Boden said to Howlett. "[Morris is] as keen for it as anyone else when he thinks it'll cut a few corners and then, when the birds come home to roost, he blames the people that let him do it. Yes, the heads will be rolling soon and part of my job, if I take it, will be to cut them off.."

When Howlett teased Boden about his own belief in keeping people on their toes and keeping them alert, Boden's reply gave a revealing insight into the management turmoil beneath the surface at Cowley. "[You] can't run an organization like one of those children's counting games and shout 'Out goes HE' every five minutes or so; people don't feel safe any more. They're alert all right, they're so alert that half of them can't sleep at night, and the other half are running around trying to make sure that someone else cops it first."

Unit construction arrives at Cowley

The Series III Twelve clearly signalled that Morris was starting out on a process of range renewal, so it was evident that the facelifted and now ohv-powered Series III Ten would have a short life. So it proved, when in September 1938 a wholly re-thought 10hp model, the Series M Ten, was duly announced.

The Series M, with its stodgily uncharismatic lines, was aesthetically something of a comedown

of a hybrid, having the new engine but the old three-speed gearbox. To allow the two to mate, the crankshaft was, however, the previous non-counterbalanced type, only fitted with shell big-end bearings.

By this stage there was no question of the Post Office being supplied with more Minor-based 5cwt vans, so the GPO leapfrogged straight to the Series Z. There was obviously some hesitancy, as the first 150 carried specially-commissioned coachbuilt bodies by Duple. Thereafter, however, the Post Office used the regular Series Z, albeit with certain specific modifications. These included carriage-type door handles, external bonnet catches, metal door inner facings, a fuel-tank stoneguard, and the deletion of fripperies such as the chrome strip on the bonnet top and down the radiator shell.

So it was that Morris entered 1939 with a trio of new or near-new models aimed at the centre of gravity of both home and export markets. On the cards, quite conceivably, was a new 14hp model for a 1940 launch, if a 1939-dated photograph of a mock-up is any guide; but with limited – and falling – sales of the existing Fourteen it is possible that this project would never have seen the light of day, war or no war. The worm was indeed turning against the penny-packet production of larger-capacity Morrises. A report on a wartime meeting to discuss future policy records Harold Ryder as saying 'I have always thought that the higher horsepowers are a nuisance to the Works.' On this there was apparently no dissent. 'This was an opinion which was unanimously agreed upon,' it was noted.

Further acquisitions: the purchase of Riley

Meanwhile, the new cars had an additional stablemate within the Morris group: in September 1938 Lord Nuffield had finalised the purchase of Riley, which had fallen into receivership thanks

to the usual cocktail of poor management, too many models, and the distractions of a motor-sport programme. Why should Nuffield have spent £143,000 to acquire the respected Coventry maker of sports cars and sporting saloons, when he already had MG in exactly that sector of the market? That was a question asked by many at MG, who were reported to be less than pleased with the acquisition.

The Post Office ordered a batch of these coachbuilt Series Z vans before settling down with the production all-steel type. (Ken Martin collection)

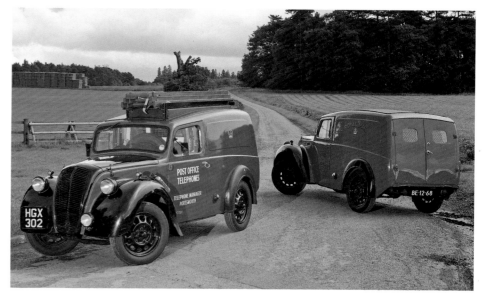

Two Post Office Series Z vans, with an engineer's van to the fore. The last left GPO service as late as 1964. (Mark Dixon)

Announced at the same time as the 'Z' was a new 10cwt semi-forward-control Series Y van (left), again of all-steel construction. The engine remained an 11.9hp side-valve. (Author)

The Series Y was also used by the Post Office, who took 34,117 for postal services and 605 for telephone engineers; this is a special linesman's van. (Author)

Not obviously related to any other Morris, this proposal for a new Fourteen dates from 1939. The Americanised front is certainly striking. (BMIHT)

Doing well – or losing focus?

Between them, the Eight, Ten and Twelve naturally enough accounted for most of Morris's sales in 1939. Despite a messy end to the year with the declaration of war in September, total Cowley despatches were up from 72,925 units in 1938's depressed market to a slightly better 76,564. Exports, meanwhile, were largely static, rising from 15,819 to 16,076 units. Still, Lord Nuffield had the satisfaction in May of seeing the one millionth Morris car off the production lines, a first for a British firm.

Looking at the figures in more detail, 54,134 Series Es were made before the war curtailed production, suggesting that sales of the 'E' were honourable but no more. In fairness, the competition was tougher, with not just Ford's smart and spacious Eight in the ring but also Standard's Flying Eight – another new introduction for 1939 – and Austin's brand-new Eight, which arrived in February that year.

The Series M, however, looked a winner: in one year Cowley despatched 27,020 units, or roughly twice the 13,719 Series III Tens – admittedly a slightly stale model – that had been made over again just a single season. For the Twelve SIII the evidence is mixed. A total of 19,465 Series III Twelves were produced, over two seasons, meaning an average of roughly 9700 cars a year – well up on the 7000 or so mainly Series II Twelves sold in 1937. The SIII certainly got off to a good start, not least in export markets, where 12hp Morris sales jumped from 2648 cars in 1937 to 3388 a year later. However, the same set of figures, drawn up by Morris Industries Exports, shows that things went awry in 1939, with export sales of the Twelve dropping to an appreciably less impressive 1148 units. Meanwhile export sales of 10hp Morrises, which had surged from 757 units in 1937 to 1604 in 1938, effectively doubled again to 3192 units in 1939, on the back of the Series M Ten.

Unless during that year there was some bottleneck in supply of the Series III Twelve – and the author is not aware of one – then the conclusion to draw is obvious. In export markets the Series III initially pulled in the customers, but once the Series M Ten came along many evidently saw no reason to spend more money on a Twelve that was heavier, more old-fashioned and only barely faster.

If one breaks down the overall production figures it becomes clear that the Twelve was indeed a one-year wonder, in the home market

When Andrews and Brunner brought up the matter, Nuffield was not very illuminating. 'Asked why he bought Riley, he replied that [Victor] Riley came to him. He was beginning to take it easy, and he seemed to want to get rid of it. The Riley had always been a good car so he took it over.' Initially Riley remained the personal property of Lord Nuffield, but this suggested a conflict of interest, with his ownership of a company that could be regarded as being in competition with enterprises within the Morris group. He therefore swiftly re-sold Riley to Morris Motors, for a nominal £100, with Victor Riley remaining as Managing Director, with a seat on the Morris board. The short-term result was a brace of new Rileys rushed into production in 1939 and sharing some parts with Morrises and Wolseleys. They proved less than reliable and the former Riley service manager memorably described them as "one of the worst series of Rileys we ever built".

Rather more useful a business expansion was the establishment in 1939 of a new Pressings Branch in Birmingham, to complement the pressings operations of Radiators Branch. Built on land belonging to Wolseley and abutting the Wolseley factory, the works was intended to bring in-house more of the group's sub-contracted presswork, especially larger pressings.

as well as overseas: of those 19,465 cars that left Cowley, a full 11,059 were despatched in the 1937–38 model year, and only 8406 in the period from August 1938 until manufacture ended in August 1940.

There are more fundamental reasons, though, to regard the SIII Twelve as a misjudgement. Strangely, it was built on a different chassis from the new 12hp Wolseley launched at the same time, although it did share in essence its basic mechanicals with its Ward End sister. More to the point, it had little in common with the all-new unitary-construction 10hp Morris that would be introduced for the 1939 season: the canny rationalisation of Morris and Wolseley products represented by the Series II generation of cars seemed to be unravelling. Confirmation comes from the fact that in 1939 Wolseley introduced a new Ten of its own, with little commonality either with the Wolseley 12/48 or with one or other of the Morrises.

It is thus hard not to be of the opinion that the Twelve was symptomatic of a renewed drift and lack of focus at Cowley. The Nuffield organisation had in fact committed two cardinal errors. It had not forward-planned so that its heartland Eight, Ten and Twelve models could share the maximum number of components. Compounding this, Morris had then pitched two of its own models head-to-head with each other, giving customers a choice between the Ten and the Twelve in a contest that favoured the lower-priced car of the two.

Worse, at its AGM in May 1939 Morris admitted that its profit margins had been eroded by product improvements the higher cost of which had not been passed on to the consumer in the form of raised prices. Demand was said to have increased as a result – sales volumes in the first three months of the year had been a record – but all the same the company was handicapping its financial health on two levels.

At the very least it could surely have kept the preceding Twelve going another year, and then introduced a related Ten and Twelve based around the unitary 10M shell, thereby amortising the considerable costs of this body over two models rather than one. Perhaps having Wolseley's 10hp and 12hp models use the same structure might have been a rationalisation too far, but as a bare minimum Ward End's newcomers could have been differently-engined versions of a shared design. In contrast Ford had brought its Eight and Ten closer together by using broadly similar bodies and chassis, Austin's new 1939 cars

were to a greater or lesser degree related to each other, and Vauxhall had based its Twelve and Fourteen on the unit-construction shell of the H-type Ten. Over at Longbridge, Leonard Lord – who understood a thing or two about production efficiency – must have been scratching his head in perplexity.

THE NUFFIELD-NAPIER RECORD PLANE

The Nuffield-Napier. Heston Aircraft made the airframe, de Havilland the prop, and Dowty the undercarriage. (Peter Seymour collection)

In early 1938 Major Frank Halford, technical director of Napier, approached Lord Nuffield about regaining for Britain the air-speed record held by Italy since 1934, and which stood at 440mph. Halford judged the new Napier Sabre engine, to be used in the Hawker Typhoon and Tempest, to be suitable, and Nuffield agreed to contribute £16,000 towards manufacture of two planes, known variously as the Heston Type 5 and the Nuffield-Napier.

The project ran into many difficulties, and meanwhile in April 1939 Germany raised the record to 469mph. By the outbreak of war, the first machine was nearly ready. The Air Ministry permitted its completion but requested the cancellation of the second plane.

After taxi-ing trials in spring 1940, it was felt that 500mph might be within reach, but the Nuffield-Napier – suffering from overheating and proving difficult to control – crashed on its maiden flight in June and was badly damaged. Given the international situation and the lack of a back-up plane, the project was abandoned.

Morris in the Second World War

The Neptune amphibian was developed by
MCC; it was good for 5 knots on water and
18mph on land. (Ken Martin collection)

The Second World War saw the group involved in a huge range of activities. There was a new Vice-Chairman and a new name, but also prominent losses in management, and a controversial attempt at making Spitfires.

As a multi-factory manufacturing business at the forefront of British industry, the Morris group was inevitably going to play a pre-eminent role in the war economy, over and above the mere provision of wheeled – or tracked – military transport. So indeed it was, with the various arms of the combine producing everything from police haversacks to Cruiser tanks – but with one particular specialism, the repair or dismantling and recycling of aircraft. In the course of the war the number of factories under Morris control, direct or indirect, rose from 12 to 63 and there were 30,000 people on the payroll at VE Day, against 20,000 at the outbreak of war.

The record is an honourable one, although there is one episode that weighs heavily on Morris's reputation: the saga of the plant set up to produce the Spitfire fighter. As this was a notably high-profile affair, and one that had its roots in an equally significant public spat in pre-war years, it is perhaps best dealt with first.

Aero-engines and 'Shadow Factories'
To understand the story behind the Spitfire factory, it is necessary to wind the clock back to the late 1920s, when Morris had just bought Wolseley and when – in common with many others – he felt that the next big thing, after the arrival of the motor car, would be a growth in the use of private aircraft. With Wolseley already having a pedigree as a manufacturer of aero-engines in the First World War, in 1929 he asked the firm to develop a set of radial power units for light aircraft. By 1935 Wolseley Aero Engines Ltd, as the operation had become that year, was ready to introduce a full range of radials.

But the anticipated civilian market did not seem to be there. The company had therefore tried to interest the government in its engines, but to no avail. In mid-1935 Lord Nuffield intervened personally, suggesting to the Secretary of State for Air, Sir Philip Cunliffe-Lister, soon to become Lord Swinton, that the two meet. His approach was somewhat abruptly dismissed by Cunliffe-Lister, and Nuffield felt affronted. Eventually a meeting took place, in November,

Lord Nuffield in uniform, as Director-General of Maintenance at the Air Ministry. (Author's collection)

but did not bear fruit: the government did not judge the Wolseley engines sufficiently powerful, with one possible exception, and felt that the existing four aero-engine manufacturers with which it had contracted had more than enough capacity to cope with all eventual needs under its rearmament programme. When Nuffield offered as an alternative to acquire the licence to build Pratt & Whitney engines, or any other unit the Air Ministry specified, the suggestion was equally rejected. Nuffield reputedly left the meeting with the words "God help you in case of war". He then fired off a letter to Lord Weir, an adviser at the Ministry, saying that if the government didn't buy his radials he would close down Wolseley Aero Engines, after which he left for one of his cruises to Australia.

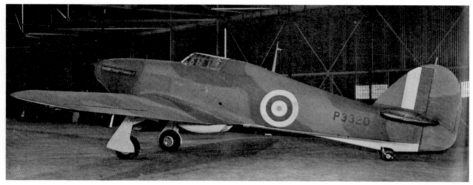

Before and after: a Hurricane that was rebuilt by 1 CRU at Cowley. (Author's collection)

In his absence the government forged ahead with its Shadow Factory scheme, as mentioned in Chapter 15. The scheme was launched in April 1936, and was rigidly constructed around the manufacture of Bristol aero-engines. Nuffield judged the concept flawed – or so he said – and felt that because he had a brand-new tooled-up factory to make aero-engines this should be used instead of new factories being set up at great government expense. Eventually he offered to make entire Bristol engines at Wolseley, but this proposal was also turned down. He then pulled the company out of the Shadow Factory scheme and took the decision to close down Wolseley Aero Engines. Ironically, at virtually the same time a government contract for the supply of 300 Scorpio engines was sent to the company, in what one assumes was a last-minute bridge-building gesture. Apparently brokered by Leonard Lord, the contract had arrived too late: by the time it reached his desk, Lord Nuffield had made up his mind.

This whole dispute was ventilated in public, with Lord Nuffield making a statement to the press and the matter being debated in Parliament. For *The Economist* the 'Nuffield-Swinton affair' was 'a major controversy of State' – and one from which Nuffield, whose grandstanding they did not appreciate, did not emerge creditably. 'One cannot read the published documents without gaining the impression that a certain dictatorial temper coloured Lord Nuffield's attitude to the whole question, and that at the same time less than the maximum possible tact was shown by the Air Ministry in overcoming this obstacle. It would also appear from the simultaneous changes of personnel and policy in the Morris organization that there was more than one school of thought among Lord Nuffield's subordinates,' it wrote, suggesting that in the matter of the Scorpio engines at the centre of the dispute Nuffield 'seems to have a very weak case'. The paper hoped that an independent enquiry would clear the air so that he could be brought into the tent – although 'not on his terms but on those of the Ministry'.

What was behind all this? Quite possibly a sincerely-held belief in the unsoundness of the Shadow Factory scheme; possibly also a desire by Lord Nuffield not to have his somewhat opaque personal finances pored over as part of the vetting procedure for the scheme. But there was also surely a desire to salvage something from an aero-engine venture that by 1936 had cost him personally an estimated £410,000 – not far shy of £20m in today's terms. If a juicy government contract could put money back in his purse, so much the better. Personality also entered into it, one can reasonably deduce. Nuffield expected to get his way, and was a touchy individual. He also didn't like being patronised, and it is quite likely that he felt the upper-class nabobs of the Air Ministry had condescended to him; that Cunliffe-Lister had suggested in his first letter that a dinner invitation was more important than meeting him can only have ruffled his feathers.

The Castle Bromwich affair

There was now a situation where Britain's top industrialist had refused to co-operate with the government – and a war was brewing. 'What an infernal nuisance these Captains of Industry are. They are temperamental almost to the extent of being female,' Air Chief Marshal Sir Cyril Newall memorably wrote to Swinton. The government sought a way to repair the breach, and when the more emollient Sir Kingsley Wood became Air Minister in 1938 a deal was stitched up with Nuffield – on his conditions and with no prior discussion in Cabinet. Nuffield was to build

Tiger Moths were produced at Cowley at a rate of 40 a week. (Author's collection)

and run a factory for large-scale production of the Spitfire, at a rate of 60 machines a week. The first purpose-built factory to mass-produce aircraft with semi-skilled labour, it would require substantial investment in jigs and tooling – and standardisation of componentry. The initial contract was for 1000 planes, and Nuffield stipulated, in a letter from Oliver Boden, who would be in day-to-day control, that 'there should be the minimum amount of interference... from the Air Ministry, to enable the position to be tackled in a somewhat different way to the present shadow scheme of the Ministry.' Not only was there to be no government interference, but Nuffield and Boden kept other company executives, including Miles Thomas, at arm's length.

A site was acquired at Castle Bromwich, purchased at what was said to be more than twice its market value, and construction began in July 1938. Two years later the factory was still not fully finished, estimated costs had doubled early on, and in the interim the government had come to discover that the whole venture was a continuing disaster. Boden, overworked trying to run the regular Morris businesses in tandem with Castle Bromwich, was buckling under the strain, and was to die of a heart attack in March 1940. Even before the Spitfire project he had not impressed Newall. 'He is old, looks flabby, is suffering from a swollen head and did not impress me at all as a mastermind or organizer,' the Air Marshal had written to Swinton in 1936. Meanwhile Lord Nuffield did not seem to know what was going on: "When you put Nuffield on

CASTLE BROMWICH: AN ALTERNATIVE VIEW

As a friend of Oliver Boden, John Howlett of piston-ring manufacturer Wellworthy observed at first hand his struggles at Castle Bromwich. 'He was on the site all the time, nursing that factory up from its foundations, planning it, cursing it, cursing himself – putting his very heart into the job and getting it done faster than anyone had believed possible. He spent every Sunday supervising the building, and for that purpose would return to Solihull on a Saturday night after he'd spent a day with me fishing,' recounts Howlett in his biography.

'It wasn't that things went wrong with the new Birmingham factory, but rather that the requirements kept changing all the time. First it was for sixty Spitfires a week, then for thirty so that bombers could be built as well. Then the Ministry couldn't decide on the type of bomber it wanted, drawings were changed and so on and the emphasis shifted to making parts for Vickers Supermarine. And there was Boden trying to get tooled up!...

'I saw very little of him in the early days of the war, but what I did see made me unhappy. The man was rushed off his feet... He was up to his ears with Air Ministry work, and he had no resources left... It made me angry the way Nuffield used people up... Only Len Lord and Arthur Rowse stood up to him and survived as free agents. Poor little Cecil Kimber was just one of the great majority who seemed to give their very souls into his keeping, and Nuffield, for all his great public benefactions, was a rather awkward sort of god in private.'

The prototype Cruiser tank, photographed in 1937; it was inspired by American practice. (Author's collection)

A MkI Light Reconnaissance Car dating from 1941. (BMIHT)

Then the situation changed. On 14 May 1940, by which stage not a single Spitfire had been built, the aggressive and abrasive Lord Beaverbrook was given charge of a new Ministry of Aircraft Production by Winston Churchill. Three days later he was on the phone to Nuffield, taking away from him the running of Castle Bromwich. Nuffield appealed to Churchill, gauchely citing the sums he had donated to the Conservative Party, but Churchill was unmoved.

Beaverbrook commissioned a report, from which a gruesome picture emerged. Building work was not yet complete, and an ineffectual architect and a bloody-minded and obstructive site foreman meant some construction work was almost at a standstill. Magnificent machine facilities were lying idle, along with huge amounts of materials. There was poor stock-keeping. Some parts had been needlessly re-tooled and others were still not in production. There was supine management and a lazy, skiving, ill-disciplined workforce, forever in dispute over money. 'It is, I regret to say, a picture of extravagance and an inability to understand the problem of aircraft production, coupled with an unwillingness to learn from those who do,' commented the writer of the report, an admittedly not disinterested Sir Richard Fairey, of the eponymous aircraft company.

Under the new government regime 195 Spitfires were delivered by the end of October, and ultimately nearly 12,000 Spitfires would be made at Castle Bromwich – more than half the total built. Nuffield's involvement had not been to his credit, and could have had grave consequences, as Leo McKinstry spells out in his history of the Spitfire, on which the author has drawn for much of the foregoing. 'Given Nuffield's promise to make 60 planes a week, the contract for 1000 Spitfires should have been easily fulfilled by the time the Battle of Britain reached its peak in September. If he had come anywhere near to meeting his pledge, the position of the RAF would have been transformed. Every squadron in the two front-line groups in the south of England could have been equipped with Spitfires, and there would have been enough for reserves and training... The "narrow margin" of the Battle was partly of Nuffield's creation.'

Nuffield and his senior management felt that much of the blame for this debacle lay with the constant changes in Spitfire specification, making it impossible to tool for production of parts. The abstraction of components by Vickers

the spot and asked him questions about the day-to-day running of the factory he just fell down," Reggie Hanks told Andrews and Brunner. Production was intended to start in April 1940, but that looked a forlorn hope.

Blame was on both sides. The technical drawings the factory needed were late and were constantly being altered, while at one stage the government, losing faith in the Spitfire, pondered on having Castle Bromwich produce another plane instead. Then, as the factory moved towards aircraft production, representatives from Supermarine, already building the Spitfire, started commandeering parts from Castle Bromwich. Meanwhile the inventory at the factory was a mess, with a large number of unbalanced sets of parts, plus huge stocks of raw materials. Vickers director Alexander Dunbar paid a visit and found the factory operating well under capacity. He wrote of 'a general slackness throughout the shops' and of 'the impression that employees were not really working because none of them knew what to do'.

was also cited as a factor. But even loyalist Miles Thomas admitted that 'Beaverbrook, of course, was right' to take control of Castle Bromwich, pointing out that one additional problem was that Boden simply did not bring in good production men from Morris to help him. Had men such as Woollard, Rowse and Lord been involved, perhaps the story would have been different, one can't help thinking. As it was, says Thomas, the Castle Bromwich affair in his opinion marked 'the turning point in Nuffield's personal career' – his chief 'had begun to sulk in his tent'.

Miles Thomas takes control

With the death of Boden, Miles Thomas was appointed Vice-Chairman in May 1940 – unexpectedly, he writes in *Out on a Wing*, as he had been envisaging the job going to Harold Ryder, whom he describes as 'a mature administrator in the Brummagen pattern'. Nuffield said he would 'leave it all' to Thomas but 'would like to know what was going on' – an arrangement that had Thomas seeing him once a week, for an hour and a quarter before lunch.

'It took me a long time to pick up all the threads,' writes Thomas. 'I sat down and tried to draw an organizational chart of what I was proposing to call "The Nuffield Organization"... The organization was far from tidy from the aspect of personnel. There were far too many faithful old servants who had done well in the early days when the whole business was run on personal first-name lines, but whose duties were now undefined. There was need for a much tauter control with proper lines of functional and administrative responsibilities.'

Repair and recycle – the CRO organization

Whilst the Castle Bromwich drama was playing out, Morris was developing a very different role in matters of aircraft. At the outbreak of war, Lord Nuffield had been asked to take control of all repair work for RAF, and was appointed Director-General of Maintenance at the Air Ministry. What was called the Civilian Repair Organization was then set up as a new unit of the RAF, under the civilian control of Morris Motors. A network of repair facilities was soon covering the country – ultimately 1500 in all – with No1 Civilian Repair Unit being at Cowley, based in the Car Despatch Department. A new Flight Shed was built, and a small airfield.

By the time of the Battle of Britain, there was a 1200-strong workforce, on a seven-day week. 1

The Salamander was a still-born amphibian with torsion-bar front suspension and 4WD. (Nuffield College archive)

The motorised canister in its second form had a seat for the driver. (BMIHT)

Rather more practical – and doubtless rather more fun – was this mini-DUKW amphibian. (BMIHT)

CRU was not just repairing planes, but was also cannibalising them to create one good plane from several damaged ones. During three key months of the Battle of Britain, it put 150 planes back into the air, with an average of 1800 man-hours put into each fighter. In the July–December 1940 period the CRO as a whole returned 4196 planes to battle – at about a third of the cost of a new plane. This was vital work, at a time when production of Spitfires had been hit by German bombing. In all, 35 per cent of aircraft issued to fighter squadrons during the Battle of Britain

CECIL KIMBER'S DISMISSAL

Slipped into a volume of Morris boardroom minutes is a single sheet of paper. It is the resignation letter of Cecil Kimber, dated 26 November 1941.

It opens with a coldly impersonal 'Sir' rather than a more personal 'Dear Lord Nuffield'. The letter simply reads: 'Will you please accept my resignation as a Director of the MG Car Company Limited and Morris Motors, Limited.' It is then signed 'Yours faithfully', with Kimber's characteristically neat

Lord Nuffield inspects an MG chassis on the assembly line at Abingdon, with Cecil Kimber in the background. (Author's collection)

signature in his trademark green ink. There is no reference to happy days creating and building up the Morris Garages marque, to shared memories of those pioneer times, immortalised by so many photos of the two men together, smiling for the camera. Kimber had been sacked, and he wasn't disposed, it is evident, to waste his time on niceties.

So how did this sad state of affairs come to pass? Esssentially because Kimber secured on his own initiative a government contract for MG to build the front section of the Albemarle bomber, at a time when Abingdon was scraping around for war work and reduced to making fish-frying pans and the like. Doubtless Kimber had exceeded his authority. But it seems that there were personal factors at play.

The Albemarle affair surely entered into things, but it was probably merely the final straw, in that for some time Kimber had been seen as exalting his own personality, and forgetting that within the Morris group there was only one hero to be worshipped – and that was Lord Nuffield. In particular, Kimber had run a series of very personal MG advertisements before the war, each one signed with his name. "He put all the directors at Cowley against the MG because of that," Carl Kingerlee told Andrews and Brunner. "Kimber... was tactless, and got so that he rather forgot that if it had not been for Lord Nuffield he would not have been able to do it.... It was Kimber says this and Kimber says that, and

he was advertising himself."

Miles Thomas, ever the courtier, would inevitably have picked up on Lord Nuffield's feelings on the matter, and the disgruntlement of other high-ups in the Cowley vipers nest. It is also pretty clear that Thomas did not warm to Kimber. According to former MG chief John Thornley, one of the things that irked Thomas was the very fact that Nuffield and Kimber got on so well together. "Kimber went on the basis of petty jealousy. I don't think there's any doubt about that," Thornley told the author. "Thomas was green-eyed about the extent to which 'Kim' had the Old Man's ear... Getting the aircraft contract gave Miles Thomas the excuse to fire him."

In *Out on a Wing* Thomas describes the sacking as 'the first of several unpleasant executive duties I had to perform'. Talking of the MG founder as an incorrigible individualist, he goes on to say that 'when Kimber wanted to maintain his acute individualism after the war had broken out and adopt a policy of nonconformity when he was supposed to be working to Ministry specifications it was clear that there must be change... I therefore went to see him at Abingdon in November 1941, and told him that he had better look for another outlet for his energies because he did not fit into the war-time pattern of the Nuffield Organization.'

He said that he felt sorry for Kimber. 'He was completely unorthodox, even in his domestic life, which did not endear him to Lord Nuffield or, in particular, to Lady Nuffield.' Thomas was alluding to what almost certainly was another element to the dismissal. Quite simply, Kimber had an affair, and then separated from Rene Kimber, at a time when his wife was seriously ill. He then married the object of his affections – a divorcee, to boot – a mere two months after Rene's death in April 1938. This would have been pretty racy by the standards of the time – and not least for Lady Nuffield, a notable prude.

Lord Nuffield was evasive when he received Kimber at Cowley. "He had me in his office for an hour...but he wouldn't let me get anywhere near the issue I'd come to talk to him about. He talked generalities for an hour," Kimber told Wellworthy's John Howlett. "He just kept me talking about things he wasn't interested in to stop me from saying what I'd come to say. And then he indicated it was time for me to go. He evaded me. He tiptoed all around me. He didn't give me a chance." It was presumably on closing the door after this fruitless interview that Kimber dictated that terse letter, heavy with unspoken words.

were repaired. Some aircraft were flown directly to Cowley by their pilots, for 'while-you-wait' repairs – and there were some that came back two or three times in a week. 1 CRU soon came to specialise in Spitfires, and could have up to 70 planes in at any given time; it also overhauled an average of 24 Lancaster engines per week.

Around the country other CRUs were set up, along with Repairable Equipment Depots to stock airframes, instruments, radio and signal equipment and the like, and distribute them for repair. RAF Maintenance Units were set up to bring in crashed planes, with the largest being run by Morris Motors. What was not repairable could of course be salvaged. Two major Metal and Produce Recovery Depots were set up by the Morris organization, one of these giant breaker's yards being at Cowley and the other at Eaglescliffe near Stockton-on-Tees. These salvaged metal, rubber, textiles, electric cable and other materials. Above all, though, there was a need for plentiful supplies of aluminium, and Cowley can claim to have pioneered its reclamation, through melting it down and removing its impurities.

The achievements of the CRO were impressive – 80,000-odd aircraft repaired during the war, for starters, and in all more than 16 million items of equipment repaired and returned to the RAF. What is not said in the history of the Morris group's war effort, *Calling All Arms*, is that while the work carried out at the Nuffield Organization plants was undoubtedly highly laudable, it is considered that the CRO only really became a dynamic and effective operation after Beaverbrook took control away from Lord Nuffield in 1940, along with the Spitfire factory, transferring responsibility from the Air Ministry to his new Ministry of Aircraft Production – at which stage Lord Nuffield ceased to be Director-General of Maintenance, a post that in any case he had found tedious, thanks to the continual need to deal with the government's bureaucrats.

'Just as with the Spitfire factory, the motor baron allowed the organization to slide into chaos, but resented any attempt at interference,' comments Leo McKinstry. Yet again, if this is a fair judgement, Nuffield would appear to have been out of his depth – or at the very least out of his comfort zone. 'In the matter of procrastination and delaying decisions, the Nuffield Civilian Repair Organization could give points to any Government department,' wrote Supermarine's Alexander Dunbar to Sir Charles Craven of Vickers.

The Morris Ten tilly, of which 4442 were made. It had various engine mods, different gear ratios and a stronger gearbox. (Royal Corps of Signals)

This Z-based tilly might well have been a one-off. (BMIHT)

Despite such views, it is possible that there was an element of sour grapes involved. Up until summer 1938, the Air Ministry thought repairing aircraft was neither feasible nor economically desirable, and when it changed its mind, initially it did not envisage using private industry. Nuffield pushed for Morris Motors to be the hub of the CRO, and as well as companies already in the aircraft business, many of the firms involved were sales and service operations connected with Morris; this was perhaps resented.

Tiger Moths, torpedoes and tanks

At the other end of the aviation spectrum from repairing Spitfires, an important wartime activity for Cowley was making complete Tiger Moths at a rate of 40 per week. In total, over 3200 were made, on production-line principles – using engines supplied by De Havilland – whereas previously De Havilland had been making no more than 200 Tiger Moths a year.

Cowley also made naval torpedoes. According to *Calling All Arms* the Navy ordnance factories took 897 man-hours per torpedo, and Cowley took 135 man-hours – prompting Cowley methods to be adopted by the Royal Navy's factories. Cowley in addition chalked up more than half

This Y-type started off as an open-lorry ambulance and was rebodied in 1942 with an alloy body over an ash frame. (Author)

the total output of Beaufighter and Lancaster power-unit modules, manufactured sundry small items, from hand winches to ammunition drums, and carried out work ranging from the painting of tents for D-day to gear-cutting for tanks and the machining of tracer bullets and shell fuses. Cowley also made the tail units for Horsa gliders, out of fabric-covered wood, in the factory sawmills.

Not primarily a Cowley activity was the manufacture of tanks; however, it is important here to underline the Morris involvement in the development of WW2 British tanks. William Morris had already shown an interest in tanks back in the 1920s, and had collaborated with tank expert Lieutenant-General Sir Giffard le Quesne Martel on the creation of the Morris-Martel light tank. On a visit to the Soviet Union in 1936, Martel and Field-Marshal Lord Wavell had been impressed by the Soviets' fast light-medium tanks, which were modelled on the US designs of Walter Christie. Martel had a word with Morris, and a Christie tank was shipped over from the States – without its turret and described as a tractor, in order to get around American legislation forbidding the sale of war material to foreign countries.

Christie visited Britain in 1937, and the tank was demonstrated to the top brass, who were particularly impressed by Christie's suspension system, with its large wheels, swinging arms and compression springs. Morris acquired rights to this suspension, and Oliver Boden, as an ex-Vickers man with an interest in armaments, oversaw the

design of a new tank around the suspension. At the end of 1937 Nuffield Mechanizations & Aero Ltd was set up in Birmingham, next door to the Wolseley works and bringing together elements of the Wolseley aero-engine business and core staff from Morris Commercial Cars who had been working on the tank.

The first two production examples were delivered early in 1939, powered by a re-jig of the old US-designed Liberty aero-engine that dated back to the previous war. With this not totally satisfactory engine and inadequate armour-plating, the first Cruisers and the later Crusaders – under-gunned into the bargain – were clearly in need of further development, as was proven by desperate reliability problems encountered when they were used in the desert. Improved Cavalier and Centaur variants followed, before the definitive Cromwell arrived in 1943. With its de-tuned Meteor version of the Rolls-Royce Merlin engine, it was one of the fastest tanks of the war. Nuffield Mechanizations built 205 Cruisers and 300 Crusaders, and had overall responsibility, as 'parent' of the design, for the 5300 Crusaders, 500 Cavaliers and 113 Centaurs made by a total of nine different companies.

Lighter metal: from scout cars to motorised wheelbarrows

Rather less heavy-duty was the Morris Light Reconnaissance Car, a project in which Alec Issigonis was very much involved, along with his long-time collaborator, draughtsman Jack Daniels. Initially envisaged as a small one-man armoured car, in its first form it had unitary construction, four-wheel drive, and all-independent suspension using a bent torsion bar at the front and coils at the rear. The design never made it to production in this form, but instead evolved into the three-man rear-drive Light Reconnaissance Car MkI of 1941. This had a rear-mounted 3½-litre 25hp MCC four-cylinder engine, independent front suspension by coil springs with an anti-roll bar, and a leaf-sprung rear axle; the tall kingpin arrangement with threaded trunnions was similar to that later found on the post-war Minor. In 1943 the MkII was introduced, with four-wheel drive and a leaf-sprung rigid front axle. In all 2200 Morris Light Reconnaissance Cars were built.

Issigonis also designed a miniature air-portable vehicle intended to be dropped by parachute in a cylinder – a sort of motorised wheelbarrow with an air-cooled motorcycle

LORD NUFFIELD'S WARTIME BENEFACTIONS

In the run-up to war, Lord Nuffield turned his attention towards the welfare of Britain's armed forces. In 1938 he gave £50,000 to the sports board of the Territorial Army. When conscription was introduced in 1939, it became clear to him that there would be a need for extra recreation facilities for regular troops, especially for younger conscripts. Accordingly he set aside £1.65m in Morris Motors Ordinary stock to form the Nuffield Trust for the Forces of the Crown, along with two additional gifts of £50,000 to cover initial expenditure; the charity still exists today.

The Trust handed out annual grants to each service, to spend as best it judged fit, the money being used on everything from radio sets to tennis courts. It also funded various clubs, the best known being the Nuffield Centre, a recreational club in London for all servicemen and women below commissioned rank which enabled those on leave to enjoy London facilities at affordable prices. It was to stay in operation, with various changes of premises, until 1980. There was also the Nuffield Club for Junior Officers, which again long survived the war, only closing its doors in 1976.

Another initiative Nuffield funded was the Nuffield Aircrew Leave Scheme, for RAF and Dominion air forces. Established in 1943 and wound down at the end of the war, it encompassed 30 hotels offering leave facilities mainly for bomber crews. Finally, sundry donations during the war included sizeable sums to the Red Cross and St John's Ambulance organizations and a substantial £250,000 to the RAF Benevolent Fund.

On a rather more banal level, Morris's personal ledger books record a £1000 payment to British American Tobacco, in 1940, for the provision of one and a half million Woodbine cigarettes for members of the armed forces.

---

engine, designed to carry a 300lb load, with the soldier walking behind, operating the steering by tiller. This developed into a sit-on version, and there was an amphibious spin-off which was a bit like a miniature DUKW. At the other end of the scale, Daniels worked on the 85-ton Tortoise, a still-born project for a mega-tank that used no fewer than 32 eight-foot-long torsion bars.

Needless to say, whilst all this was going on, manufacture of motor cars was very much a minor activity. The last Series Es and Twelve Series IIIs were made in August 1940, but Series 10Ms continued in small numbers until February 1941. In essence, all cars on the lines went to the services. Thereafter, production was restricted to a 10M-based pick-up or 'tilly' for the armed forces, Y-type vans built as ambulances, and Z-types and Y-types for the Post Office. Additionally, Cowley assembled 15cwt Ford and 3-ton Dodge lorries for the Army.

THEY ALSO SERVED...

To give a detailed account of the war work of the Nuffield Organization would require a second book. Although inevitably partisan, the Morris-sponsored account of the combine's war activities, *Calling All Arms*, is a good starting point for readers wanting to know more. The author's name, Ernest Fairfax, is a pseudonym, incidentally: the book was written by a well-known motoring journalist, with Miles Thomas very much in the editor's chair. Here, meanwhile, is a round-up of the contribution to the war made by the other subsidiaries of the Morris group.

Morris Commercial Cars

Morris Commercial Cars had a long tradition of supplying the armed forces, principally with the six-wheeler trucks it had first produced for the War Department in 1925 and which had become a mainstay of the British and Indian armies. During the war it supplied in particular large numbers of the 'Portee' vehicle, used to transport the two-pounder field gun. As well as these light-gun tractors, MCC made Crusader tanks, travelling platforms for mobile anti-aircraft guns, six-pounder gun carriages,

The Morris Quad was used in large numbers by the British army, to tow field artillery. (BMIHT)

CONTINUED >

amphibians, anti-submarine weapons, aero-engine components, transmission units for torpedoes... and, naturally enough, vehicles for the Post Office. Late in the war it began development of the Neptune amphibious carrier, which was designed to have a five-ton payload and carry a 17-pounder anti-tank gun or a three-ton truck and be operable in heavy surf. Propelled by its tracks, it was capable of five knots in water and 18mph on land, and used rubber-in-torsion suspension.

Large numbers of Carriers of all types were made by Wolseley. (Author's collection)

Nuffield Tools and Gauges Ltd

This was established in 1942 by acquiring an existing firm, and specialised in the manufacture of small tools and gauges.

Morris Engines Branch

The Meteor V12 engine was a derivative of the Merlin, and built by Morris Engines. (Author's collection)

Centaurs being converted into bulldozers at the MG factory in Abingdon. (Author's collection)

Engines Branch stuck to its last, making various engines, including 8hp units for portable water pumps, engines for ambulances, and marine engines for lifeboats, in addition to gears for machine tools, components for anti-aircraft installations, and accessories for the 'power eggs' of Beaufighters. Additionally it instituted the conveyor-belt manufacture of steel tank-track links, using a new technique for casting manganese steel – important and pioneering work. Above all this, though, it was the production centre for the Nuffield-Liberty tank engine, developed from the US-designed power unit, and in 1943 set up a new plant to build the Rolls-Royce Meteor tank engine.

Wolseley

The principal role of Wolseley was the manufacture of what are generically – but incorrectly – known as Bren Carriers. During the course of the war the company made over 22,000 Carriers of all types,

making it the largest producer of tracked vehicles in the country. It also took over production of Morris six-wheelers from Morris Commercial, and made nearly 6000 in all. Rather less heavy-duty was the conversion of 600 secondhand cars into pick-ups, for use as ambulances, and several hundred further cars into vans for the Royal Corps of Signals. Wolseley also did much work for the Admiralty, including the manufacture of sea-mines and sinkers and depth-charge pistols. Rather differently, it was the parent company for the four companies making wings for the Horsa glider.

MG

Abingdon started out reconditioning Matilda light tanks and armoured cars, and moved to the assembly of Crusader tanks and Oerlikon and Bofors anti-aircraft guns and the conversion of tanks to other uses such as flail minesweepers, mobile bridges and bulldozers. Eventually it became the production centre for nose sections for Albemarle bombers.

Riley

The Coventry firm specialised in aircraft components, the undercarriage for the Beaufighter night-fighter being a major contract. It also made parts for midget submarines, operated as a shadow factory for SU and in addition set up its own shadow factory to make aircraft carburettors in Leicestershire.

SU Carburettors

A relatively small business, with just 700 employees at the outbreak of war, SU initially supplied all the carbs for Spitfires and Hurricanes, amongst other planes, and also made the supercharger casing for their Merlin engines. It additionally developed a fuel-injection system that was lighter and simpler than that used by the Germans.

Morris Motors Body Branch

Unsurprisingly, Bodies Branch did what it did best, making bodies for troop-carriers, ambulances, tractors, anti-tank guns, and mobile military headquarters. It also made millions of jerrycans, adopting the German design after examples of the fuel can had been captured by the Desert Rats. Other products included seat panels for utility buses, canopies for army vehicles, shell carriers, transport crates, compressor boxes and toolbags.

Radiators Branch

Radiators Branch devised a new radiator for the Spitfire that was more efficient, weighed less and could be easily mass-produced. Its use soon spread to the aircraft industry as a whole and from then on Radiators produced most radiators for Merlin-equipped Beaufighters, Lancasters, Mosquitoes and Spitfires. It also made radiators for motor vehicles, naturally enough, and specialised in rads for tanks. Other aircraft work included an intercooler for the Merlin engine, which raised the operational height of fighters and bombers by several thousand feet, and a new exhaust system conceived so no flames would shoot out to betray the aircraft's position to the enemy. Radiators also made ¼ million steel helmets, ½ million mess tins, and field cookers, baking dishes, Sten-gun magazines, 25-pounder shellboxes and headlamp masks.

Pressings Branch

Set up just before the war to make car bodies, Pressings Branch in Birmingham made aircraft components, not least cowlings for the Beaufighter and Lancaster, along with shell-boxes, jerrycans and the like. When it needed more factory space it set up a plant at Llanelli, on a greenfield site in an area of high unemployment; it was the first modern flow-line light-engineering works to be built in South Wales.

Nuffield Mechanizations

Centred on Nuffield Mechanizations, the Morris group produced more than half of all UK-made Bofors anti-aircraft guns. This was done off Lord Nuffield's own bat when, in 1938, concerned by Britain's poor AA defences, he sent Boden and Landstad to Sweden to arrange a manufacturing deal with Bofors. Following on from this, in 1941 Miles Thomas, drawing on his experience in the previous war, initiated the design and production of self-propelled Bofors guns, convincing a sceptical War Office that the Bofors-Quad could bring its gun into action in 6.4 seconds from a speed of 30mph. Eventually becoming a standard design, the Bofors-Quad played an important part in the British advance across Germany. As well as its tank work and that of assembling various armoured cars, trucks and other vehicles, Nuffield Mechanizations also made torpedoes, shell fuses, tracer bullets and sundry other items. It was additionally the home of the Oxford Vaporizer 'iron lung' sponsored by Lord Nuffield and redesigned for mass-production by Gerald Palmer from the original created by Robert Mackintosh, the Nuffield Professor of Anaesthetics at Oxford. In all, 2700 were distributed by Nuffield, and the device is still in use today.

Morris Industries Exports

In 1940 MIE's buildings were converted into production lines for the assembly of sea-mines and sinkers for Admiralty; 8000 mines were ultimately made. Towards the end of 1941, it switched to the manufacture of Crusader tanks, of which it made more than 650, including observation-post tanks with dummy gun barrels and anti-aircraft tanks based on Crusader and Centaur hulls.

A standard SU car carburettor is dwarfed by one built for an aero-engine. (Author's collection)

Years of turmoil 1945–48

Derived from the 'Intermediate' body and dating from 1946, this is a proposal for the Wolseley 18/25 version of the Morris Imperial/Viceroy. (BMIHT)

The immediate post-war period was hugely challenging. Not helping matters, there was constant dispute over the next generation of cars. In the end there was a management purge, but precious time had been lost.

It was a very different world in which the Nuffield Organization had to operate after the end of the war. Britain was heavily indebted, in need of foreign exchange, and beset with materials shortages. Key parts were not always available, and production would often be interrupted. Steel was rationed – 'on allocation' – and even items such as leather were not always obtainable. The workforce was restive. Overshadowing all this was a Labour government with a strong belief in industrial intervention and a wish to nationalise key sectors of the economy. There was pressure to export, yet Nuffield products were overpriced and not readily saleable in many overseas markets, even if retailed at minimal profit.

Sales in Britain were throttled, both by the government demand for exports above all else and by a high rate of Purchase Tax – imposed, Labour admitted, as a way of killing the home market; Sir Miles Thomas, as he had become in 1943, was to spend an inordinate amount of time trying to fend off requests by would-be queue-jumpers trying to obtain one of the few cars released for sale. In April 1946 there would be outstanding orders for 65,000 cars. The black market became a real problem, and would represent about 10 per cent of deliveries in 1946.

An Eight, a Ten – but no Twelve
Car production re-started once the government had given the necessary authorisations, which in the case of Morris was for 50,000 cars in the first year – against 1939 production of 76,564 units. Deliveries began in September 1945, in which month just 19 Eights and 62 Tens left Cowley. After their poor sales pre-war, the larger cars were understandably enough not reintroduced. In any case, materials shortages meant that manufacturers perforce had to concentrate on a smaller number of models. So it was that only the Eight and Ten figured in the post-war range.

Initially it had been intended to reintroduce the Twelve after the war, in an improved specification with independent front suspension and rack-and-pinion steering; this was the same set-up as had been rejected for the 10M and which would ultimately surface on the Y-type MG. Providing

With its new front, teardrop headlamps and split screen, it is difficult to recognise this 1943 exercise as being based on a Series M Ten. (BMIHT)

With its symmetrical layout and central grille, the dashboard is pure Issigonis. (BMIHT)

a possible impulse to re-start production, as early as 1944 George Lloyd, Nuffield's main man in Australia, was pressing for a supply of 12hp chassis, to be bodied as utilities. However, the pre-war sales figures clearly made some senior managers queasy. During a wartime discussion about whether to uprate existing models or just reintroduce them as they were, pending new designs, Miles Thomas said that he envisaged re-starting production of the 8hp, 10hp and 12hp. "I think we can forget the Twelve," was the tart rejoinder from Morris Motors joint-MD Harry Seaward.

Clearly spun off from the 1943 Ten restyle, this is a suggested facelift of the 'M' for the Hindustan. (BMIHT)

This position was maintained as the war drew to a close, Seaward informing Thomas in February 1945 that very little material was available for manufacture of the Twelve and that because it was impossible for Fisher and Ludlow to supply the necessary panels, it would be better not to include the model in Morris's post-war programme; surplus engines and gearboxes could go to the Service Department. Despite this, in June 1945 Miles Thomas is on record saying that the Twelve was intended to go back into production in early 1946. As the Nuffield Organization grappled with the multiple challenges of the immediate post-war period, this never happened.

The cars were largely unchanged. The Ten had been given detail modifications in October 1939, and when reintroduced after the war it had many minor improvements – including extra front-end bracing, the introduction of which suggests that in service the monocoque was less clever than it appeared on paper. During 1946 a rounded radiator shell would be fitted, giving the 'M' a touch more elegance; this had been originally conceived for a version of the Ten to be made in India, as the Hindustan, by the Birla industrial group. The deal with Birla had been signed in December 1944, and it was envisaged that the company would be supplied with completely-built and Semi-Knocked-Down (SKD) cars until full Indian production could start. Expediting this, in July 1945 a Cowley engineer was sent out to

Hindustan Motors. It had been intended to restyle the car more comprehensively for India, not least with headlamps in the wings, but in the end the likely cost and the delay that would be caused militated against this.

To diversify – or not?

In the later stages of the war and the early days of peace, the board considered various diversifications from the manufacture of motor cars. One long-running possibility was to become involved with government plans for steel-framed or pressed-steel pre-fabricated housing. Harold Ryder feared that the houses would be jerry-built, and suggested instead making baths, sinks, lavatory cisterns, gas stoves and electric-cooker surrounds, making use of Morris expertise in vitreous enamelling. He saw this as part of a putative Nuffield Special Products division, making everything from filing cabinets to washing machines, and taking in the existing marine and industrial engines operation. Also mooted were an electric car, a helicopter (rapidly discounted), and – more realistically – a residential caravan.

Most fascinating of all these still-born projects was a proposal to return to the company's roots, and make a bicycle, initially as a way of picking up market share in Europe and elsewhere previously held by the Germans. By 1944 there was talk of an 'Oxford' bicycle, seen as a high-grade lightweight machine with the various models named after different Oxford colleges. In spring 1945 the first prototype was ready for Lord Nuffield to inspect. 'It is certainly light,' commented Miles Thomas, of what was evidently a mould-breaking design. This slightly concerned Vic Oak. 'There are so many points about the frame and forks which are unorthodox that I think we should do all we can to prevent Lord Nuffield trying the machine until we have had an opportunity of carrying out tests to prove the strength of the various joints,' he wrote to Thomas.

Tractors, taxis… and a 'British Jeep'

Two projects that did make it to production were a tractor and a return to the taxi market. The Nuffield Universal Tractor went into production at Ward End towards the close of 1948. An up-market machine, it never sold in large numbers, but was regarded as a high-quality product. Construction would continue under the Nuffield name until 1969, when the tractors were rebaptised Leylands and lost their characteristic orange livery in favour of a two-tone blue. In 1962 manufacture would shift to Bathgate in Scotland, after which quality issues compromised the Nuffield's reputation. Leyland carried on making the tractors until 1982, when the designs were taken over by Lincolnshire tractor company Marshalls, who would build the former Leylands – and one-time Nuffields – until 1985. Production continued with two other firms, ceasing in 2008.

The Nuffield Oxford taxi was a new design, developed during the war and using an 1802cc dry-sump version of the Morris Twelve engine in a cruciform chassis laid out by former Lea-Francis and Riley engineer Charles van Eugen. The wood-framed body was initially a four-light design, and early examples had the archaic feature of artillery wheels; additionally the brakes were mechanical rather than hydraulic and there was an old-fashioned worm-drive rear axle. In Series II form, Easiclean wheels arrived, whilst the Series III had a six-light body. Manufacture went ahead on the basis that Nuffield would take up former cab-maker Beardmore's steel allocation, in exchange for which Beardmore would sell and service the Oxford cab.

Production lasted until 1953, by which time 1926 had been made, roughly half at Ward End and the remainder at the cab's second home, the Morris-Commercial plant at Adderley Park. It is said that the Nuffield taxi was discontinued as a result of the merger with Austin, which brought the Austin FX3 taxi into the fold. This is not the case. In August 1951, ahead of the merger, the Morris board noted that sales of the taxi – 'always small' – had stopped completely, as a result of double Purchase Tax and higher fares. It was decided to produce the remaining sanction mostly as hire cars and then get out of the taxi market as soon as the agreement with Beardmore's had run its course, which would be at the end of 1953.

One final diversion – perhaps a more understandable one – was the Nuffield Organization's involvement in what ultimately became the Austin Champ. This had started out in 1943 as a project to make a 'British Jeep'. By 1944 two prototypes had been built, pretty much along the lines of the American original. There was consideration, however, of whether what was termed a 'Chinese copy' of the Jeep was what was wanted, or something more elaborate that could be used in a larger number of roles. It has generally been said that it was the War Office's ambitious requirements that led to the unduly complex and overweight Champ. 'The

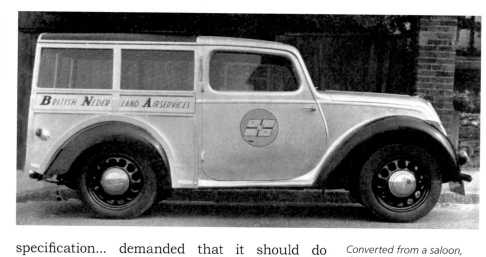

Converted from a saloon, this Series E estate was used as a crew-carrier by British Nederland Airservices in the Netherlands. (Author's collection)

specification... demanded that it should do practically everything... as some wag had it, do everything except pick coconuts and wait at table,' Miles Thomas memorably wrote in *Out on a Wing*. The design of just such a multi-function machine was embarked upon, but it seems that the Nuffield Organization was as much responsible for its specification as the Army top brass and the civil servants of the War Office, if the minutes of a meeting at Wolseley in 6 September 1944 are any guide. 'With regard to the JEEP-type vehicle, as it was extremely unlikely that the War Office had any clarified ideas of their requirements, Morris Motors Design Department (Mr Oak) will put up a suggested design of vehicle which will incorporate the performance characteristics of the JEEP but will give more comfort and protection', one can read. 'Independent suspension, chassis-less construction and a big, low-stressed engine were mentioned.'

The rounded front introduced on the Ten in 1946: it did not meet with Lord Nuffield's approval. (Author's collection)

It was advantageous in the early post-war years to export chassis for bodying abroad. This Z-type was bodied by Danish distributor DOMI. (Author's collection)

This Z-type was operated by the Nuffield distributor in Uruguay. The 'Z' would stay in production until 1953 because prototypes of the Minor van were judged too underpowered with the Eight engine. (Author's collection)

This was the starting point for what became known as the Nuffield Gutty. At least in part drawn up by Alec Issigonis, this did indeed have all-independent suspension, by torsion bars, and had unitary construction and a larger version of his original dry-sump flat-four designed for the Mosquito small car. The engine seems subsequently to have been enlarged from 1800cc to around 2500cc, and was envisaged as also being used in a light truck, and in a version of the new Morris 'Intermediate' model to be made by Hindustan. There was also talk of a Jeep for the Indian army, which may well have been another putative Hindustan project.

Soon the War Office started to intervene in the specification, which as a result never seemed to be finalised, thanks to continued suggestions for changes coming from all quarters, much to the frustration of Miles Thomas. The first prototype was completed in time for July 1947 trials, but subsequently the War Office required the Gutty to be re-designed to take the Rolls-Royce B40

four-cylinder engine, as part of its plans for a unified range of vehicles using four-cylinder, six-cylinder and eight-cylinder versions of the B-series Rolls-Royce power unit.

In this form, known as the Wolseley Mudlark, the car limped forward to production, undergoing endless trials. Despite Morris having initially hoped to win what was expected to be a 20,000-car contract to build the vehicle, in the end its manufacture was put out to tender. Austin's bid won, and its Cofton Hackett factory at Longbridge had the responsibility of making what was now called the Austin Champ. Expensive, unreliable and in some conditions dangerously unstable, fewer than 12,000 Champs were built between 1951 and 1956.

Planning the new generation

New-model development hadn't stood still during the war. Obviously the amount of time that could be devoted to such an activity was limited. But under Technical Director Vic Oak, the talented Alec Issigonis – less of a calculated eccentric in those days – was working on a new small car that would ultimately provide the template for a full range of post-war vehicles.

When the project was initiated in 1941 it was seen not as a replacement for the Eight but rather as a small 6hp two-to-three-seater in the mould of the Fiat 500 Topolino. For a little buzz-box, the name Mosquito bestowed on the car seemed appropriate. Initial explorations centred on use of a 488cc opposed-cylinder two-stroke with a belt-driven supercharger. Thought was also given to an orthodox four-stroke in-line 'four'. Apparently at least one such engine was built, and seems to have been a side-valve unit of roughly 600cc.

The Mosquito was intended to be part of a three-car Morris range, minutes of a meeting of directors in February 1944 confirmed. The Mosquito was described as a 'chassis-less two-seater with occasional seating for four, non-opening boot, fixed screen... fitted with either a flat-four, flat-twin or four-cylinder in-line engine of approximately 750cc'. Next up would be the Minor, 'a chassis-less four-seater family car, in effect a modernised version of the present 8hp car, giving slightly more body accommodation by reason of the incorporation of a flat-four-cylinder engine of approximately 1100cc'. Finally there would be the Major, a 4/6-seater 'in general conception a modernised and slightly enlarged version of the present Ten' and powered by a 1250cc or 1500cc flat-four. Each model would

popular than the Series M Morris 10 – and we now propose to drop it from our range.'

Causing further anguish was the July 1947 announcement of the Standard Vanguard and the proclamation of Standard's 'One Model' policy, in response to government pressure for manufacturers to focus on a single type of car. If Morris went down this road with the 'Intermediate', they risked committing commercial suicide, by handing lower-horsepower sales to the opposition at a time when the company had orders for over 144,000 Eights and Tens, including 5cwt and 10cwt vans, and further orders were coming in at a rate of approximately 2500 a week, wrote Vic Oak to Thomas. Even if half these orders were 'just scraps of paper', fulfilling demand would take at least 18 months – and 10,000 of those orders were from fleets, who wouldn't want larger vehicles. Such custom should not 'just be thrown aside purely and simply to follow what after all is to a large extent a shadow'. Following the Vanguard policy would be 'most dangerous and unsettling to the retail side of the industry... [In] all instances without exception there is the hope that the Nuffield Organization will not indulge in what would appear to be purely a political stunt.'

The worries of Hanks and Oak seem to have hit home. Whatever his hopes for the Mosquito and 'Intermediate', Thomas felt the need to reassure the trade. 'We would like to make it quite clear that it is not proposed to take out of production the current 8hp and 10hp types for a very considerable period – indeed, not until sales factors warrant a change, which they certainly do not at the moment,' he wrote to all distributors and dealers in August 1947.

Dreams of Empire: the Imperial and Viceroy

Whilst this debilitating maelstrom of decisions and counter-decisions was playing out, still in the picture was a a large six-light saloon. This had evolved out of the initial proposition for a model for 'Empire' markets, as enthusiastically promoted by Lord Nuffield. The car was intended to counter the American manufacturers, and in a July 1944 memo Vic Oak cites its nearest competitors as being the Nash Ambassador, Studebaker Champion, Hudson Six and the V8 Ford – as well as the very American-looking Opel Kapitän. 'The Nash is the most modern production effort... and, in the main, fulfils the specification we propose,' wrote Oak, so it is perhaps no accident that one of the post-war mock-ups has a slight ressemblance

The Imperial engine was seen as a 'six' with shaft-and-bevel drive to the overhead camshaft – as would be the case with the new-generation Wolseley engines. (Nuffield College archives)

The original idea for an Imperial for export markets was presented as a top-of-range member of the Mosquito-Oxford family. (Nuffield College archives)

to the six-light Nashes of the period.

Both Morris and Wolseley versions were envisaged, the latter possibly with a Cotal gearbox, and the power unit was initially seen as being the 2¼-litre ohc 'six' – although consideration was also given to the Morris having the flat-four engine of the 'British Jeep'. There would only be a three-speed gearbox on the Morris, which was to be considerably cheaper than the Wolseley, and to keep costs down it was proposed to manufacture both cars at the Wolseley plant. By early 1947 there was discussion of a 4-litre version, to be called the Viceroy in its Morris form. 'The good reputation built up by the 25hp Wolseley may make it desirable for the Organization to offer a high-powered high-performance car of similar, or

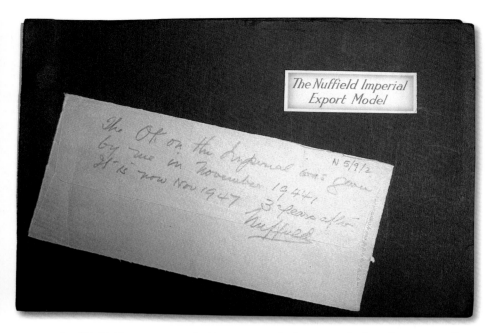

The Nuffield Imperial Export Model

Lord Nuffield was disgruntled about the lack of progress with the Imperial, which was a pet project of his. (Nuffield College archives)

even better, general characteristics. From a policy point of view it may be undesirable to leave this particular field to the Humber/Hillman, Vauxhall and Austin Companies,' wrote Miles Thomas to Wolseley MD Charles Mullens. The 4-litre engine would be a new unit developing over 100bhp and mated to a Cotal gearbox, but as the cost of the new engine and a revised front end would be substantial, Thomas suggested waiting to see how the 2¼-litre version performed before going ahead. The project was still 'live' in October 1947, by which time the bigger engine had returned to the picture, only in 3¼-litre form. Ultimately, though, the venture was quietly abandoned.

Exit Sir Miles...

Miles Thomas wasn't around to oversee the fulfilment of the new-model programme for which he had fought. In November 1947 he parted company with the Nuffield Organization. The account given in *Out on a Wing* can be succinctly summarised. Thomas could see that relations with Nuffield had become tense, not helped by Nuffield resenting the loss of his loyal private secretary Wilfred Hobbs, whom Thomas had appointed Company Secretary. At one of their regular meetings Thomas suggested either that he be given the freedom to manage as he saw fit or else that he step down; Nuffield indicated that the second option was more what he had in mind.

There was rather more to it than this. During 1947 Thomas had been asked to join the Board of Colonial Development. Apparently – although he denied this – Thomas accepted without informing

Lord Nuffield, who read about the appointment in the papers, complete with Thomas being quoted as saying it was only a 'part-time' job. Infuriated by the implication that he must therefore regard the Vice-Chairmanship of the Nuffield Organization as a less than full-time job, Nuffield asked for his resignation. "Thomas was a silly man because he let his name appear in the papers more than Nuffield's, and there is no doubt Lady Nuffield asked who was running the business – [Nuffield] or him," commented George Dono. So it was that another talented senior executive was lost to the Morris business – and anyone who has read Miles Thomas's surviving papers will know that he was anything but a part-timer.

... and enter Reggie Hanks

Reggie Hanks took over as Vice-Chairman. A former Great Western Railway apprentice, Hanks had joined Morris in 1922, in the technical services department. General Manager of Nuffield Metal Products from 1941 to 1945, he had also run 1 CRU and Nuffield Mechanizations. In 1945 he was given responsibility for Nuffield Exports, and he had joined the board in August 1947. Steam enthusiast Hanks was regarded by his colleagues as a bit of a plodder. 'He hadn't the vitality of Miles... he was very steady going,' Issigonis told author Paul Skilleter.

But if Hanks was, in the words of George Dono, "a sweet-tempered man", he had iron in his backbone. A far-reaching management re-shuffle followed his appointment, with several long-serving directors leaving, including Hans Landstad, Carl Skinner, Harry Seaward and Victor Riley, and a new smaller board being constituted. Cutting out the dead wood was long overdue. "Seaward was no good, Riley was sick, Shaw was quite nice but impossible [and] did not carry enough weight," sourly commented Leonard Lord. The move was presented as being on Lord Nuffield's initiative, and as proof of his continued vitality and vision. He was quoted as saying that the aim was 'to vest control in a smaller directorate, and to bring the younger generation to the fore.' That may well be, but in fact the purge was insisted upon by Hanks, and was initially resisted by Nuffield. "Rome is burning," Hanks told his Chairman.

Hanks was determined that under his command there would be a new broom. He was sickened by the backbiting and plotting that had prevailed in the upper echelons of Cowley management – not least when Nuffield was away on one of his voyages. "There was always some sort of domestic row to settle when he came back from away," he told Andrews and Brunner. When he had achieved his clear-out of senior management, he said, "Nuffield could go away and come back and he would never find a breath of trouble when he came back, and it hurt [me] that Nuffield never had the slightest appreciation of that."

Relations in fact remained prickly. Hanks said his colleagues tried to get him to see Nuffield more. "It was excellent advice, but he got his head blown off every time he went into his office. Why should he stick his neck out to have his head blown off when the business was going extremely well and there was no justification? Frankly, [I] did not got on very well with Nuffield in [my] period as Vice-Chairman... [He] was very harsh, with exactly those people to whom he was beholden. Issigonis, for instance, was a brilliant man... but Nuffield never did anything but curse him."

Hanks told Nuffield he wanted him to be 'a benevolent head' of the business. There were so many people to whom he should say 'thank you' and speak a word of praise to, here and there, while he could deal with any unpleasantness. It didn't work out, he said. "All they got was cursing and swearing – and usually over quite unimportant things, like the Morris band."

The Organization reorganizes

Starting in 1948, the business was reorganized around four groups, and production tidied up by moving manufacture of Wolseley cars to Cowley and of Rileys to Abingdon. Wolseley at Ward End was to become the machining centre for the group and to be responsible for the tractor, and would henceforth be known as Tractor and Transmission Branch; the Riley works would become part of Engines Branch; all sales departments would be centralised on Cowley, except that for Morris Commercial Cars. This was part of a programme proposed by George Dono, who in a statement of the blindingly obvious said that the administration of the Nuffield Organization was 'unnecessarily cumbersome and expensive'. One particular example was Wolseley, who before the war were making 400 cars per week but in 1948 were on less than half this. Yet Morris and Wolseley at the end of 1948 were both gearing up to produce essentially the same car. Cowley had got over the 'bulk of teething troubles' with the Oxford, said

Hans Landstad was one of the 'old faithfuls' who lost his place on the board in the 1947 purge. (BMIHT)

Dono, and here was Wolseley just about to start independently with its 4/50 and go through the learning process all over again – a complete waste of money. Transferring Wolseley production to Cowley was not just a question of production, either: there was the added cost of transporting cars to Cowley for export, with interim storage sometimes at Castle Bromwich. Then there were bodies being produced by Pressed Steel and then transported to Birmingham.

'I cannot believe that Mr SV Smith and his colleagues [at Cowley] are any less able to produce a Wolseley car having the same qualities of finish and distinction as when it is made in Birmingham,' Dono was recorded as saying. 'At the present time between 60 per cent and 75 per cent of our customers are abroad, and I find it impossible to believe that they care whether the car is made in Birmingham, Oxford, or (for that matter) Aberdeen!'

Dono envisaged that when Wolseley had been absorbed, MG and Riley production could also move to Cowley; Andrews and Brunner hint that the Nuffield Organization could indeed have consolidated all car manufacture at Cowley had the Town and Country Planning Act not prohibited further growth of the site.

Even without this ultimate reorganization, the group was now in broadly sound administrative order. It had been beaten to the market with new cars by Austin, but at the first post-war Motor Show, in October 1948, the Morris conglomerate would have a range of five new models on display. The clock was set fair for a return to rude good health, under a revitalised management team.

AUSTRALIA: DREAMS AND NIGHTMARES

In the 'Export or Die' climate of post-war Britain, Lord Nuffield's enduring obsession with Australia suddenly seemed forward-thinking and in tune with the times. As had been his fashion when building up his business, he acted decisively: in September 1945 he contracted to buy – out of his personal purse – a site in Sydney on which to build a factory for local assembly of Morris cars.

FOR ECONOMY AND
RELIABILITY

To-day's Outstanding Utility . . .

The New
MORRIS
8/40 SERIES E

DISTRIBUTORS FOR NEW SOUTH WALES
YORK MOTORS PTY. LTD. (INC. IN VIC.)
101-111 WILLIAM STREET, SYDNEY. PHONE FA 6621

York Motors in Sydney offered this smart 8/40 Series E roadster-utility, bodied by Richards of Adelaide. (Author's collection)

It had by this stage become evident that the Australian government would do everything it could to promote motor manufacture in Australia rather than expensively importing vehicles. In 1944 Nuffield had tried to buy Ruskin Motor Bodies, who were one of those Australian coachbuilders who had bodied Morrises before the war. In March 1945 he had pulled out of the evidently frustrating negotiations, citing Ruskin's obstructiveness. "I have never been so humbugged in my life," he exclaimed.

Working in harness with thrusting Morris distributor George Lloyd, Nuffield established relations with the Australian prime minister and ended up being offered the chance to buy the Victoria Park racecourse in Sydney. It was supposedly an outstanding site, and surplus land could be sold off to amortise the purchase.

The rear lights on the survivor shown here are a later addition. (Kerry Kaehne)

But after a formal announcement of the intended purchase in November, things started to go off the rails. There was talk of the Sydney Turf Club wanting to re-start horse-racing, and the New South Wales premier refused to undertake that this would not happen, the Australian Jockey Club having a lease on the property until the end of 1947. A very public row between the local prime minister and Nuffield ensued, and in March 1946 Nuffield said he would postpone the project indefinitely and use a South Australian firm to body cars on the company's behalf. Back at Cowley, where there were continuing worries about the economic viability of the Australian market, this was greeted with a sigh of relief – 'three rousing cheers' cabled Miles Thomas to Lord Nuffield.

The snag was that the company in South Australia was Richards Industries Ltd of Adelaide, and Morris's collaboration with the company soon turned into a catastrophe. Richards had pitched for the Nuffield Organization's business in 1943. But the situation was unmanageable, as there was insufficient bodybuilding capacity in Australia to cope with demand: by the beginning of 1947 there would be 20,000 chassis in the country awaiting bodies, and an industry capable of only producing 3000 bodies a month, for a market needing more than three times that number.

As a result, Richards were over-extended trying to service too many clients – including Standard, which rankled with Cowley. Consequently they were not meeting production targets for Morris. Not only that but twice they demanded more money from Morris. Finally in May 1947 they said that they would not have facilities to cope with manufacture from CKD kits of the new generation of integral-construction Morris cars, and wanted to end the Morris contract by the close of 1948 – it being generally understood that this was because the company was now financially controlled by Chrysler and wanted to work exclusively or near-exclusively for the American firm. Lloyd was furious – the situation was 'insufferable' and Richards were guilty of 'distinctly unethical conduct'.

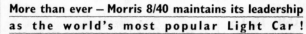

More than ever — Morris 8/40 maintains its leadership as the world's most popular Light Car !

There's more than superb appearance to the new Morris 8/40 for 1946. There's magnificent performance . . . extreme economy . . . ample accommodation . . . and all the time tested Morris advantages in engineering and design that make Morris 8/40 the No. 1 car in sales performance throughout the British Empire year after year.

MORRIS 8/40 FOR 1946

This tray-back roadster-utility is probably the work of Hopes Body Works of Brisbane. (www. classiccarsforsale.com)

The Richards Series E tourer was an elegant job – but relations with the firm turned into a nightmare. (Kerry Kaehne)

No less unhappy were the Nuffield distributors who had bankrolled the Adelaide coachbuilder and felt they had been kicked in the teeth.

If Nuffield wanted to stay in the Australian game, urgent action was needed: General Motors, Ford and Rootes all had Australian assembly plants, and the Nuffield Organization was being left behind and risked gradually losing the Australian market. As it was, the group was losing traction: Nuffield Exports shipments in the first three months of 1947 had totalled 3577 units, putting Cowley behind Austin, Standard and, above all, Vauxhall. Not only that, but the British-bodied Morris Ten was distinctly uncompetitive, at £647 against £543 for a locally-bodied Vauxhall Wyvern and £477 for a Ford Prefect that was again bodied in Australia. By November 1947 the Victoria Park project had been re-started, and the factory would become operational in March 1950.

Fitted with a pick-up body, this Series Z was used by a market gardener in New Zealand. (Author's collection)

MORRIS *Coupe Utility* 5-CWT.

A LONG-LASTING, HARD-WORKING, ECONOMICAL UNIT

This coupé-ute is another Australian-bodied 'Z' – one of various types offered by different coachbuilders. (Kerry Kaehne)

The New Generation – Minor, Oxford and Six

The basic shape of the MO had been finalised by 1945, when this photo was taken; the grille, however, clearly needed some further thought. (BMIHT)

With the Minor, the company had a modern and well-received small car. The verdict was mixed for the larger Morrises. Everything was, however, to change with the shock merger of the Nuffield Organization and long-time rival Austin.

The new generation of Morris and Wolseley cars finally took their bow at the 1948 Motor Show, the first to be held after the war. The Morris Minor, known internally as the Series MM, was accompanied by the Series MO Oxford and the Series MS Six, while Wolseley fielded 4/50 and 6/80 derivatives of the two latter cars. All five cars had unitary construction, independent front suspension by longitudinal torsion bars, and a conventional leaf-sprung rear. It was a nicely integrated range, with much component commonality. In particular, the 4/50 engine was essentially an overhead-cam version of the MO's side-valve – or, if you like, a four-cylinder version of the 6/80 and Morris Six engine.

Template for the range – the Minor

Cornerstone of the range was the Morris Minor, which was initially offered solely in two-door and tourer forms. Without the flat-four engine, it was a less radical car than its designer had intended, but was still one of the most advanced British cars of its day – perhaps bested only by the Jowett Javelin. Spacious and sweet-handling, it was to become a reference amongst small cars, above all on account of its secure and rewarding road behaviour.

A keen amateur racing driver in his younger days, Issigonis had indeed placed good road manners high up his requirements for the new car, and this naturally enough meant having independent front suspension – along with the novelty, for the period, of rack-and-pinion steering. Building on the experience of the Ten Series M, chassis-less construction was retained. Considering these two features together – and with a sidelong look at the inspirational Citroën 'Traction Avant' – led to the use of longitudinal torsion bars. These gave a suitably supple ride, and were made long enough to feed suspension loadings – already reduced, thanks to the length of the bars – into mounting points on a central crossmember. It was an elegant solution, especially when used in conjunction with a long threaded upright which put the upper link of the front suspension sufficiently high for its loads

The original 'lowlight' MM saloon. Issigonis was mortified about having to lose the lowline wings, especially as they were more aerodynamically efficient. (Author)

The Minor interior was drawn up by Issigonis, and he remained proud of it; it was clearly as American-influenced as the exterior. (Author's collection)

In its original form the convertible had lift-out rear sidescreens and was known as a tourer. (Author's collection)

The four-door was always a 'highlight' and from the start had one-piece bumpers; for the first year only the rear screen had a chrome surround. (Author's collection)

Distinctive features of the four-door interior were rear-door armrests, and a chrome strip on the door trims. (Author's collection)

Home-market cars received one-piece bumpers just ahead of the standardisation of the 'highlight' wings in January 1951. (Author's collection)

In the end a plan to use torsion bars for the suspension of the live back axle was discarded, apparently after this had been briefly tried on the initial prototype, and conventional leaf springs were employed instead. Another feature to be abandoned was torque-tube location of the axle, in conjunction with a split propshaft. This would have allowed a less obtrusive transmission tunnel, but would have added to cost, weight and complication. Ultimately a much greater contribution to space-saving was achieved through use of unusually small 14in wheels – at a time when 17in rims were more normal. Wheelarch intrusion was thus limited, and the small wheels also reduced unsprung weight and harmonised better with the car's overall proportions. 'The new Minor turns out to be a small car which is unique in one respect,' Issigonis wrote in a launch-time article. 'This type of vehicle has always in the past been associated with a degree of passenger huddling... We have achieved our objective in giving you big car comfort, so far as elbow room inside the body is concerned, to a degree unheard of before in the field of small cars.'

Inherited from the Morris Eight Series E, the 918cc side-valve engine was mounted well forward to give secure nose-heavy handling and maximise interior space; it developed a quoted 27.5bhp at 4400rpm, with maximum torque of 39lb ft at 2400rpm – sufficient to give the Minor a top speed of 62mph. "It was a terrible old thing, but, well, we had no option," author Paul Skilleter reports Issigonis as remarking. Cooling was initially by thermo-syphon, but from late 1950 a water pump became available, enabling North American cars in particular to be supplied with a heater as standard equipment; on home-market

to be fed into a robustly-constructed bulkhead. Issigonis had recognised the main flaw of the Citroën system, namely that the location of the lower arm was not sufficient to resist torque under braking. He therefore added a diagonal radius rod to triangulate the arm. Furthermore, the layout was conceived so that there would be no need for a front anti-roll bar.

A 'highlight' car with split bumpers, as here, has to be a North American export vehicle – Canada also receiving the raised-headlamp front during 1950. (Author's collection)

cars the water pump and heater were an option. A clever detail, of which Issigonis was very proud, was an aperture in the back of the headlamps to illuminate the engine compartment.

Initial production was to a large extent for export, and herein lay a rub: it was discovered that the low-set headlamps so beloved of Alec Issigonis were not high enough to comply with United States legislation due to be introduced at the beginning of 1949. As a result a new 'highlight' configuration was hurriedly developed specifically for the US market. Morris, already trailing Austin in shipping new product to the car-hungry American and Canadian markets, thus suffered a further hold-up. With production slow to gather pace, there was exasperation at Nuffield's failure to supply dealers across the Atlantic with adequate stock. Not only that, but every car sent across the Atlantic meant one fewer for the loyal Morris markets in Australia and New Zealand. 'I am afraid there are just not enough to go around,' wrote Nuffield Vice-Chairman Reggie Hanks to Sir William Welsh, the Society of Motor Manufacturers and Traders representative in Washington. 'As evidence of our attempts to satisfy Canada and other hard-currency markets, our position in the Australasian countries has slipped from No.1 down to No.6 – a very distressing fact.'

By 1950 annual Minor production at Cowley had hit 48,000 cars, a level at which it was to remain for a further two years before making a big jump in 1953 with the arrival of the Series II models. These figures include production of CKD ('Completely Knocked Down') kits for assembly abroad – notably in the Irish Republic, Australia, New Zealand, South Africa and the Netherlands, but also in India, another key market, where four separate companies assembled the Minor.

From 1950 these and other export markets received priority for a new Minor model, a four-door saloon; from the start this had 'highlight' wings and one-piece bumpers. It was the arrival of this heavier variant that underlined the need for a more potent power unit than the old Morris Eight side-valve which had always constituted the Minor's biggest weakness. By this stage the Minor had considerably evolved from the 'lowlight' original of 1948, having undergone a goodly number of detailed modifications while remaining mechanically unchanged. The most obvious was the standardisation of the 'highlight' front in January 1951. Also during 1951 the Tourer was

In June 1951 the tourer lost its side-curtains in favour of integral glass rear windows – the model henceforth being known as a convertible. (Author's collection)

given integral glass rear side-windows in place of lift-off celluloid sidescreens, and was renamed the Convertible, while all models received a longer bonnet that extended further into the scuttle and right back to the door aperture.

This MO has the later style of grille. Bumper overriders were standardised from late 1952. (LAT)

The MO and MS has rubber rear-window surrounds whereas the Wolseleys has a chrome-framed window. (LAT)

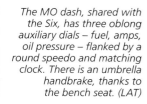

The MO dash, shared with the Six, has three oblong auxiliary dials – fuel, amps, oil pressure – flanked by a round speedo and matching clock. There is an umbrella handbrake, thanks to the bench seat. (LAT)

The side-valve engine develops 40.5bhp – or 41bhp on cars made after a cylinder-head mod in 1950. Fuel consumption was 25–30mpg. (LAT)

Morris's mid-sizer: the 'MO' Oxford

The larger cars were very much extrapolations of the Minor. When the author talked to Jack Daniels he had very little to say about them. To him they were nothing more than a scaling-up of the smaller Morris's engineering and styling: all the donkey work had been done. "The Oxford went extremely simply," he said. "As far as I recall, it just happened. The six-cylinder cars were a bit more difficult, because you had to get that longer length of front in there and find some way to mount the dampers."

Looking first at the Oxford, this deviated the least from the template laid down by the Minor, retaining rack-and-pinion steering and having its front lever-arm dampers anchored to the bulkhead. One departure from Minor practice was the incorporation of a Panhard rod to help locate the rear axle; another was that there was a column change for the four-speed gearbox.

Developing only 40.5bhp, the 1476cc all-iron side-valve engine featured a Fabroil timing wheel rather than a timing chain; required to haul along 21.3cwt of six-seater saloon, it made no better a fist of the job than did the old Morris Eight engine in the Minor. 'The power unit has been specifically designed to match the characteristics of the new car. Both revolutions and maximum power output have been deliberately restrained, but on the other hand great pains have been taken to obtain the highest possible torque to aid top-gear acceleration,' wrote Alec Issigonis in a launch-time review of the car's engineering – going on to say that the improved aerodynamics of the new car made overhead valves unnecessary. This was surely special pleading, even if the modest 65lb ft of maximum torque did come in at a low 2000rpm. In its road test of the Oxford *The Motor* recorded a maximum speed of only 67mph and a glacial 38.9 seconds to spool up to 60mph. The findings of *The Autocar* were worse, the magazine achieving a 0–60mph time of 41.4 seconds, whilst the 18.3 seconds taken to accelerate from 30mph to 50mph in top was exactly the same as the magazine had recorded for the pre-war Ten Series M.

As soon as more modern rivals joined the fray, the Morris began to look distinctly disadvantaged. Although no lighter, the Ford Consul introduced in 1950 had a revvy oversquare pushrod engine, and on 47bhp was according to *The Autocar* good for 75mph and 0-60mph in 31.1 seconds.

Perhaps for many buyers the Oxford's lethargy didn't matter. With its excellent rack-and-pinion steering, generous track and well-controlled torsion-bar front suspension, the Morris could be cornered with a brio you'd be hard-pushed to achieve in say a box-steered Austin Devon, whilst at the same time offering comfortable accommodation for all the family, helped by the bench front seat that was always part of the specification. An honest and essentially sturdy car, it was in the tradition of what people bought Morrises for, as Eric Lord acknowledged to the author. "That old slogging side-valve engine

The LCVs used the Cowley name; this rare surviving van has a Martin Walter Utilavan conversion. (Author)

Early LCVs were photographed with black-painted wheels and hubcaps. Body colours were beige, blue, dark green and grey. (Author's collection)

The pick-up had a generous length of load-bed. A chassis/cab was also available. (Author's collection)

The Oxford and Minor Travellers were visually very similar but the MO boasted 10in more loadspace length with the rear seat down. (Author's collection)

There were no rear reflectors on the Traveller, as these only became a legal requirement in October 1954; the rear doors were aluminium-panelled. (Author's collection)

These half-ton vans assembled in South Africa have a squarer rear body. (Author's collection)

where you almost needed pedal-assistance to pass anything! But it just kept slogging on – which is what a lot of people wanted, of course."

From October 1952 a woody MO 'Traveller's Car' was also available, with a wood-framed and aluminium-panelled rear body built by Morris Bodies Branch, in Coventry – home also of the wood-framed bodies for the Nuffield Taxi, the Riley RM and the MG T-type. Looking near-identical to the Minor version that would be launched a year later, only 5550 would be made. Additionally a half-ton van and a pick-up were on offer from 1950, along with a chassis-cab. Current until 1956, the LCVs ('light commercial vehicles') used a separate chassis, in the style of the Morris Minor van and pick-up; Cunard offered their own 'woody' on this commercial base, while Martin Walter of Folkestone sold a Utilavan estate conversion on the van. In all, 43,600 LCVs were produced.

The MO was largely unchanged throughout its life. For 1950 the rear axle ratio was lowered and for 1951 angled telescopic dampers were fitted

at the rear, bringing with it the deletion of the Panhard rod. In 1951 the central instrument panel changed from a crackle finish to plain gold cellulose, and the following year a bolder design of grille with a protuberant stainless-steel frame was introduced; the LCVs, however, retained the painted version of the original mazak grille they had always worn.

If the Minor became the best-known of the five 1948 debutantes, the Oxford was certainly no sales disgrace: between 1948 and 1954 Morris produced an impressive total of 154,932 MO saloons, against 232,034 Minor saloons and tourers in the same period. Most, especially in the early days, went to export, and sales remained relatively steady as the model aged: peak output of 32,584 cars in 1950 dropped to just over 28,000 in each of the Oxford's final two full years of life, 1952 and 1953. The car was also assembled as the Hindustan 14 in India.

Disappointment: the Morris Six

The final model in the new Morris range, the Six, was more closely related to its Wolseley sister, sharing its overhead-cam engine and differing only in its level of trim and its frontal treatment. Recalling pre-war Wolseley practice, the 2215cc in-line 'six' used a shaft-and-gear drive to the camshaft, with the bottom of the shaft driving the oil pump and the top the distributor; to ensure constant meshing of the gears, these were split in two and spring-loaded. The camshaft acted directly on hardened steel discs threaded onto the valve stems and incorporating a vernier adjustment whereby each click equalled one thou of valve clearance – a clever if fiddly feature.

Developing 70bhp, this engine, again mated to a four-speed gearbox with column change,

AUSTRALIA – A MARKET FOR BMC TO LOSE

At the formation of BMC, Austin and Nuffield cars dominated the Australian market. Between them they held a 30.4 per cent share in 1951, as Empire loyalty, a scarcity of American dollars, and the British government's policy of Imperial Preference kept out the previously-popular American cars. But the market was a rapidly expanding one, and one not likely to be bound by Empire ties if more suitable vehicles from elsewhere came along – especially if those vehicles were to be of an all-Australian make.

As much as anything, this was because, as elsewhere in the world, British vehicles, frantically exported under government pressure, soon proved themselves less than ideally suited to 'colonial' conditions. Without the right product, matters weren't going to change with the arrival of local assembly. And so, as the General Motors Holden established itself, buyers began to turn away from BMC. Holden's market share rose from 23 per cent in 1951 to 41.7 per cent in 1957, while BMC's share fell to 17.5 per cent.

Quite simply, the Holden was the sort of car Australians wanted. Once initial problems, such as a lack of body rigidity, had been tackled, it rapidly became an Australian institution. With no real competition, it became entrenched in the market, as high volume kept prices down and made it difficult for any would-be challenger to become established.

BMC sat back and let this happen. Yet as early as 1950 Lord Nuffield, always keenly interested in the Australian market, had recognised the threat posed by the Holden. On his orders a Holden was shipped back to Cowley. Talking to the author, Charles Griffin, later to become

Chief Engineer at Cowley, recalled Nuffield – "a very wise old bird" – telling him "that's the sort of car we should be making".

This was not an unfamiliar tune: in 1947 Lord Nuffield had cabled Cowley from Australia to state the urgent need for a six-cylinder vehicle to compete with those offered by other manufacturers. In 1948, too, consideration was given to a 'Coupé Express' 15cwt pick-up based on the Morris Six – a 'ute' of this sort being just the thing the Australians loved.

The snag was that to produce a Holden rival would demand investment – not least in a new engine, as Nuffield's only small 'six' was the complex and unreliable overhead-cam unit found in the Morris Six and the Wolseley 6/80. To produce a car specifically for the then-small Australian market simply didn't look viable – and doubtless also evoked memories of the catastrophic Empire Oxford of the late '20s. There was also some doubt about whether the notion of needing a big rugged car to go bush-whacking was just an antipodean affectation, according to Griffin. "Management took the attitude, I suppose, that any European going to Australia would take – that the Australians were always talking about the outback but never going there." So Lord Nuffield's suggestion was taken no further.

In retrospect this appears a crucial mistake, as the investment would almost certainly have paid off in the longer term. In case, what price a widened Morris Six with a simplified pushrod variant of its 2.2-litre ohc power unit. Such a car would even have looked a bit like the original 'Humpy Holden'...

This drawing of an MS-based pick-up dates from 1948, at which stage consideration was given to such a model; it would have been ideal for Australia. (BMIHT)

This 'king cab' conversion of the MO-based half-tonner was carried out by the Morris distributor in Chile. (Author's collection)

Danish distributor DOMI devised this removable top for the pick-up. (Author's collection)

This Cowley LCV was built up in Finland as a hearse. (Author's collection)

The Cunard Utility Car had four doors; it was ash-framed and panelled in oak-faced ply, with a wood-lath roof. (Author's collection)

was mounted in a longer-nosed version of the MO bodyshell, with the wheelbase extended by a substantial 13in to 9ft 1in and overall length up 10in to 14ft 9in. Minor-inspired torsion-bar front suspension was retained, along with a leaf-sprung live back axle damped by lever-arms and again controlled laterally by a Panhard rod. The front dampers – initially, at least – were again lever-arms, a twin-arm type sitting on a

turret and serving as the upper wishbone of the suspension system. A key difference, however, was that unlike the Minor and the MO, the Six, in common with the 4/50 and 6/80, used a Bishop cam-and-peg steering box, as the engine was too bulky to allow room for a rack. This gave the Six notably cumbersome steering, at four turns lock-to-lock.

In service, the Six and its Wolseley 6/80 sister were a disaster. The longer-wheelbase 'sixes' folded in the middle if driven with too much gusto on unmade African or Australian roads, while all models suffered from weak dampers and the knock-on effect of inner wings that deformed as a result of the pounding the bump-stops received. "The body structure was very weak – so much so that if the dampers faded slightly it was one of the few independent-front-suspension cars that suffered from wheel wobble. We were telling 'Issi' about this and he wouldn't have any of it," Morris development engineer Charles Griffin told the author.

"They were bumping about in the outback, and the next thing they knew was that they couldn't shut the doors because the vehicle had sagged in the middle. I think the Old Man was in Australia at the time, and all hell broke loose," recalled Morris engineer Mark Yeatman-Reed in a 1997 interview. "Cables went back and forth. Issigonis got a team together and they designed a brace to make the whole thing stable. And they sent about a dozen people all over the world to fit this, in the outback or wherever. It went on for about 18 months in all. The joke at Cowley was 'Issi gone yet?'. The Old Man was absolutely flaming mad about it." To remedy things, the body was indeed reinforced, with two triangular braces from the inner wing to the bulkhead; substantial numbers of cars were recalled to Cowley to have the braces retro-fitted. Additionally in 1949 telescopic dampers were fitted at the rear, followed during 1950 by an unusual two-per-side telescopic installation at the front.

According to Griffin the modifications to the Six and its Wolseley sister transformed it, to the point where it developed a reputation for ruggedness. "It became known as the No.1 car for durability. It would stand up to outback roads – unmetalled roads – very well. The car that had the reputation for standing up to outback conditions before we straightened up the Wolseley was the old Chevy. We made our thing match that."

But these traumas were only half the story. The expensive-to-produce ohc engine was not only poorly cooled – despite a revised cylinder head introduced in 1952 – but was notoriously prone to burning out its exhaust valves, a problem made worse by the low-quality fuels and oils of the time. Valves lasted 15,000 miles if you were lucky, 5000 miles if you were unlucky. The police, heavy Wolseley users – in both senses of the word – had replacement heads built up ready to be installed on their 6/80s at the slightest hint of trouble. Stellite hardening pushed valve life up to maybe 25,000 miles, but Nuffield never adopted this process. The problem was inherent in the means of valve actuation, which prevented the valve from rotating as it opened and closed, and in despair Morris Engines began to develop a related pushrod unit.

Two hits, three misses

With the Holden available in Australia from roughly the same time, the Six was never likely to make much of an impact in its principal export market, especially given its early problems. So it was: only 12,400 Sixes were made before the model was axed in 1953. The Wolseley 6/80, which stayed in production until 1954, managed rather better, with 25,281 made. The significant numbers bought by the British police helped, but equally the car had a greater appeal to private buyers than the Morris. The Wolseley grille and the superior interior appointments counted for something, yet the price premium over the Six was a realistic 12 per cent.

In contrast, the smaller 4/50 was a far less attractive proposition. At £904 in 1951, it was a full £206 – or nearly 30 per cent – more expensive than a Morris Oxford, and was actually undercut by the £883 Morris Six. Consider, too, that a

Zephyr Six cost £740 and a broad-shouldered Standard Vanguard £857. In return you got a posh radiator grille, some wood and leather, and marginally less slothful performance than the flathead Oxford offered: the 4/50 weighed a substantial 2cwt more than the MO, so the extra 8bhp or so delivered by the ohc engine hardly made much of a difference. By 1951 sales had collapsed, production falling from 1950's 3214 cars to a miserable 1342 units. When it was discontinued in 1952 a mere 8925 had been made, representing a paltry 5.3 per cent of combined MO and 4/50 output.

All things considered, this wasn't a happy scenario for the Morris business. Of its five keynote models, arguably only two had been a success. Worse, despite all the investment in a unified range of new power units, not a single one of the cars had a satisfactory engine.

In 1951 there was consideration of a grille similar to that on the Morris Minor; it didn't quite work aesthetically. (BMIHT)

Another possible facelift was this wraparound rear screen tried by Nuffield stylists in 1952. Again this never made it to production. (BMIHT)

The Six had a traditional vertical grille – supposedly at the insistence of Lord Nuffield. (LAT)

The extra length of the Six's bonnet is clear in this shot. The big Morris was claimed to offer 'Powerful, luxurious motoring at modest cost'. (Author's collection)

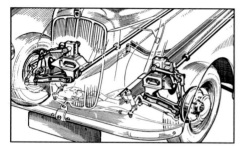

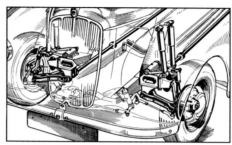

The original MS front suspension used lever-arm dampers that were not up to the job. Note the length of the torsion bars and the system of relays for the steering. The revised installation used an upper wishbone and paired telescopics – a big improvement. (Author's collection)

Cowley was keen to demonstrate that the big Morrises and Wolseleys were now suitably robust. This photo was taken at the Army's tank-testing grounds in Surrey. (Author's collection)

This Morris Six was entered in the 1951 Monte Carlo Rally by Dorset dealers E Channon & Son. It did not figure in the results. (Author's collection)

Rubbing salt into the wound, Wolseley, once a reasonably well-burnished jewel in the corporate crown, was looking an increasingly tarnished asset. Sales in 1937 were 15,313 units, or 14.6 per cent of combined Morris and Wolseley sales; in 1950, output of 9079 Wolseleys was just 8.4 per cent of this figure. Meanwhile, sales of Rileys were

on a downward trajectory from 1951, output of the old-fashioned MG Y-type saloon was dwindling, and after peaking in 1952 the sales of Abingdon's bedrock T-type sports cars would fall away sharply in 1953 and 1954.

It is hard not to conclude that the Nuffield Organisation was again losing traction. In compensation, it was still capital-rich: after a patchy 1948, profits before tax had jumped from £1.4m to over £7.2m in 1950, and rose again, to £8.7m in 1951. That year the accounts showed over £3.7m of retained profits, so if there were failings in the product range, at least Morris had the pounds-shillings-and-pence firepower to address the problem.

Merger with Austin

We are, however, jumping ahead of ourselves. By the time that Cowley was in a position to deliver a final judgement on the MM-MO-MS trio and their Wolseley spin-offs, the Nuffield Organization had ceased to exist as an independent entity. What to many eyes was unthinkable – and to others was simply unforgivable – had actually come to pass: Nuffield had merged with principal rival Austin.

Already the idea had been explored, directly after the departure of Miles Thomas, and following on from a re-establishment of relations between Lord Nuffield and Leonard Lord. On 10 October 1946, Nuffield's 69th birthday[1], Lord had rung up Nuffield's office and asked personal secretary Carl Kingerlee to pass on his best wishes. Kingerlee had suggested that Lord speak directly to 'WRM' and within a few minutes a friendly rapport had been re-established.

Kingerlee told Andrews and Brunner what happened next. "When Thomas went, Lord came down to see [Lord Nuffield], Nuffield having asked him to come in when passing. Things were very difficult. Nuffield decided he would not have another Vice-Chairman, but run the factory himself, with Reggie as his Managing Director. Then they talked about amalgamation. It was argued by the Board. Then Nuffield did something which he rarely does – started having these blokes up individually and [we] could see he was hesitating about it. Hanks and [the] others all wavered and that was the failure of that one. There was also the financial angle..."

[1] This is the date given in the Andrews and Brunner transcripts. In Wealth Well-Given, Tony Lewin cites a date of October 1947. Graham Turner, in The Leyland Papers, puts the phone-call as being in October 1950. Kingerlee's chronology is coherent and was furnished in a 1954 interview, when the events described were fairly recent. It thus stands a chance of being correct, although a 1947 date, tying in with Nuffield's 70th birthday, might be more plausible.

THE J-TYPE VAN

The replacement for the Y-type semi-forward-control van duly arrived in 1948, in time for the late-autumn Commercial Motor Show. The sliding-door 10cwt Morris J-type had a separate ladder-frame chassis, a beam front axle, a 36bhp version of the 1478cc Oxford MO side-valve engine, and a pre-war three-speed gearbox.

Fully forward-control, the J-type's most novel feature was its heavily-offset engine: to keep the van suitably narrow, Morris engineers rejected a central location for the power unit, and instead put it right over – and well forward – on the passenger's side, with the rear axle having the differential offset to match. Left-hand-drive versions have a mirror image of this arrangement.

The Post Office was a major user of the vans. As was its practice, it requested various items of special equipment, including rubber front and rear wings to cut down on panelbeating bills following arguments with gateposts and the like. As a consequence, GPO vans have the headlamps and sidelights mounted on the body rather than on the wings.

From 1957 the 'J' used the BMC B-series engine and accompanying four-speed gearbox. In this later 'JB' form it was also offered as an Austin 101, with a different radiator grille. Production ended in early 1961, by which stage 48,621 J-types had been made.

An early J-type with the MO engine; the later JB had a 42bhp B-series unit. (LAT)

Reggie Hanks – who was in fact appointed Vice-Chairman – recalled how he had dissuaded Nuffield from going ahead. "Morris's were at a very low ebb at that time – their model policy and everything else was not settled. Then Nuffield and Lord were talking about this merger. [I] persuaded Morris out of it, saying 'Let us present a Nuffield merger which is presentable' and suggested [I] should be given 3–4 years before they talked about it."

Possibly as a way of retrieving something from the wreckage of these negotiations, in October 1948 a joint announcement was made:

Lord Nuffield and Mr LP Lord have recently had a series of talks which have resulted in an arrangement whereby there is to be a constant interchange of information on production methods, costs, purchases, design and research, patents and all other items which would be likely to result in manufacturing economies.

The object is to effect maximum standardisation coupled with the most efficient manufacture, and, by the pooling of all factory resources, a consequent reduction of costs.

What this meant was another matter. The press judged the proposed co-operation to be a preliminary step towards a merger. It was, said *The Autocar*, an 'almost breath-taking' announcement. It would surely result in lower prices, and maybe the two companies might set up joint assembly plants abroad. At the very least it should allow commonalisation of electrical components and other bought-in parts. Perhaps, though, things might evolve further. 'One can conceive that in the course of time an engine, for example, made at Longbridge might find itself being assembled into a chassis at Cowley, or conversely that a product of the Nuffield engine factory at Coventry might be fitted in a chassis at Longbridge,' pondered the magazine.

But it wasn't long before the old rivalries re-asserted themselves and in mid-1949 a joint statement was issued, to the effect that the two companies would go their own ways. By this time, in any case, a Standardisation Committee had been established, pulling together all the major manufacturers, so there was less need for Austin and Morris to work together. The results of this committee were undeniable: to give just one example, it was reported in 1952 that the 48 distinct types of dynamo used before the war had beden whittled down to a mere three.

But by this juncture it was clear to people such as Kingerlee that Nuffield was no longer really fit to be at the helm of a modern conglomerate. "[We] had a new Board and I and Nuffield went to Australia. I came back and realized Nuffield was very retrospective in his outlook. He was still back in the days of coachbuilt motor cars in his own mind and I began to get very worried about it. Reggie was tired to hear [of] little troubles – another characteristic of old people. Instead of worrying about steel he worried about a man cleaning windows... Reggie said it could not go on."

Eventually Kingerlee tried again to bring Lord Nuffield and Leonard Lord together, and in late 1951 the two met at Nuffield Place. This time there was an agreement to merge the two companies, this being duly announced at the end of November that year. 'Both industrial and financial circles were taken completely by surprise,' wrote *The Motor*. So it was that at the end of the year the British Motor Corporation – or BMC – came into being, with Lord Nuffield as Chairman and Leonard Lord as Deputy Chairman and Managing Director; after six months Nuffield would step down, to become Honorary President, leaving Lord as Chairman. In 1951 Austin and Morris between them built 243,211 cars. In 1952, output would be slightly lower, at 235,777 units, but the fact that Ford that year turned out 93,499 cars gives an idea of the dominant position the new combine held.

This was little consolation for those senior executives who felt that they had been sold down the river. "There was a lot of bitterness... chiefly because, other than Dono, they were all frightened for their jobs," commented Kingerlee. Whether Reggie Hanks was frightened for his job or not, he was furious that the whole deal had been tied up behind his back. He was also vehemently against the fusion of the two companies, telling Andrews and Brunner that for Lord Nuffield it was "another escape from not knowing what was going on in his own business... but there was no reason from the balance sheet for Nuffield to be anything but proud and happy, but since he was so aloof he got into feelings of fidget and worry..."

The act of a fool – or a visionary?

For Leonard Lord, the coming-together of the two companies was 'natural' but at the same time "arose out of the fact that [Nuffield] knew little about his own organization. Morris was not doing so well. He cast around and found no one in his own opinion who was the right person to talk over his organization with, so he came back to me. I was in his debt because he took me up from nowhere and I had to help him. [There was] no discussion about it – [it was] all done over a cup of tea. He was getting old and asked if I would think about [Morris] joining up with Austin. I had responsibilities to Austin and so had to make sure it was right and proper, so said I would see him in a week's time. [I] then said it seemed reasonable [and] said [the] only way to do it is to make a straight swap of shares – 'If that is all right for you, it is all right for me.' [We] never discussed anything about the price of shares or anything. It was just like that – [there's] no story behind it."

Asked by Andrews and Brunner about the reasons for making one of the most determining decisions of his career, Nuffield was singularly vague in his response. '[One] could not say so but in fact he got tired of being misled by people not telling him things,' his biographers noted after a 1954 interview. 'Basically, however, it was the same story as before – that an amalgamation would reduce costs, that you could buy better, and so on.' Tellingly, he returned to an old *leitmotif*, implying that he had never had the right lieutenants since the death of the much-admired Lancelot Pratt, saying that if Pratt had lived, he would never have done it.

It is tempting to condemn the merger as an act of resignation by a tired old man who had lost interest in the increasingly arduous struggle to run a complex company in complex times. But there is another argument, namely that Lord Nuffield was ahead of the curve, with a visionary appreciation of the new industrial realities. In global terms, Austin and Morris were relatively small fry, and they were devoting a lot of energy to fighting each other. Nuffield, by mentality a buyer rather than a creator,

This 1950 advertising artwork clearly shows the family resemblance of the three Morrises. Note for sociologists: real men smoked pipes back then. (Author's collection)

Hanks (far right) was against the merger, talks for which Lord Nuffield had conducted behind his back. Carl Kingerlee is far left in this 1950 photo, with Charles Mullens, Overseas Director and former Wolseley MD, between him and Nuffield. (Author's collection)

could see that to compete with the US firms that were now expanding rapidly in Europe, and with state-supported companies such as Renault and Volkswagen, it was necessary to drive costs down by sharing components, so that they could be bought or produced in greater numbers, and thus more cheaply. He also surely recognised that Leonard Lord, who had once already turned his company around, remained one of the best-regarded production engineers in the motor industry, and could do the same thing again. Creating the world's fourth-largest motor-manufacturing business could be judged as the crowning achievement in a dazzling career, and one calculated to ensure the survival and continued development of the enterprise he had created.

It can also be pointed out that he had heeded Reggie Hanks's advice, and waited until the business was financially strong, As the most profitable UK-owned car operation, the Nuffield Organization was in better health than Austin, and could reasonably expect to be the more powerful partner in the merged company. On the other hand, however, Austin had invested substantially in up-to-date facilities. The CAB 1 ('Car Assembly Building 1') installation finished in 1951 was claimed to make Longbridge the most modern plant in the country and had the capacity to make 100,000 cars a year. Ironically, former Morris engineer Frank Woollard was involved, and proudly asserted that it featured probably more automatic transfer machines than any other British factory.

In all this, what is equally true, of course, is that revisionist historians can look at what happened next and come to the unprovable but nonetheless attractive conclusion that Morris would have been better off staying independent. Alternatively, perhaps it might have been better allying itself with a weaker company, still achieving economies of scale and buying market share, but with the Nuffield Organization much more clearly the dominant partner. In 1950 Reginald Rootes apparently approached Hanks, a personal friend, about a possible merger with the Rootes Group; it is interesting to speculate what might have been the outcome of such a union.

The Minor Series II and Minor 1000

The slatted grille introduced for 1955 modernized the Minor a little. It was body-colour until early 1959, exccept on black cars, where it was in Birch Grey; thereafter a Pearl Grey was standardised, with no exceptions, giving way to Old English White for 1961 and to a brighter Snowberry White for 1968. (Author's collection)

The Minor would evolve steadily over the years, after it was given a new Austin-derived engine. Attempts to replace it came to nothing, and it remained a well-loved and emblematic model – especially the wood-framed Traveller.

It was the Minor that felt the consequences of the merger before any other model. In late 1950 it had been decided to fit the overhead-valve Wolseley Eight engine to the Minor – apparently after briefly re-considering making do with a bored-out 980cc version of the 918cc side-valve unit. The idea was that a limited number of engines would be available towards the end of 1951 for the four-door Minor and the still-to-be-launched LCV vans, for which the ohv engine would provide the improved performance required. Full-scale production would then begin in early 1952, with the engine accounting for roughly 40 per cent of Morris Engines output.

Death of a 'beautiful' engine

This programme soon began to slip. By July 1951 modifications to the body to take the new engine had not been finalised and by October that year – by which time the ohv Minor should have been announced – the transfer machinery was still not in place, and was not likely to be in operation before January 1953. The reasons were various. The Korean War had deflected the machine-tool industry into armament production. Then the change of tack from a 980cc side-valve to a 918cc pushrod unit had meant that design work on the transfer machinery had to start again, and a further delay had been occasioned by a decision to switch from metric to SAE threads. Meanwhile, Austin had pinched Morris's place in the queue at machine-tool supplier Archdale. The best that could be hoped for, the board was told, was building engines for stock on the existing machinery, for the debut of a re-engined four-door at the 1952 Motor Show. This never happened: in July 1952 the export four-door Minor was given the Austin A30's pushrod engine, as a prelude to it being standardised across a revised SII Minor range. The ex-Austin power unit was of just 803cc and developed 30bhp at 4800rpm, with maximum torque of 39 lb ft at 2400rpm. In January 1953 the last four-door Series MM was made, and a month later the last two-door and convertible MMs. Henceforth all Minors would be to Series

II specification – physically identical to the MM but for a new bonnet-top mascot and a long-tailed bonnet badge.

John Barker, who was an engineer in the Morris Engines Branch experimental department at the time, confirmed to the author that the transfer machinery for the Wolseley engine did in fact arrive at the Morris engine plant at Courthouse Green. "We'd reached the stage of getting the transfer machines ready for it to go

There is little to distinguish this early SII from an MM. The painted grille and longer bonnet were both introduced on the MM during 1951. (Author)

The 'cheesegrater grille' Traveller only lasted a season. Once a De Luxe specification arrived for 1954, standard Minors in Black and Clarendon Grey had a body-colour grille. (Author's collection)

The LCVs lacked the bonnet coachline moulding and the 'Morris Minor' bonnet-side badging, while the tail-less MM-series front badge and accompanying bonnet-top strip were retained. This is a Utilavan estate conversion by Martin Walter. (Author's collection)

Rare beast: a surviving first-series SII pick-up. The optional tilt cover was always in buff canvas, right through to the end of pick-up production. (Author)

A rubber-wing GPO engineer's van; the wings are attached by self-tapping screws and spring clips. An opening windscreen for the driver featured on split-screen Post Office vans almost to the last. (LAT)

into production. We were a long, long way down the road – imagine the amount of space all the machines took up on the factory floor and the planning that would have to have gone on to install them. Sid Barron, the Chief Planning Engineer, was assured the engine was going into production, and then overnight 'The Austin' had its way, and the A30 engine took over. He was very, very bitter. He had done so much work to get the Wolseley engine into production. He was terribly upset, and really felt very let down."

In terms of the economies of mass-production, the decision had strong merits. Austin had tooled up for extensive production of a modern pushrod engine, while Morris was lagging on its tooling-up, and this for an engine which was essentially an adapted pre-war unit. The elimination of the Wolseley engine was all the same a hurtful blow to Nuffield engineers. "It was superb – it was a beautiful engine which really made the Minor," Jack Daniels once told the author. "I drove the prototype Wolseley-engined Minor a lot – probably more than anybody. Once I borrowed it for a holiday in the West Country, and I had the best ride across Bodmin Moor that I've ever had. I loved it. It went very well – the traffic was nose-to-tail and I took everything in sight. There was nothing to stop me. It was a really nice little car, with a good performance. I'm still of the opinion that had we been able to put the 918cc ohv engine in the Minor that would have been magnificent."

Series II – and three new models

As a stunt to promote the new Series II, Morris took a four-door to Goodwood race track and ran the car for 10,000 miles non-stop, over ten days. When servicing, re-fuelling or a driver change were required the car was hooked up – always under power – to a special U-shaped trailer towed by an adapted Morris Cowley half-ton pick-up. Continuous running of the car was thereby possible, with changing of a rear wheel achievable thanks to a lockable differential. At an average speed of a little over 45mph, the Morris turned in fuel consumption figures of between 39.4mpg and 43.0mpg; the only failure was of a voltage-control regulator.

Notwithstanding their participation in this venture, Nuffield men regarded the Series II Minor as a grossly inferior vehicle to the stillborn Wolseley-engined Minor. They had a point, and not only in that the Austin engine had a weak bottom end; even without this, it was only capable of giving the Minor acceptable performance as a result of oddly-spaced gears and a low final drive. One unimpressed *Motor Sport* reader calculated that if both cars were run in top gear, when a Volkswagen had attained 70,000 miles an 803cc Minor, with its low overall gearing, would have notched up a mere 43,000 miles for the same number of engine revolutions. Nor was the Austin back axle, fitted across the range from the beginning of 1954, anything like as robust as the Morris unit it replaced.

But the fact remains that the old Morris Eight side-valve had bestowed on the Minor pretty lacklustre acceleration and only gave of its best with meticulous tuning. The A-series Austin engine endowed the Minor with a touch of sparkle, and was probably reliable enough for the average take-it-easy British motorist. Further afield, proof that the Series II didn't necessarily leave its big ends in the road after 20,000 miles was furnished by a four-door SII *petit taxi* in Fez, Morocco, that in 1955 was reported as having covered 72,000 miles in 18 months with only a decoke and a valve grind.

Equally to the point, the Austin engine allowed Morris to go ahead with launching first the light commercial vehicle (or LCV) versions of the Minor and then the wood-framed Traveller. The van and pick-up were announced in May 1953. They were built on a separate chassis – although the front end followed the same lines as the unit-construction passenger Minors, and retained their torsion-bar independent front suspension. One beneficial change was that at the rear they used more efficient telescopic dampers, lightly angled inwards to aid axle location. The axle itself was the 5.375-to-1 Austin unit of regular SIIs – quite low enough for most purposes.

Whitewall tyres give an unusual look to this slatted-grille four-door, photographed at the 1956 Paris show alongside an MG Magnette ZB. (Author's collection)

This 1954 proposal for a Minor replacement marks a clear break with the Issigonis era, but seems too clumsy to have been created under the aegis of the artistically talented Gerald Palmer – who denied all knowledge of the design when the author tackled him on the subject. (BMIHT)

The LCV was also available as a chassis-cab unit, with or without a cab back, allowing outside coachbuilders to construct tall gown-vans, their own design of van, or even a different interpretation of Minor estate car. Relatively few people availed themselves of this opportunity, only 460 chassis-cabs – both open and closed – being despatched in 1954, against 14,583 vans and pick-ups.

As might be expected for Nuffield's major fleet customer, vans for the Post Office were to a unique specification. The most obvious feature of cheesegrater-grille models was the use of rubber front wings, as had also been specified for the GPO's J-types. These brought with them exposed 'bug-eye' wing-top headlamps, as first seen on at least one LCV prototype.

The Minor 1000 as a two-door. Amazingly, trafficators were retained until 1961, making the Minor the last British car to be so-equipped. (Author's collection)

The A-series engine came good as a 948cc unit; in this form it developed 37bhp, rising to 48bhp in bored-and-stroked 1098cc guise. (Author's collection)

October 1953 saw the announcement of the Morris Minor Traveller's Car – as it was originally called. Based on a part-completed two-door shell, rather than on the separate LCV chassis, it used the wider doors of the two-door body. From the start the Traveller had the Austin three-quarter-floating back axle. The Traveller was offered in basic and De Luxe forms, both having a one-piece rubber floor mat rather than carpeting. It's worth pointing out that the Traveller put the British Motor Corporation ahead of the game: it was the first series-production small estate car from a British manufacturer that was not a converted van. It was also launched a year before the estate version of the Standard Ten and two years ahead

of Ford's van-derived Escort and Squire models. Given this pioneering role, it is perhaps easier to understand why Cowley did not tool up for a full pressed-steel body – something it surely came to regret, as discussed later.

With van, pick-up and estate variants on offer, and a steadily more prosperous home market, the revised Minor proved an undoubted success, with sales on a constant upwards curve in the years 1953–55. Thus BMC could afford to mark time with nothing more than a superficial facelift, this duly arriving in time for the 1954 Motor Show. Essentially this comprised a new front panel with a horizontal-slat grille and a new dashboard with a single central dial. The revised frontal treatment – bringing with it reshaped front wings – certainly modernised the Minor's looks, but the new dashboard was a debatable improvement. Mechanically the car was unchanged, although the addition of an adjustable engine steady-bar did help reduce clutch judder. Interior trim was as before, too, so all things considered the 1955 model-year Minor was no great advance; what it really needed was a more broad-shouldered power unit, with more sensible gearing.

The 'New Minor' that never was
It had never been intended, pre-merger, that the Minor would still be in production in 1955, largely unchanged. Alec Issigonis and his team had been busy working on the next generation of Morrises, not only evolving a new body style

– similar to that seen on the 1954 Series II Morris Oxford – but also investigating front-wheel drive. When Issigonis left to work for Alvis, in 1952, his successor Gerald Palmer carried on refining the design proposals left behind, and by 1954 a remarkably ungainly 'New Minor' had been created by the Cowley styling department. Perhaps fortunately, this horror, envisaged as being powered by a 1200cc version of the ex-Austin B-series engine, was passed over in favour of a proposal by Austin's stylists under Dick Burzi. Conservatively inoffensive, this made its way towards production, based on the Minor floorpan, only for BMC to change its mind: with Minor sales still increasing at a gratifying rate, and with an improved 948cc version of the A-series engine ready to go, it was decided to keep the old favourite in production.

All the work on a 'New Minor' was not wasted, however: instead the car metamorphosed into a brace of more up-market vehicles, the Wolseley 1500 and Riley One-point-Five, that retained in their essentials the entire Minor understructure and suspension. It does seem, though, that there were some hesitations, because right up until 1957 a stripped-out lower-powered Morris variant, the Morris 1200, was on the cards as a big brother to the Minor; indeed, 5568 such cars were sold in the Republic of Ireland.

Maturity – the Minor 1000

The October 1956 Motor Show marked the Minor's coming of age, with its transformation into the 948cc Minor 1000. This didn't come a moment too soon. After peaking at an estimated 106,439 cars and LCVs in 1955, Minor production slipped to an estimated 83,943 vehicles in 1956. The Series II had served its purpose, but there was only so much you could achieve with such an under-engined compromise, especially in ever more competitive export markets.

The heart of the Minor 1000 was the revised and enlarged 948cc engine. This had a new block with siamesed bores, but more crucially used lead-indium instead of white-metal bearings – a major contribution to improved durability. Developing 37bhp at 4750rpm, it was mated to a revised gearbox with more sensibly arranged ratios, better synchromesh, and a particularly effective remote change. Other mechanical changes were stronger swivels (except on some very early 1000s) and a higher final-drive ratio.

In the 1000, Morris at last had a Minor with an engine and gearbox worthy of its chassis,

The centre-dial dash of the 1000 had two lids until late 1961, when both were deleted; that on the passenger side returned with the restyled interior for 1965. (Author's collection)

This convertible has the bigger rear window introduced with the 1000. In 1959 the soft-top accounted for 5.7 per cent of Minor sales, but this would dwindle. (BMIHT)

and the raft of improvements that came with the new powerpack gave the car a new lease of life – not least a modernised body with a one-piece windscreen and an enlarged rear window. With the peppy new engine and its snappy remote-control gearchange the Minor was immeasurably more pleasant to drive, while the interior appointments would arguably become the best they would ever be during the six-year currency of these first-generation 1000s.

The Minor Million, of which 350 were made. The millionth Minor was supposed to have starred at the 1960 Motor Show, but production was delayed by unofficial strikes at some BMC factories, and the car, with a build date of 22 December 1960, officially only came off the line on 3 January 1961. (BMIHT)

weeds were starting to grow up through the floorboards," top Californian dealer Kjell Qvale once told the author. Yet interest revived during the later-'50s import boom, and it was only in 1959 that sales in the States had their best year, with Minors forming the lion's share of the 14,991 Morrises sold in the US that year.

Qvale was one of those who was happy to ride the wave. "I liked the damn car, that was the trouble, so I kept dragging it back. You wouldn't think that you could quit something for two or three years and then bring it back again, and still sell it. But people loved that little Station Wagon. That was the cutest thing you ever made. The Minor was a goofy car, a funny little thing. I don't know – there was something about them. They were a kind of clever little car..."

Clever, cute or whatever, Minor sales in the US tumbled after 1959, and had again evaporated by 1962: imports to the States that year of 348 Morrises was a long way from the near tenfold jump to 4375 cars in 1957. Whether BMC could have done a lot better is all the same a valid question.

John Boyd of the British Consulate-General in New York wrote in 1957 to the local SMMT about the grumbles he had received from JS Inskip, the East Coast distributor. 'Inskip has complained bitterly to the Embassy about BMC's failure to supply this market with sufficient Morris 1000s,' reported Boyd. 'He apparently said that the BMC dealers throughout the USA had got together and were prepared to order at the rate of 2200 a month, but that the factory were only supplying 600 a month. I understand... that even this figure may not be maintained.' Perhaps BMC was merely being prudent: Renault burnt its fingers badly with the uncontrolled import of Dauphines into the States, ending up with a year's stock of cars deteriorating in storage pounds around the States.

Celebrating the millionth Minor
Once the Mini had arrived in 1959, the Minor took second place at Cowley in terms of production volume. Whilst the new Issigonis model might have represented a big step forward in terms of motor-car technology, it didn't do much good to BMC's finances: company figures the author has unearthed, relating to US-market vehicles for 1963, give a 1961–62 cost of production for a US-spec Mini De Luxe of £241.13s.1d (£241.65), against £238.12s.9d (£238.64) for a US-spec Minor two-door De Luxe. This was when the Minor

The market responded. Despite the Minor being ten years old at the time, sales peaked in 1958, with 113,699 passenger versions leaving Cowley, and went on to crack the one-million barrier in 1960 – the first time a British vehicle had achieved this milestone. Admittedly a year earlier Volkswagen had produced its three millionth Beetle. But it is only fair to point out that it took until 1958 for Renault to breach the one-million mark with its little 4CV, first on sale in 1947, while Citroën's millionth 2CV only arrived in 1962, nearly 13 years after its 1949 launch. Given the extended range of cars produced by Nuffield and by BMC, the company had every right to feel proud.

Riding the import wave: Stateside revival
Amazingly, part of this latter-day success was a resurgence of Minor sales in the States, after they had crumbled to virtually nothing in the 1954–56 period. "We had a real slow-down, and at one stage I had a hundred in a lot, and the

The 'Morris-Healey'

One of the more oddball Morris Minors was a one-off fitted with Austin-Healey 100 mechanicals. Created by the Donald Healey Motor Company and using part of the 100's chassis, according to Geoffrey Healey it was built in 1953. "It was done when we were looking at the problem of producing bodies and the thought was that it might be possible to take the Morris Minor and use it as the basis for a motor car. It was quite a good car but whether you'd have sold a great many would have been another matter. It would have been a way of producing a low-cost sporting car..."

The car is also remembered by Healey stylist Gerry Coker. "They used it as a runabout. As far as I remember, it was a 100 with a Morris Minor body on it. It was a two-door black saloon – like a Q-ship... I think the bonnet was a bit longer, and that was all, so when you were sitting at the lights people thought you were in a Morris Minor, and then you'd floor it. As far as I know it wasn't anything more than a fun job."

This Morris hot-rod – 95bhp in a Minor has surely to be pretty tasty – had been brewing for some while, evidence suggests. According to the memories of early Healey collaborator 'Sammy' Sampietro, as recounted to author Paul Skilleter, during the days of the Riley-engined cars Donald Healey gave consideration to a Minor fitted with the Riley 2½-litre power unit. This is corroborated by a reference in Morris boardroom minutes for May 1949 to Healey being in touch with George Dono of Nuffield Metal Products, with a view to the possible supply of Minor panels. Whether such a car was ever built has not been documented; most likely it remained a paper project.

retailed at £601 in Britain, and a Mini De Luxe at £535. With the Minor's healthy contribution to company profits, helped by its low warranty costs, one can understand BMC's reluctance to drop the model, as discussed below.

To celebrate the millionth Minor, in 1961 BMC came out with a limited-edition Minor, of which only 350 were made – including 30 with left-hand drive. Appropriately enough, the cars carried 'Minor 1000000' badging; less appropriately,

perhaps, the colour was a somewhat startling lilac, matched to ivory leather trim. Jack Field, then Nuffield sales promotion manager, can take responsibility for selecting the colour for the Minor Million, as he related to the author.

"Donald Harrison, the sales manager, said we were going to build the millionth Minor. I asked whether they wanted any particular colour. 'Yes,' he said. 'They want gold or silver.' So I got hold of the paint superintendent and he said we'd better

Laborious hand-building of the Traveller drove up costs – and the materials bill was equally elevated. (BMIHT)

go to ICI. So off we went, and I put my story. 'Well, we can't do gold,' they said. What about silver? 'We could do it,' I was told. 'But it would only last three months.' So I asked what colour I could have. 'Any colour in our regular range' was the reply. So that was that. It was agreed that the plant would do six or seven Minors in various

In 1956 BMC studied a four-door all-steel Traveller, in round-back and square-back styles. This would have shaved costs, but demanded an investment in tooling, for a model likely to have a short life: the usual bind. (BMIHT)

The 948cc LCVs were called the Series III, and always had silver wheels. Chassis-cabs were still available, but few were ordered, and production would finally end in 1967, in which year only 36 were made – after a mere eight in 1966. (Richard Barton)

The van retained small rear windows until the '62 arrival of the 1098cc Series V LCVs. This is a late SII GPO van, manufacture of which continued until January 1959 – with the opening screen only phased out in 1958. GPO SIII vans kept the 803cc engine. (Author)

colours, one being that lilac. I know I did an orange one, as Donald Harrison had a passion for orange, and I thought he'd choose that. And I think there might have been a kind of pale blue. The idea was that the directors would come down, see the cars displayed in the showroom, and then choose the colour they thought best. Unfortunately, they came down after lunch, and were in no state to make up their mind. All of them went except Donald Harrison, who asked me if they'd chosen a colour. 'No,' I replied. 'Have you?' When he said he hadn't, I asked him what he wanted me to do. 'Please your bloody self,' he said. So I chose the colour. It was generally acclaimed – you have to remember that this was a time when women were beginning to have more influence in colours being chosen."

Amidst all the 'Millionth Minor' junketings there was the predictable reassuring talk about production carrying on. "BMC have every confidence and faith in the continuance of the Minor and it will be manufactured so long as the general public want it," said Harry Roberts, manager of Nuffield Metal Products. It was stressed that BMC was still investing in the Minor, with a new draw die for production of the bonnet due to be installed and improvements to the making of the doors in hand.

But it was evident that the Minor's moment in the sun was drawing to a close. Alec Issigonis and his team – more particularly Charles Griffin at Cowley – were well on the way to launching the car intended to replace the Minor, the front-wheel-drive 1100; meanwhile, sales had dipped in 1960 and were to fall sharply in 1961. Thereafter they were to be in a continual steady decline.

The long goodbye: the 1098cc Minors

The last significant upgrade to the Minor came at the 1962 Motor Show, when the Minor received a 1098cc version of the A-series engine. This was a logical piece of rationalisation, the same engine being simultaneously standardised in the Austin A40 and the Sprite/Midget alongside its introduction in the 1100 saloon.

Mated to the new power unit via a larger clutch was a stronger gearbox featuring more efficient baulk-ring synchromesh and recognisable by its more rigid ribbed casing. Uprated brakes remained drum all-round, despite the use of front discs on the 1100: the front drums increased in diameter by an inch, to 8in, and there was a reduction in the bore of the rear wheel cylinders and the master cylinder.

Lesser phases of development saw new lights for 1964, and new interior trim for 1965, but in essence the Minor was left alone for the final nine or so years of its life. The 1100 had been supposed to replace it, but BMC suffered from a constitutional inability to rationalise its range, and kept the Minor in production without modernizing it – alongside the barely less old-fashioned Austin A40 and such antiques as the A35 and A55 vans. Whereas Ford had three basic ranges of car in 1966, BMC offered eleven different passenger vehicles – yet another reason for the poor state of its finances. This was typical of BMC's muddle-headed management: either the Minor should have been axed, in the name of manufacturing efficiency, or it should have been updated to keep it competitive in an increasingly hard-fought market.

One man who urged the latter course was old Issigonis friend and sometime BMC consultant Laurence Pomeroy. In December 1962 'Pom'

It is thought that Danish importer DOMI only built 50 or so of these Minor De Luxe vans, in both SII and 1000 guise; the body is in steel. (Anton Kamp Nielsen)

A MINOR MADE BY MG

Between 1960 and 1964 the MG factory at Abingdon assembled Travellers and LCVs. Making Minors helped compensate for a severe dip in sports-car sales. MGA output fell sharply in 1960 and really tumbled in 1961, to little more than a quarter of its 1959 peak, while Sprite sales fell in 1960 and didn't pick up in 1961 despite a new model and the arrival of the MG Midget; as for the Big Healey, production dropped by nearly an eighth in 1960 and then halved in 1961. Abingdon was catching a bad cold, not least as it was no longer making Magnettes or Rileys, and so was more than happy to add to Minor output.

A total of 10,818 Travellers were assembled at the MG works, the greatest annual production being 4268 cars in 1963. As for the vans, Abingdon built 9147 of these in the 1960–63 period, output peaking at 4439 units in 1961; in contrast, only 49 pick-ups were MG-made, all in 1962. Helped by Abingdon's contribution, overall output of the LCVs, which had been pretty steady, rose measurably in 1960 and quite substantially in 1961. Annual Minor production in the three full years of Abingdon manufacture was relatively stable, ranging from 6389 units in 1961 to 4562 units in 1963.

The penultimate – '64-only – version of the Traveller, with larger front flasher/sidelight units but still with the duotone seats introduced for the 1962 season. (Author's collection)

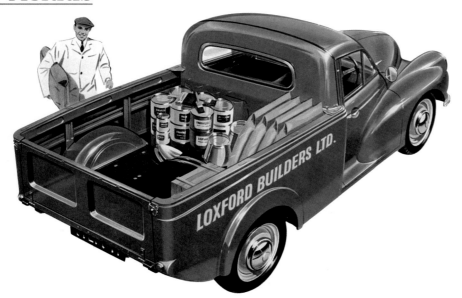

Half-timbered car, half-baked economics

Traveller output slipped a little during the life of the 1098cc Minor, but after a blip in 1964, when output jumped to 17,083 cars, annual production settled at a gently-rising 12,000 to 13,000 units for the 1965–67 period. In 1968 another jump saw 13,485 Travellers made, the most since 1964 and representing 41.9 per cent of all Minors produced that year. In 1970, the Traveller's last full year, an output of 10,062 cars out of total Minor production of 22,981 units represented 43.8 per cent of the total and was an increase over 1969's tally of 9567 Travellers. Given that it was unlikely any profit was being made on the model, thanks to its labour-intensive

The LCVs were always popular, and production in fact peaked in 1971; pick-ups hit their maximum annual output in 1969, with 3974 made, or 16 per cent of total LCV production. (Author's collection)

Silver wheels became standard across the range for 1968. The four-door sold in much smaller numbers than the two-door: in 1968, only 4315 would be made, against 14,067 two-doors – and a mere 346 convertibles. (Author's collection)

wrote to PR chief Reg Bishop suggesting a revised Minor with the 55bhp twin-carb Midget/Sprite engine and disc brakes. At a suggested cost of £556 including Purchase Tax, a two-door Minor to this specification, said Pomeroy, would offer 'substantially over 80mph' and would have 'the highest performance of any small closed car in Europe' – while costing £43 less than a Ford Anglia 1200. Perhaps on less firm ground, the exuberant Pomeroy also proposed painting the Traveller wood in body colour – imagine the maintenance nightmare – and fitting simulated cane inserts, along with full-diameter wheel discs, plated door hinges, and an improved rear light cluster.

construction, there must have been sore heads in the accounts department as the Traveller took an ever-increasing proportion of Minor sales.

"The body, with all that ash, cost us an arm-and-a-leg to put together," former Cowley manager Eric Lord told the author. "The only Minor we never made any money on was the Traveller... It was a very expensive car to assemble, because we had to bring the bodies in, and lift them up, one at a time, into what we called 'the loft'. Down below there was a feed line which we ran all the car production down, from the paintshop right down to the bottom of the assembly line, and you'd be standing in the loft with a hoist and you had to time the feed line so there was a gap so you could let the back end down to allow the car to be assembled. That was the problem, to get the front end and the back end together on a feed line that was running at the same speed as all the assembly lines were. It took a bit of timing... By the time we'd bought the body, brought it in, and assembled it, it had cost us money. If we'd put it together for nothing we'd still have lost money on it. I could not get the sales people to put the price up. Which was ridiculous – because the car was selling quite well, really. But they decided they wouldn't do it."

Confirmation of how the Traveller must have contributed to BMC's financial mess comes from those 1963-dated figures quoted earlier. Referring to US-market cars for the 1961–62 period, they show that the Traveller cost 18.3 per cent more to produce than the saloon, at a time when a Mini Countryman cost 7.8 per cent more to make than a Mini saloon. This was despite the costs for the Minor not including any write-down for amortiseation of tools. The breakdown of these figures is very interesting. Labour costs on a Traveller were calculated as being 26.7 per cent higher than on a two-door Minor De Luxe, and material costs as being 18.6 per cent higher. Yet in September 1963 the Traveller cost £606 in the UK, against £540 for the two-door. In other words, it sold at a 12.2 per cent premium. To reflect the extra cost of production, it should have cost £100 more, not £66 more. Admittedly it was already marginally more expensive than a £593 Ford Anglia De Luxe Estate. But a Triumph Herald Estate commanded £662, so the Traveller probably could have stood a higher price.

At last, the curtain...
Part of the dilemma with the Minor was that although sales were on a downward slide they still remained more than respectable, holding relatively steady in the 1964–67 period and only suffering their first sudden big drop in 1968. But the writing was on the wall, and the last convertible was made in June 1969, the last saloon in November 1970, and the last Traveller in April 1971; despite this, the two-door and the Traveller were still included in the Morris price list at the time of the 1971 Motor Show.

The commercials, meanwhile, outlived the private cars, continuing in production until February 1972. They had gained the 1098cc engine and transmission at the same time as the passenger cars, becoming known as the Series V. During 1962, just after production of these

revised LCVs had begun, manufacture moved to Adderley Park, the former Wolseley plant that from 1932 had been the home of Morris Commercial Cars Limited. This liberated more room at Cowley for the production of the Mini and the 1100, and it also saved a lot of transportation of bodyshells around the Midlands.

Indeed, from July 1969 the LCVs were joined at Adderley Park by the Traveller, a move that made obvious sense, given that both the front and rear of the latter's body were made in the Coventry/Birmingham area, along with most of the mechanics. One consequence of the transfer was that Birmingham-built Travellers were often painted in different colours from their Cowley siblings – including latterly a series of gruesomely inappropriate BL colours dreamed up by an ex-Ford colour man who had joined the company in the late 1960s along with various other former Ford staff.

From the late '60s the police used 1098cc two-doors, in Bermuda Blue with white doors and generally also a white forward section of the roof. This car has the larger rear lights introduced for 1964. (BMIHT)

Last twist in the tale: having always been sold exclusively as a Morris, in 1968 the Minor van and pick-up became available with an Austin badge and a 'crinkle-cut' Austin grille. Minor LCVs always had a shorter bumper blade, painted silver. (BMIHT)

The Oxford Series II and family

1954–60

Two examples of the Isis: the Series I wears the mesh grille that was introduced in May/June 1956, and the Series II has the duotone paint available from February 1957. (Classic and Sports Car)

Arguably the last true Morris design, the Series II Oxford and its six-cylinder Isis sister had a relatively short life in Britain – but a derivative of the last SIII Oxford is at the time of publication still being made in India as the Hindustan Ambassador.

In May 1954 the first new Morris of the BMC era was unveiled – a replacement for the MO Oxford. Known retrospectively as the Series II Oxford, it was swiftly followed by a lower-priced Cowley model and then a year later by a six-cylinder variant, the Isis. These three cars were to be the last Cowley-designed stand-alone Morrises: corporate Longbridge-originated models would replace them, and the Morris marque would cease to have any meaning as BMC imposed a policy of badge-engineering whereby essentially identical models were sold under the different brand names of the group. It is ironic, therefore, that the Series II Oxford family ended up outliving not only all other Morrises, but also the parent company itself: the car is still in production in India as the Hindustan Ambassador.

Thankfully the droopy grille on this prototype was not carried forward to production; DO 1033 is the Oxford's internal Drawing Office designation. (BMIHT)

Initial proposals for the Isis were for it to have a vertical grille; this photo dates from 1953, at which time the car was badged as a Morris Six. (BMIHT)

Series II – the Oxford re-modelled

Design of the new range began under the aegis of Alec Issigonis, before he left BMC to join Alvis in 1952. The Series II was an extrapolation of MO practice, and thus retained swivelling-trunnion torsion-bar front suspension and rack-and-pinion steering, with the added enhancement of all-round telescopic dampers – a major advance over the ineffective and costly lever-arms with which the Minor remained saddled. At the front this meant that there was now a proper pressed-steel upper arm.

The wheelbase was unchanged, at 8ft 1in, as was in essence the track, there being a nominal half-inch extra at the front end. Despite the bulky look of the new body, essentially the work of draughtsmen Bert Rayner and Tom Ramsay, the overall dimensions were in fact pretty much as before. The width was unchanged and the length grew by just three inches; the kerb weight remained the same, too, at 21.5cwt. However, the Series II was a true Issigonis car, in that it had generous interior room for its size, something emphasised by the sparse far-away dashboard that was so typical of his cars; it is interesting to note that both the exterior and the interior bear some resemblance to what he later created for his still-born Alvis V8 saloon.

If the chassis and the body were informed by Nuffield practice, the engine and transmission were pure Austin, with the same 1489cc B-series engine as would be found in the rival A50 Cambridge, mated to an Austin four-speed column-change gearbox and driving an Austin back axle. Had the merger not happened, the Oxford would of course have retained a Nuffield engine, gearbox and back axle, and evidence suggests that the power unit would have been an overhead-valve version of the MO's side-valve unit,

possibly of 1750cc. Jack Daniels remembered this engine being installed in an Oxford – in all likelihood an MO rather than a Series II – and its virtues being vigorously demonstrated by Charles Griffin, who was no mean driver.

"Charlie had a 1750cc version, I think, of that ohv engine put into an Oxford, and he was trying it out, and he was saying what a good job it made of the car. I can accurately recall that in that car we went five-up to the Frankfurt Motor Show... Charlie drove it on the autobahns, and he was actually scaring people off. He was sitting right on the back of Mercedes-Benzes, and they were giving way. We were doing about a ton – an enjoyable ride, that was!"

The SII was the first Morris to benefit in full from testing at the new Motor Industry Research Association test-track at Nuneaton, successfully completing 1000 miles on the pavé section. Morris's test régime, under Chief Experimental Engineer Walter Balding, was regarded as more rigorous than that followed by Longbridge, but the car also profited from all the lessons learnt the hard way with the MO and MS. Another contribution to the car's sound design was that it was developed with one eye on the Holden that Lord Nuffield had insisted be imported from Australia, and which spent some time in the Experimental Department. "I would say that the main benefit we gained from the Holden was its ruggedness – its suspension and structure," Nuffield engineer Peter Tothill told the author. "I think that was built into the Series II."

Whilst the axeing of that Nuffield ohv engine might have been mourned by Cowley, there was no arguing with the corporate planning logic behind standardising on the B-series. As with the A-series, in its early days Morris engineers were shocked by its lack of durability, notably in its original 1200cc form. "In endurance testing of the 1200 we found that by 30,000 miles the big ends had given up," former experimental engineer Jim Lambert once told the author. But the 1489cc 'B' was a sturdier unit, and in the Oxford it did a pretty reasonable job. On just 50bhp, it transformed the car. Whilst the MO had struggled up to 60mph in 41.4 seconds and topped out at 67mph, *The Autocar* found that the Series II romped to 60mph in 29 seconds and

had a mean maximum speed of 72.5mph. At last Morris's emblematic mid-size saloon had a power unit worthy of its roadholding and handling.

Cowley and Isis join the range

In July 1954 the Oxford was given a lower-cost stablemate, the Cowley, powered by a 1200cc B-series developing 42bhp – or barely more than the MO's old side-valve unit. Recognisable by its unchromed screen and window surrounds and by the elimination of bumper over-riders and the side chrome strips, the Cowley was equally bare inside, lacking carpet, a heater and a water-temperature gauge and having fixed front quarterlights and plain door trims.

Such austerity motoring had relatively little appeal, as the sales figures would show, but the Cowley was not without its friends, including Richard Barton of the Barton Motor Company in Plymouth, who at one stage rallied one of the cars. "The Cowley went, even though it only had a 1200cc engine, because it had lower gearing. It would outcorner an Oxford easily, too," Barton once reminisced. "I said this to the chaps at Morris, and they said 'Don't be silly – it's the same car except for the engine.' But it wasn't. It had cheaper tyres, and these improved the handling immensely. A little bit later all Oxfords had these cheaper tyres..."

As might have been expected, a Traveller version of the Oxford soon joined the range, being announced at the '54 Motor Show. At first glance the car retained the wood-framing of the preceding MO Traveller and its Minor sister. This was deceptive. Although the rear structure was still bolted in place, the actual framing was of steel box sections, with the wood being largely

The Cowley was a miserably austere-looking car, lacking even the upright chrome strips on the grille. (LAT)

Richard Barton in his Cowley, near Carlisle, on the 1954 MCC/Redex National Rally. (Richard Barton)

The on-stilts stance of the Isis was aggravated by use of 15in wheels, as opposed to the 14-inchers on Oxfords. The long torsion bars were hard to adjust for a level suspension 'trim'. (Author's collection)

The hefty C-series engine put out 86bhp in the SI Isis – and 124lb ft of torque at a low 2000rpm. (LAT)

ornamental; the exception was the top rail, which remained of timber and to which the aluminium roof was pinned. The doors also remained wooden-framed and alloy-panelled. Arguably, then, the SII Traveller was no real advance at all, as it continued to have rot-prone timber and a labour-intensive form of construction that perforce resulted in a less rigid shell than a one-piece steel unit.

From the rear, only the badging gives this first-series car away as an Isis; in fact the bonnet, front wings and front bumper are all different. (Classic and Sports Car)

The interior of an SI Isis. The dials have golden faces and a clock inset into the speedo; they are mounted in a plastic panel with a striking weave pattern. (Classic and Sports Car)

The Traveller in Isis guise. Relatively few were made, but there are survivors. (Author's collection)

After the failure of the Six, it would have been understandable if Morris had abandoned the idea of a six-cylinder version of the SII, but in July 1955 the Isis was announced, powered by an 86bhp single-SU version of the 2639cc BMC C-series engine that had been designed by Morris Engines – none too cleverly – and had already found a home in the Austin A90 Westminster. It would also end up in the Austin-Healey, somewhat to the disgust of Geoffrey Healey, who gave the author a colourful impression of the unit's inadequacies. "We put an early 'six' into a car and it was horrifying, really, because everything used to thrash about on the early engines. They used a very thin backing plate between the engine and the gearbox, and there was a complete lack of beam strength... At 4500rpm you felt the crank was going to drop out. They persevered and found the answers, but it didn't get going until it became a three-litre... There were always certain inherent problems, though. It was never going to be an economical engine... and there was a horrible mixture spread between all the cylinders, regardless of what you did – and you had to run the mixture rich enough to keep the weakest cylinder firing. It was pretty diabolical."

To accommodate this large lump of cast-iron the Isis had 10½in let into the wheelbase, betrayed by the car's lengthened front end. To prevent the body from folding in the middle there were diagonal box sections running from the A-post to the front of the chassis, reinforcements at the front toeboard, and two braces in the engine compartment. Other than bigger brakes with a claimed 40 per cent larger swept area, the only other change of significance was to swap the Oxford's rack-and-pinion steering for a cam-and-peg layout. Pretty soon, however, came one definitely worthwhile enhancement of the Isis specification: during the later part of 1955 overdrive became available as an option. Operating on the top three gears, this Borg-Warner set-up incorporated a freewheel and was slightly bizarre in its functioning. Engaged via an under-dash T-lever, the overdrive operated automatically at speeds over 32mph, cutting in when one lifted one's foot and disengaging if one kicked down. If speed fell to below 27mph the overdrive automatically cut out, and the car freewheeled with the throttle released, allowing low-speed clutchless gearchanging.

In all, the Isis was a competitively-priced and unostentatious 'six' that at £844 undercut the more luxurious Wolseley 6/90 by a healthy £220 and was in the same ballpark as Vauxhall's Velox and Standard's Vanguard Phase III. Ford's soon-to-be-replaced Zephyr MkI was a tempting £90 cheaper, but that difference could be eroded if you specified the stripped-out basic Isis, which made do without the leather-faced seats of the De Luxe, or such niceties as a heater, a clock or opening front quarterlights. There was also an Isis Traveller; unlike its Oxford sister, this had the pioneering feature, for a British estate car, of a rear-facing fold-up jump seat, making it an eight-seater.

Industrial strife – and a new look

These were not happy times, either for Morris or for the motor industry as a whole. In 1956 the economy was slowing down, and a credit squeeze hit car sales hard. Stock piled up on airfields and the waiting lists that had been such a feature of the post-war years evaporated. In reaction to this, in June 1956 BMC dismissed 6000 workers across the company. There had been an evident lack of communication. "We were told that the order books were full – we were taking on new labour and they were expecting the whole factory to go on overtime. Within a fortnight notices were printed and put up throughout the departments to say every man with less than three years' service would be made redundant. Now that shook us rigid after what we had been told," Cowley trade union leader Arthur Exell told the Television History Workshop. In *The Times* BMC's action was deemed 'unjustified provocation' and Prime Minister Anthony Eden was openly critical of management conduct. The result was a bitter

This one-off four-door Isis Traveller was built by Sussex dealer Caffyns for the headmaster of Eastbourne College. (Author's collection)

With the fold-up jump seat in use, the spare wheel was secured on the side of the car, in its cover, so the wheel well could be used for the passengers' feet. (Author's collection)

The rear doors of the Travellers continued to be wood-framed and alloy-panelled. (Author's collection)

and violent strike at Morris that ultimately led to full union recognition at the plant. With the power of the shop stewards enhanced, the stage was being set for the labour disputes of the 1960s and onwards that would have such a disastrous effect on the company.

It was against this background – and with the Suez Crisis adding further gloom – that in

The SIII Oxford gained finlets and peaked headlamp cowls, and along with the Isis SII there were chrome-plated strips on the wing crowns. (LAT)

The Oxford Traveller in SIII form, identifiable by its scalloped bonnet. There are no known survivors. (Author's collection)

In 1956 consideration was given to all-steel Minor and Oxford Travellers with more rakish lines; this is the Oxford proposal. (BMIHT)

This more practical – if less elegant – 'squareback' Traveller seems to have been a running prototype; again it dates from 1956. (BMIHT)

The final result, the Series IV, was one of the more pleasing estates of the era. (Author's collection)

October 1956 the Cowley-Oxford-Isis family was restyled. The lines were firmed up by modest fins at the rear, deep fluting of the bonnet and – on the Oxford alone – the use of cowled headlamp rims. The hair-shirt austerity of the cockpit was also addressed, with a new dashboard incorporating two lidded gloveboxes and the arrival of a dished steering wheel. Additionally the Oxford's engine was boosted to 55bhp and standardised on the Cowley. This was not enough to revive sales of Morris's bargain-basement model. Output had fallen from just over 10,000 in the 1955 model year to roughly half that for the 1956 season, and it would halve again, to 2355 units, for the August 1956 to July 1957 period.

At the other end of the range, the Isis also gained a little power, the C-series now developing 90bhp thanks to a similar hike in its compression ratio to that given to the four-cylinder cars. Making this easier to enjoy – at least in theory – the frankly sub-standard column gearchange of the Isis was replaced with a right-hand floor change, as on the Riley Pathfinder and Wolseley 6/90. The shift was an improvement, but still rubbery and vague. "The side gearchange was always a nightmare to adjust. There was so much lost motion in the linkage. I know we tried to eliminate some of the lost motion, to get a better change," Peter Tothill told the author. Owners might have been better advised, therefore, to consider the newly-available option of a Borg-Warner three-speed auto, which made the Isis – now dubbed the Series II – the cheapest automatic on the market. On the Oxford saloon, meanwhile, a Manumatic automatic clutch was now offered – a fairly dreadful device that had robust-spirited MG boss John Thornley writing a brisk memo to Technical Director SV Smith advising that it be immediately discontinued before BMC ran into 'a packet of criticism, if not trouble'.

Final modifications... and an all-steel Traveller

In their facelifted form the Oxford Series III and the Cowley 1500, as they were now called, were made until March 1959. After the over-production of 1956 it was only to be expected that sales would fall, and this was indeed the case: output of the Oxford for the August 1956 to July 1957 season crashed to 20,274 units, a fall of nearly 48 per cent from the preceding year's 38,684 units. The Oxford gained two-toning, broken by a chrome strip, as an option from February 1957 and both it and the Cowley received a floor gearchange in March 1958; sales tickled slightly

upwards, with 23,364 Oxfords made during the season. The Isis also went two-tone in '57, and was given a range of duo-tone leather-and-nylon interiors. It was calculated that would-be Isis owners now had the choice of 44 different colour or trim combinations; the opportunity to profit from such largesse was, however, limited, as in March 1958 the Isis was discontinued. Although sales had stabilised after a fall of roughly 60 per cent in 1956–57, making fewer than 3000 of the Isis per year – or approximately 2 per cent of total output at Cowley – was hardly a viable exercise.

In the interim, one final improvement had been made to the range: in August 1957 the half-timbered Oxford Traveller had given way to an all-steel four-door Traveller, the only Oxford to carry the Series IV label. With the burgeoning market for estate cars, this made a lot of sense, even if the tailgate opening was relatively small and the load floor set quite high. The Series IV Traveller continued after the saloons had been replaced by the Farina-styled Series V Oxford, only being deleted in April 1960.

The figures that tell the story

Over their relatively short life the Series II-III-IV Oxford and its various evolutions acquitted themselves adequately well. Morris racked up output of 167,494 Oxfords and Cowleys, plus a further 16,500 or so commercial derivatives. With 17,413 Cowley Series IIs sold, against 87,341 SII Oxfords, the budget model pulled in 16.6 per cent of Series II sales, so evidently it had its fans.

THE CAR THAT WOULD NOT DIE: HOW THE OXFORD LIVES ON IN INDIA

The MkII Ambassador (1) had a new grille, replacing the old Morris item, and was offered with various different bodies, as depicted in these 1970 catalogue images (2–5).

MkIIs are still to be seen in India; this example (6) was photographed in Chennai (formerly Madras) in 2004, serving as a taxi. All these cars have an Indian-made version of the 1489cc BMC petrol engine. (Author/Nairn Hindhaugh)

Hindustan began production of the Series II Oxford in 1955, as the Landmaster, advertising it as offering 'Low-cost luxury motoring'. The old side-valve engine of the MO was retained, so the motoring must have been as leisurely as it was supposedly luxurious.

In 1957, the Landmaster was replaced by the first of the Ambassadors, with the 1489cc B-series engine and the SIII fins. This became a MkII in 1962, at which stage it gained a cross-hatched grille. In this form it continued until 1974, with various other body styles being available, albeit in fairly small numbers.

A third style of grille arrived in 1974, for the mechanically unchanged MkIII. In 1979 came a further facelift, with a bolder grille and square front indicators, this constituting the MkIV Ambassador. This lasted for ten years, along the way becoming available with a derivative of the BMC B-series diesel, a 1489cc unit developing just 37bhp.

With a further revision to the grille, which now had horizontal slats, the Ambassador Nova arrived in 1992. This generation of Ambassadors was still available with the BMC diesel, but the petrol engine was now exclusively an 1800cc Isuzu unit, mated to a five-speed Isuzu gearbox; additionally a 2000cc Isuzu diesel engine was offered. There was also a new plastic dashboard, replacing the old Oxford SIII type.

From 2000 the Nova was renamed the Classic and was joined by the first attempt to modernise the old Morris shape, in the form of a luxury model called the Ambassador Grand. This had plastic body-colour bumper shields and other cosmetic changes; equipment additionally included a remote-control gearchange, power steering and disc front

7

brakes, along with a front anti-roll bar and a Salisbury back axle. A further evolution came in 2003 with the arrival of a third model, the Avigo. Intended to evoke the BMW Mini, this had a completely new front end and a redesigned dashboard inspired by that of the Mini. The Classic and Grand are still marketed, only without these names being used, with engine choice being 1500cc diesel, 1800cc Isuzu petrol or 2000cc

8

Isuzu diesel. Cars to run on Compressed Natural Gas (CNG) and LPG are also offered.

The 'Amby' has become a national emblem in India and over four million have been made; attempts to complement it with another retired British design, the FE-series Vauxhall Victor, came to little, with the resultant Hindustan Contessa being withdrawn after a very short production run.

Sales of the Ambassador sharply diminished after

9

the Indian car market was liberalised in the 1980s, and today most sales are to government or to taxi drivers. The introduction of more stringent anti-pollution norms in 2011 dealt the Hindustan a further blow, meaning that it could no longer be purchased for taxi use.

In 2012 production was approximately 5000 units. Although the Ambassador might seem to be reaching the end of its life, plans are afoot for a three-stage revival. A revised 1500 common-rail diesel is expected during 2013, followed

10

11

by a variant with a truncated tail to conform to preferential legislation for cars of under 4-metre length. Finally, during 2014 a restyled Ambassador is promised, on the old Morris floorpan but with updated suspension. Additionally, manufacture of up to 10,000 cars per year is planned in Bangladesh. When the Hindustan finally ceases production, with it will disappear the last direct link to the pre-BMC Morris company, one that can be traced back to the MO Oxford from which the Ambassador ultimately derives its underpinnings.

The Porter (7) was a pick-up, this being a c.1982 MkIV fitted with the BMC B-series diesel.

The Trekker (8) was Ambassador-based; van versions are sometimes encountered. Most common in India are Novas or later Classics with round rather than square flashers (9).

The Grand (10), here a government car, has plastic bumpers and a different grille. Rather more radical is the Avigo (11), of which this is a prototype. (Author/Nairn Hindhaugh)

The duotoning introduced for 1958 was bolstered by a chrome side spear in the style of the '55 US Fords. (Classic and Sports Car)

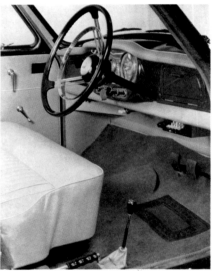

The dashboard of the SIII – or the SII Isis, as here – is closer to the driver; dials are grey-faced. (Classic and Sports Car)

The handbrake was always a pull-up item beside the seat; here the side change identifies a SII Isis. (Author's collection)

This was for real. The duo-tone interiors on the late Isis were very American. (Author's collection)

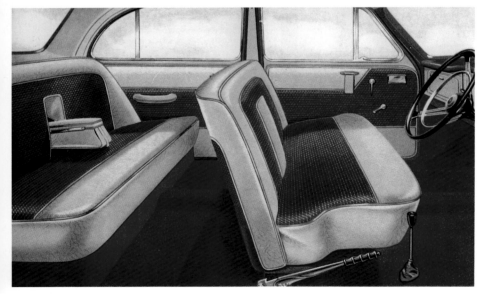

As a 1500 it fared substantially worse, with 4623 made, against 58,117 Series III and Series IV Oxfords, representing 7.8 per cent of the total.

What of the Isis? Certainly the production figures make pretty poor reading: 8541 first-series cars left Cowley and only 3614 of the be-finned Series II model. Relative to the 55,000 or so of Austin's A90/A95/A105 made between 1954 and 1959, those 12,000-odd Morrises look small beer indeed – never mind the 166,504 E-type Crestas that Vauxhall made between 1954 and 1957. Look a little closer at the figures, however, and a different story emerges. Although manufactured for less than three years, the Isis outsold the longer-lived Wolseley 6/90, 11,852 of which were made between 1954 and 1959. Take the SI Isis alone, and the Morris compares even more favourably, those 8541 cars being well ahead

This grotesque 1956 model suggests thought was given to making an Oxford out of the A55 Cambridge. (BMIHT)

of the 5776 MkI 6/90s made during the roughly comparable 1954–56 currency of the Wolseley.

What all this boils down to is that the Isis might not have set the sales charts ablaze, but it was not the catastrophe it is often said to have been. After all, it took Cowley nearly twice as long to sell approximately the same number of its Morris Six predecessor. The explanation is probably simple. When a Wolseley 6/80 cost only 12 per cent more than the related Morris Six, the extra luxury on offer made the Wolseley look a better buy than its Cowley sibling. But the next generation of Nuffield cars saw roles reversed: the bigger 6/90 came in over a quarter as expensive again as the Isis, making the Morris the more attractive proposition this time around, for those who could do without the Wolseley's walnut trimmings.

But we are talking here of the borderline irrelevant. What matters is that of the half-million or so BMC four-cylinder 'middies' sold, the lion's share was constituted by Austin Cambridges, at 299,533 units including vans and pick-ups. BMC's combined Austin-Morris output of Cambridges, Cowleys and Oxfords compares pretty well with the 651,661 MkII Fords made between 1956 and 1962, even before you add in the various six-pot BMC siblings. But the Morrises, more expensive than the Austins, even if they were demonstrably better, simply failed to sell as well as their Longbridge equivalents – and that was by a significant amount. In such a situation it was easier for BMC management at Longbridge to promote an evolution of the Cambridge as the basis for the new generation of Pininfarina-styled 1500s that would be introduced during 1958 and 1959.

There was also a pick-up variant. Builders tended to prefer the Austin rival, as it had a longer load bed. (Howard Dent)

In 1956 a half-ton van derivative was announced; current until 1960, it always had the SII Oxford style of bonnet. (Richard Monk)

The BMC years

Old favourite, new best-seller: a four-door Minor and the Morris 1100 intended to replace it. In the late 1960s the 1100 at times held nearly 15 per cent of the British market. (Classic and Sports Car)

Under BMC the marque names were devalued by the practice of 'badge engineering' but the Morris name lived on – with some oddball variants and unique re-branding in some parts of the world.

At the time of the merger announcement, *The Autocar* had speculated on the likely evolution of the amalgamation between the Nuffield Organization and Austin. Most likely, the magazine felt, was that there would be a pooling of sales and service operations in export markets and perhaps some shared overseas manufacturing plants. They expected some standardisation of components, and later 'in some aspects of design', but judged it unlikely that this would entail 'any loss of individuality in either the design or the appearance of the various marques'.

The arrival of 'badge engineering'

The magazine's journalists must therefore have felt a sense of bemusement – embarrassment, even – when asked in late 1958 and early 1959 to attend separate launches for each of a range of new mid-sized models that were mechanically and physically near-identical, but for their radiator grilles and interior presentation. There had been undoubted need for rationalising the corporate parts bin, and for a more logical model range. To the outside eye it must have seemed mad to have had three separate designs – the Austin Cambridge, Morris Oxford and the Palmer-designed Wolseley 15/50 and related MG Magnette – all competing with each other in the same broad market sector. But at the time of the merger these models had been too far down the road to commercialisation to be cancelled. It had at least been possible, however, to standardise on the B-series engine and its matching gearbox and back axle – although in its original 4/44 format the Wolseley had retained Nuffield units.

Now, though, what became known as 'badge engineering' had arrived: the Austin A55 Cambridge MkII, announced in January 1959, and the Morris Oxford Series V, launched in March that year, were effectively the same car, and had Wolseley, Riley and MG clones, as well as six-cylinder Austin and Wolseley spin-offs. Not only that, but under their crisp Pininfarina styling was a reworking of the narrow-gutted Austin A40-A50-A55 Cambridge platform, complete with weak and expensive lever-arm

Trim, grille and tail lamps on the Oxford Series V differed from those of the equivalent Austin Cambridge. In all, 87,432 were made. (LAT)

The Wolseley 15/60 was the sister car to the Series V, and was developed into the 1622cc 16/60 in 1961. (Author's collection)

dampers and steering by box rather than rack. Slightly improving things, in 1961 the cars were given a longer wheelbase and a wider track, along with a 1622cc engine for the four-cylinder models. The Austin would last in this later A60 form until 1969, but the Morris Oxford Series VI would continue until 1971.

The 'Farina' series was a retrograde move for Morris; as for Riley enthusiasts still mourning the old RMs, they must have been crying into their Single Malt. The separate makes were on the way to becoming meaningless. Only MG retained a certain individual stature, thanks to its continuing manufacture of stand-alone sports cars, even if nobody took the be-finned 'Farina' Magnette too seriously. But the tears of marque loyalists were less the point than the fact that the cars were technically backward in a European market that was now becoming more

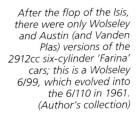

open. Relative to a Peugeot, Borgward or Volvo, the BMC 1500s were distinctly old-hat – and in the course of their over-long life would come to be seen as risible relics.

Few would have argued with the abandonment of Morris's sadly inadequate range of engines, but the wholesale imposition of Austin components was another matter. MG boss John Thornley, a former accountant who was certainly nobody's fool, spelt things out to the author in a 1989 interview. "To assemble an axle there was a piece price, and that was the price which went into the costing. What actually happened was that on the line the chargehand issued pink tickets that represented chargings over and above the piece rates – and the pink tickets were ignored by Austin's accountants. But somebody had to pick up the tab at the end of the year...

"When BMC was formed, a great exhibition was created in the dungeons below the 'Kremlin' administration block at Longbridge. The equivalent Nuffield and Austin components were laid out side by side, with their production prices. Of course the Austin price beat the Nuffield price all the way down the line, and the Austin parts were chosen.

"The engineering of a lot of the Nuffield stuff was superior, and the prices included every damn thing. If you costed that into the Austin part, you really were in the gravy. This to a very large extent contributed to the downfall of BMC."

Morris Major: 'the best thing we ever made'

Here is not the place to discuss the detailed evolution of models that were corporate products, rather than cars with a distinctive Morris identity. But if 'badge engineering' was devaluing the Morris name in the home market,

there were other parts of the world where it still had sufficient worth to end up being used exclusively on a particular model – as well as on one or two vehicles that were not sold elsewhere as Morrises. We are talking here primarily of Australia, which had already been home to a Morris-badged Austin A95, the Morris Marshal – not to mention a Morris version of a locally-bodied Austin A50 pick-up.

Even as late as 1957 BMC retained sufficient strength in Australia for it to be able to mount a challenge to Holden. By autumn 1957, when the Wolseley 1500 entered production at the ex-Nuffield plant in Sydney, it was clear that the firm was at last ready to confront the challenge. The factory had been newly expanded, and equipped with the latest machinery, and had the capacity to produce 50,000 cars per annum, rising to 100,000. This was when the total Australian market was around 155,000 cars per year, so when BMC began talking of an all-new '100 per cent Australian' model, it was immediately presumed that it had a pretty exciting product up its sleeve. Expectations were further boosted when Leonard Lord announced his intention to take 30 per cent of the Australian market.

All this fun and games came to a rather low-key end with the March 1958 introduction of the Morris Major. This was nothing more than a 1489cc version of the Morris 1200 that had originally been planned as a new Morris Minor. Externally identical to the Wolseley 1500, apart from a simplified grille and a revised lamp configuration, the Major – billed as 'the friendly family car' – was also mechanically the same, and differed only in having a more spartan interior. There was also an Austin version, called the Lancer. After all the bally-hoo, the disappointment was palpable.

In July 1959 the two cars were substantially revised, and became much more acceptable vehicles. The wheelbase was extended by 6in and the rear remodelled to take American-style fins and a larger squared-off boot; overall length was up 9in. Frontal styling was also made more angular. In addition to the restyling, dampers (still lever-arm) were uprated, wider wheels fitted, and the body beefed up with extra box sections; the interior was also restyled and the cars given a front bench seat, with the handbrake on the right. The 50bhp 1489cc B-series engine remained as before, but the rear axle ratio was lowered, to give a little extra acceleration. The changes could have been more radical: an independent rear designed for possible use in the Minor, and featuring semi-trailing arms and a transverse laminated torsion bar, was offered to the Australians. But they chose to stick with the existing leaf-sprung live back axle, as they found that the more expensive IRS set-up offered only a marginal improvement to the ride.

Thanks to a thorough pre-production proving regime, the re-modelled cars offered rugged and reliable transport for those who didn't feel the need to smoke around in a six-cylinder Holden or a Ford Falcon. Judged 'the most improved car of the year' by *Modern Motor* magazine, the Major acquitted itself honourably in the marketplace, and the dealers were happy, because little went wrong. In 1960 BMC sold 11,045 Majors and Lancers – although to put that in perspective, Volkswagen sold almost 18,000 Beetles and GM-H knocked out 107,690 Holdens.

In early 1961, de luxe versions of the Lancer and Major were announced. These had more chrome, revised two-tone paint schemes, and improved equipment levels. The final development of the Major – but not of the Lancer,

which was deleted – came in April 1962, when the Major Elite was introduced, with a Zenith-carb 58bhp 1622cc engine and telescopic rear dampers, as well as a restyled grille and interior. "We decided we would fix every known problem – and we did," recalls former BMC-Australia engineer Roger Foy. "The car was an almost immediate success. We didn't change the final-drive ratio, and it went like a rocket. At the traffic lights you'd be burning off the VWs." Colleague Chris Rogers agrees. "With the 1622cc engine it was a real goer. It was an excellent vehicle. I thought it was the best thing we ever made – a very nice motor car." The press concurrred, *Modern Motor* deeming the Elite 'hard to beat – both as value for money and as a car that gets you places quickly and is a pleasure to drive'.

The car stayed in production until spring 1964, when it was replaced by the Australian-built Morris 1100, and there are stories of people paying more for a used example than the last list

The Oxford dashboard was unique to the Morris, and was the same on both the Series V and the Series VI. (Author's collection)

The Traveller version of the Oxford – here a Series VI – had a two-part tailgate and always kept the original sharp-tipped rear wings. (Author's collection)

The Morris Marshal was an Australian-assembled A95 with the bonnet modified to have a shovel-like air intake. (Nairn Hindhaugh)

The Austin A50 Coupé Utility was also sold as a Morris; its Australian-built body used the A55 saloon rear window. (Nairn Hindhaugh)

A Marshal estate version was also offered. Current from 1957 until 1960, relatively few Marshals were made: in 1959 a mere 379 were sold, and in 1960 a final 227. (Nairn Hindhaugh)

The first series of Morris Major failed to make much of an impact, and was replaced in less than two years by the much-improved SII. (Author's collection)

This 1957 photo shows that consideration was given to an Americanised front to match the rear. (BMIHT)

price when the cars were available new. All the same, as the Sydney plant had been equipped by 1958 with all the new tooling necessary to build a fully indigenous design, the Major – 96 per cent Australian content by the time of the Elite – nonetheless constituted a disturbing miscalculation. "The Major was ill-conceived and badly contrived," according to Charles Griffin. "We couldn't succeed [in Australia] making the cars we were making."

One more effort to adapt a British design to the Australian market was however made, when the 'Farina' Cambridge-Oxford was given an Australian-built six-cylinder version of the B-series engine. The resultant Austin Freeway and its Wolseley sister, the 24/80, were not a success, although old BMC hands in Australia praise the car's qualities. By this stage, however, BMC-Australia had changed tack. The locally-assembled Mini had proved an unexpected success, and the 1100 was to do even better, in some months being Australia's fourth-best-selling car, displacing the Beetle. With an Australia-assembled Austin 1800 available from 1965, BMC turned its back – at least for a while – on the idea of directly rivalling Holden.

Back in 1961, the practice of having separate Austin and Morris dealerships had been abandoned – ahead of any other country – and as a result the Mini was sold solely as a Morris, as was the 1100. The name thus had a certain capital in the country. Alas, this was squandered with the next BMC-Australia product, the Morris Nomad and its saloon sibling, the Morris 1500. Hastily developed, on a minimalist budget, this duo was intended to replace the 1100, and had the 1478cc Maxi E-series engine shoehorned into the same bodyshell, which for the Nomad was given a new hatchback rear. The trouble was that the Maxi five-speed cable gearchange gave enormous in-service problems: the Australians were appalled by the deficiencies of this wretched system, and struggled to make it work. All the goodwill generated by the Morris 1100 was dissipated. Indeed, there are those who consider that it was the Nomad that sealed the death warrrant of BMC/BL in Australia – and not the almost equally problematic Kimberley/Tasman 1800 updates or the unfortunate P76 big saloon that British Leyland launched in 1973. A year earlier, in any case, the Morris name had been dropped in favour of universal Leyland branding.

In the end, the front of the SII stayed very similar to that of the SI. An estate was mooted but never made it to production. (Author's collection)

In other territories, as mentioned earlier, the Morris name still counted. This was particularly the case in New Zealand, where separate distribution networks continued into the 1970s. To cater for this, Australian-assembled Austin Freeways and Austin Kimberleys and Tasmans also bore the Morris nameplate in New Zealand, as did Australian-sourced Austin 1800s, including the pick-up that BMC-Australia had developed. NZ-built Minis kept their Austin and Morris identities until the end of 1971, with in the interim the odd peculiarity, such as Australian-sourced Morris Minis being sold as Austin Mini-Minors – complete with the Morris grille.

The Morris badge also had some worth in Denmark, where the Morris Minor had been a best-seller. At first the Mini was sold as the Austin Partner and the Morris Mascot, with the Austin later being known just as the Austin Mini. But in 1971 the Austin importer closed, and henceforth former Morris concessionnaire DOMI used only the Morris name on the Mini – right through until imports stopped in 1981.

Cowley in BMC's brave new world

More relevant than such diversions is to look at the role of the Cowley factory in the development of the British Motor Corporation. By this time the company's easy dominance of the British market was starting to melt away. In 1959 the company as a whole was to make 431,247 cars, but Ford was closing the gap, making a record 314,793 units that year. It is the profit figures, however, that are more revealing: Ford turned in £32.2m and BMC £21.4m, meaning that Ford was making £102 profit per car, against BMC's average of £44.

Meanwhile, a brave new British Motor Corporation was emerging. Under the technical direction of Alec Issigonis, and encouraged by Leonard Lord and his deputy, George Harriman, the company was to shed its conservative reputation, and espouse the technological avant-garde with a range of front-wheel-drive transverse-engined designs. Henceforth its mission was to outflank the US-owned competition by offering cars that were sufficiently advanced to stay in

The grille on the Elite was intended to make the car look wider. There was no Austin version of the Elite. (Nairn Hindhaugh)

Originally it had been planned to give the Elite a squared-off rear roofline, but with the 1100 on the way the investment was not thought worthwhile. (Nairn Hindhaugh)

Until Leyland badging arrived, the Mini was always sold in Australia as a Morris, with the cars initially being called the Morris 850. (Nairn Hindhaugh)

The Australians were the first to fit wind-up windows to the Mini, on the 1965 De Luxe. (Nairn Hindhaugh)

and MkIV Magnettes – in other words all the 'Nuffield' variants – the Cowley plant assembled some A55/A60 Cambridges and some A99/A110 Westminsters. Latterly it became the sole site for all the 'Farina' cars, as BMC eventually started putting some order into its hotch-potch production arrangements.

This meant that Cowley constructed what was supposed to be BMC's most prestigious private car, the Vanden Plas Princess 4-litre R, with its Rolls-Royce engine. Part of a planned model-sharing project with Rolls-Royce that ultimately came to nothing, the car was in fact an unsaleable disaster, with desperate in-service problems, not least from the inlet-over-exhaust aluminium Rolls-Royce power unit. In the end fewer than 7000 were made, over a life of almost four years. "The Vanden Plas Princess 4-Litre R was awful. We had more problems getting that engine right, getting it cleared through the engine tuning department, than any other model we built," Cowley plant manager Eric Lord told the author. "I remember [Technical Director] SV Smith having a go at me. 'It's ridiculous,' he said. 'It's a Rolls-Royce engine, and look at your costs on it.' I said 'That's the problem. The pushrods aren't fitted in properly, this isn't right, that isn't right. The trouble is that Rolls-Royce are trying to mass-produce an engine and they're not up to it.' We had a lot of the 4-litre R sitting around. We had them over on an airfield. Customers who decided to buy a new one were finding the chassis number was earlier than the one they'd just got rid of, because we'd had the cars in stock for so long."

Advantages and handicaps

Despite such unwanted low-volume diversions, Cowley acquitted itself well in the later BMC years. In the period between the August 1956 to July 1957 model year and the August 1967 to September 1968 model year, annual production at Cowley jumped from 130,979 units to 326,818 units, whilst output at Longbridge increased from 166,627 units to 348,664 units. That equates to a rise of 109.2 per cent for Longbridge and of 149.5 per cent for Cowley, suggesting that the Morris plant was the more productive of the two factories.

"In terms of vehicle assembly, Cowley was more efficient than Longbridge," former BMC Deputy Director of Production Geoffrey Iley confirmed to the author, attributing this to practices imposed back in the days of William

production for a longer period, thereby amortising their higher costs. So it was that in 1959 the Mini was launched, followed by the Morris and MG 1100 in 1962. From the outset the Mini was available with both Austin and Morris badges – with Riley and Wolseley twins from 1961 – but the Austin 1100 only arrived in 1963, followed in 1965 by the inevitable Wolseley and Riley versions. In accordance with BMC's turn-and-turn-about policy, the 1800 was launched first as an Austin and only 17 months later joined by a Morris version that was identical but for its grille and badging.

The Mini was made at both Longbridge and Cowley, until production was concentrated at Longbridge during 1969. The 1100 was made throughout its life at both plants, whilst the 1800 was made at the two works until 1968, when it too became a Longbridge-only product. In compensation, Cowley was given the 1969-launched Austin Maxi in exclusivity, and the ill-fated Austin 3-litre. As for the older generation of rear-drive cars, as well as making all the Morris Oxfords, Wolseley 15/60s and 16/60s, Riley 4/68s and 4/72s and MkIII

Morris. "There was very rigid control of the flow of parts through the system. It was calculated in terms of how long it took to have a typical incoming component going out of the door in a car that had been paid for..."

According to Eric Lord a degree of rigour was built into planning processes at Cowley. "When I was Branch Manager, every Monday morning on my desk there was the complete costing of every car we produced – material costs, labour costs. You had your finger on the pulse all the time – you knew what was happening. If one department was showing an increase in cost, that was the one you went to on your rounds, to find out what had gone wrong. You knew something had gone wrong. The superintendent would say 'Bloody Hell! You can't get away with anything these days.' I suppose it was a legacy of the Nuffield days, when if something cost tuppence more you had to explain what had happened. Lord Nuffield knew what something was costing, and where it was costing, and that attitude didn't change dramatically with the merger."

Rigorous accounting practices at Cowley were accompanied by lower labour costs, but that wasn't the whole story, says Lord. "I know the Mini we produced at Cowley we produced at a lower cost – which stuck in Longbridge's throat... There was rivalry between Morris and Austin. It wasn't unhealthy. But we reckoned we were making a better car than Austin, at a lower price – and Austin suspected that this was true. It used to upset them no end. The thing that really got up their nose was that on the same model the warranty costs for those cars produced at Cowley were lower than for cars produced at Longbridge – which to my mind showed that we were taking more care putting the thing together. And we were always told by the trade – who were selling both Austin and Morris – that a car made

The Australian Austin Freeway was sold in New Zealand as a Morris. (Nairn Hindhaugh)

The Morris 1500 had a revised grille and recessed door handles; the five-speed gearchange was a catastrophe. (Nairn Hindhaugh)

The Nomad was inspired by the Renault 16. The tail lights are from the Wolseley 18/85. (Nairn Hindhaugh)

Interior space in the Nomad was generous; note the continued use of a bench front seat. (Nairn Hindhaugh)

at Cowley would fetch a better price. How much of that was kidding us on I don't know, but that's what the trade was saying.

"I think we used to do a pretty good job at Cowley. We used to take a car off the assembly line, at random, after it had passed, and then subject it to all sorts of road tests – mileage, hills, dales, fast running, stop-start, cold conditions – to see if we had any problems with it. And if we did, it might take us a fortnight to find out, but we found it out before we'd got very many cars showing that fault

Another Australian Austin to be badged as a Morris for New Zealand was the 1800 Utility. (Nairn Hindhaugh)

1st class worker
Morris 1800 Mk. II Utility.

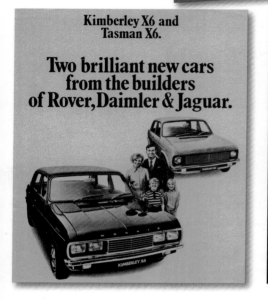

Kimberley X6 and Tasman X6.

Two brilliant new cars from the builders of Rover, Daimler & Jaguar.

Even the Kimberley and Tasman – re-jigged 1800s with the E6 six-cylinder engine – took on a Morris identity for New Zealand. (Nairn Hindhaugh)

Right to the end of imports in 1981, the Mini was sold in Denmark as the Morris Mascot. (Georg Mikkelsen)

The MkI Mini was built at both Longbridge and Cowley. A quirk was that at Longbridge the ignition key went in one way up, and on Cowley-built cars it went in the other way up. (Author's collection)

Austin Morris **Morris Mascot 95** Pick-up og Varevogn

More Mini-magic!

MORRIS MINI-MINORS NOW WITH **HYDROLASTIC SUSPENSION**

share of a £10m expansion programme begun in 1954. "I was left running plant that was clapped out," Lord told the author. "We were still making quite a good motor car, but with very clapped-out equipment. We were using the old chain-operated conveyor system, because I couldn't get the money to modernise it, and the paint plant was old. We really were struggling. It was exasperating that when we became BMC, Austin would cream off money to build new plant – their CAB facility and so on. The profits we made at Cowley were all going into Longbridge to be spent on equipment that we'd earnt at Cowley – that we should have had, to increase our efficiency."

The problem was all the more acute, according to Lord, because Cowley had already been parsimoniously treated before the merger. "Lord Nuffield's attitude was 'If it's still working, why do you want to change it?' He could never be persuaded to invest in machinery. It was 'What do you want to spend all that money for?' The money he was giving away should have been reinvested in the plant. We weren't allowed to waste paint. 'It's alright – it's not peeling off very much, is it?' was the attitude. He wanted every square foot of that factory to be producing money. 'I'm not heating it and looking after it for nothing – it's got to pay its way,' he'd say…"

Cowley and the coming storm
It was against this backcloth that Cowley picked its way through the '60s, as the Austin-Morris combine gradually slipped beneath the waves. Its popular but expensive-to-produce small front-wheel-drive cars had high warranty costs, whilst its rear-wheel-drive models were old-fashioned, heavy (and thus again costly to build) and increasingly unwanted. Then there was the fundamental misjudgement of the Austin 1800, which had been intended to replace the mainstream four-cylinder 'Farina' range and generate sturdy profits. But when the 1800 came along – over-sized, over-priced and under-endowed – it proved a sales catastrophe, selling in a fraction of the numbers around which production had been planned; as a consequence the Cambridge-Oxford family was kept in production.

Worse, BMC seemed to have a constitutional inability to chop out the dead wood, and had a ridiculously large range of frequently unrelated motor cars, several of which were selling in penny-packet numbers. In 1966 it had eleven basic models, against Ford's three. In addition

– because immediately a problem showed up and was reported we could take action. We didn't need to ask anyone's permission to take action, as we had to later on."

Cowley's performance was all the more praiseworthy given that its plant was less modern than the Longbridge facilities, which had not only benefitted from the substantial investment in CAB 1 but also from the lion's

The Italian-built Innocenti IM3 version of the 1100 was badged as a Morris; it had a delightful up-market interior. (Author's collection)

to this, it was still making vans based on the old Austin A35 and on the A55, plus two different forward-control light commercials, over and above the Morris Minor and Mini vans and pick-ups. Ford, in comparison, was making only the Anglia-based Thames van and the Transit.

What this amounted to was that all the volume was in smaller-sized lower-margin cars, principally the Mini and 1100 families. By 1965 sub-1100cc models were accounting for almost three-quarters of BMC's ouput. "On the Mini I reckon we were making £5 a motor car – which was ridiculously low," Eric Lord observed to the author. "It was much too low, because it didn't allow for any margin of error, for anything that could go wrong – and it didn't take warranty costs into account. Eventually we were making more than a fiver a car, but we never made very much money on the Mini."

BMC had the arrogance to think that its dominance of the British market – led by the Mini and the top-selling 1100 – made it immune to the basic laws of economics. The figures said otherwise. Writing in 1964, Peter Wilsher of *The Sunday Times* pointed out that while BMC had 38.5 per cent of the market, against Ford's 25 per cent, it had made only £15m profit in 1963, in comparison to the £35m Ford had made. That meant that Ford was making roughly two and a half times as much per car, averaged out. The figures in 1964 looked superficially better, with profits of over £21m. But this was not much more than BMC had achieved in 1958, when it had made 280,000 fewer vehicles. In 1955 BMC had been making an average profit of £40 per car; ten years later, it was making half that. Having begun the decade making nearly £27m profit on sales of £346m, in 1967 BMC recorded a £3m loss, on sales of £467m. With a Labour government keen to see industrial consolidation, the combine was looking distinctly vulnerable.

An early Canadian-market 1100; in its time the car was the most advanced small/medium saloon in the world. (Jaguar North American Archives)

Meaningless 'badge engineering' saw the arrival in 1966 of the Morris 1800; the grille on MkI and MkII cars was different from that on the Austins. (Author's collection)

The Vanden Plas 4-litre R had engine and other quality problems; one service engineer said he virtually lived at Vanden Plas for several months. (Graham Robson)

British Leyland and the Marina

For its last year in the States the Marina was sold with ugly impact bumpers. (Jaguar North American Archives)

With the Marina there was again a Morris with a stand-alone design. But the mid-sized fleet contender was a rushed and ill-considered project. Despite that, it had a long life and can be regarded as a modest commercial success – at least in its home country.

In 1968 the last merger in the history of the British motor industry took place. The Leyland Motor Corporation, which had acquired Standard-Triumph in 1961 and absorbed Rover in 1967, joined with British Motor Holdings, as BMC had become following its own acquisition, in 1966, of the Jaguar group of companies. The resultant combine, headed by Sir Donald Stokes – or Lord Stokes as he became in 1969 – was named the British Leyland Motor Corporation, but was more commonly known as BL.

The end of BMC: decadence and decay

This was not a partnership of equals. Triumph and Rover were essentially large-scale specialist manufacturers whilst Leyland had developed out of a tight-knit Lancashire maker of trucks; BMH, meanwhile, was a major-league mass-producer. Yet behind this apparent mis-match was a very different reality, one that BMH chairman George Harriman was too complacent to realise. French BMC importer Jean-Pierre Richard had uneasy forebodings after a dinner in Paris with Sir George and Lady Harriman.

"There was an Irish chap there, whose name I forget. Lady Harriman said 'Sir George has a lot of work at the moment, because we are in the process of taking over Leyland.' I always remember this sharp little Irishman who turned round and said to Lady Harriman, 'One should always watch out, your ladyship, for those snakes that swallow bigger animals whole.' Harriman had a somewhat distant air about him. After the dinner a colleague of mine said 'There's something that worries me. Sir George is frightened about what's happening on the stock exchange with Leyland.' We only knew afterwards what the situation was – but Harriman really thought BMC was absorbing Leyland."

The truth of the matter was that for BMC the game was up. The company was rotten to the core. Stokes himself was tempted to walk away, once he had discovered the degree of decay in what was supposed to be a national flagship. The company was run on the basis of what might be termed 'Management by Agreeable Luncheon', whereby alcohol-infused decisions were taken in the senior dining room by Harriman and technical director Alec Issigonis and then relayed to the minions outside.

Even after the merger, the whole atmosphere at Longbridge was 'Last Days of the Raj', recalls Ray Bates, an ex-Leyland engineer who joined the board in 1970. "I think they sat on their backsides - it was 'We've got 40 per cent of the market, the money's rolling in, that's it boys, we're home and dry.' The attitudes I encountered were Victorian. I was entitled to eat in the executive dining-room – a great honour. There was gin, scotch or whatever you wanted. I remember Charles Griffin saying to me, 'You're the junior member, you'll have to carve.' It was like sitting in a gentleman's club, watching the world go by..."

The sheer scale of the BMC shipwreck is mind-boggling. The financial figures can be dismissed in a line: in 1966–67 BMH had made a loss after tax of nearly £4m, its cash resources had halved from £28m to £14m, and its overdraft had risen

The Maxi was only made at Cowley; its widely reported gearchange problems helped torpedo sales. (Author's collection)

The initial Roy Haynes proposal for what became the Marina; note the use of Cortina MkII hubcaps and wheeltrims. (Roy Haynes)

Two mock-ups from 1969 show both the saloon and coupé most of the way to their final design. The grille of the saloon is very Ford-like. (John Sheppard)

to titivate BMC's ageing best-sellers; when the MkII Minis and 1100/1300s were announced at the 1967 Motor Show, supplies of the restyled grilles and rear lamps had not arrived, and nor had the bigger engines.

On the commercial-vehicle side, built up on the back of the once-successful Morris Commercial business, the company had lost £1.25m in the 1966–67 season, had recorded its lowest-ever market share of 18 per cent, and had a plant utilisation rate of under 40 per cent, thanks to the unsaleability of BMC's outdated and unreliable trucks and light vans. All the while, as discussed earlier, there was the yawning hole in the centre of the firm's car range, thanks to the debacle of the 1800. Rounding off this hellish picture was the familiar backcloth of disastrous labour problems, over-manning and antiquated facilities.

The man with a plan

At Cowley there had been some efforts to redress things. Former Pressed Steel MD Joe Edwards, a highly-respected ex-Austin senior manager, had returned to BMC in 1965 with the acquisition of Pressed Steel and was soon Managing Director. On his watch a significant number of staff had been recruited from Ford, and a new dynamism was being implanted in the company. Or so it was hoped: in fact there was a definite measure of ill-will towards many of the newcomers, who were regarded by old BMC hands as being know-it-all smart-alecs who had probably jumped ship because they had been no good at Ford. Whether there is an element of truth in this is not for the author to say; what is the case is that some of the senior ex-Ford men imposed a new and much-needed rigour of thought upon BMC.

One of these men was Roy Haynes, who had been appointed Director of Styling for BMH after being Assistant Chief Designer at Ford. Based at the Pressed Steel Fisher body plant in Cowley, Haynes established a new styling department independent of the Longbridge studios run by Austin's Dick Burzi. Haynes knew that the way to pull the combine out of its death spiral was to rationalise the huge number of models and put in place an American-style cross-marque platform-sharing strategy, based on a mid-range car at the heart of the car market – and nicely positioned to take fleet sales from Ford and Vauxhall. This was the start of what would become the Marina. Complex charts were drawn up, showing how a Jaguar or an MG could be spun off from the same underpinnings as a Morris. At this stage the

from £1.6m to £23m[1]. Meanwhile, Issigonis had been amusing himself by working on a smaller Mini for Italy, a miniature 4x4 called the Ant, and a large Hydrolastic-suspended sports car irreverently nicknamed Fireball. Although the 'Mini-Mini' would evolve into the potentially brilliant 9X would-be Mini replacement, this was a classic case of fiddling while Rome burnt.

Alongside such marginalia, in 1967 the company had been pushing forward to production with three cars nobody would much want when they ultimately hit the market: the Maxi, the MGC and the Austin 3-litre. Valuable engineering time and resources were being tied up in this trio of underdone turkeys, and only at the last moment was it decided to do something

[1] *Figures quoted in* The Leyland Papers, *by Graham Turner.*

nature of those underpinnings was not known, but obviously Haynes didn't envisage taking a Morris Minor and dolling it up to be a Jaguar.

"Roy locked himself away and started what was in effect a corporate plan. Because there were so many products, he set about doing a plan which was based on the GM route, where you had an 'A' body, a 'B' body, a 'C' body and a 'D' body, and there was interchangeability between the different marques. They all shared the same underpinnings but looked different, and you could also swap the engines around," remembers future Austin-Morris styling head Harris Mann. "Roy had this masterplan in his office. We were all involved in doing little drawings to put on the wall, so you could see where Austin was going, where Morris was going, where MG would be going, and you could see the relationship between one and the other, how they overlapped, and how you could take a Jaguar engine, say, and put it in a top-line Rover. It seemed a good way forward – using the whole of the organisation to bring together a logical plan for the company."

From Maxi to 'New Minor'

Work duly began on a conventionally-engineered mid-size car, drawing on Haynes's intimate knowledge of the highly successful MkII Cortina, which had been designed under his direction. "I said to Harry Barber, the MD of Pressed Steel, that we were going to undercut the Cortina in every respect," recalls Haynes. "This was when the MkII's body-in-white weighed less than 500lb and cost less than £100. Barber said they'd never built a car like that. The best they'd managed was the Hillman Hunter and that was way above £100 and weighed nearly half as much again."

In the middle of all this came the merger. The incoming ex-Leyland managers discovered that the new-model cupboard was bare but for the Austin Maxi, which was supposedly near-ready for production at Cowley. Originally thought of as a sort of 'Super-1100' – and at first known internally as 'ADO16+' or 'ADO16⅜' – this had evolved into something more like a cut-down Austin 1800 and had its costs and its aesthetics handicapped by the stipulation that it be based around the 1800's doors. The car looked a fright, had yet another set of mechanicals unrelated to other BMC cars, and was manifestly only half developed. With thoughts already turning to an orthodox rear-drive car, this was the final straw: with the Maxi, Issigonis had signed his own death warrant.

The new Morris Marina, beauty with brains® behind it.

Two bodies, one set of front doors; the 'plank' grille insert of 1.8s was a way of doing something different from the opposition. (Author's collection)

Canadian-market Marina with sheep – possibly from the discarded photo-shoot described in the text. (Jaguar North American Archives)

A crash programme was initiated to make the car less awful – but at its 1969 launch the Maxi was still unsatisfactory, and became notorious for its dreadful cable-operated gearchange. "I have never driven such a load of garbage in my life – and they'd had a year re-working it by this time," remembers ex-Ford man John Bacchus, later to become director of Product Planning for Austin-Morris. "You had a history of the Mini, the ADO16 – still the gem, in my opinion – and then the 1800, which... was commercially a load of rubbish, and then this Maxi, which was a disaster in every way. So one fought against the absolute block of prejudice towards Alec Issigonis."

The MkI 1.3 Marinas had a split front grille; De Luxe and Super de Luxe versions were available. (Author's collection)

The pick-up was only available with the A-series engine. (Author's collection)

The 1.3s had twin-dial instrument packs, the 1.8 Super de Luxe and TC a three-dial cluster with rev-counter. (Author's collection)

Eric Lord recalls the gloom that descended on Cowley. "The first Maxis we had off the Cowley production line, we knew we were in trouble. With the cable selectors you couldn't get the gears. I remember going to George Turnbull and saying 'We're going to get a dreadful reputation with this car. There is nothing we can do to adjust these cables so they will stay adjusted. It's got to come to a rod change. Can you please stop production until we've got a rod change? Otherwise we'll get a terrible reputation for poor gearchanges.' We found this out within the first week of production, but we still went on making the things, when we knew that what we were making was rubbish.

The Maxi never really recovered from the bad name it got during those first months."

As warranty costs stacked up, and sales flat-lined, further impetus was given to the design of a conventional rear-drive model, with Eric Lord being among those who pressed for a reversion to tried-and-tested mechanicals. "I wrote a paper about the Maxi saying 'For Goodness sake would we please stop working from a clean sheet of paper. Let's learn from our mistakes on the cars we're making and develop these – let's put a new dress on them.' I pleaded that the Morris Minor should have a new dress, but remain basically the same, while we had a chance to catch our breath. It was a reliable car, it didn't cost a great deal to assemble, and warranty costs were low."

John Bacchus was one of those who could see the appeal of such a scheme. "There was a desperate need for a fleet-market car... Casting around, there it was – the Morris Minor. It had a fairly stable structure, rack-and-pinion steering – and a conventional leaf-spring rear suspension, of course, but so had Cortinas and a lot of other cars. We needed a quick and dirty programme. So why not just drop a new bodyshell on the Minor? Bingo! It would only have to live for 4–5 years, anyway..."

So it was that under BL the idea of a 'New Minor' gathered momentum, with the target – notwithstanding Roy Haynes – being less the Cortina than the Escort and the Viva. The new car would be a Morris, and henceforth orthodox rear-wheel-drive cars would carry the Morris badge, whilst front-wheel-drive models would exclusively be Austins. Superficially this seemed an elegant solution to the old issue of 'badge engineering'.

Into the fleet-car heartland

After proposals from Michelotti and Pininfarina had been rejected, the styling was worked up by a team including ex-Ford designer Harris Mann. "Roy was the instigator, getting the project up and running, with his knowledge of how much the Escort was costing, as opposed to the 1100. There was a big difference, I think – in those days it was a big sum – there was a £30 difference in the suspension alone. The Hydrolastic cost a lot of money. We were out to produce a vehicle which was a competitor to the Escort – not the Cortina – and which gave the company some profit. It was a quick programme. There must have been some urgency about getting it out. There wasn't any 'back to the drawing board' or 'you'll have

LABOUR AND MANAGEMENT PROBLEMS IN THE MARINA YEARS

Labour relations at Cowley in pre-war days had not been enlightened. Post-war, the unions were eventually recognised but soon the extreme left started their infiltration, as former TGWU official David Buckle acknowledges in his memoirs. 'Having obtained jobs in Morris Motors, a small group of Trotskyites laid low for a time. When the opportunity came for the election of shop stewards, they put their names forward, claiming they could, and would, achieve far more than line representatives and the few shop stewards had managed to do. Most of the very militant stewards made sure members had no idea about their real motives.

'Having been elected for two years, their tactic was to persuade a small group of members to stop work until their demands were met. Anyone who carried on working discovered later that the stewards had informed management the work done during the dispute was "black" and could not be worked on when the dispute ended. This in turn had a much wider effect on many others elsewhere in the plant... In effect, the extremist union stewards were trying to run a union within a union and eventually became a greater danger to their members' job prospects than the inefficient poor management.'

With management prepared to cave in just to keep the lines running, the extremists made hay, without either side able to break out of this vicious circle. 'Neither management at Morris Motors nor the militant stewards seemed to have any idea how to talk and agree with one another,' writes Buckle. Exacerbating matters was the move to Measured Day Work in time for the launch of the Marina. The abandonment of piecework was judged a disaster by both unions and local management.

"Measured Day Work was alright, but it wasn't properly measured," says Eric Lord. "They went into it too quickly. Those stories about clocking on and going home were quite true. There were cases of three men being employed where one was sufficient, and the others going off and having a kip. They appointed people who didn't know what the hell they were doing. They took no notice of the old rate-fixers who had to know the job in order to fix the rate for the operation. These whizz-kids came in and made an absolute mess of it – and of course the costs went sky-high."

In an interview for the Television History Workshop, John Power, a former TGWU shop steward, admitted that the company needed to move away from the piecework system, and said that many unionists would have preferred a standard payment with a bonus. Management, he says, wanted Measured Day Work or nothing and forced a five-week strike to impose it.

'They were actually able to boast to the men [...] "Why are you striking? Because we are offering you more money to do less work." But they were the architects of the destruction of BL, the people who had this obsession with setting up a single corporation at all costs, out of different companies, with different histories and backgrounds, and then trying to bring a pay structure into all of its plants that didn't suit it and actually cost more money in most of the plants.' Former Cowley engineer Roy Davies confirms this. "Measured Day Work effectively lifted the hourly rate from 12s to £1 without

any extra effort. Lord Nuffield would immediately have seen the pitfalls..."

Leyland management was in fact depressingly incompetent, says Eric Lord. "The biggest problem with BL was that they tried to centralise everything. You can't control quality centrally. You have to get the people in each plant to do it... And then the Cowley plant no longer know how much each car cost – because it was all centralised. The poor bloke who was manager of Cowley had no idea of his costings.

"The obsession with paperwork was terrible... I remember having a letter from Brigadier Maple, who was made the director in charge of quality-control... and it said that in future any problems should be reported in duplicate or triplicate on such-and-such a form. There was to be no direct contact made with engineering. Can you imagine it! In the meantime the

lines were running at 30 cars to the hour and things were happening. But you had to go through a system and a procedure. I'm afraid we deserved to go down the slot."

Production engineer Peter Tothill recounted one episode to the author. "A lot of this centralisation was completely destructive. I was in the office of Des North, the Cowley plant director in the mid 1970s, and a call came through from a high-placed person at BL in London, tearing him off a strip for spending £3000 without authorisation, after he'd installed a line of cable throughout the shop after a power failure. Des said, 'Look, I've got responsibility for making 5000 Marinas a week. The plant broke down at 1500hrs and I got it up again by midnight and I was still in the factory at midnight.' He was told, 'Well, you should have applied for a sanction to spend that money.' Des said, 'I don't care whom you report it to – I've done my job. My job is to keep the plant running, and I've done it.' And this guy said he hadn't applied in triplicate...'

All this impacted on labour matters, says Eric Lord. "We had one man who was responsible for labour relations across the firm. He'd got an impossible job, because the whole lot would land in his lap, and he had to decide what was to be done. Unless you had your finger on the pulse and you knew the people you were dealing with, you couldn't really control it. This was where Leyland absolutely went up the spout. The thing that brought Austin and Morris together more than anything else was Leyland. Austin and Morris suddenly discovered that they rather liked each other after all – and to hell with those bastards from Leyland. The tribal instinct is terribly strong."

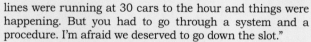

The new assembly facility was accompanied by new working practices that caused many a problem. (Author's collection)

Much designers' ink was expended on coupé versions of the Marina. This is one of a series of 1968 proposals. (Paul Hughes)

Another Hughes proposition for the 'Condor' coupé project: it could have become an MG Magna. (Paul Hughes)

Harris Mann wanted to modernise the idea of how a Vanden Plas should look; this is his proposal for a Marina version. (Harris Mann)

to change this'. It was only nit-picking. [Austin-Morris Engineering Director] Harry Webster had some input and I think he and Stokes considered the rear pillar on the two-door as being too wide, so we had to slim it down."

Mann judges the Marina a satisfactory design. "The Marina was alright for the time. People don't realise what was around with it – the Viva, the Avenger, the Escort. Put them all together and there's nothing about it where you could say 'Oh that didn't fit the bill for the time.' You couldn't be adventurous in any way – no way at all. It was fitted into a marketplace where there were three rivals in there. It was a case of 'Don't offend anyone – just do it'..."

The excitement would come later, had the Haynes masterplan survived, as sporting versions of the new BL mid-sizer were very much in the picture. The modular planning matrix Haynes was working on included use of the Rover V8 engine, and there were hopes of a car that could be a sports coupé in the mould of the Australian Holden Monaro, but more the size

of the Opel Rekord coupé, a car Haynes much admired. A modern MG-badged V8-powered Capri-eater would have been a nice high-profit earner for the company. But BL wasn't ready for such bold forward-thinking, and after falling out with Harry Webster, Haynes left BL in 1969. "He got so completely uptight at being controlled by people who just didn't – in his mind – see the future, who just didn't get it," recalls Mann, who at this stage took over as chief designer. As for Haynes, his time at BMH/BL and the company's failure to implement his master plan constitute, he says, "the tragedy of my life".

The prostitution of engineering

Meanwhile, excitement was anything but in order when it came to the hardware chosen to underpin the new model. In terms of its mechanicals, the car was envisaged as using the 1100cc and 1300cc A-series engine and the 1500cc E-series Maxi unit, with the gearbox being the new corporate rear-drive four-speeder that would first be seen in the 1970 Triumph Toledo. The rest of the running gear would be Morris Minor, and here was the first major mis-step.

At the heart of the Minor was its torsion-bar front suspension, which used lever-arm dampers as a key component, feeding all their loads into the bulkhead. Used in conjunction with threaded uprights, the set-up was expensive, inefficient, and had basic failings in engineering terms – failings which could have easily been palliated by the use of telescopic dampers and a conventional upper arm. "With lever-arm dampers, you have no noise insulation from the road, and once you've put them on, you're restricted to one supplier," comments Ray Bates. "They were just a nightmare. I can't think for the life of me why they carried over the lever-arm damper. We should have done better. We were carrying over too much Morris Minor stuff..."

Worse was to come. For what seems to have been a combination of reasons, the E-series engine was axed from the programme. According to Bates this was because the Cofton Hackett facility would not be able to produce the engine in sufficient numbers. Given that at this time the E-series was only being fitted to the Maxi, which at its best would only sell in a quarter of the numbers planned, this is hard to believe. John Bacchus feels that another possible explanation is that it was decided to sell the Marina in the States, and the E-series was not homologated under US exhaust-emissions regulations.

The only other mid-size Austin-Morris engine available was the heavy and old-fashioned B-series. So this was schemed into the project, which was as a result now mutating into the Cortina rival that Roy Haynes had originally envisaged. The first snag was that the transmission tunnel had been laid out for the '58.5mm' Triumph gearbox, and the B-series transmission would not fit. The Triumph unit thus had to remain. This was in the full knowledge that this re-hash of a gearbox that had started life in the 1953 Standard Eight was simply not strong enough to withstand the torque of the B-series engine. The second consequence of installing the B-series was that the antiquated Minor suspension system couldn't cope, as the motoring press would later discover. There was a further irony to this twist in the story, says Eric Lord. "In the end the only bit of the Minor that was carried over to the Marina wasn't made to drawing anyway – the suspension had been altered and changed but the drawings had never been updated..."

Admittedly BL's engineering resources were shockingly deficient in comparison with those at Ford or in other European companies. Also it did not help that Webster and Stokes had made the decision to split the mid-size market two ways. Engineers were therefore spread too thinly, across not just the Marina but also the new fwd car that would emerge in 1973 as the Austin Allegro, thereby compromising the design of both cars. But across the corporation there were men of talent and ability. This sort of fiasco should not have happened. Part of the reason was that BMC engineers wedded to front-wheel-drive were asked to create the cut-price Marina against their will; equally, though, the car started out as one thing and ended up as another. "We'd got product planners on board, mainly from Ford, and that was their idea of a motor car," says former senior BL engineer Ron Nicholls. "There was a complete lack of communication. Why were things happening the way they were? They made the decisions. You kept your head down. But you can't just evolve things as you go along. Marina was meant to be a cheap car, but it was sold as an expensive car. It sort of lost its way, and the engineering was prostituted to keep the cost down. It ended up totally underbraked; the wheel bearings weren't up to the job. The whole thing was totally inadequate. It was designed to compete in a certain part of the marketplace and then it suddenly had to compete with cars

The estate was initially only available as a 1.8 Super De Luxe; a 1.3 version followed later. (Author's collection)

properly designed for the job. Had it been just a 1300 it would have worked. Not that brilliantly, but it would have worked."

Dislike for the abrasive Harry Webster didn't help matters, but nor did the unwillingness of the engineers to look beyond their own companies and think about how best to use the over-stocked corporate parts-bin available to them. Had the new car been based on Toledo underpinnings, to cite the obvious example, then it would have had modern strut front suspension, a coil-sprung back axle – and a design with a development future. But with everyone fighting their own corner that was never going to happen. Ray Bates recalls a commonalisation committee of senior engineers from each company, and of which he was secretary. "We never achieved anything. They always wanted to support their own particular design areas. If we commonalised a few plain washers that's probably all we did."

Of sheep and suspension

So it was that in April 1971 the ten-car Morris Marina range was announced, after a total investment of £45m. This included £7m to create a new gearbox facility at Longbridge and a complete re-fit of Cowley, taking in new assembly lines, a new paint plant, and a covered link between the Pressed Steel works and the main factory. The whole programme had taken two and a half years, or a year less than the industry average at the time. Not only that, but Haynes's target had been met: the Marina body-in-white weighed less than 500lb and cost less than £100 to make.

The arrival of the new Morris was as ill-starred as its conception – even down to an embarrassing publicity goof which suggested that the car had been designed by a bunch of sheep. "Ahead of the Marina launch some of us were asked to see the press material," remembers Eric Lord. "There was a picture of the Marina in a country setting, and the slogan 'Beauty with Brains Behind It'... and in the background were these sheep. I said to Harry Barber, 'Harry – they're having us on. It's supposed to be Beauty with Brains Behind It, and there are bloody sheep behind the car. We got hold of the publicity people and said, 'Are you out of your mind? You can't publish that.' Tens of thousands of catalogues had to be dumped..."

That was the least of BL's problems. Rival motoring weeklies *Motor* and *Autocar* were so appalled by the road behaviour of the 1800cc Marina that quite unprecedentedly they joined forces to tell BL that they would damn the car in print unless something were done about it. "We drove the car independently... and we both thought it was pretty bloody awful," former *Motor* editor Charles Bulmer told the author. "Later we got together and said, 'We ought to say something about this.' The thing was a terrible bodge in its first form. Well, it was fairly dangerous – tremendous understeer and very low cornering power. It was so different from the sort of cars they had been producing. It was an enormous disapppointment. I don't remember anything like that happening before or after. We were both at Dorset House but we preserved the old rivalry, so we didn't collaborate."

A rapid modification was made to the kingpin inclination on 1.8 models, with a BL service engineer being despatched with new front suspension uprights for the press cars; subsequently the mod was phased in on the 1.3-litre cars. It was a bad start to the Marina's life, and in service the car was not to be much better. "The body leaked like a seive, there was trouble with halfshafts breaking, and the gearbox made at Longbridge was a nightmare from the quality point of view," remembers Cowley production engineer Roy Davies. "We couldn't get the cars to roller-test without jumping out of gear... and if a car passed, it had problems when it got to the dealer. Longbridge wasn't renowned for sticking to tolerances and they were not building to spec – on top of which the gearbox couldn't cope with the power, and chucked oil out of the back."

The experience of John Bacchus confirms that the gearbox was – in the words of Eric Lord – "a

The Marina 2 featured one style of grille for the entire range; top models had inset foglamps. (Author's collection)

This Marina 2 is a 1.8 Super; the twin-carb variant was now called the GT. (Author's collection)

The sweepaway dashboard was ergonomically a little peculiar; it was the work of Paul Hughes. (Author's collection)

Available as a De Luxe and a Super de Luxe, in 1.3 and 1.8 forms and as a twin-carb 1.8TC with the 95bhp MGB engine, the Marina was offered as a two-door coupé and four-door saloon, BL cleverly saving costs by the coupé sharing the saloon's front doors. With drum brakes on the front of the 1.3 and a leaf-sprung Triumph rear axle with no further location but the sharply-angled telescopic dampers, the Marina was basic to the point of rusticity.

In 1974 BL unveiled a trio of Experimental Safety Vehicle Marinas; the engine was moved forward to aid body deformation. (Jaguar North American Archives)

Interlocking door and sill structures gave strength in side impacts. (Jaguar North American Archives)

boy doing a man's job". After analysing warranty costs on the Marina gearbox by engine type, he discovered a fault incidence on the 1.8 TC of 108 per cent – meaning that on average every car had at least one fault on its gearbox. On the 1.3 the figure was 33 per cent, which was hardly more reassuring. Meanwhile the drum brakes on the 1.3 were proving totally inadequate, something it took some time for the engineers to make Harry Webster accept. In the end disc brakes were standardised, but only on MkII 1.3s – although quality control was sufficiently lax that one London dealer received a car with a disc brake on one side and a drum brake on the other.

As was only to be expected, the range soon grew. In August 1972 a van and a pick-up arrived, with 7cwt and 10cwt payload options for the van and the choice of 1100 or 1300 engines – the latter being standard wear on the 10cwt van. In October the same year a 1.8 estate arrived. Thereafter the Marina was largely unchanged until October 1975, when the Marina 2 was announced. This had revised suspension with anti-roll bars front and back, the modifications prompting *Autocar* to comment that the Morris 'now handles very acceptably for a car in this class'. Other changes were a new dashboard, oddly with the radio curving away from the driver, and restyled grilles.

Whatever the crudities of its design, the Marina was not a sales failure. In 1972, its first full year, it was third in the UK sales charts, with 104,986 cars registered, against 187,159 for the first-place Ford Cortina. The following year it did even better, UK registrations of 115,041 units putting it in second place, with 6.9 per cent of the market. Sales dropped back to 81,444 cars in the troubled year of 1974, and to 78,632 in 1975, putting the Marina in fourth position in the charts – but still well ahead of the Austin Allegro, whose sales were never anything but disappointing.

Hard sell: the Austin Marina

The year 1975 also marked the end of the Marina's inglorious career in the US, where – as in Canada – it was sold with Austin badging. Bob Burden had the job of mounting the advertising campaigns for the car. "The Triumph gearbox was just god-awful – the gearlever would vibrate like hell. It just wasn't very good at anything. It was mediocre. The Japanese made a better product, and price-wise we were struggling – there was no competitive price advantage. It was a sedan being sold in sports car market. The press savaged it. For their cover picture *Car and Driver* put the car in the centre of an auto-wrecking yard. My boss Graham Whitehead, who would roll with the punches, just went absolutely ballistic. Nobody liked the car – it had no class-leading areas. We knew we needed volume, and you kind of hope things are going to get better."

Even the name worked against the car, says Burden: while for the English the word 'marina' conjures up images of beautiful people swanning around in posh yachts, for an American it's a grubby place where chaps in overalls fettle rusty

The low front of the more styled SRV2 was intended to minimise pedestrian injuries. (Author's collection)

The Australian Marina had a different grille. This treatment was carried through to the South African version. (Author's collection)

The Australians wanted their own mid-size design; this model is of the car at its P82 stage, pictured with stylist Michelotti. (BMC-Leyland Australia Heritage Group)

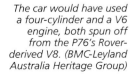

The car would have used a four-cylinder and a V6 engine, both spun off from the P76's Rover-derived V8. (BMC-Leyland Australia Heritage Group)

boats. "Why did the company call it the Marina? Don't land yourself with a name that has no meaning – the Austin Boatyard! Why are you starting me off with a handicap? Give me a name I can make something of, give me something I can work with – particularly when you're not giving it to me in product..."

BL's Stateside PR man, Mike Cook, was no more impressed by the car. "The Marina was supposed to be powerful enough and reasonably-priced enough to take a piece of the sedan market. But it was so crude and so ordinary-looking that even if it had been a tremendously value-for-money beautifully-built car it wouldn't have sold. What were you thinking of? It was reasonably priced, but it was cart-sprung, it didn't handle, it wasn't comfortable and it was cheaply finished. There

was a lot of stuff that was wrong with it. It didn't always start, it didn't always run, and the engine was rough – even at 65mph on the highway there was always a little vibration.

"It was a real piece of junk. Everybody drove them for company cars – we had 'em coming out of our ears. The last year we had them – 1975 – we were stocked up to the ceiling and we knew we weren't going to sell them. So we did a price cut of $400, and sold them out – only to get fined by the US government for dumping."

Down-under dramas

The Marina's career in Australia was even shorter, being curtailed by the 1974 winding-down of BL's car assembly operations in the country. It had not been the intention of BL-Australia to make the Marina. After the disasters of the Nomad/1500 and Kimberley/Tasman, it had decided that the only way forward was to stop adapting British designs and built a range of rear-wheel-drive cars aimed directly at Holden and Ford. The idea was that there would be a mid-sized 'Model A' to take on the Holden Torana and a larger car, the 'Model B', to tackle the full-sized Holden and the Ford Falcon. To reduce costs, both cars would share a considerable number of parts, these where possible being proprietary off-the-shelf-units. In the early stages of developing the larger car – which would become the P76 – the company in the UK persuaded the Australians that taking the Marina would be a short-cut to get into the mid-size market. The 'Model A' was therefore put to one side. It remained in the background, however, as it was always felt that the Marina would be no more than a stop-gap, and work quietly continued on the project, latterly under the P82 label.

As the Australians no longer made the B-series engine, local-content requirements meant that the BL-Australia Marina would need to use the E-series, which was in production in Australia in both four-cylinder and six-cylinder forms. It wasn't long before the suggestion came up that as well as the 1500cc and 1750cc 'fours' the 'six' could also be used, to give BL a competitor to the Falcon-engined Cortina MkIII and the six-cylinder Holden Torana. This was where the project started to come off the rails, as the 2.6-litre E-series developed for the P76 was schemed into a car that had started life as a rebodied Morris Minor.

"That was the marketing people," says former Leyland-Australia engineer Bruce Elson. "The engine was too heavy for the front end. But the six-cylinder Cortina was a bastard, and the later six-cylinder Chrysler Centura was a bastard. We just joined them. Everybody had a small six-cylinder saloon so we had to have one. It was a pig of a car. We shouldn't have got into it."

Diverting engineering time to sorting the Marina Red Six for its November 1973 launch was possibly what killed Leyland in Australia, says Roger Foy, who worked on the car. "It was sold to David Beech, who was director of engineering, that the 'six' would be no problem – that it would just pour straight in. Whatever they measured up wasn't what we measured up. Almost the complete car was changed, back to the windscreen. What this did was take all our best people to work on the design and fitting of this engine into the Marina. It wasn't a simple thing to do. This took the emphasis off refining the P76 before it went into production, and that was the genesis of the failure of the P76, because we no longer had the manpower to ensure that the P76 was right as well as to design this engine into the Marina."

The re-jig to take the E6 engine was all the same restricted largely to structural modifications, given the limited time and resources available: lever-arm front dampers were retained and the back axle tamed merely by a pair of radius rods. Although Foy says that if one accepted that the car was a 'straight-line rocket' it was perfectly adequate, he confirms that the Red Six – standard transmission a three-speed Borg-Warner manual 'box – was as one might expect a pretty crude device. "The structural stength of the Marina body was bloody dreadful. If you got any front wheel/tyre radial run-out you got the whole front of the car shaking up and down." Fellow former Leyland-Australia engineer Chris Rogers recalls that the body required extensive strengthening, not least as the specified spot-welds were insufficient in number. "We still got scuttle shake. It was so bad that we actually had to shave the front tyres after assembly, to make them dead round."

Meanwhile the four-cylinder Morris Marinas had been doing adequately well, after their April 1972 launch; indeed production had to be ramped up after a few months. Models offered were the coupé in 1500, 1750 and twin-carb 1750 TC forms, and the saloon just with single-carb 1500 or 1750 power. Renamed the Leyland Marina during 1973, the car ended its first full year on sale with over 10,000 examples registered, the best result for some time for a BMC/BL car in Australia. In 1974, faced with supply problems and uncertainty about Leyland-Australia's future, sales dropped to 8109 units, of which 2852 were

The big bumpers and spoiler of the third-generation Marina did not flatter the car. (Author's collection)

ADO77 started off being closely based on the Marina – note the doors on the bare shell – but ended up a bigger car. (Ray Bates/Keith Adams)

six-cylinder models. Production of the Marina ended in Australia in December 1974, with the last of the 30,000 or so cars that had been made being sold to the Australian government as part of a package deal tied up with the disposal of the factory.

Few tears were shed. "It was the worst car we ever made," former chief engineer Bill Serjeantson told the author. All the tooling was shipped to Leyland's South African operation,

The Ital restyling wrung a few more years of sales out of the Marina. (Author's collection)

where manufacture was re-started in 1975 and continued until 1978. Just over 4000 ex-Australia Marinas were made, against approximately 13,000 – mostly LCVs – built in South Africa from UK-sourced CKD kits.

A life prolonged

If the Marina had run its course in the USA and in Australia – and it was never going to be a starter in Europe – then back home it continued to sell steadily, although it never met its production target of 5000 cars per week. In 1976 it stuck at fourth place in the UK market before moving back up to the number-three slot in 1977. Of course the car, designed as a stop-gap, was never intended still to be in production after 1975 – or perhaps 1976 at the latest. From the end of 1972 the engineers at BL had been looking at improving the design, studying a telescopic conversion for the front and a Toledo four-link coil-sprung rear axle – in other words what the car should have had in the first place. There was also a trial of a leaf-sprung rear axle with a torque tube and a Panhard rod, and of another set-up using Hydragas units, radius arms and a Panhard rod, but which was soon deemed too complex and costly. These experiments evolved into a new car to replace the Marina, under the model code ADO77. "Having done the Marina, the next thing was to put it right with ADO77," observes Ray Bates.

As well as a new body, a strut front was at the top of the list, plus a more sophisticated rear suspension, with coil springs, a torque tube and four-link axle location. The B-series engine would also be ditched, in favour of BL's ohc O-series unit, and in place of the 'Toledo' gearbox would be a more robust '66mm' unit. Because the Marina floorpan was inadequate, the car would have had no carry-over, the price paid for not getting the Morris right in the first place. The project also started to get out of hand, says John Bacchus, with the car getting bigger and more elaborate.

But this was all delusional stuff. Wracked with labour problems, lacking investment money, under-resourced as ever in engineers, BL was still not thinking like a coherent corporate whole. While Austin-Morris engineers were toying with a future new Morris, Rover-Triumph, proudly separate, was working on exactly the same sort of car in the form of the SD2 – 'Specialist Division 2' – as a replacement for the Triumph Dolomite. Eventually sense prevailed. Rover designer David Bache would continue with SD2, essentially a cut-down Rover SD1, and a Morris version would be spun off from this. Tagged TM1 – for 'Triumph-Morris 1' – the venture didn't get very far down the road before the cold-shower reality-check of the end of the 1970s saw thoughts focus on what would ultimately become the Maestro/Montego.

The revised tail was inoffensively neat; the Ital was not available as a coupé. (Author's collection)

The van and pick-up also gained the new Ital front. (Author's collection)

Meanwhile the Marina had continued to be manufactured, turning into more and more of an antique as more modern competitors arrived on the market. Only limited improvements were ever going to be feasible – or affordable – and so the principal change was merely to swap the B-series engine for the 1.7-litre O-series unit in September 1978. At the same time there was a light restyle, with bigger bumpers and the suppression of the front quarterlights. It is tempting to be dismissive of the Marina by this stage, but fleet sales continued to keep the car afloat: in 1978 a total of 82,638 were registered, making the Morris Britain's third best-selling car, behind the Escort and the first-place Cortina. Nor was the gap between the Marina and the Cortina that huge, the Ford taking its crown with 139,204 registrations. It is a salutary fact, too, that the advanced wedge-shaped Princess staggered into eleventh spot in the UK sales chart that year, with a mere 36,813 cars registered. The Marina might have been an old relic, but it was at least a modestly successful old relic.

End of the line: the Ital

The Morris's moment in the sun was not to last. By 1979 it had slipped back to fourth place in the UK charts, with a sales drop to 62,140 registrations. BL was hanging on until it had launched the Metro and could bring the Maestro and Montego to market, so to keep the Marina in contention the car was facelifted front and rear in 1980. This was supposedly the work of Ital Design, but in fact Harris Mann's team at BL was responsible, with Ital merely productionalising the new look. Despite this, the car was renamed the Ital. As well as the new look there was also a re-jigged and much-improved A-Plus engine and better soundproofing. Additionally, from October 1980 the option of a 2-litre version of the O-series was offered alongside the 1700cc unit for the range-topping HLS model; the big engine was only available with automatic transmission, doubtless a tacit acknowledgement that the old 'Toledo' gearbox couldn't cope with the 2-litre's power output. Sales continued to fall away and by 1982 – when the slow-selling 2-litre was dropped – they had slumped to 23,228 units.

The end of production was announced in December 1983. In February 1984 the last Ital officially rolled off the lines. This was at Longbridge, to where production had been moved in 1982 in order to allow Cowley to be refitted for the Maestro and Montego. In fact manufacture continued on a small scale for another six months, to fulfil fleet contracts for the van and estate. In all 1,338,392 Marinas and Itals had been produced, over nearly 13 years, making it the best-selling car made by British Leyland. That over 2.1m 1100/1300s had been made over a roughly similar time-span puts that figure in perspective.

Intriguingly, that was not the end of the story. BL came close to selling the production line to India, and then to Pakistan. While both these deals fell through, eventually at the end of 1990s the Ital re-entered production – in China. In 1998 the Chengdu Auto Works began assembly of the Huandu CAC 6430, formerly the Ital estate, along with a pick-up and two versions of the Ital van. Powered by the BL O-series engine, the cars were apparently only in production for a year or so, with sales largely restricted to the western regions of China.

The end ...
and a new beginning

A lightly re-skinned Honda Accord, the Rover 600 was a high-quality 'junior executive' but its life was short. (Author's collection)

The Morris factory produced cars under many identities in the late 1970s and 1980s, but none was the hoped-for success. Despite the decline and collapse of the Rover Group, today the site has taken on a new life under the administration of BMW.

Cowley wasn't just home to the Maxi and the Marina in the 1970s. Leaving aside the ill-fated Austin 3-litre, production of which ended in early 1971 with just 9992 cars made, the former Morris works was also the manufacturing site for BL's last great white hope, launched in March 1975 as the 18–22 range.

Given radical wedge-shaped lines by Harris Mann, the car was a replacement for the old 1800/2200. With Hydragas suspension and a modern and stylish body, it was well received by the press but soon the usual BL quality and reliability issues emerged. Announced as an Austin, a Morris and a Wolseley, the 18-22 marked a return to meaningless 'badge engineering' that in the context of the time seemed completely witless. Just six months later all three marque names were removed from the car in favour of a new identity as the Leyland Princess. After 1977, sales fell away, output hitting a nadir in 1980, when a slender 14,612 Princesses were made. A re-jig in 1982 gave the car the hatchback for which it had always been crying out, and the re-named Austin Ambassador had a brief moment in the sun, with sales that year jumping by 70 per cent.

'The New Cowley'
The Ambassador was phased out in early 1984, when the second stage of what was described as 'The New Cowley' reached fruition. The first stage was the complete factory re-fit for the March 1983 launch of the Austin Maestro. With more than a hundred robots, it made Cowley BL's first plant with automated glazing equipment. With a new paint shop and a raft of computer-controlled machinery, the one-time Cinderella of the combine was now the most advanced factory in the group. Stage Two was the April 1984 introduction of the Montego, a booted derivative of the Maestro. The Montego was in effect a replacement for the Ital, and with the new BL fleet-market contender carrying the Austin badge, this was the end of the line for the Morris name, at least on private cars. Some time before, there had, however, been a rather startling announcement: BL had

The new Morris 1800, 1800 HL and 2200 HL.
The car that's got it all together.

The Morris version of the short-lived 18-22 series was recognisable by its round headlamps and contrived raised grille. (Author's collection)

apparently discovered that people associated Morris more with commercial vehicles than with cars. As a consequence, in 1982 the badge had been appended to the Metro van and the Sherpa range of light commercials. When this policy proved nonsensical, in 1985 the Morris name was finally laid to rest.

Acclaim – The Japanese Triumph
Alongside the Maestro and Montego, Cowley was also at the time producing two very contrasting cars under other badges: the facelifted Rover SD1, which had started to roll off the lines at the end of 1981, and the Triumph Acclaim, manufacture of which had begun in time for an October 1981 launch. Not only did the Acclaim mark the beginning of BL's partnership with Honda, but it also heralded a sea-change in the quality of the company's cars.

"The way the Triumph Acclaim was engineered was fantastic – it just fell together," veteran Cowley production engineer Peter Tothill told the author. The workforce was no less impressed when the first kits of parts arrived from Japan,

Bizarrely, the Metro van was briefly badged as a Morris; the policy of using the name for light commercials did not last. (Author's collection)

The second-generation SD1 – here a Vitesse – had higher quality when built at Cowley than at Solihull, which alas was not saying much. (Author's collection)

The Triumph Acclaim initiated the collaboration with Honda and introduced previously unseen quality standards for a Cowley product. (Author's collection)

Consolidation – and a move across the road

The collaboration with Honda was to gather pace, with the Acclaim being replaced by the Longbridge-built Rover 200-series in 1984 and the launch of the Cowley-produced Rover 800 in 1986. This was followed by the 1988 government disposal of BL into the private sector, with its purchase by British Aerospace. There now began a period when the future of Cowley seemed to some to be under threat. It was announced in July 1988 that the South Works would close with the end of Maestro/Montego production – which in truth was some good way in the future. North Works would stay open to make the Rover 800 and its successors, and meanwhile 46 acres would be freed for redevelopment. In November 1989, however, it was announced that North Works would also close, with production of 'executive cars' to be concentrated on the Pressed Steel site. An investment of £130m was spoken of by Rover Group, as the company had been re-named in 1986. With a further 41 acres now available for lucrative commercial redevelopment, it looked like a classic asset-stripping operation.

Production and jobs seemed sure to be run down, and various figures were bandied about in the press – not least that the workforce risked shrinking to 2500–2800 people. There was even talk of car manufacture ceasing entirely. Given that in 1973 the numbers working in motor manufacturing and associated businesses in Oxford had peaked at roughly 28,500 people, and that by the end of 1989 the workforce at the Cowley factories numbered just 8300, there was clearly legitimate concern.

There was, however, no escaping the laws of economics. Cowley might have made roughly 40 per cent of Rover's total output in 1988, but the 49,894 Rover 800s and related Honda Legends, 79,316 Montegos and 67,406 Maestros hardly required two sizeable factories – especially as the two latter cars had failed to set the market alight and sales were in constant decline.

For a while it looked as if Cowley was indeed doomed. As the partnership with Honda deepened, there was talk of the joint-venture replacement for the Montego being made either at Longbridge or at Honda's Swindon plant. In the end this didn't happen, and the new car went into production at Cowley in 1993 as the Rover 600. By this stage all car production had indeed shifted, in 1992, to the former Pressed Steel body plant across the way from the original Morris works, with a total of 4500 employees retained.

as trade-union leader David Buckle relates in his memoirs. 'The foreman gave the workers crowbars and hammers to break open the crates and remove the parts. I was told that as the crates were so well made the workers refused to damage them and opened them very carefully. When I asked, "What about the quality of the parts?" I was told "They actually fit first time." The point about parts fitting first time is very important so far as line speeds and productivity are concerned.'

Re-birth under BMW

In 1994 came the big shock – the author remembers it well, as on the day of the announcement he was driving to Cowley in his Morris Minor to visit the small facility where the MG RV8 was being hand-assembled. The bombshell was that Germany company BMW had bought Rover Group for £850m – a nice return for British Aerospace, who had paid £150m for the business just a few years earlier. Less happy was Honda, who felt it had been treated shabbily.

BMW put a new Rover, the 75, into production at Cowley, after a substantial investment in new plant. Even the unions were impressed. When on a visit with the Duke of Kent, David Buckle was asked by the Duke how industrial relations were at the plant, relative to the turmoil of earlier times. He replied, "A lot better than when I worked here, because it is quieter, cleaner and safer, due to the massive investment by BMW, which BL denied it in the past. The conditions you see now are what we begged for in the 1950s and 1960s but could not obtain."

Sadly, though, sales of the 75 were disappointing, despite the acknowledged quality and competence of the car and its intelligent interpretation of traditional Rover values. As is well known, BMW failed to turn Rover Group around – although arguably it was well on the way to assembling the model range to do so – and in the end it withdrew in 2000, leaving the rump to the Phoenix consortium led by John Towers.

For once, it was the former Austin plant that had drawn the short straw. BMW retained Cowley for production of the new Mini, completely refitting the one-time Pressed Steel factory in time for a production start-up in April 2001. Meanwhile, the Rover 75 lines were moved to Longbridge, and set up again by MG Rover, as the last remains of the old British Leyland combine were now called.

In 2012 BMW made 199,276 Minis at what it now refers to as 'Plant Oxford'. Projected output for 2013 is the same 200,000 or so units, manufactured by a workforce that at the time of writing numbers 3700 people. This is below the peak of 268,424 fully-built vehicles turned out by Cowley in the 1963–64 model year, but is being achieved with only one type of car – albeit in various forms – and with much reduced manpower. Equally to the point, those Minis are being produced in factory conditions of which the workers in William Morris's day could only have dreamed.

The Montego was another BL 'nearly car' produced at Cowley; it suffered aesthetically from being based on the Maestro centre section. (Author's collection)

The Rover 800 in its second form, with a prominent chrome grille. All the hard points of the 800 were shared with the Honda Legend, as part of the 'XX' project. (Author's collection)

The Mini assembly line features cradles so the underside can be worked on without operatives having to bend or crawl underneath. (BMW)

APPENDIX I: THE NUFFIELD BENEFACTIONS

No book on Morris would be complete without a look at Lord Nuffield's substantial benefactions, which ultimately became more newsworthy than anything occuring in his motor business. His first known gift was in 1917, to help establish the Oxford Military Orthopaedic Centre, and by his death he had given away a total of about £30m – say at least £800m in today's money. More than 90 per cent of his fortune, this puts him in the same league of philanthropists as Bill Gates and Warren Buffett. Broadly speaking, the benefactions concentrated on three key areas: health care, further education and support of the disadvantaged.

Nuffield had a life-long obsession with his own health, and this translated into a fascination with medicine. In later life he said he had always wanted to be a surgeon, although some sources suggest that this was said more for effect than anything else. Nuffield's first post-WWI donations in this field were to help what became the Wingfield-Morris Orthopaedic Hospital; re-named, it still exists as part of the Oxford University Hospitals NHS Trust. Then in 1929 he bought the Observatory site in Oxford and financed the installation there of the Radcliffe Infirmary and the School of Medicine. In 1937 came the creation of the Nuffield Department of Clinical Medicine and on the back of this the establishment of four Oxford University chairs, later increased to five. These included – unprecedentedly – one in anaesthetics at a time when such an idea was regarded as ridiculous. It was the first such chair in the world. Similarly innovatory was his support in 1944 for the creation of a Plastic Surgery unit with an attached professor; this played a leading role in adapting wartime techniques to the treatment of civilian patients and was integrated into the NHS in 1957.

Guy's Hospital was another favoured recipient, Nuffield ultimately becoming president of the governing body in 1944. He led the search for new funds, galvanised management, and financed a substantial extension in the hospital's facilities. He was also to sponsor other hospitals around the country.

Nuffield had a long association with the provident movement, going back to when he helped finance Oxford and District Provident Association. When most of the societies amalgamated into BUPA in 1947, a guarantee from him for up to £250,000 helped BUPA come into being. In 1957 he founded the Nuffield Nursing Homes Trust to establish the BUPA nursing homes, today known as Nuffield Hospitals.

Meanwhile the Nuffield Provincial Hospitals Trust, created in 1939 to coordinate hospital services during the war, laid some of the foundations for the setting-up of the NHS, and in the post-war years helped establish various health centres around Britain. Another valuable service to medicine was a substantial grant by the Trust to further penicillin research. On a more modest but no less appreciated level, Nuffield financed the Talking Book Library for the Blind, starting in 1935. In the same field, in 1941 he established a fund for research into ophthalmology.

Benefactions to the University of Oxford began in 1926 with the funding of a chair in Spanish. As well as the medical chairs mentioned above, Nuffield also endowed scholarships at various Oxford colleges. The culmination of his association with the university was his sponsorship of a new college to bear his name. Despite his generosity towards the University of Oxford, his relationship with it was ambivalent. This was largely a result of the saga of his gift to establish Nuffield College.

The first Oxford college to be set up in modern times by benefaction of a private individual, it was the subject of much wrangling between the 1937 inauguration of the project and its 1955 completion. Nuffield, who wanted the college to specialise in engineering, was strong-armed into accepting its status as a post-graduate centre for social studies – a science he undoubtedly despised – and when he saw the initial Mediterranean-flavoured proposals for its architecture, by the former Government Architect for Palestine, he threatened to pull out. In the end the college was built in a style he found acceptable, drawing on an austere 'Cotswold vernacular' presentation that has ultimately aged much better than some of the more modern architecture inflicted on the university in the subsequent decade.

Away from the cloisters of Oxford, a major benefaction of £2m was used to establish the Nuffield Trust for Special Areas – "one of the most useful things [I have] ever done", Nuffield told Andrews and Brunner. It did much to revive industrial life in South Wales, Jarrow and Cumberland. Nuffield was particularly proud of his hand in reviving the mining town of Whitehaven.

The crowning achievement in this history of public-spirited generosity was the establishment in 1943 of the Nuffield Foundation, with £10m of Morris Motors shares. It grew to be one of the major foundations in the world. Operating in the fields of health, social well-being, care of the aged and the advancement of education, the Foundation still thrives today and has assisted in countless research projects, sponsored research and fellowships, and helped establish such diverse institutions as dental schools and Departments of Industrial Health at several universities, and bodies such as the Centre for Policy on Ageing. In modern times it has been an important player in many fields, from the study of disease in fish to work on non-sectarian integrated education in Northern Ireland.

Nuffield's benefactions were substantial enough before the 1936 part-flotation of the company, with about £1m having been given away by 1935. But after 1936 the donations became a major activity. Indeed, they are certain to have been one of the motivations behind the share issue. By 1943 Lord Nuffield had given away nearly all the 8m five-shilling shares in Morris Motors that he had retained, this representing £15m at the time, or over £550m in today's money.

It is legitimate to ask whether his motor business might have had a more robust future had at least some of that money been ploughed back into improved production facilities, engineering research and the like. On the other hand, the history of the British motor industry suggests that however healthy a firm he might have bequeathed to the newly-formed BMC, his legacy would inevitably have been squandered by the under-endowed incompetents who ran the combine and its successor companies.

In that context, it is more pertinent to note that people can benefit from Lord Nuffield's benefactions at every step in their life. As a child one can be cared for in the paediatric ward of a Nuffield Hospital. One can study a Nuffield syllabus at school, be supported in one's research by the Nuffield Foundation, and carry out post-graduate work at Nuffield College. One can have one's wisdom teeth extracted in the Nuffield House wing of Guy's Hospital (as did the author), and be looked after in later life through a BUPA scheme that owes its existence to a Nuffield gift, before spending one's last days in a Nuffield Care Home. The Morris motor car might be no more, but the impact on modern life of that jaunty businessman-viscount in the cheap suit can be seen all around us. It's not a bad memorial to William Richard Morris, one-time bicycle-maker and garage-owner.

APPENDIX II: STATISTICAL TABLES

Production by model, Morris passenger cars	
White & Poppe Oxford	1,475
Continental Cowley	1,450
Bullnose 1920–26 model years	151,424 est
Flatnose 1926–31 model years	201,692 est
Empire Oxford	1,741
Six	3,470
Minor ohc 1929–31 model years	34,599
Minor ohc 1932 model year	4,500
Minor side-valve, 1931 model year	5,435
Minor side-valve 1932–34 model years	41,546
Isis 1930 & 1931 model years	3,939
Isis 1932 & 1933 model years	2,381
Isis 1934 model year	552
Isis 1935 model year	149
Twenty-Five 1933 model year	228
Twenty-Five 1934 model year	300
Oxford LA 1930 & 1931 model years	23,646
Oxford LA 1932 & 1933 model years	8,636
Oxford LA 1934 model year	3,255
Oxford Sixteen/Twenty	3,501
Major 1931 model year	4,025
Major 1932 model year	8,936
Major 1933 model year	5,533
Cowley-Six 1934 model year	3,960 est
15-Six 1935 model year	3,525 est
Ten Four/Six 1933 model year	14,080
Ten Four/Six 1934 model year	20,905
Ten Four/Six 1935 model year	14,153
Cowley 1932 & 1933 model years	24,205
Cowley-Four & Twelve-Four	7,985 est
Eight Pre-Series & Series I	159,358[1]
Eight Series II	50,900[2]
Ten/Twelve Series II	59,366
Ten Series III	13,721
Series II Fourteen	8,505[3]
Series II Sixteen	2,443
Series II Eighteen	4,385
Series II Twenty-One	829
Series II Twenty-Five	2,229
Series III Fourteen	4,092[4]
Series III Twenty-Five	848
Eight Series E to August 1941	54,575
Eight Series E post-war	65,859
Ten Series M to February 1941	27,020
Ten Series M 'Tilly'	8,671
Ten Series M post-war	80,990
Twelve Series III	19,465
Minor	1,619,958
Oxford Series MO	159,960
Six Series MS	12,400
Cowley 1200	17,413
Cowley 1500	4,623
Oxford Series II	87,341
Oxford Series III & Series IV	58,117
Isis Series I	8,541
Isis Series II	3,614
Marina/Ital	1,338,392

Morris production by year 1913–51	
1913	404
1914	908
1915	316
1916	705
1917	126
1918	197
1919	387
1920	1932
1921	3076
1922	6956
1923	20,042
1924	32,910
1925	53,582
1926	48,330
1927	61,632
1928	55,480
1929	63,522
1930	58,436
1931	43,582
1932	50,337
1933	44,049
1934	58,248
1935	96,512
1936	90,949
1937	89,859
1938	72,925
1939	76,564
1940	8633
1941	5903
1942	5076
1943	3253
1944	3746
1945	6078
1946	41,182
1947	54,702
1948	54,712
1949	67,061
1950	98,481
1951	92,141

These figures are for deliveries (actual financial sales) and are for model years (August to July).

Source:
Carl Kingerlee for Andrews and Brunner.

Car-derived commercials included, except Series Z

Sources: BMIHT/Anders Clausager; pre-1920 figures Jarman/Barraclough. Some extrapolations by author.

[1] Includes 5cwt vans
[2] Additionally 10,679 5cwt vans made to SI spec, August 1937 – February 1940
[3] Includes 469 Fourteens converted to Series III
[4] Excludes 469 Fourteens converted from Series II

MOTORGRAPHS
Quality Prints from the Archives

The **British Motor Industry Heritage Trust** has made thousands of archive images from its unique photographic library available online as high-quality prints suitable for framing. Click on www.motorgraphs.com and begin your nostalgic trip through history of the motor industry.

CLASSIC MARQUES
MG, Morris, Austin & Austin Healey, Mini, Rover & Land Rover, Triumph.
BRITISH MOTOR FACTORIES
A glimpse behind the scenes at iconic factories like Abingdon, Cowley, Longbridge and Solihull.
MOTOR INDUSTRY PERSONALITIES
William Morris (Lord Nuffield), Cecil Kimber, Syd Enever, Alec Issigonis, the Wilks brothers among many.
ADVERTISING & FASHION
From the Roaring Twenties to the Swinging Sixties.
RACING & RALLYING
The glamour of motor sport on road and track.

The British Motor Industry Heritage Trust is an educational charity, custodian of unique Vehicle and Archive Collections, based at the Heritage Motor Centre in Gaydon near Warwick. Find out more about us at www.heritage-motor-centre.